AMERICA'S TOP TRIAL LAWYERS

Who They Are & Why They Win

AMERICA'S TOP TRIAL LAWYERS

Who They Are & Why They Win

by
Dr. Donald E. Vinson, PhD

PRENTICE HALL LAW & BUSINESS

Requests for permission to make copies of any part of the work should be mailed to:

Permissions
Prentice Hall Law & Business
270 Sylvan Avenue
Englewood Cliffs, NJ 07632

ISBN 013-356635-8

Printed in the United States of America.

To Ginny
Katie
&
Mark

About the Author

Donald E. Vinson, PhD

Don Vinson holds a BA in Economics, an MS in Marketing Research, an MA in Sociology, and a PhD in Marketing and Consumer Behavior. He initiated his first career as a college professor at Louisiana State University, UCLA, and as Chairman of the Marketing Department at the University of Southern California. In 1976, he created the shadow jury concept for one of IBM's major antitrust cases and launched a new industry—the field of jury consulting—and a new career. Vinson is widely recognized as the nation's foremost expert in the field of jury research and trial strategy. Over the years, he has worked with trial lawyers throughout the country on hundreds of high profile cases. He is chairman of DecisionQuest, Inc. which provides consulting advice to trial lawyers on jury issues, trial strategy, and the design and production of courtroom graphics. He resides in Los Angeles with his wife and children.

America's Top Trial Lawyers

Thomas D. Barr, Esq.
Cravath, Swaine & Moore
New York, New York

Fred H. Bartlit, Jr., Esq.
Bartlit, Beck, Herman,
  Palenchar & Scott
Chicago, Illinois

Maxwell M. Blecher, Esq.
Blecher & Collins
Los Angeles, California

David Boies, Esq.
Cravath, Swaine & Moore
New York, New York

James J. Brosnahan, Esq.
Morrison & Foerster
San Francisco, California

Philip H. Corboy, Esq.
Corboy Demetrio Clifford
Chicago, Illinois

Robert B. Fiske, Esq.
Davis Polk & Wardwell
New York, New York

Joseph D. Jamail, Esq.
Jamail & Kolius
Houston, Texas

Arthur L. Liman, Esq.
Paul, Weiss, Rifkind,
  Wharton & Garrison
New York, New York

Patrick F. McCartan, Esq.
Jones, Day, Reavis & Pogue
Cleveland, Ohio

James F. Neal, Esq.
Neal & Harwell
Nashville, Tennessee

Harry M. Reasoner, Esq.
Vinson & Elkins
Houston, Texas

Stephen D. Susman, Esq.
Susman Godfrey
Houston, Texas

Robert S. Warren, Esq.
Gibson, Dunn & Crutcher
Los Angeles, California

AMERICA'S TOP TRIAL LAWYERS:
Who They Are & Why They Win

TABLE OF CONTENTS

PART II: WHY THEY WIN: STRATEGIES AND TACTICS

Chapter 3: Evaluating the Engagement:
Pretrial Considerations

Chapter 4: Structuring the Case

Preface

There are many people who I would like to thank for assistance and cooperation with this book. First, I would like to thank my partners at DecisionQuest who have tolerated the dispersion of my energy necessary to complete this project. This has been a time-consuming venture, and they have been supportive and enthusiastic at all stages of the work, offering encouragement and interest.

I am also indebted to all those friends in the legal profession and lawyers I did not personally know who were willing to take the time and effort to provide me with their nomination for candidates to be included in the book as well as their viewpoints as to what it takes to be a truly great participant in the world of high stakes, big-time litigation. Peter Frank at Price Waterhouse played an important role in helping me acquire the survey data for the study. He and his staff were absolutely first rate in collecting the material from the participating lawyers and in all of the follow-up details involved. I am very grateful for their assistance. My administrative assistant, Rita Plantamura, has provided her usual invaluable help. I would like to thank her for her sublime patience and word processing skills on this, the second book on which she has assisted me this year. Special thanks to Eric Sikola and Norma Silverstein for their assistance with research and manuscript preparation. I would like also to thank my publishers, Lynn and Steve Glasser, and Dan Mangan, Vice President, Editorial, at Prentice Hall Law & Business. I also gratefully acknowledge Noah J. Gordon, Executive Editor, for his editorial expertise and contributions and to Tracy Smith for her assistance in making this book a much better final product than she first encountered.

Finally, I would like to express my gratitude and appreciation to the fourteen men in this book who gave me their time, shared their insights, and extended their trust and confidence to allow me to undertake this project. The time I spent with them was truly enlightening and was a wonderful experience that I enjoyed very much.

Donald E. Vinson
Los Angeles, 1994

Introduction

*They possess an uncommon degree of judgment, sense
of humor, judgment, intelligence, judgment, likability,
quickness, judgment, courage, common sense, physical and mental toughness, judgment, discipline. Did I
mention judgment?*
      —John S. Martel, Survey Respondent

The Survey

Working with gifted trial lawyers is a fascinating experience.
In my eighteen years as a trial consultant, I have known a
large number of attorneys. As in any profession, there exists
in the litigation arena a spectrum of skill, talent, and reputation. Over
time, I became intrigued with the question of what separates the great
from the merely good. Are there defining characteristics that differentiate truly gifted trial attorneys from the rest of the profession? Do the
great ones all have something in common? Or, are they in some way
unique? At first I decided to pursue this question at the law library. I
spent weeks reading accounts of legendary trial lawyers from the
American Revolution to the present. And I read the books written by
them. While this effort was interesting, it produced only anecdotes
and generalizations and very little empirical data or serious analysis. It
became apparent that if I were to obtain meaningful answers to my
questions, it would be necessary to undertake my own research.
Rather than an historical perspective, I decided to focus my attention
on contemporary trial lawyers of national repute.

My first task was to select a group of great trial lawyers to study. To
help me in this endeavor, I enlisted the assistance of prominent people
in the legal profession whose experience and judgment I valued. They
included senior partners of medium to large firms, as well as a few

solo firms, known for their trial experience. I also contacted the presidents of law societies and associations on the state and national level; bars of those states with major urban centers, e.g., New York, California, Texas, Illinois; twenty federal and state judges; and corporate counsels of major American companies. In all, four hundred letters were sent containing these two directives:

1. In my view, the following individuals possess national reputations as exceptionally skilled trial lawyers.

2. Is there any specific trait or characteristic that you believe is common to these people?

The Results

Based upon the results of this survey (hereinafter referred to as the Profession Survey), I selected fourteen men who constitute the trial lawyers studied in this book. Why fourteen? I wanted the sample to be large enough to find similarities and differences but not so large to be unmanageable. Originally, I had intended to select fifteen but regrettably Robert Hanley passed away as I began the research for this book. He was a truly gifted trial lawyer who would have made a tremendous contribution to the study. His death was a great loss for this book, as well as for the legal profession.

The fourteen lawyers nominated by their peers as superstars and who are the subject of this book are Thomas S. Barr, Fred H. Bartlit, Jr., Maxwell M. Blecher, David Boies, James J. Brosnahan, Philip H. Corboy, Robert B. Fiske, Jr., Joseph D. Jamail, Arthur L. Liman, Patrick F. McCartan, James F. Neal, Harry M. Reasoner, Stephen D. Susman, and Robert S. Warren. As it turned out, I knew all of them except Arthur Liman and Joe Jamail. While I relied heavily on the Profession Survey's responses, the responsibility for selecting the participants was ultimately mine. Will there be critics who disagreed with my methodology? Should I have selected more than fourteen for my sample? Have I omitted candidates who should have been included? In the final analysis, many things could have been done differently. However, looking back on the intent of my study and what it accomplished, I am comfortable with the process and pleased with the results. There are many excellent trial lawyers in the United States, but I believe that I have included fourteen of the best who are practicing trial advocacy today.

An interesting issue, as well as a potentially critical point, is the demographic composition of this group of lawyers. *All are white males*. This is an artifact of the legal profession itself. These lawyers are in their fifties and sixties. All of them entered the legal profession in the decade following World War II. Without the experience accrued in their thirty to forty years of practice, they would not enjoy the national reputation or landmark litigious opportunity that places them in this group. There are at present many successful and extremely talented trial lawyers who are women and members of minority groups. Today, half the students in many law schools are women, a vast change from the period when these men received their legal education. If this study were to be replicated fifteen years from now, the composition of this group of superstars would undoubtedly reflect this difference.

It is important to note that the fourteen lawyers selected for inclusion in this book practice primarily in the area of civil litigation. Even though many began their careers in the US Attorney's office or with a district attorney, most are recognized for their accomplishments in the civil arena. Jim Neal, Arthur Liman, Jim Brosnahan, and Bob Fiske practice in both areas and are frequently associated with high-profile criminal cases or investigations. Irrespective of their area of specialization, all fourteen are consummate courtroom advocates whose reputations are associated with major cases that have had a significant impact on society as a whole.

Evaluating the Fourteen

Once I made the selection of my fourteen subjects, it was necessary to employ a series of objective measures for defining their personality and performance characteristics. For this purpose, I decided to use portions of a number of standard psychological tests that would enable me to gain insight into these lawyers' attitudes, beliefs, and values. These were contained in four lengthy questionnaires (presented in Appendix 2) that included in-depth inquiries into personal background and lifestyle issues. The participants also completed a 240-item NEO-R Personality Inventory, containing questions that assessed work and personal values, as well as self-evaluation adjective checklists. On the basis of these more "objective" measures, inferences, and conclusions were drawn about the personality constellations of the fourteen.

The questionnaires required anywhere from eight hours to two days to complete. Because of the personal and sensitive nature of some of the questions, the group was guaranteed anonymity. Each respondent selected a personal ID code that was used to identify his set of questionnaires for tracking purposes. They sent their completed responses to Peter Frank of Price Waterhouse. Peter knew the ID codes for each lawyer, but did not see the submitted contents. He forwarded the questionnaires to me, identified only by the ID codes.

When I began reading the responses, I knew the fourteen had taken their task seriously. They were committed to candor, and many of their answers were reflective, open, and immensely personal. The information collected on their personal data has been statistically analyzed and presented in the aggregate as a group profile. The results are compiled in tables and charts in Chapter 2.

The second major source of information for my research was an in-depth interview with each attorney. These interviews ranged from seven to eight hours in length. Using an extensive Interview Guide (see Appendix 3), I probed personal history, lifestyle, philosophy, and a wide range of topics relative to their practice of trial law. Early on in the project, I realized the enormous value of the interview material. Not only is it interesting, but it also captures the inimitable characteristics and personalities of these fourteen fascinating and accomplished professionals. Simply to have digested and summarized this material would have lost valuable (and oftentimes colorful) commentary as well as diluting the full flavor of their unique points of view. In order to preserve the spontaneity of these personal encounters, I have included much verbatim material with only minor changes to facilitate interpretation.

As we shall see in the following chapters, the traits of great trial lawyers identified by the responses to the Profession Survey and the study of the fourteen individuals included in this book are closely related to their professional achievements. Even though each possesses a unique style and approach to trial law, there are strong similarities as well. In general, the lawyers share a number of characteristics essential to their success. These include a practical intelligence, the ability to communicate to different types of people, charisma, mature decision making, the love of competition, self-discipline, leadership, the capacity to self-monitor, and luck.

In undertaking this study, I have not attempted to produce a clinically objective or balanced analysis of the life and character of the men in this book. Could I have identified personal flaws, weaknesses, or limitations? Even they would offer a resounding "yes" without hesitation. My goal however, has been to examine positive qualities that can contribute to an explanation of their success. I have attempted to provide the reader with insights into their background, prominent cases, philosophies, and courtroom strategies that reflect their approach to the practice of law. To accomplish this, I have painstakingly distilled the surveys, questionnaires, psychological inventories, and my interview materials of the past two years to identify the salient personality and performance characteristics that have caused their peers to consider them to be among the very best at what they do. There are more than 800,000 lawyers in this country, 65,000 in the Section of Litigation of the American Bar Association, but only a handful of these people have achieved "superstar" status. This book modestly proposes to evaluate the multiple dimensions of these fourteen trial lawyers, discuss the traits and factors that have contributed to their status, and present a primer on the courtroom strategies and tactics where accomplishment meets its venue.

Organization of the Book

The first part introduces our *dramatis personae*. Selected cases from the ensemble's vast repertoire along with their brief biographies are sketched in Chapter 1. Chapter 2 reveals the salient personality and performance traits shared by the men profiled. Numerous tables and charts are also included here. Chapters 3 through 9 is a fascinating discussion of their insightful, oftentimes unorthodox approach to trial law. From accepting a case to winning it (and losing), all fourteen decant advice with remarkable frankness. Chapter 10 presents their perceptions on what makes a great trial lawyer. For the reader interested in reviewing the statistical information derived from the psychological tests and inventories, these data are presented in detail in Appendix 4.

PART I:

WHO THEY ARE

CHAPTER 1 ███████████████

The Fourteen: Biographies and Selected Cases

> *There is no feeling in the world... sitting there when the jury is coming back in. You don't know what it's going to be...There's nothing like it—not sex—not anything in the world.*
>
> **—Jim Neal**

Our age of rapidly changing technology has witnessed aggressive innovation in product manufacturing, corporate restructuring, financial endeavors, and other multi-million dollar concerns. Occasionally in the process, there are seriously injured parties. Questions of justice and equity arise. And these questions are primarily asked and answered in the courts and through the actions of the legal profession. In 1990 alone, the cases from both civil and criminal courts were *equivalent to one court case for every other adult in the country.*[1] From what and how we buy, the news we see and read, the lifestyle and technology we enjoy, for better or for worse, have been influenced by the legal profession. Trial lawyers are at the center, influencing our lives in overt and subtle ways. And if a single word can be used to sum up the importance of these fourteen trial attorneys nominated by their peers, it is impact.

Consider the following: On the morning of September 29, 1982, 12-year-old Mary is given an Extra-Strength Tylenol by her father to fight off a cold. In a few minutes she is comatose; hours later, she is dead. Her parents hire Phil Corboy. Six others will die from cyanide-tainted

---

[1] *State Court Caseload Statistics: Annual Report* 1990.

3

Tylenol. Capsules were removed from the package, opened, tampered with, and reassembled without arousing suspicion. Who did this? There is no way to find the perpetrator of this heinous crime. Corboy and an associate decide to prove that the manufacturer's packaging was unreasonably dangerous. Under pressure from seven consolidated lawsuits, Johnson & Johnson changed the packaging. As a result of Corboy's undertaking this legal engagement and formulating his particular theory of the case, over-the-counter pharmaceutical products are much safer today.

Joe Jamail is also responsible for taking several products off the market that he believed to be unsafe. In one case, it was the Honda ATV. He won a giant verdict against the manufacturer in a personal-injury case. In another, he gained a record-breaking settlement and managed to have Remington Arms recall 200,000 guns.

Consider too the case against Michael Milken and Drexel Lambert. The government's prosecution of Milken and Drexel ended what some have referred to as an era of unrestrained greed. David Boies and Tom Barr collected $1.5 billion, including over $1 billion for their client, the FDIC. And what did Arthur Liman get for his client, Michael Milken? A reduced jail sentence and a chance to start over.

The aggressive and numerous corporate takeover attempts of the last decade were battled in court with far-reaching results. Joe Jamail effectively ended what he considers the bad corporate behavior of Texaco when he won a *Guinness Book of World Records* judgment totaling nearly $12 billion on behalf of Pennzoil. This verdict had a chilling effect on the whole tender-offer movement, as well as leading to the serious restructuring of one of the nation's largest oil companies. Another corporate takeover attempt, also dealing with oil, was Mobil's endeavor for Marathon. It was short-circuited by Pat McCartan representing Marathon as a plaintiff. He prepared this $6.5 billion case in sixteen days, and won.

Several of the men highlighted here have effected changes in America's media. A notable case was David Boies' defense of CBS of libel charges from General William Westmoreland. This case helped to define the parameters of responsible reporting on controversial political information. When Tom Barr defended *Time* magazine against libel charges from Israeli military leader, Ariel Sharon, the case compelled the news media to analyze its journalistic practices, particularly the use of confidential sources. In a less-publicized but important and unique case, Bob Warren defended Dow Jones when the *Wall Street Journal* was sued for libel by Ramada Inns in a case lasting nearly six months.

Both Jim Neal and Arthur Liman played key roles in the two great domestic political events of the last twenty years, Watergate and Iran Contra, respectively. For six months Bob Fiske acted as special counsel to probe the Whitewater and related investments of President Clinton and his wife, Hillary. His findings caused considerable consternation in Congress.

No one can deny that sports are a major part of the American scene. Lawyers in this study have made an impact here too. Maxwell Blecher represented noted sports entrepreneur and owner, Al Davis, in successfully defending the move of the Oakland Raiders to Los Angeles against the wishes of the National Football League owners and the City of Oakland. Bob Fiske defended the National Football League against a suit brought by the United States Football League. Although the jury found the NFL to be a monopoly, it awarded damages of only one dollar. This case affected the manner in which antitrust law is applied by the courts regarding professional sports.

The American trial lawyers discussed here also engage in cases of international scope. David Boies successfully defended Westinghouse when a new government in the Philippines tried to recover the $2.5 billion paid to Westinghouse for a nuclear power plant that never operated. Jim Brosnahan took a case with international consequences when he successfully defended a man who allegedly plotted against Ferdinand Marcos. Later he found himself representing an alleged member of the Irish Republican Army accused of murder.

Serious antitrust disputes have been a feature of American civil litigation since the passage of the Sherman Antitrust Act. In recent years, many of these have focused on the billion-dollar computer industry over patents and pricing. Probably the most important realm of the computer antitrust cases are those cases brought against IBM by its competitors. Tom Barr has been the chief trial attorney for IBM in all of its litigation. David Boies was lead counsel in the fourth civil case that proceeded to trial. Steve Susman won what might be considered the first billion-dollar judgment in a predatory pricing case against Corrugated Container. Harry Reasoner secured a $200 million settlement for his clients, Houston Natural Gas and Ranchers Exploration and Development in the uranium cartel litigation and secured a judgment of over a billion dollars against six railroads that were trying to block his client, ETSI, a coal slurry pipeline. Fred Bartlit is the man who is called in at the eleventh hour to represent major clients with hundreds of millions or billions of dollars at risk. General Motors hired Bartlit to handle the Mosley case that involved truck fuel tanks. After almost ten years in litigation, Shell Oil asked for his help in the MDL-150 Antitrust Case brought against it by the City of Long Beach and the State of California. The case settled soon after.

A number of important civil suits have arisen out of industrial accidents. New York attorney, Bob Fiske, successfully defended Babcock and Wilcox, the manufacturer of the reactor at Three Mile Island, in a suit by General Public Utilities asking for $4 billion in damages. Jim Neal represented Exxon in the tragic oil spill when the tanker *Exxon Valdez* went aground in Alaska.

The great trial lawyers have both destroyed and saved reputations. Jim Neal began the government's juggernaut against trade unionist Jimmy Hoffa. On the flip side, Neal saved the reputation of the officers of the Ford Motor Company when they were charged with criminal homicide in an accident involving a Ford Pinto. Jim Brosnahan earned a judgment of $9.7 million in favor of Ben Ford, a member of the Detroit Ford family, one of the highest awards ever made to an individual. Bob Fiske put Nicky Barnes, one of the most notorious drug dealers in America, behind bars. Fiske also destroyed Anthony Scotto, the head of the International Longshoremen's Association in New York, accused of racketeering. Fred Bartlit was special counsel to investigate corruption in the Cook County court system; many members of the bar and bench have been indicted.

The impact these men have on the legal profession has been and is profound, both through case law precedent and through their views on litigation in general. This chapter introduces the fourteen with brief biographies, and furnishes synopses of their more challenging and important cases. The cases are presented not only for their interest, but to anchor later chapter discussions on trial strategies and tactics.

THOMAS D. BARR

Tom Barr is partner in the New York law firm of Cravath, Swaine & Moore. His litigation practice is primarily large, complex cases for both plaintiffs and defendants.

Barr was born January 23, 1931, in Kansas City, Missouri. He received his BA degree in History in 1953 from the University of Missouri at Kansas City. He had fully intended to pursue graduate education in history to become a professor. However, soon after graduation, he joined the Marine Corps and in due course became a first lieutenant. It was there that he was introduced to law when he was assigned to conduct court-martials and was appointed prosecutor for the regiment. He found he was good at it and he liked it. He attended Yale Law School and received his LLB in 1958.

Perhaps Barr's most prominent cases as well as the most interesting are those involved in the thirteen-year defense of IBM against the

United States, the European Economic Community, and a number of private actions. *United States v. IBM* received banner headlines in the *New York Times,* "Government Quits after Seven Years of Trial." The cases began when Barr was the firm's newest litigation partner and David Boies was a young Cravath associate. *United States v. IBM* was an antitrust action for divestiture and injunction relief. The trial was especially noteworthy in that it developed into a series of increasingly bitter confrontations. Barr and Boies again and again gave writs of mandamus to the judge. This process was necessary in order for the judge to accept papers for filing that he disagreed with and to permit the IBM lawyers to interview government witnesses. They also had to give writs of mandamus to the judge after the Department of Justice filed its notice of dismissal from continuing the case without a plaintiff. Throughout the trial, the judge interrupted their cross-examination of government witnesses to warn the witness of possible traps and to suggest answers—in general disrupting cross-examination. It was an example of how a judge can seriously undermine courtroom proceedings. The private cases were brought by Greyhound, then Telex, then CalComp—all antitrust cases against IBM for monopolizing the market for certain peripheral computer devices.

Ariel Sharon's Quarrel with *Time* Magazine

[*Ariel Sharon v. Time*]

In 1986 Barr defended *Time* magazine in a $50 million libel suit brought by Ariel Sharon, a leader in the Israeli Defense Force. On February 21, 1983, *Time* published a cover story about Sharon. In his suit, Sharon objected to one paragraph in particular. It discussed his role in the slaughter of 700 Palestinian civilians in two Beirut refugee camps by Lebanese Christian Phalangist militia as well as the findings of Israel's Kahan Commission that subsequently investigated the 1982 massacre. The paragraph said, in part, that on the eve of the massacre, Sharon met with Lebanon's militia and "discussed" the need to avenge Lebanese President-elect Bashir Gemayel's assassination that had occurred two days earlier. The trial would hinge on how the jury interpreted the disputed paragraph. Barr went to Israel to take Sharon's deposition.

Sharon and I had a macho conversation privately, a sort of, "I understand you were a Marine and you were a fighter, and you know these things have to be done." That kind of thing. When he came for his deposition...I sat across from him and I put both feet up on the table. He lost it, absolutely lost it. I showed him the soles of my feet. It is a mortal insult in the Near East. Don't ask me why it is. He went bananas. We had a very tempestuous deposition. Sharon was a controversial character in his own country. People in Israel either hate him or love him. He's either a hero or a fiend. What I did, basically, was to take him through two things. Just force him step by step through the findings of the Kahan Commission, as to what he said, where he was, what he did, and so forth. And I didn't care whether he admitted it or denied it. This came before the *Time* article. Whatever they said, whether it was true or not true. If it was true, it meant he was a bastard. If it was not true, they're the ones who hurt him, not *Time*.

Sharon continued to appeal to Barr as a former Marine.

"Mr. Barr, you're a military man, you should understand the military situation. Let me explain the military situation to you." I'd say, "Military, wipe it out. I'm not interested in that." We went back and forth on that basis. As I remember it, there were a lot of, "You know what you would have done under the circumstances." What he was trying to do was to get me into that argument and I never got into it. I just said, "Look, General, I'm here to ask you questions and you're to answer them. That's all we're here to do."

In his five and half-hour closing argument, Barr sought to convince the jury that the words in the paragraph in question "simply don't mean what the plaintiff says they mean." Sharon was "stung," according to Barr by the Israeli commission report that found him "indirectly responsible" for the massacre but could not sue it. Instead, Barr pointed out to the jury, he picked out *one* paragraph buried in the middle of a *Time* story, gave it one meaning, as a way of retaliating against the Kahan Commission.

Sharon got what he wanted [a chance to tell his story, even though], *Time* was not held liable. Sharon was trying to regain his reputation by trying *Time* magazine in the United States and trying it in the newspapers in Israel. I think some of the jury liked Sharon and some of the jury definitely disliked Sharon. I'm quite sure that if the jury had been asked...if we had found *Time* liable and been asked to award damages, they would have awarded him a penny or no damages at all. I mean, there are a hundred newspaper stories before *Time* was ever published that called him murderer, assassin, accused him of killing, bulldozing houses with people in them, killing helpless people all over the world—this is not a nice guy.

FRED H. BARTLIT, JR.

Fred Bartlit is senior partner at the law firm of Bartlit, Beck, Herman, Palenchar & Scott in Chicago, Illinois. His principal area of practice is high-risk and complex litigation.

Bartlit was born August 1, 1932 in Harvey, Illinois. He received his BS degree in Engineering from the United States Military Academy, West Point, New York. He served four years in the US Army, including service with the US Army Rangers. He attended law school at the University of Illinois College of Law. He received his JD degree in 1960, graduated first in his class, with the top academic record in the history of the College of Law. He was also editor of the law review.

Bartlit holds the singular distinction of performing more actual on-trial days before juries than any other large-firm business lawyer in the United States. In a recent year he has spent thirty weeks on trial before juries in four trials ranging from the Virgin Islands to San Jose,

11

California. He is also one of the few lawyers whose practice consists of being retained for tough cases in jurisdictions other than at home.

Bartlit considers one of his most memorable trials to have been the case in Scotland when he represented General Motors (Allison Gas Turbine) in a United Kingdom civil proceeding. This concerned the British Department of Energy report that claimed Allison jet engines ignited a gas cloud that resulted in the $2 billion Occidental Piper Alpha 1988 North Sea platform explosion. In the disaster, 166 lives were lost. He was invited to participate in the proceedings by the trial judge, Lord Cullen. He was given full rights of audience and was the sole trial counsel for GM. Bartlit was the only non-UK lawyer. The rest were leading members of the Scottish and English bars. He was given full rights of cross-examination, which he exercised by cross-examining over thirty experts and other witnesses. The proceedings were highly technical from a scientific and engineering standpoint, with experts in every discipline from three-phase gas flow to computer simulations of explosion overpressures and flame fronts. "The final result was a brilliant opinion by Lord Cullen, covering every aspect of the incident. Allison Gas Turbine was found not responsible in any way...The case is unique in that, to my knowledge, no other US lawyer has been accorded rights of audience in the UK."

Another large case in which Bartlit was engaged, the General Motors Fleet Discount Case (*United States v. General Motors*), took place in 1974. This was a case involving billions; in today's dollars perhaps as much as ten billion. It began with a a criminal indictment of GM, Ford, and Chrysler, claiming price fixing on vehicles sold to Hertz, Avis, and state and local governments. Bartlit says the case was interesting, not only for the large monetary amount involved, but because of the witnesses who included Lee Iacocca, John DeLorean, Henry Ford, Lynn Townsend, Ed Cole, and other big names in the auto industry. The case was tried to a jury for four months. Bartlit secured an acquittal for his client.

Recently Bartlit was retained by General Motors in a last-minute decision to defend it in a case where a young man died in a fiery crash involving a GM truck. The plaintiff alleged design defects in the vehicle's fuel tank. The jury ultimately returned a verdict of more than $100 million against the company. Many observers felt that with the particular facts and the intense emotion of the case, it simply could not be won. Nevertheless, Bartlit accepted the engagement and waged a spirited defense for his client. The nature of the case, and Bartlit's research into the customary tactics of opposing counsel, dictated a strategy focusing on the use of *in limine* motions to set up critical issues for appeal, and protecting these issues on a daily basis during trial. As this book went to press, the entire $100 million plus jury verdict was set aside by the Georgia Appellate Court.

Bartlit has continued to be the eleventh-hour trial lawyer in big cases. In 1993, he was called in after most of the discovery was complete to represent FMC in a $50 million environmental case against Lloyd's of London. In 1994, he was retained at the last minute to represent Miles in a $60 million laser-optics patent defense against Johnson & Johnson. In both cases he secured jury verdicts for his clients.

Operation Greylord

In 1986, the US District Court for Northern Illinois appointed Bartlit to be special counsel and gave him subpoena power to investigate alleged misconduct of lawyers implicated in the Greylord judicial bribery scandals. Bartlit was named because "he's a methodical, meticulous investigator who is tenacious as a bulldog and not political," according to one federal judge. About 300 lawyers testified in bribery trials, have been named in testimony, or have been indicted in a widespread Justice Department investigation of corruption in the Cook County court system. The code-named investigation, Operation Greylord, resulted in the convictions of six state court judges, thirteen attorneys, sixteen police officers, and court personnel on extortion and bribery charges. The federal judges exercised the rare move to appoint an outside counsel because of disillusionment with the Illinois Supreme Court that oversees attorney discipline. According to one unnamed US district judge, "A lawyer can do anything short of assassinating the entire Illinois Supreme Court and still get his license back."

(Source: Larry Green, *Los Angeles Times*, July 16, 1986)

For the past few years, along with his full trial schedule, Bartlit has been leading an initiative to revolutionize the way litigation is handled in the United States. He considers this to be perhaps the most important aspect of his professional life. He is attempting to abolish lawyers' time-based billing. He believes that litigation is the single most inefficient business process in America. The hourly rate rewards inefficiency and penalizes efficiency. He proposes to put the economic incentives where they should be, and reward results and efficiency, not hours. *Both* lawyer and client should be at risk not just the client. He acknowledges that many law firms think he is out of step with big-firm mentality, and ask, "What if a law firm made a bad deal and the case cost more than they thought it would?" His response is, "This happens to businesses all the time. Lawyers are the only people who expect that every business deal will be profitable and have the same high-profit margin." The concept is catching hold in some areas and Bartlit has been contacted by senior management of Fortune 500 companies who want to work with him to bring this concept to fruition.

*Fred Bartlit in the US Army during
active duty.*

*Fred Bartlit with wife and daughter
in Vail, Colorado.*

MAXWELL M. BLECHER

Max Blecher is managing partner of Blecher & Collins law firm in Los Angeles, California. His principal area of practice is antitrust litigation.

Blecher was born in 1933 in Chicago, Illinois. He attended undergraduate school at the De Paul University from 1951 to 1952, and received his LLB from the University of Southern California in 1955. Upon graduation from law school, Blecher worked as trial attorney for the Antitrust Division of the US Department of Justice in Los Angeles. In 1963 he became associated with the Law Offices of Joseph L. Alioto in San Francisco. During that period, he was trial counsel on behalf of Mayor Alioto in the first jury trial of Alioto's libel suit against *Look* magazine.

The way in which Blecher became an antitrust lawyer was somewhat accidental. It occurred because he had worked throughout law

Max Blecher with trial team.

school and of necessity arranged his classes to accommodate his work schedule. He needed a class to start at 8:00 AM, and the only class offered at that time was antitrust law. He took the class and found it interesting. "I took a shine to it because it seemed like an area that was just in the process of being developed. One could bring some creativity to the process; whereas, other areas of law were well cut and dried; rules had been decided and they seemed pretty mechanical to me." Although he barely passed the course, with encouragement from his professor he continued with antitrust law. Upon graduation, he immediately went to work for the Antitrust Division in the Department of Justice and at the age of twenty-eight became lead lawyer in the criminal prosecution of General Motors. He tried the first merger case under the new statute in California. Due to his extensive trial experience, he was selected into the American College of Trial Lawyers in 1973 at the age of forty.

Although he tries both prosecution and defense antitrust cases, Blecher believes it has become much easier to win as a defendant than as a plaintiff, particularly as the law has evolved in the last decade. In the period from 1960 until 1980, being a plaintiff was relatively easy. It was easier to blend law and facts and to create inferences of conspiracy or monopolistic conduct. However, with the advent in the 1980s of what was called the "New Era," and what he refers to as "The Dark Ages," the law shifted dramatically in favor of the defendant. "Today it is difficult to win an antitrust case as a plaintiff. Then if you win, you've got the judge and a court of appeals looking over your shoulder, scrutinizing the record to find a basis to reverse."

Los Angeles Memorial Coliseum Commission v. National Football League

Blecher's most publicized case was on behalf on the Los Angeles Memorial Coliseum that found itself without a team when the Rams decided to move down the road to Anaheim. The Coliseum Commission, after trial, wound up with a final judgment, including interest and attorneys' fees of nearly $30 million and an injunction that prohibited the National Football League from interfering with the then Oakland Raiders proposed move to Los Angeles.

Another of Blecher's most challenging cases was *Handgards, Inc. v. Ethicon, Inc.* The case was important to him because it is an example of the use of litigation as an effective way to stifle competition. As a result of the patent litigation brought against his client, the client's company was unable to operate effectively. The client could not make a public offering due to the impending litigation and it stifled possibilities for a joint venture with Revlon. At the time the case was begun, the legal theory was not developed and everyone thought it would be impossible to win. But the jury wound up giving Blecher's client exactly what he had asked for. The whole process took about thirteen years. "It was the most gratifying victory because it was the hardest case from a legal and factual point of view. The other side never credited the case with having any possibility of success and never made an offer of settlement."

His two most successful defense cases were both tried in the federal court in San Francisco. One involved the defense of Syufy Enterprises in a case brought by the Department of Justice charging a violation of the anti-merger and monopoly laws when Syufy acquired all of the first-run motion picture theaters in Las Vegas. The trial court found for the defendant and the ninth circuit affirmed in a much-cited opinion written by Judge Kozinski that cited 200 motion picture titles. Considering the damages that were claimed, the nature of the charge, and the evidence they had, he thought it was a very successful result for the client. In another matter, Blecher represented Continental Baking Company as a defendant in a case brought by two small competitive southern California bakers who had gone out of business alleging this was a result of Continental's low prices. There had been a precedent in northern California where a baker had gotten $14 million on the same kind of claim. But in this case, the jury awarded the plaintiff $300,000. His client was delighted.

DAVID BOIES

David Boies is a partner in the law firm of Cravath, Swaine & Moore in New York. His litigation practice is primarily large complex cases for both plaintiffs and defendants.

He was born March 11, 1941 in Sycamore, Illinois. After completing high school in Southern California, he received his BA degree in History from the University of Redlands in 1962. After completing most of his undergraduate work at the University of Redlands, he received his BS degree from Northwestern University in 1964. He received his LLB from Yale University, magna cum laude in 1966.

Upon joining the Cravath, Swaine & Moore firm Tom Barr became his mentor; and in the 1970s they together tried a number of high-profile cases, including the *Telex v. IBM*, *United States v. IBM*, and *California Computer Products (CalComp) v. IBM*. In 1978 Boies, on leave of absence from Carvath, Swaine & Moore, served as Chief

*David Boies wearing one of his famous
"Christmas ties."*

David Boies during the Westmoreland case.

Counsel and Staff Director of the Senate Antitrust Subcommittee; in 1979 Boies served as Chief Counsel and Staff Director of the Senate Judiciary Committee. One of his recent large defense cases involved his representation of Westinghouse in *Republic of the Philippines v. Westinghouse*. The issues in the litigation and the amount of money at risk made this an extremely important case for his client. On the plaintiff's side in the *Computerized Reservations Systems* antitrust litigation, he recovered more than $200 million for his client, Continental Airlines. Representing the government in the *FDIC v. Drexel and Milken* case, Boies and Barr again joined forces to collect approximately $1 billion for their client. The suit was filed on behalf of failed savings and loans that bought junk bonds from Drexel. At the time Cravath was retained, the FDIC said that a $200 million recovery would be considered a successful result. Time was of the essence. For years the FDIC had tried unsuccessfully to make a case against Drexel and Milken and statutes of limitation were in danger of running out. However, within six months of their retention, Boies and Barr had reached a settlement with Drexel that included, in addition to cash payments, the right to sue Milken and others for any liabilities they might have to Drexel, and commenced discovery against the Milkens in the California action. A year later, they negotiated settlements. (Boies' and Barr's hourly rate began at $300; but once they collected $200 million in judgments or settlements, the success fee kicked up to $600 an hour.)

From the *Guinness Book of World Records* (1993):

Heaviest Fine: The largest fine ever was one of $650 million, which was imposed on the US securities firm of Drexel Burnham Lambert in December 1988 for insider trading. This figure represented $300 million in direct fines, with the balance to be put into an account to satisfy claims of parties who could prove they were defrauded by Drexel's actions.

The record for an individual is $200 million, which Michael Milken agreed to pay on 24 April 1990. In addition, he agreed to settle civil charges filed by the Securities and Exchange Commission and is now serving a 10-year prison sentence. The payments were in settlement of a criminal racketeering and securities fraud suit brought by the US government.

Westmoreland v. CBS

Boies' first libel case was the much-publicized Westmoreland suit against CBS. General Westmoreland was seeking $120 million in damages against CBS and Mike Wallace for a CBS News television documentary, "The Uncounted Enemy: A Vietnam Deception" aired January 23, 1982. In the documentary, CBS accused the general of misleading his superiors including President Johnson and Congress about enemy troop strength at a crucial period in the Vietnam War.

There was a newspaper story every day. We tried the case for seventy-five days and there were ninety newspaper articles. It was from the beginning a perfect case for the lawyer. It was two years from filing to trial, which is a short case for something like that. When I took on the Westmoreland case...that was the first libel case I'd ever done. My wife, who was then a vice president at CBS, was getting a lot of flack from some of the people who thought they ought to have retained a libel lawyer instead of me. They said to her, "What does David know about libel? About the First Amendment?" She replied, "Well, it's a very short amendment."

The specifics of the case were that there had been a CBS broadcast that alleged that Westmoreland and other high officials had distorted enemy troop strength in Vietnam in order to make it appear that we were winning the war. That is, they had overstated people who had been killed and understated the existing enemy strength in an attempt to show progress. They had concealed these figures from the American people, the Congress of the United States, and perhaps even the President of the United States...

Dean Rusk, Robert McNamara and the like...were prepared to come in to testify that Johnson knew everything...that if there was any deception, it was Johnson who was doing it...There was on the surface, substantial doubt both as to the truth of the broadcast and as to CBS' state of mind. But I sat down and I read every Supreme Court case from the time the United States was founded to the present that dealt with defamation. There were fewer than you think. Only about twenty cases. And out of that came a legal argument...no high government official had ever successfully sued for libel, ever, in the history of our country. If you are alleging that what they are doing as a high government official is wrong, that is absolutely protected free speech and you ought to be able to engage in it without having to worry about whether you're going to have to convince a jury later that you were either right or had the right state of mind.

By far the most interesting part of the case was the cross-examination and some of the depositions. I took the depositions of Dean Rusk, Robert McNamara, Walt Rostow, and four different CIA directors, and Westmoreland himself. His went on for fourteen days spread over seven months, which was a terrible mistake from their standpoint because they just kept letting us come back at him and come back at him. By the end of the deposition, I had him saying so many contradictory things, it almost didn't matter what he said on the stand. I had something to contradict him with.

On direct, however, his lawyers had done a wonderful job of preparing him right down to an emotional speech about how he cared about the boys over there and he was bringing this lawsuit because of the memory of all of the soldiers who had fought and died for American freedom in Vietnam and his reputation was now tarnished. It was a wonderful direct examination.

And my normal inclination with a witness once the direct is over, is to try to damage the witness's credibility right away, both because that will unnerve the witness and because it will demonstrate to the jury that the witness has been wrong or inaccurate or deceptive in one respect and will precondition them to what they can expect is going on...I really couldn't do that with Westmoreland...there were some things I could have just taken him apart on...I was afraid the jury would not like it. In the first dozen times I caught him in inconsistencies, I was very gentle with him. I said, "Now, you said this but in your deposition you said something quite different, didn't you, sir?" "Well, I don't remember that." Then I would show it to him and I would say, "Isn't that quite different?" "Well, I don't know that's different." I'd go, "Well, let's look at it. In the trial you said this and in your deposition you said that and don't you really agree that those are two different things?" And the more that he would try to get out of it and admit some, you could tell the jury was now getting uncomfortable with him, and by the second day, he was under real pressure...the next morning his lawyer came in and said he had back spasms and couldn't continue, so we recessed for a few days. And when we continued and he was just really not able to keep up…he was really broken.

The general contradicted himself or his former officers twenty to twenty-five times during nine days of testimony. The *Washington Post* reported that the press corps in the courtroom had taken to humming quietly the theme to *Jaws* when Boies rose to cross-examine witnesses. Prior to trial, CBS had offered to pay Westmoreland's legal expenses and give him air time to present his views if he would drop his case. Half-way through the trial, Westmoreland's counsel sought to accept the offer. CBS, on Boies' recommendation, told Westmoreland that the offer was no longer open. Westmoreland later dismissed his case with no money, no apology, no air time, and the scant comfort that CBS agreed not to pursue him for court costs.

In spite of his busy work schedule, Boies has written the book, *Public Control of Business*, as well as numerous articles.

JAMES J. BROSNAHAN

J im Brosnahan is senior partner with the law firm of Morrison & Foerster in San Francisco, California. He is a specialist in civil and criminal trial work.

He was born January 12, 1934 in Boston, Massachusetts. He obtained his BSBA degree in Business/Economics from Boston College in 1956. He received his LLB degree from Harvard Law School in 1959. In 1961, at the age of twenty-six, his post-law school career led to five years as an Assistant US Attorney prosecuting federal cases in Phoenix, Arizona and in San Francisco, California. As Assistant US Attorney, he specialized in both civil and criminal trials. He greatly values that experience. "I was in the courtroom all the time for five years. I probably tried sixty cases in that time. So the courtroom held no terrors for me. It was a natural place for me to be. I understood how it worked and how judges preside over things, a little bit about juries. That experience was invaluable."

Brosnahan's jury cases have spanned the gamut of civil and criminal subject matter and he is equally experienced as both prosecutor and defense counsel. He has argued many civil and criminal appeals in state and federal court, including two cases in the United States Supreme Court. A partial list of his case subject matter demonstrates the diversity of his trials. He has tried cases on patent, libel, murder, antitrust, personal injury, product liability, interstate transportation of explosive materials, bank embezzlements, real estate fraud, narcotics, and obstruction of justice, among others.

His largest plaintiff's case was undertaken for Benson Ford, Jr. of the Detroit automotive family in 1988. The defendants in that trial had been charged with professional misfeasance. He obtained a cash settlement of $9.7 million.

Brosnahan considers himself more of a defense than a plaintiff's lawyer. He regards the 1989 acquittal in San Francisco Federal District Court of Steven Psinakis his most important defense verdict. Psinakis was charged with interstate transportation of explosive material. (Psinakis had helped to overthrow Marcos in the Philippines. He was a close ally of Benigno Aquino, Jr., who was assassinated in 1983 in Manila.)

NIEMI v. NBC

Another prominent trial was his defense of the National Broadcasting Company in 1978. The plaintiff's charges arose as a result of an assault by a group of teenagers who said they got the idea for the assault from watching a television movie, "Born Innocent." The plaintiff claimed that because the perpetrators of the vicious attack got the idea by watching the movie, NBC ought to be responsible because they had aired the program. In that case, he and Floyd Abrams received a directed verdict in favor of the defense at the end of the opening statement.

Brosnahan was also appointed by the Office of Independent Counsel as the lead prosecutor in *United States v. Caspar Weinberger*. Because President Bush pardoned Mr. Weinberger along with other Iran-Contra defendants, the case never proceeded to trial.

Jim Brosnahan relaxing at a ranch in the high Sierras.

In spite of his busy schedule, Brosnahan has published a book, *Trial Handbook for California Lawyers*, and he is currently writing another entitled *Trial Advocacy Test*. He has published over thirty articles on the theory and application of the law.

Brosnahan feels that he owes gratitude to the people who taught him how to try cases, and that for young lawyers in the United States, it is crucial to have people to teach them, and that means having a strong trial bar. "In a democracy you've got to have these people. As long as you have people who are trained to stand on their feet in a time of adversity and say, 'You know, I really don't agree with you and if you give me half a chance I might prove you're wrong.' I believe this is important. That's why when people talk about hating lawyers, the first thing I think about saying to them is, 'May you experience being somewhere where there are no lawyers. Try it out. See how you like it. Because the first time you open your mouth—you're out of there.' It's important to train good trial lawyers."

PHILIP H. CORBOY

Phil Corboy is the founder of the law firm of Corboy Demetrio Clifford in Chicago, Illinois. He specializes in the area of plaintiff's personal-injury and wrongful-death litigation.

Corboy was born August 12, 1924 in Chicago, Illinois. After attending high school in Chicago, he graduated from St. Ambrose College in Davenport, Iowa following a year at Notre Dame. While in the Army, Corboy also studied engineering at Baylor University and Sacramento Junior College. He received his JD cum laude from Loyola University of Law in 1949 where he graduated first in his class. In 1978 he was presented with an Honorary Doctor of Law Degree from St. Ambrose.

The *Chicago Tribune* has called Corboy a "high-soaring local legal eagle for whom million-dollar verdicts are not unfamiliar and who is known for training top talent in the unofficial Corboy College of Law that is his firm..." Corboy is known for consistently receiving the highest verdicts for his clients. (Headline samples: "Brain-Damaged Boy Awarded $6 Million," "Jury Gives $8.2 Million to Bicyclist Who Fell at Train Crossing.") It is interesting to note that his firm has had 225 cases that have resulted in verdicts and settlements in the amount of $1 million or more. Corboy Demetrio Clifford is the largest plaintiff's personal-injury firm in the country. With 32 members, it far eclipses boutique firms and large firms in their speciality because they restrict their practice to representing plaintiffs in personal-injury and wrongful-death cases.

Although he is publicly recognized more for his professional accomplishments, Phil Corboy has been extremely active in philanthropic activities as well. Over the years, he has donated significant amounts of money to charities such as the "Big Shoulders Fund" of Chicago to help educate inner-city children.

Tylenol Packaging Case

[*Eliason v. Johnson & Johnson*]

Corboy has tried literally hundreds of tort cases resulting in large verdicts. He is one of the lawyers who has had serious impact on societal changes in this country. One of his more famous cases, ironically, did not go to verdict but was settled just before trial. This was the most publicized and far-reaching product-liability case of the last twenty-five years. It legally questioned firmly established liability on the part of a product manufacturer for the intentional misuse of a product by a third person to harm others. The cases were settled the day before trial was to begin, May 13, 1991.

(The following is an abstract of that case excerpted from newspaper articles and the court file.)

By October 3, 1982, seven deaths had been linked to the ingestion of tainted Tylenol. The nation was in a panic as copy-cat poisonings and false alarms were reported almost daily. Hospitals and poison control centers were flooded with calls by consumers about what to do with Extra-Strength Tylenol in their possession. The FDA announced a recall of what was now two suspect batches of Extra-Strength Tylenol... Tylenol products were cleared from shelves across the country. The FBI was brought into the investigation....

"The Tylenol Task Force" determined that the tainted bottles came from five separate batches manufactured at two separate sites and the cyanide in all of the tainted capsules came from the same source...For the concentrations of cyanide found in tainted capsules recovered by investigators as well as the amounts of cyanide found in the blood of the victims to be so high, literally thousands of pounds of cyanide would have had to be introduced during the manufacturing process. In addition, while McNeil [Johnson & Johnson's parent company] did use cyanide in its laboratories, it was quickly determined that the cyanide found in the tainted capsules were not the same as the cyanide used in McNeil's labs. More and more the evidence pointed to a third party perpetrator, not contamination during the manufacturing process.

Investigators surmised that the capsules were tainted most probably by one person with possibly one or two accomplices who bought some of the Extra-Strength Tylenol, took it to an outside location, emptied the Tylenol from the capsules and refilled the capsules with cyanide. Forensic psychiatrists surmised that the killer was in his or her late twenties or early thirties, intelligent, devious and acted out of cowardice and with no remorse.

The most important question, and the one that later proved to be the most crucial for the plaintiff was how did the tainted capsules get into the bottles on the shelves? Were they placed in bottles outside the stores and then put on the shelves, or were the tainted capsules placed into containers that were already on the shelves? Law enforcement reports pointed to both conclusions...

[Although there was one suspect in the killings, the file on the Tylenol deaths is still open.]

On October 6, 1982, the first suits were filed against Johnson & Johnson...The seven actions were consolidated for trial...The complaints sounded in strict liability and negligence alleging both that the product was unreasonably dangerous when it left McNeil because it was open to tampering once it left McNeil's control, because McNeil failed to properly package its product and failed to warn of the possibility of tampering, and because the cyanide in fact was somehow placed in the capsules during the manufacturing process....The theory that the cyanide entered the capsules during the manufacturing process was quickly publicly discounted and little was found during the discovery process to support that theory. McNeil was able to get those counts of the complaints dismissed early in the litigation and admission of what little evidence Corboy had regarding that possibility was later barred.

Corboy realized that to be successful McNeil's negligence would have to be stressed; proof would be required that the company knew that its or other companies' products could and had been tampered with after leaving its control and that it took the deaths of seven people to force it to take precautions to prevent such tamperings and their resulting injuries...

Corboy was successful, by utilizing motions *in limine* in preventing McNeil from referring to the deaths as "murders" and "terrorist attacks" during trial. Corboy knew that these phrases had been burned into the minds of Americans through McNeil's advertising strategy in response to the poisonings. From a practical standpoint, Corboy had to convince a jury that McNeil not only knew that tamperings could occur but it made the conscious decision not to do anything to prevent them until they were forced to by seven deaths...

Through discovery, Corboy found that literally dozens of forms of what would eventually be called "tamper-resistant" or "tamper-evident" packaging were readily available to McNeil and other manufacturers prior to 1982. Patent research established that many forms of "safety packaging" had been around since the early twenties...Corboy and his staff also found fifty *reported* cases of injury-producing product tampering occurring prior to the Tylenol deaths. All these tamperings were thought by the FDA to have occurred once the product left the manufacturer...

Through the use of discovery and Freedom of Information Requests to the FDA, Corboy discovered that McNeil had received literally hundreds of consumer reports of Tylenol products allegedly being tampered with on the shelves...Given that the FDA itself has reported that statistically, for every one consumer complaint received by it and the manufacturer, there are ten instances that are not reported, it adds up to quite a number of prior tamperings.

Virtually all the experts agreed that both the gelcaps and the caplets were virtually tamper-proof...McNeil had ignored the most obvious way to prevent or at least deter tampering—discontinue use of the capsule...Internal records showed that the only reason they chose the capsule over some other dosage form was marketing—the public believed that the capsule allowed the medicine to work faster and made the medicine stronger—two consumer misconceptions that McNeil never disputed in its advertising and in fact promoted and capitalized on…Even McNeil's experts had to agree—using a dosage form other than the capsule was by far the best way to prevent tampering. After taking well over 100 depositions and having prepared over 125 exhibits for trial and being ready to vouch for the credibility of the packaging experts, Corboy was ready to go to trial.

The jury was in the box on the morning of May 13, 1991. In Corboy's words, "jury de-selection" was about to begin. Settlement was reached, however, before the case come to trial. McNeil argued that divulging the amount of the settlements would promote copy-cat tamperings and put the public at risk. Corboy, at the very moment of this settlement, was proposing state legislation which would prohibit secret settlements. Johnson & Johnson and McNeil had made seven specific improvements in the packaging of Tylenol. These improvements have been picked up by the packing industry in America. Today, the tamper-evident changes initially sponsored by McNeil and Johnson & Johnson have made America a safer place for people who ingest over-the-counter products. The policy reasons against entering into a secret settlement in this case were gone. McNeil had corrected the defects in its product. Corboy and his clients agreed to keep the amount of the settlement secret.

Corboy has been chosen by The National Law Journal as one of "The 100 Most Influential Lawyers" since it began publishing *Profiles in Power* in 1985. The Journal publishes the *Profiles* every three years, and Philip H. Corboy was featured as one of "The 100 Most Influential Lawyers" in 1985, 1988, 1991 and 1994. Corboy belongs to an organization of 100 lawyers called "The Inner Circle." Membership is by invitation only and the bare minimum for consideration is that the lawyer has acquired a million-dollar verdict in compensatory damages for one person. An additional requirement is that the lawyer knows how to "get the shoes tied within the confines of the litigation system." Philip Corboy does not trip on his laces.

Phil Corboy delivering opening address at the
International Institute in Newman House,
University College, Dublin, Ireland, May 18, 1993.

ROBERT B. FISKE, JR.

B ob Fiske is a senior litigation partner in the firm of Davis, Polk & Wardwell in New York. His principal area of practice is complex civil litigation and white-collar criminal defense.

Fiske was born December 28, 1930 in New York City. He graduated from Yale University, in 1952, receiving his BA in 1952. He attended law school at the University of Michigan, receiving his JD in 1955. His memberships included Order of the Coif and associate editor of the *Michigan Law Review*. After law school, he worked for two years at the firm of Davis, Polk, Wardwell, Sunderland & Kiendl. Then followed four years at the United States Attorney's Office for the Southern District of New York during which he served as Assistant Chief of the Criminal Division and head of the Special Prosecutions Unit on Organized Crime. In 1961 he returned to Davis Polk. In 1976 he was appointed United States Attorney for the Southern District of

New York. He served a four-year term returning to Davis Polk in 1980. He is past president of the American College of Trial Lawyers.

As an Assistant United States Attorney Fiske learned his trial skills by prosecuting criminal cases. These gave him significant trial experience at an early age that was not otherwise available in large-firm private practice in New York. He also developed an immense respect for the importance of public service that would greatly influence the course of his career. As United States Attorney, he had the opportunity to lead the office, set criminal and civil priorities, and try major cases himself, all the while training many of the best young lawyers in New York in trial skills and the value of public service.

Putting Away Harlem's Biggest Drug Dealer

[*United States v. Leroy Barnes*]

The most satisfying case without question, was convicting Nicky Barnes. He was the largest drug dealer in New York City, probably in the country. He had been indicted four times in the New York State system and acquitted four times by trials in the Bronx...In 1977, when I was US Attorney, our office indicted him and fourteen others on federal charges. He had fourteen others running this big drug ring. Originally I was not going to try the case.

But in June (in rather dubious journalism I thought) the *New York Times* magazine section had a cover story about Nicky Barnes. There he was on the cover in this arrogant pose and it said this is "Mr. Untouchable." The article was about how he had become a role model in Harlem because he had run this drug ring. He flaunted it. He had two penthouse apartments in New Jersey. He had thirteen automobiles—a Ferrari, Porsche, Jaguar, BMW—two hundred suits. He used to carry a roll of thousand-dollar bills in his pocket...There was this story about how he had led the police on this high-speed chase and they followed him around and he went into the men's room. They were just tailing him all the time. The cop follows him into the men's room and when the cop is reaching for a paper towel, Barnes reaches into his pocket and peels off about five one-thousand dollar bills and says, "Hey why don't you dry your hands with these?"...He had become a folk hero in Harlem because of his ability to be above the law. The thrust of the article was that the state tried four times and

---

now the feds were taking a shot. The bet in Harlem was nobody was ever going to get Nicky Barnes.

This article came out on a Sunday. Monday morning I am in the office about eight-thirty and the phone rings, it is Griffin Bell, the Attorney General. He said, "Bob, I just got a call from the President. The President has just read this article yesterday in the *New York Times*. I hope we've got a case against this guy...And I said, "Well, I think it is a good case. It actually has its problems, but I think it is a good case." And he said, "Well, the President wanted me to tell you that he considers this the most important case in the country because if we can't put away somebody like this in the federal system, then our whole system of justice is all lopsided." And I said, "I think I get the message." So I went out and tried the case and fortunately we convicted him.

It was the first time in a trial jurors' names remained anonymous. Witnesses had been killed and it was believed jurors would be in jeopardy if their identities were known. Barnes was convicted (along with eleven of his colleagues) and received a sentence of life without parole. Fiske says the significance of the case was not only the destruction of the most efficient drug ring in New York, but also the destruction of Barnes' image of invincibility and his celebrity status as a role model for young black children in Harlem and the South Bronx.

The following year, Fiske prosecuted Anthony Scotto (*United States v. Anthony M. Scotto and Anthony Anastasio*), head of the International Longshoremen's Association (ILA) in New York, on racketeering charges. The Scotto case was significant because of his prominent role in the New York waterfront and in both state and national politics. His union had been a major contributor to candidates of both political parties. In addition to testifying in his own defense, he called a number of prominent character witnesses, including former New York City mayors John Lindsay and Robert Wagner, Lane Kirkland, head of the AFL-CIO and the then New York State Governor, Hugh Carey. Scotto and Anastasio were convicted of RICO charges for taking payoffs from companies whose employees were members of the ILA. The implicit, if not explicit, threat was that unless the payoffs were made, there would be slowdowns and other labor problems potentially damaging to the companies.

In January, 1994, Robert Fiske was selected by Janet Reno, the US Attorney General, as the Whitewater Special Counsel because "he is a ruggedly independent lawyer who brings a reputation for fairness . . . ." In reporting the appointment of his successor, Kenneth Starr, *USA Today*, said "Fiske was the perfect independent counsel, a legitimate nonpartisan figure and one of the great prosecutors."

Bob Fiske running the New York City Marathon,
October 26, 1980.

Bob Fiske backpacking with his son, Robert B. Fiske, III.

JOSEPH D. JAMAIL

Joe Jamail is the sole owner of the law firm of Jamail & Kolius in Houston, Texas. His principal area of practice is trial work for all kinds of cases.

Jamail was born October 19, 1925 in Houston, Texas. He obtained his BA degree from the University of Texas in 1950. He attended law school at the University of Texas, receiving his JD in 1953.

Jamail knew he wanted to become a trial lawyer after he skipped school to watch Percy Foreman and A.C. Winburn face each other in an Austin criminal trial. Foreman was defending two men for murdering a Mr. Tony Valone. Valone had been killed in a gang-type slaying. Winburn was the prosecutor. "I knew right then and there, this is where the action and drama is." Upon graduation from law school, he was hired by a local firm and his employment lasted all of twenty minutes. He understood immediately that if he were to remain

Joe usually gets the "last laugh."

Joe Jamail at his favorite bar in Galveston.

Joe Jamail relaxing in Galveston.

there, he would be years from a courtroom. So he left the firm, and was appointed to a position with the DA in district court. He worked there for one year. "We tried sometimes two cases a week. I know I tried sixty to seventy-five felony cases. That was the greatest learning experience of my young career." Ironically, he wound up working for Winburn in the Criminal Courts Building and later, when he opened his own office, had clients referred to him by the great Percy Foreman.

Pennzoil—The Mother of all Judgments

[Pennzoil Company v. Texaco, Inc.]

One of Jamail's most stunning verdicts occurred in the 1985 Pennzoil and Texaco trial. A case experts said was not winnable. His client, the plaintiff Pennzoil, received the largest civil damages award in legal history according to the *Guinness Book of World Records*: $10.53 billion ($7.53 billion in actual damages, plus $3 billion in punitive damages and interest. Altogether $11.12 billion with accrued interest). The Texas jury found that Texaco wrongfully interfered in a planned merger between Pennzoil and Getty Oil Company. Pennzoil had entered into an agreement with Getty Oil to buy Getty stock at $110 per share. The deal was not completed and Getty stock later sold to Texaco at $128. Pennzoil claimed that since Texaco had interfered with the Getty deal, Pennzoil had a right to recover damages. The case made an important statement about the limits of corporate greed. "Pennzoil was gratifying because it did something...and nobody thought we could win it. We prevented them from continuing to carve up corporate America. And that's the God damn truth. And anybody who writes about this will tell you that. They stopped. They got frightened to death."

An out-of-court settlement in 1987 was reached after two days of negotiation for $3 billion. It behooved Texaco to move quickly: The uncollected judgment owed by Texaco to Pennzoil amounted to *$3 million a day.*

Jamail's courtroom style is flamboyant and truly his own. He considers himself enough of a "ham" to enjoy the spotlight. He knows how to play to his audience, the jurors. He recalls one instance, where opposing counsel was intent upon pointing out how much his fees would amount to if his client won. "The jury kept looking over at me in astonishment, because it was a lot of money. Finally, the other lawyer asked, 'What do you think Mr. Jamail's going to do with that money?' Well, that invited me: 'Your Honor, he's now invited me to tell you and this jury what I'm going to do with my fee. Most of it I am going to give to Galveston charities for underprivileged children,' and I sat down. My client won."

Jamail recalls the first time women were allowed to serve on juries in Harris County. He was trying a case in the mid-1950s. "There were three women on the jury. I was late. The jury was in the box, the judge was on the bench, and he was frowning because I was late. The city attorney was grinning like he wants to turn me in to the principal. I hit the swinging door. The place was crowded with people. I said, 'Your Honor, you can see I've had an unfortunate accident. I have broken my zipper and I hope it doesn't distract any of the women on this jury.' Well, everybody cracked up. I had on a pair of red shorts and...They gave me more than I sued for."

Jamail says there is not one thing he dislikes about being a trial lawyer. He loves the limelight, helping other people, and hearing other people say, "There's Joe." His notoriety, however, has caused some problems. Once a juror told the judge, "Well, I've read about Mr. Jamail. And I wouldn't believe him if he was representing the Virgin Mother." Laughing, he thanked her for her honesty.

John Coates v. Remington Arms

In yet another case, according to the *Guinness Book of World Records*, Jamail's client received the largest individual cash settlement in the history of tort law at the time (1978).

> Remington made a shabby rifle. A little boy was holding it in a deer blind when it went off and paralyzed his father. Kid said the gun went off when he was sliding the safety into position. Remington Arms said it was impossible. I put a guy from the company in front of a camera for a videotape, pointed the gun at him. I had it on safety. I nudged the safety button. The thing exploded, guy dove for cover. They didn't go to trial, wrote us a check for six million, eight-hundred thousand.

As a result, Remington Arms recalled 200,000 rifles. "A lot of my cases have social ramifications like those recalls. I take a lot of pride in something like that."

ARTHUR L. LIMAN

A rthur Liman is a partner in the law firm of Paul, Weiss, Rifkind, Wharton & Garrison in New York City where he has been a trial lawyer and appellate advocate on complex cases for over twenty-five years.

Liman was born in 1932 in New York. He grew up in a suburb of New York City. He received his AB from Harvard University in 1954, graduating Phi Beta Kappa, magna cum laude. He received his LLB from Yale Law School in 1957, graduating first in his class, magna cum laude, Order of the Coif.

Ollie North and Iran-Contra Hearings

Liman holds the singular distinction of having his courtroom performance watched by more Americans than any other lawyer in history (with the possible exception of Perry Mason and the lawyers involved in the O.J. Simpson murder case). As Chief Counsel of the Senate Select Committee on Investigation of Military Sales to Iran-Contra in 1987, the television cameras brought the hearings and him into the homes of millions of Americans. The country watched as he interrogated Oliver North, John Poindexter, and Richard Secord about their involvement in the affair, and overnight, Liman became a reluctant celebrity, requiring police protection during the hearings. "It was terrible. They would stay under our house with their police radios on all night and I couldn't sleep."

Liman on Oliver North:

> North is a person with an enormous presence, television sense, and an ability to read what the questioner is going to do...there was a question that I was going to put and it would have been embarrassing to him and have gained nothing, just an irrelevancy, but it would have embarrassed him. And I started, and I probably didn't get two words out and I switched. There wasn't anyone in the room, I think, including [North's attorney] Brendan V. Sullivan, who knew what I had done, and at the next recess, I had a handwritten note from Oliver North, "Thank you for not asking that question."

> North was sort of a rogue and a likable one and you couldn't believe Ollie's yarns. When Ollie would tell a yarn and you knew it was a yarn, he had a great imagination. He was way over his head in the task that was assigned to him but there was a warmth in Ollie and I believe that Ollie could have worked for Carter as easily as Reagan. I mean, Ollie got involved in whoever he was working with. Ollie was not an ideologue. Maybe he has become one now, but he was not an ideologue then. Poindexter was much more of an ideologue. Poindexter I could see pushing the button. Oliver North, no. And so I understood them both and I think as a trial lawyer, I try to understand every witness.

Liman arrived at an interesting psychological profile of North:

> I understood North. I think that North basically had father figures throughout his life and in the period that I studied him, the first father figure was Bud McFarlane who was the National Security Advisor. He lost all respect for Bud McFarlane when McFarlane tried to kill himself because that

was a weak thing. Casey was a father figure...Secord was a father figure for a period of time—strong, very tough guy. Secord flew over the Ho Chi Minh Trail at tree-top levels dropping calgonite so that in the rainy season the Viet Cong would slip off the trail...I mean, for anyone to be nuts enough to do that...but that was Secord.

By the end of the hearings, Liman observed that North's attorney was the latest in the parade of Ollie's father figures.

And so ultimately the father figure became Brendan Sullivan. Ed Williams told me that he was worried that Brendan was becoming too close to North. But Oliver North needed a strong authority figure and he found them throughout his life.

Liman walked a tightrope as Senate Counsel. He could not express his opinion of witness credibility lest he polarize the Senate committee into party components. It meant he had to cover his prosecutorial style with a velvet glove.

I was able to do it the way I would have done it were I trying a case with one exception, that as a counsel to the Senate, and a bipartisan counsel, something they had never done. I was very conscious that I wasn't a Senator. [If] I tried to steal the show and start to express my own judgments in the form of questions on credibility, I would have polarized the committee that I was sworn to represent as a whole. And, indeed, at one point on Poindexter, I ran into that trouble.

The difficulty took the form of some casual talk to the press.

I was almost the only person in Iran-Contra who was impeached because at the recess all the mikes are supposed to be off. The press comes up and talks to you [about] what are you trying to do...I was talking to them...in response to some question about what I thought of Poindexter's story. I said it was BS and the mike was on. And some of the Republican House members attacked me mercilessly when we went back on and the Senators defended me and, of course, I said that wasn't what I was intending to refer to, I was a good boy...

It was a fairly demanding situation in which Liman had to exert considerable forbearance.

All of my examinations had to be restrained in that I could not express my judgment. All I could do was test the witness and present the witness so that if they wanted to express their opinions, they could, but it would have blown the thing up if I tried to do what Walsh [Joe Walsh in the McCarthy hearings] did. My role was different.

Although he has obtained a number of prominent defense verdicts, he says that he relishes the plaintiff's role because he feels that in high-stake cases plaintiffs are more willing to try cases to verdict than defendants. Liman's legal career is unique in that he has been equally at home with both civil and criminal cases. He says that the criminal cases, the ones where at the end of the day someone might go to prison, are the ultimate test for the lawyer.

PATRICK F. MCCARTAN

Pat McCartan is managing partner of Jones, Day, Reavis & Pogue, an international law firm with nineteen offices world-wide (and ranked as the world's second largest law firm).

He was born August 3, 1934 in Cleveland, Ohio. He received his BA degree in 1956, magna cum laude, from the University of Notre Dame and his JD from Notre Dame Law School in 1959, graduating first in his class. During law school, he was editor-in-chief of the law review. Upon graduation, he clerked for Justice Charles Evans Whittaker of the United States Supreme Court during the 1959 term prior to joining Jones Day in 1960.

The son of a Youngstown policeman, McCartan grew up in a tough town and worked in a variety of jobs while attending high school and college, including summer employment in a steel mill, on construction crews, and in an aluminum plant. He credits those experiences with providing him with an understanding of working people, the kind he often finds on juries. He joined Jones Day in 1960 in order to practice corporate law because "corporations don't cry when they lose a case."[2] However, when he first joined, the firm's hierarchy wanted him to specialize in federal taxation. McCartan knew he wanted to try cases, so he soon went on to accumulate his own docket and began trying cases in Common Pleas Court before anyone could stop him. He was extremely successful, and became one of the firm's top trial lawyers. Featured in the *Wall Street Journal*, the *American Lawyer*, the *Institutional Investor*, and named by the *National Law Journal* as one of the most influential lawyers in the country since 1985, McCartan's trials include antitrust, taxation, takeovers, officer and director liability, and various kinds of securities and shareholder litigation. He has also been active in the product liability and consumer-class action areas, having defended mass-tort litigation for several manufacturers throughout the United States. McCartan is one of few lawyers to have sued one President of the United States and defended another. He had Jimmy Carter's gasoline tax declared unconstitutional and successfully defended Ronald Reagan's right to $29 million in federal election funds when the Carter-Mondale campaign tried to block the money headed for his 1980 presidential bid.

Marathon Oil Co. v. Mobil Corp.

McCartan's most significant case is the one he brought on behalf of Marathon Oil Company to enjoin Mobil Corporation's hostile tender offer for Marathon in 1982. "It isn't often you're given only sixteen days to prepare a six and-one-half-billion dollar antitrust case, but we did it. Of course, we had a team of approximately fifty lawyers working around the clock, but if I had been given three years to get ready, I don't think there is much I would have done differently." The president of Mobil, William Tavoulareas, had called Marathon late on a Friday afternoon in November of 1981 to advise that Mobil was going to make a tender offer for Marathon when the market opened on Monday. McCartan was advised around dinner time on Friday. He assembled a team

---

[2] *Cleveland Plain Dealer*, November 8, 1992.

and went to work, and by 11:30 Sunday evening had a temporary restraining order against the tender offer and a young lawyer on an airplane Monday morning to New York to serve Mobil with the order before trading opened on the New York Stock Exchange. "I think it was one of the most enjoyable professional experiences that I have ever had in my life." (It wasn't the young lawyer speaking, was it?) McCartan relates. At issue in the case was whether the acquisition of Marathon, a transaction that would have been the largest horizontal merger in history, would violate the federal antitrust laws. During the hearing on Marathon's motion for a preliminary injunction, McCartan's cross-examination of Tavoulareas was so intense that the trial judge threatened them both with contempt, but McCartan proved his case, and the court enjoined Mobil's tender offer.

Perhaps McCartan's most satisfying case was the defense of The Firestone Tire & Rubber Company in the protracted oil-extended rubber patent litigation brought by General Tire & Rubber Co. against the US tire industry. Every tire company except Firestone settled General, and the amount each settling defendant had to pay was conditioned on the outcome of the Firestone case. After losing the case to a trial judge, who said Firestone's arguments "couldn't stand the light of day," and facing more than $100 million in damages, McCartan convinced the Sixth Circuit Court of Appeals to reverse the trial court and to enter judgment for Firestone.

Another one of McCartan's most difficult matters was the successful defense of the Corvair direct-air heater litigation, a series of class actions and individual personal-injury cases. In one of the last Corvair cases tried in the United States, a Cincinnati man had burned to death in a Corvair crash. The family sued GM, claiming numerous design defects, specifically the direct-air heater, the positioning and protection of the fuel tank, the integrity of the entire fuel system, the door locks, and the interior trim on the automobile. "These product cases, in addition to presenting some rather complex technical issues, have an additional emotional layer because of the human tragedy that is so often involved. That makes them very challenging and difficult cases to defend, particularly when you have a major corporation as a defendant."

53

McCartan takes the most pride, not in his incredible trial record, but in the development of the largest and most effective litigation capability in the world. The Jones Day Litigation Group, with almost 500 members, has responsibility for a firm-wide docket of 4,000 matters pending in state and federal courts across the country and before international arbitral tribunals in Geneva, London, Paris, Stockholm, and The Hague. He took over the group in 1976, at which time there were twenty-five people in what was a quality regional litigation practice. "I have always maintained that being the best is a process, and not an event, and I expect the group to get even better in the years ahead."

Pat McCartan interviewed when he represented President Reagan.

Pat McCartan at Rancho Encantado, Santa Fe, New Mexico.

Cartoon appeared in the Cleveland Plain Dealer, 1982, depicting Mobil's takeover attempt of Marathon.

JAMES F. NEAL

Jim Neal is a senior partner in the firm of Neal & Harwell in Nashville, Tennessee. His principal area of practice is white-collar crime.

Neal was born September 7, 1929 in Sumner County, Tennessee. He attended college on a football scholarship and received his BS degree in Education, from the University of Wyoming in 1952. Upon graduation, he became a captain in the United States Marine Corps and was sent to Korea during the conflict there. It was during his military experience that he "volunteered" to study law and happily found that he liked it. He received his LLB from Vanderbilt University School of Law in 1957. His memberships included Order of the Coif and editor-in-chief of the *Vanderbilt Law Review*. He was also awarded the prestigious Founders Medal at Vanderbilt in 1957. This award is bestowed upon the student achieving the highest grade average for the

Dr. and Mrs. George Nichopoulos with defense counsel, Jim Neal.
"Dr. Nic" acquitted of over-prescribing drugs to Elvis Presley.

Jim Neal, John and Deborah Landis, "Twilight Zone" trial.

"I have many regrets in my life. Hiring you to defend me
is the one decision I will never regret."
—John

Jim Neal making a point regarding the
Exxon Valdez *case to law students.*

Picture of Judge John J. Sirica, with note to Jim Neal,
Associate Special Prosecutor, Watergate.

"With an expression of my highest regard for James F. Neal,
a great trial lawyer — Your friend, John J. Sirica."

entire law school period. In 1960 he received his LLM in taxation, from Georgetown University School of Law.

United States v. Jimmy Hoffa

In 1960, Neal met Attorney General Robert Kennedy who was looking for bright young men to bring into the Department of Justice. He was offered a position and he accepted. A few days later he was approached again by Kennedy who asked him to become Special Assistant Attorney General to prosecute major criminal cases. Soon, he found himself trying the Teamster giant, Jimmy Hoffa. He told Robert Kennedy that he had little or no experience in these types of cases. Kennedy said to him, "Well, I've had no experience being Attorney General either."

The case against Hoffa is not only one of Neal's many high-profile cases, it was one of his first cases. Jimmy Hoffa, head of the Teamster's Union, had been the subject of a great deal of not very pretty publicity over the years. (Neal was consulted during the filming of the 1992 movie starring Jack Nicholson as Hoffa.) In the early 1960s, Hoffa and a union colleague created a truck company and put the stock in their wives' names. Neal contended that they had violated the Taft-Hartley Act. After some further investigation, he uncovered some misuse of pension funds to develop an alleged Teamsters' retirement community to be known as Sun Valley. However, he felt they had only enough evidence to indict on the Taft-Hartley violations, so he pursued that. The violations were all misdemeanors. "It was only Hoffa who managed to escalate that into a felony by attempting to bribe jurors during the course of the trial."

> I think Hoffa had the best raw intellect of anybody I had ever seen. Very bright, very aggressive, very hardworking, all those admirable qualities. No education. Came up a terribly hard life. Got in a position of power and decided he'd do anything to keep it. Hated the Kennedys. I sort of had a grudging respect for Hoffa, thinking that he was evil all along, but I certainly could see some admirable qualities... It's been said before, but there is an enormous similarity of characteristics between Bob Kennedy and Jimmy Hoffa. Bob Kennedy had advantages, took advantage of those advantages. Bob Kennedy was, as far as I'm concerned, a very honorable man, but he was also very bright, very aggressive, very

> hardworking. Hoffa had the ability to charm. And I am sure with people who associated with him under a different ambiance, he had great ability to charm. I didn't see much charm from my perspective.

It was a colorful and dangerous time for Neal. He jokingly said that he allowed his wife to start the car in the mornings. A shooting had actually occurred in the courtroom.

> I turned around and this guy, with a trench coat on, collar turned up, was pulling a gun out of his pocket and the gun just keeps coming out, you know, the barrel seemed so long. He pulls the gun out and looks over at me, turns and starts shooting at Hoffa. The lawyers all jump into filing cabinets and behind chairs. But Hoffa jumps up and swings at the guy. Then his bodyguard takes over and just beats the devil out of him. So, if you look at the trial transcript, there is this dull argument going on and then the next line is, Judge Miller: "Will somebody please wipe up all that blood."

In 1964 Hoffa was eventually convicted in two separate trials for jury tampering and fraud. He was imprisoned in 1967. Despite the fact that he was incarcerated he remained president of the Teamsters until 1971 when President Nixon commuted his sentence with the stipulation that he not engage in union activity until 1980. In 1975 James Riddle Hoffa disappeared. It is assumed he was murdered.

Neal's high-profile cases read like a collection of front-page headlines from the *Daily News*. He was Chief Trial Counsel in the Watergate Special Prosecution Force, he defended the Ford Motor Company in the much-publicized Ford Pinto criminal trial (see box), he defended the movie director John Landis in the "Twilight Zone" criminal trial (*State of California v. John Landis, et al*), he defended Governor Edwin Edwards of Louisiana (*United States v. Governor Edwin Edwards*), he defended the Exxon Corporation in the civil and criminal cases involving the *Exxon Valdez* oil spill (*United States v. Exxon Corp. and Exxon Shipping Co.*), and in one very highly publicized case, he was asked to defend Elvis Presley's personal physician (*State of Tennessee v. Dr. George Nichopoulos*).

Henry Ford II
Chairman of the Board

Ford Motor Company
Renaissance Center
P.O. Box 43345
Detroit, Michigan 48243

March 13, 1980

Mr. James F. Neal,
Neal and Harwell,
800 Third National Bank Building,
Nashville, Tennessee 37219

Dear Jim:

I want to extend my personal congratulations
on the victory in Winamac and express my deep
appreciation for the total dedication and
effort you gave to bring about this result. I
know it was a tough assignment, and I don't
think anyone could have done a better job
than you did in representing our interests.

Some people can be expected to criticize
the verdict in Winamac. The charge could be
that now we are off the hook, we can forget
about product quality and safety. I don't
see it that way. I think the vote of confidence
from the jury in Winamac will serve to
encourage our management and our engineers
to redouble their efforts to achieve the
highest possible levels of quality and safety.

Thanks again for an outstanding job.

Best Regards

Henry Ford II

HFII:jc

*Letter from Henry Ford to Jim Neal,
"Ford Pinto" trial.*

*Jim Neal, (pictured third from the right)
Special Assistant to Robert F. Kennedy,
US Attorney General.*

The Indiana Pinto Case—The Car that Never Got to Goshen

[*State of Indiana v. Ford Motor Co.*]

Criminal charges were brought against Ford alleging that a 1973 Ford Pinto's faulty gas tank ruptured and led to the tragic deaths of three young women.

> My ultimate strategy was to show that whatever you may think about the Pinto, it was as good as any subcompact built at the time and better than some. Couple that with the fact you don't get the protection with a Pinto you get with a Lincoln Town Car and everybody with any sense has to recognize that. You don't pay near as much and there is a trade-off.

> The girls were on their way to a church service at night. But the car was headed the wrong way when it was hit. They left Elkhart, Indiana on the way to Goshen, Indiana. They never made the church that evening in Goshen, Indiana. The car was hit in the rear when it was headed in the direction back to Elkhart. Why was that car headed back? The prosecutor made no effort to determine that. And that just bugged the hell out of me and bugged the hell out of me. I knew that the 1972 Chevrolet van that hit the Pinto in the rear ruptured the gasoline tank—gas everywhere, a spark, and burned the girls up. I knew that the van driver admitted going fifty miles per hour. He had looked at his speedometer and he was going fifty miles an hour and he reached down to get a cigarette, then the Pinto was right ahead of him.

> There were seven eye witnesses who said the Pinto was traveling at about thirty-five miles per hour, making a closing speed of fifteen. The gas tank should not have blown up at that closing speed...the rear of that Pinto sure as hell didn't look like that was just the closing speed, but these seven eye witnesses swore to it. Shows you the problem with eye-witness testimony when you have a tragedy like this, at least.

Neal discovered, however, that one of the victims had told a different story to a hospital orderly just before she died.

> I scoured the world for that orderly. Sent somebody to Costa Rica because that's where we heard he was. Finally, we heard that he had moved to the peninsula up in Michigan. And I'll never forget, it was hunting season. And I sent a couple of guys up there, red and all that, because they were terrified. They found the guy.

His story proved invaluable. The orderly related the crash victim's story.

> "She told me that they were in this Pinto and they were driving to Goshen and they happened to look and see that they were about out of gas. So they pulled up at this self-service station, took the gasoline top off, put it on the top of the Pinto, filled it up with gasoline, and drove on their way to Goshen. As they were driving down, they happened to look back and the gasoline cap was rolling across the highway and they saw it roll across on the other side, and there happened to be a curve up there on this particular highway. The gasoline cap came to a stop. We looked in the rear-view mirror, made a U-turn, drove up to the cap, and we stopped." And she was the driver who was speaking. "I just started to open the door to get out and I happened to look in my rear view mirror and say, 'That truck is not going to stop.' And with that she expired."

Neal convinced the jury that the Pinto was hit at a closing speed of fifty miles per hour. He then simulated the crash using a Chevy van, and a number of comparable subcompacts, a 1973 Pinto, a Dodge Dart, a Gremlin, a Toyota. The results were the same— ruptured gas tank. Total destruction. The simulation was repeated with full-size cars with the same result. The prosecutor was shocked by Neal's surprise witness.

> They put on their case. All the eye witnesses, everything. We did what we could, but what can you say when a guy gets up there and says, "I was right across there. The Pinto was going twenty-five miles or thirty-five miles or whatever it was." We got on our case, we called our first witness. We called the Seventh Day Adventist [the orderly], put him on the stand. He gave the most moving testimony of how he had talked to this girl. Of course, we immediately handed a brief on dying declaration and all of that. The court admitted it. Talked about the girl, what she had told him, everything. The Pinto was stopped. If they believed him, we stopped the Pinto and we followed that up by showing the crash tests. The prosecutor, he just died over there, grabbing at anything, and he says, "When did you come up with this story?" implying it was a recent fabrication. "When did you get with Mr. Neal and come up with this story?"

The witness held his ground.

He says, "I didn't come up with this story. This was such a tragic event for me that I went to my church that following Sunday, two days later. We have this practice of telling people of experiences in our lives. I stood up and told everybody in church about what had happened, what this girl had said to me." Well, I got up and said, "Ladies and Gentlemen, we've got a bus outside," and we were ready, [if the prosecutor] "wants to continue this claim that this guy is fabricating this story," I said, "we will bring a bus load of people from that church down here to testify about what they were told two days later." We got to the bottom line. Having established the closing speed was fifty miles an hour, whether cars should be made to withstand that or not, they weren't. The jury was still out three days even then. During the trial, the jury was sequestered and Johnny Carson would come out and talk about the Pinto, the mobile stove. The first vote was ten to two for acquittal on all charges. But two people held out for two and a half days. They finally just capitulated.

HARRY M. REASONER

Harry Reasoner is managing partner of the law firm of Vinson & Elkins in Houston, Texas. His principal area of practice is general litigation, including antitrust and securities litigation. Reasoner was born July 15, 1939 in San Marcos, Texas. He graduated from Rice University in 1960. He received his BA in Philosophy. A National Merit Scholar, he graduated Phi Beta Kappa, summa cum laude. He attended law school at the University of Texas at Austin, School of Law. There, he was editor of the *Texas Law Review*. His memberships included Chancellors and Order of the Coif. He graduated first in his class in 1962. He also completed post-graduate education at the University of London as a Rotary Foundation Fellow studying international law and comparative law of competition and monopoly. He then clerked for Judge Charles E. Clark on the United States Courts of Appeals for the Second Circuit.

Reasoner's initial interest in law was in the area of taxation. However, when he joined the firm of Vinson & Elkins, the senior partner immediately enlisted his efforts in a large antitrust case that was getting ready to go to trial. He found he loved the work, and as he put it, "I simply never got around to trying tax law." That first case was *United States v. Continental Oil.*

One of Reasoner's most important plaintiff's cases was an early one involving a uranium cartel. He represented the then Houston Natural Gas and Rancher's Exploration and Development in the State District Court in New Mexico. They had sued Gulf Oil Corporation for its participation in the uranium cartel. The case settled on the eve of trial, for a value of $200 million.

Reasoner's largest plaintiff case tried to verdict was the ETSI case (*ETSI Pipeline Project and Houston Lighting & Power Co. v. Burlington Northern, Inc., et al*). ETSI was a joint venture of Bechtel, Texas Eastern, KN Energy, and Enron, planning to build a coal slurry pipeline. Reasoner had sued six railroads that had conspired to prevent ETSI from building the coal slurry pipeline from Wyoming to supply the utilities in Texas and Arkansas. All of the railroads settled with Reasoner with the exception of Santa Fe. There were rumors in the legal community that Santa Fe could have settled the case for $25 millon but declined to do so. The jury verdict against them was $1.035 billion. The case was important because it attacked the most effective way to frustrate competition in the United States: the misuse of administrative and judicial processes to create barriers to entry. It was also a case demonstrating brilliant trial strategies and tactics and Reasoner's innovative use of electronic visual technology in the courtroom.

One of his most memorable plaintiff cases occurred when he was appointed to represent the inmates of the Texas prison system as a class (*Guadalupe Guajardo, Jr., et al v. W.J. Estelle, Jr., et al*) with regard to the infringement of their First Amendment rights. At that time the prison system routinely read attorney/client communications, refused to allow prisoners to write to the media, and followed a wide line of restrictive practices as to what inmates could read or with whom they could correspond. His firm still serves as special counsel to monitor compliance in the Texas Department of Corrections. "It is far too easy for our prisons, which are under-funded and overcrowded, to slide towards truly barbaric conditions," Reasoner has observed.

Harry Reasoner with legal assistants during ETSI Pipeline Project and Houston Lighting & Power Co. vs. Burlington Northern Inc., et. al. *in Beaumont, January 1989.*

Harry Reasoner and wife, Marcey, receiving the Anti-Defamation League's Torch of Liberty Award.

Harry Reasoner (left) the night before ETSI verdict with Tom Farhner and Dalton Taulin playing poker.

Times Herald Printing Co. v. A.H. Belo Corp.

On the defense side, Reasoner considers the trial in which he defended the *Dallas Morning News* when it was sued by the *Dallas Times Herald* under the Texas antitrust laws, as one of his most important. The *Times Herald* had claimed that when the *Morning News* contracted with Universal Press Syndicate to obtain twenty-six syndicated comics and columns (Dear Abby, Erma Bombeck and Doonesbury, among others) that had been running in the *Times Herald*, and transferred them to the *Dallas Morning News*, it had violated state antitrust laws. The *Times Herald* was a smaller newspaper, in desperate economic condition, therefore able to create an underdog sympathy. The *Times Herald* claimed that the act had hurt them enough to send them into a death spiral and sued for $100 million. The jury deliberated for seven days and returned with a take-nothing verdict in favor of the defense. Reasoner obtained the defense verdict by persuading the jury that honest competition was a tough game that benefitted consumers and, if the *Dallas Morning News* was not allowed to compete for comic strips and columns, those who had the comics and columns under contract could treat their creators like serfs. He felt that a take-nothing verdict is a major accomplishment because it is difficult to make a jury understand the difference between hard competition and unfair conduct, and it is difficult to overcome sympathy for an underdog. At the time Reasoner was quoted as saying in the *Houston Post*, "We went out and competed with them for these features and paid a better price. Did we go out and pay a better price? You betcha. Did we tortiously interfere and violate the law? No."

Reasoner is currently Chair of the United States District Court for the Southern District Civil Justice Reform group, which advises on developing plans to lessen court delay. He is a civic-minded citizen in his Houston community and active in Democratic politics. In 1992 he and his wife, Macey, received the Torch of Liberty Award from the Southwest Region of the Anti-Defamation League in recognition of their charitable and professional efforts to oppose bigotry and advance the cause of human rights. "Law is only a worthy profession if lawyers become involved in civic affairs for other than venal reasons," he has stated.

STEPHEN D. SUSMAN

S teve Susman is a partner in the law firm of Susman Godfrey in Houston, Texas. His principal area of practice is commercial litigation.

Susman was born January 20, 1941 in Houston, Texas. His mother was a lawyer and his father had been a trial lawyer. He received his BA in Honors English from Yale University, magna cum laude in 1962. He attended law school at the University of Texas, where he graduated first in his class in 1965. His memberships included Order of the Coif, Chancellors, and Friars. He was editor-in-chief of the *Texas Law Review* and was Phi Delta Phi's outstanding graduate. He served as law clerk to Judge John R. Brown of the fifth circuit and Justice Hugo Black of the United States Supreme Court. After a brief stint as a partner with a large Houston law firm, Susman considered becoming a law professor. But at the urging of his wife and friends, he began his

*Susman jogging with Bill Clinton in New York City's
Central Park during the Democratic Convention.*

*Susman family. Left to right:
Steve, Karen, Harry and Stacey.
Sculpture by Dean McNeil.*

*Susman bicycling with
daughter Stacey and son
Harry in Burgundy, France,
at the beginning of their
three-and-a-half month
world trip.*

successful commercial litigation practice as a plaintiff's antitrust lawyer.

Susman's first widely reported victory came as lead counsel for the plaintiffs in the *Corrugated Container Antitrust Litigation*, a class-action suit in 1980. He sued forty corrugated-box makers for price-fixing and obtained a jury verdict that almost topped a billion dollars and settlements in excess of $500 million (and garnered $7 million for his litigation group). He represented former Speaker of the House Jim Wright in his ethics fight (see box), and the Hunt brothers in their lender liability case against twenty-five US and international banks. On behalf of his clients, he sued the banks for $1.5 billion. The lawsuit, a brilliant piece of logic, claimed that the banks were not entitled to have the money repaid to them because the banks should never have loaned the money to the Hunts in the first place, they were such bad risks. As a result of this strategy, the case was dropped as part of an agreement to let the brothers emerge from Chapter 11 bankruptcy reorganization. (For this Susman received a million-dollar retainer and $600 an hour.) He has tried, and won, jury trials against Schlumberger, 3M, Xerox, and Whittaker; and for Picker International and Inter-City Products, as defendants.

In 1988, House Speaker Jim Wright had been charged by the House Committee on Official Standards—the House Ethics Committee—with taking gifts from George Mallick, a Fort Worth businessman. These gifts were prohibited because Mallick allegedly had an interest in legislation. Susman's task was to persuade the members of the Ethics Committee that they had made a legal error. His strategy was to present his argument that even though Wright was close to violating House rules, he did not. Susman's point was that the Speaker was being hanged for acts he did not commit. Wright, whom the media already considered a dead man, deserved due process and his day in court—not a "lynch mob" to respond to the sixty-nine charges. Although Wright eventually resigned, his career and reputation in shambles, Steve Susman's soared as a result of the national exposure. A prominent national newspaper covered this story:

STAND IN THE WAY OF LYNCH MOB AND DROP CHARGES, WRIGHT LAWYER ASKS

(by William J. Eaton, *Los Angeles Times*, Wednesday, May 24, 1989)

WASHINGTON – House Speaker Jim Wright's lawyer urged the House Ethics Committee Tuesday to "stand in the way of a lynch mob" and drop major charges against Wright, which he said could drive the Speaker from office without a fair hearing from his colleagues.

From the tone of their questions, however, most members of the panel seemed unmoved by the emotional and legal arguments presented on Wright's behalf by Stephen D. Susman, a trial lawyer from Houston, at a day long televised hearing.

The Speaker did not attend but watched most of the hearing on television. His wife, Betty, who is a principal figure in the committee's charges, had a front-row seat and bestowed a kiss on Wright's lawyer after his initial presentation, whispering: "You're wonderful."

ROBERT S. WARREN

Bob Warren is partner and member of the Executive Committee of the law firm of Gibson, Dunn & Crutcher in Los Angeles, California.

Warren was born on December 9, 1931 in Pasadena, California. He graduated Phi Beta Kappa from the University of Southern California in 1953, with a BA in Economics. He attended law school at the University of Southern California, graduating second in his class, in 1956. His memberships in law school included Order of the Coif and associate editor of the *Southern California Law Review.* He was admitted to the American College of Trial Lawyers in 1974, which, based upon years of practice, was the earliest date possible to be eligible for admission to the college.

Star Wars

In the latter half of the 1970s Warren handled two cases of importance for Twentieth Century Fox Film. The first involved an effort by a group of Chicago investors to claim an interest in various Fox films, including a claim that they had been fraudulently deprived of an interest in the film *Star Wars*. Needless to say, the amount of money at issue on that claim was astronomical, although the basis of the claim was weak. After extensive discovery wars in the federal court (primarily relating to the claim by the plaintiffs that all communications through their attorney negotiators were privileged), the claims were settled at a sum that was quite tolerable to the company. The second Fox suit was initiated by Fess Parker, the lanky actor who gained fame in the television series playing Daniel Boone and Davy Crockett. Parker presented one of the first of the claims by performers challenging the studio's accounting methods in computing "profits" to be paid to performers under the standard studio contract then being used. The case was litigated over a period of years, including appellate proceedings attempting to force the case into a form of accounting arbitration provided for in the contract. On the eve of trial, a change of ownership took place at Fox. The new management, deciding to put pending litigation behind it, negotiated a settlement with Parker.

Warren has an eclectic trial background, with major cases in a wide variety of areas, including securities, business-contract claims, insurance, and the First Amendment. Since the latter half of the 1960s, he has been intensely involved in the area of First Amendment litigation, causing him to be selected as chief trial counsel for the *Los Angeles Times*, the Times Mirror Company, Dow Jones, and McClatchy Newspapers. He has also been involved as senior trial counsel for other media interests, such as NBC, Twentieth Century Fox , and The New York Times Company. In the well-known case, *Ramada Inns v. Dow Jones & Co.* (1981), Warren represented Dow Jones, publisher of the *Wall Street Journal*. The paper had published an article, co-written by an investigative reporter titled, "Ramada Inns' Gambling Operations Beset by Thefts and Mounting Costs." Ramada brought suit against Dow Jones and the reporter, stating that the story was false. The trial lasted fifty-seven days. The jury returned a verdict for the defendants. The prosecution's strategy had included an attempt to discredit the reporter, who did not appear in the trial, by having the reporter's deposition read from the stand by a person who was dressed in sloppy clothes and appeared carefully prepared for the performance. They attempted to discredit his sources and to portray him as loudmouthed and abusive. However, their strategy backfired when the defense presented a photograph of the reporter and witnesses described him as a soft-spoken family man. Further, the defense had shown that there was reason to doubt the sources' denials, pointing out that it is a common journalistic occurrence for sources who have provided embarrassing information to back away when confronted with their allegations. This was a difficult case due to the length of the trial, the many interruptions that occurred during the proceedings, the fact that the reporter was not a witness in the trial, and the overwhelming importance of closing arguments.

In 1985, Warren was brought in on the eve of trial to represent Underwriters at Lloyds in the case pending in the Nevada District Court for Clark County (Las Vegas) in the cases entitled *In the Matter of the MGM Grand Hotel Insurance Litigation*. This case arose after claims settlement arising from the hotel fire when MGM attempted to collect on multiple layers of highly unusual "retrospective insurance" that had been procured by MGM after the fire. The case was presided over by a judge later removed from the bench because of alleged mental disorders. He routinely imposed "sanctions" of $5,000 to $25,000 upon counsel for such matters as failing to have exhibit notebooks properly punched and labeled. The trial commenced with row after row of counsel tables filled with lawyers for the contending parties, with seats in the rear for mandatory "local counsel" who were not to participate in the proceedings. Faced with ongoing expenses, which included paving a portion of the parking lot outside the auditorium (where the trial was held), the parties reached a settlement after empanelment of the jury.

NBC "Dateline" Crash

Early in 1993, Warren and attorney Lewis B. Kaden, were commissioned as co-investigators by NBC to report on the much-publicized faked General Motors truck crash shown on the TV program "Dateline NBC" aired November 17, 1992. The problem with the segment resulted from the inclusion of an "unscientific crash demonstration" of a GM truck in which igniters were used but not disclosed. The lawsuit had been settled with an apology only after GM filed a defamation suit. It also took a lawsuit for NBC to investigate the crash test methods. The investigation lasted one month and produced a seventy-one page report, which concluded, among other things that those who prepared the crash story "did not deliberately set out to falsify the 'test'" but that the "story of the ill-fated crash demonstrations and its aftermath is rather a story of lapsed judgment—serious lapses—by persons generally well-intentioned and well-qualified." Nevertheless, the report exposed serious journalistic blunders. And as a result of the debacle, NBC News President Michael Gartner resigned and three producers of the series also resigned the week the investigative report was issued.

Warren's most interesting cases have been the ones that attempt to blaze new trails. He gives as an example, *Sam Yorty v. Los Angeles Times and Paul Conrad*. In this trial, a famous cartoonist, Paul Conrad, skewered former Los Angeles Mayor Sam Yorty in the late 1960s, ridiculing Yorty's belief that President Nixon might appoint him to be Secretary of Defense. A libel suit followed, and Warren's motion to dismiss that suit raised important and novel issues relating to the protections of rights of free press applicable to political cartooning. The dismissal was upheld on appeal by an opinion that is still the subject of frequent reference.

He is active on the Board of Counselors at the University of Southern California Law School and has donated his time and financial resources to the Norris Cancer Center at University of Southern California.

*Bob Warren spotting mountain black bears
for Park Service.*

Bob Warren with grandchild.

CHAPTER 2 ████████████

Personality and Performance Traits Identified

> *I'm going to walk into that court and know who I am. I know that's what God put me on this earth for.*
>
> **—Phil Corboy**

How did the fourteen men reviewed in this book become an elite group? What are their strengths? What is their genius? What are the secrets of their success? Why do they get the big cases and why do they win most of them? As we shall see, the personality traits of these lawyers are closely related to their professional achievements. There are of course differences in style and personal approach to trial law among the fourteen. But they share a number of characteristics essential to their success.

Intelligence

> To begin with, there is no substitute for gray matter. I see it time and time again, day in and day out. Foot speed is the criterion for the NFL. Gray matter is the criterion in this profession. You just have to have it.
>
> **—Pat McCartan**

Not surprisingly, all of the fourteen advocates presented here are extremely intelligent. In the conventional IQ context, each one would score at the upper end of a continuum measuring intellectual ability. They were exceptionally successful in their academic endeavors, most graduating in the top of their law school class. In addition to "academic" intelligence (See Figure 2-1), they also possess an analytical intelligence; that is, the ability to comprehend abstractions and to master new and complex information quickly and accurately. Besides their "gray-matter smarts," these men have "street smarts"— the ability to apply raw intelligence to a problem *instantaneously*. The Profession Survey revealed that nationally prominent trial lawyers are not viewed as intellectuals. They were described as possessing a common-sense type of intelligence. Respondents variously described this intelligence as intuition, imagination, quick thinking under pressure, and exceptional memory. (Judge Learned Hand once described the trial lawyer as possessing a "bathtub mind." He saw good lawyers as capable of filling their heads with the myriad of pertinent facts of a case, then afterward pulling the plug, scouring away their recollection of those facts, and getting ready to refill it for the next trial.)

Undergraduate Education

- Boston College
- De Paul University
- Harvard University
- Rice University
- University of Missouri, Kansas City
- University of Notre Dame (2)
- University of Redlands
- University of Southern California
- University of Texas
- University of Wyoming
- US Military Academy, West Point
- Yale University (2)

Law School

- Harvard
- Loyola - Chicago
- University of Illinois
- University of Michigan
- University of Notre Dame
- University of Southern California (2)
- University of Texas (3)
- Vanderbilt
- Yale (3)

figure 2-1

Intelligence among the great trial attorneys is also manifest to a degree in love of intellectual stimulation. This is not a primary characteristic, however, as it would be for many academics working in an abstract field. For these lawyers, intellectual stimulation takes place in a pragmatic context. Trial law is intellectually stimulating, and that is one of its most important attractions. Wide intellectual interests allow great trial lawyers to make use of different disciplines when attempting to relate to jurors. They can, to a degree, draw upon psychology, literature, religion, sociology, history, and political science, as well as an occasional craft or trade, to relate more easily to a jury.

Intelligence, then, is basic to all of these men. Yet their intelligence is never a barrier between them and those they seek to influence. There is a strain of anti-intellectualism in American life that these attorneys well understand. They do not allow their intelligence to alienate jurors or to distance themselves from the people they must persuade.

Communication Skills

There is no greater indicator of the special kind of intelligence possessed by successful trial lawyers than their ability for nuanced communication. They are particularly expert at using different levels of language. They speak legalese fluently with judges and fellow attorneys. But they are also able to speak with great familiarity to a broad stratum of people—groups from which juries are typically drawn. Their talent in this area is akin to that of a successful popular novelist or politician. They sense a psychological pulse among jurors that is not frequently picked up by others, and talk to it directly. This effective communication, the alpha and omega of a trial lawyer's bag of tricks, depends on naturalness and sincerity.

> What's important is that it be natural...if it's not natural, you can't sustain it. And the thing that will turn a jury off worse than anything is a sense that they are being played on, that you're fooling with them, that you're not being yourself.
>
> **—David Boies**

Maintaining jury focus is the difference between good and great. Communication is important, but according to Max Blecher, knowing *what* to communicate is even more so. "The great trial lawyers know what's going to sell...the way you package and present it is what makes the difference as well as the oratorical ability to communicate. It takes those two ingredients."

An attorney must translate detailed, complex knowledge of the case into a story the jury can understand. The attorney must persuade the jury on a point he has perhaps spent hundreds of hours to master himself. The point must be stated so clearly that the jury exposed to it for the first time and with its limited background in the matter, will immediately grasp it.

The importance of psychological insight into the process of effective communication is so critical for a trial lawyer that it was surprising to find that this was not mentioned with any consistency in the Profession Survey. A few of the respondents indicated that exceptional trial lawyers have a keen sense of how they are perceived by jurors, judges, and other lawyers. But there was no overt mention that this grasp of human nature was a shared trait. Yet, the fourteen lawyers themselves felt that this ability to understand and communicate with other people was of critical importance. They believe, generally, that in order to construct a reasonable theory of a case, a believable scenario, one has to understand probable, sensible human behavior.

Juries are like children in a lot of respects. They notice far more than you think they notice. They are very good at separating people who are posturing from people who are being natural. They are pretty good at separating people who are lying from people who are telling the truth. They tend to go for simple truths rather than complicated explanations. And they understand when people like them, just like a child does. I think it's hard to fake that. If you're going to be a good trial lawyer, you've genuinely got to like people.

—David Boies

The fourteen draw upon their knowledge of people when they conduct voir dire, as well as at all times during a trial. It is critical to determine instantly whether or not a given juror will be sympathetic or hostile toward the client's position. This requires the ability to fathom a mind-set on the basis of only a few salient pieces of information. A knowledge of human psychology is essential with witnesses too. The manipulation of a witness's moods, or forcing emotion into a witness's voice, for example, is an important capability. On direct examination, a witness must be made to appear confident and credible. On cross-examination, the attorney might incite a witness to anger, or even fear, making them appear uncertain or lacking in confidence.

Knowledge of human psychology is also germane to a successful relationship with clients. A great deal of understanding and empathy is needed on the lawyer's part, especially when dealing with all the people involved. Even in the case of large corporate clients, dealing effectively with a variety of individuals from executives to in-house counsel is essential.

Finally, the lawyers attempt to maintain an approachable demeanor, not only in terms of what they say in the courtroom, but also in the way they physically appear to jurors. They are aware of their appearance and choose their attire appropriately. They do not wish to be perceived as a "dandy" or pompous clothes horse. Instead, they tend to choose clothing that communicates a statement of success and reliability.

Judgment

> The one that doesn't get mentioned a lot but I think is fundamental is judgment. That is to say, this trial is unfolding, things are happening, there is a dynamic. The judge is a certain way, your opponent is a certain way, the jury is a certain way, your witnesses are doing something, and you have to make a judgment about what to do... That's number one.
>
> **—Jim Brosnahan**

Judgment differs from intelligence. We all know incredibly bright people who possess no discernible judgment. Of course, one must be intelligent to have good judgment. Judgment includes the ability to understand the consequences of action—yours or someone else's. For example, if the lawyer files the case in federal court rather than state court, certain events may well occur to his advantage or disadvantage regarding witnesses, procedural rules, voir dire, and trial calendars. Judgment is the capacity to anticipate the response of someone else to some action, event, or situation. What is a witness likely to do if the lawyer embarks upon a particular line of questioning? How is the judge likely to rule on a relatively minor side issue that might ultimately have a major impact on the totality of his case? Judgment is understanding the available options—to be able to evaluate them and select the most appropriate, i.e., pertinent legal theory, response to opposition's counterclaims, or cause of action.

Simply, judgment is knowing what to do and when to do it. Bob Warren laments that even though they are intelligent and receive top law school grades, many young lawyers "simply can't do any-thing...I've finally decided that the most essential qualities of all are the willingness to make a judgment, and secondly, the ability to make a good judgment." Vacillating will not win a case. "They simply can't bring themselves to put their guts on the line with the choice."

One might suppose making a judgment is more of a character trait than a skill. But experience counts. The ability not just to choose, but to make the right choice is the question, and to do so quickly. Judgment is what distinguishes one lawyer from another.

It is all part of what I call judgment...the ability to know whether you go left or right when you get to the fork in the road. Now everybody will sometimes choose the wrong fork. We can't all be right all the time. But if you're right more than you're wrong, then you at least pass the judgment test. If you keep making judgmental mistakes because you can't see the issues or you can't focus on the problems or you don't have the capacity to see the story...then you're not right for this business.

—Max Blecher

While it is not normal to be paralyzed with indecision, most of us are unaccustomed to making complex decisions involving the fate of individuals or corporations, or the functioning of important economic and financial entities in our society. These lawyers have a superior ability to make decisions and then implement the imperatives. Although they receive input from associates, it is the trial attorney who makes the final decision about the legal course of action based on their own confident judgment, knowledge, and experience. These fourteen unanimously display a remarkable amount of self-confidence. Once they make a decision, they know it is right. They are not easily dissuaded from continuing on a course they have set for themselves.

Nevertheless, one important aspect of this decision-making gift is an ability to remain receptive once a course of action has been planned. Once the situation changes, once new evidence is available, these men are capable of quickly reformulating their original decision and plotting a new course. This flexibility is also part of their success.

I make up my mind very fast intuitively, not by inductive reasoning...When I feel it, when I get the sense I know what the right thing is to do, I'm going to do it unless somebody is very, very good and very fast at talking me out of it.

—Tom Barr

Self-Monitoring

A critical component in the success of these trial lawyers is their ability to know how they are perceived by others at all times, and to control these impressions. Self-monitoring is a discipline. And for Tom Barr, it is the ability to "keep his own personality in check and to use it." Altogether too frequently trial lawyers have no clue as to when they are boring a jury, angering a judge, or insulting a witness. These fourteen advocates are constantly fine tuning their performance, exquisitely aware of their affect on jurors, the judge, and witnesses. And in today's environment of televised trials, this capability extends to the media and to the millions of "courtroom junkies" watching the trial at home.

These lawyers know exactly the degree and quality of emotional valence they put into every word. Consequently, a component of their emotional stability is an acute awareness of the effect they have upon others. These lawyers are comfortable in the courtroom. They are not self-conscious or modest, which is not to say that they are never anxious or emotional. But they know how to use emotion to step up their trial performance. Self-monitoring means dealing with pressure and keeping emotion and impulsive acting out under control. Even when things go wrong, or not according to plan, the great lawyers display great agility in turning the surprise to their advantage. They think on their feet, can improvise when necessary, and take advantage of an opening that may suddenly and unexpectedly appear.

An unbridled display of anger, for example, is not something that these lawyers tolerate in themselves or in the behavior of those working with them on a trial team. Even Joe Jamail, who more than any of the other fourteen tends to engage in heated outbursts in the courtroom, says that his outbursts are well considered and intended for a purpose. These men believe that a trial lawyer does not have the luxury of a cathartic experience in front of a jury. Several said that the few times that a situation had occurred in which they had lost control of their emotions, something deleterious had ensued. Either the jurors had seen them in an unflattering light, or the opponent had used the outburst to his own advantage. Even worse, they were usually extremely disappointed in themselves for the display.

I've always been struck by Yeat's phrase, "Cast a cold eye," because I think the ability not to allow your emotions to interfere with your art is crucial. A trial lawyer who gets genuinely angry, not the use of the emotion as part of their appeal or advocacy, but where it actually starts to affect their judgment and conduct, I would not think that people to whom that happens to would be great trial lawyers...

—Harry Reasoner

Social psychologists have documented the relationship between emotional arousal and performance. The relationship is so constant it is assigned the distinction of law, one of the few that exists in the realm of social psychology. The law states that there is a minimum amount of arousal necessary for optimal performance at any given task. Too little arousal, and the individual does not do well at the task. Too much arousal and the individual also performs poorly. The amount of arousal needed for optimal or best performance is greater for simpler tasks. This seems counter-intuitive at first. But it means that, when an individual is engaged in a task that is simple, one that he or she has practiced over and over and is good at, he or she needs a greater amount of arousal to perform well. It can be conjectured that the individual who is not aroused sufficiently is simply too bored to do well.

For experienced trial lawyers the basic courtroom tasks are well learned and somewhat elementary. In order to perform at an optimal level, they need to "psyche" themselves up to a level of arousal, both mental and physical, which will allow them their best performance. Without this ability their effectiveness would be diminished. In fact, one of the lawyers speculated that an important distinction between a good trial lawyer and a great one who continues successfully to try cases for twenty or thirty years, is the ability to maintain intensity about a trial.

Controlling fear is another important element in self-monitoring, but fear can become a positive force. It is fear that drives Tom Barr to a higher level of thinking. Winning decisions are driven by emotion tempered by detachment, the lawyer's magic formula. Barr *knows* where he stands at all times in court. "I know when it's stepped up and I know that's the time when I feel like I could really make all the decisions and they're going to be right." Harry Reasoner adds, "You have to caution yourself not to overreact. You are exposing yourself in a vulnerable way when you're trying to sell and persuade people." These men are aware of their emotional state at all times, and can control the projection of anger, satisfaction, or dismay. Because they are "plugged in," they are highly receptive to continuous information and cues; and are therefore more agile in courtroom maneuvering. "Be self-confident but receptive," advises Bob Warren, "to receive information and to act on it and to adapt to the environment." And finally, a point Tom Barr emphatically makes, is knowing when to "do nothing . . . And many, many people never, ever learn that. They just get up and shoot their mouths off."

> When a lawyer decides that he wants that spotlight in the courtroom on himself, that he wants to be the star of the show, he is going to fall on his ass every time. [It gets] in the way of your case. It's letting that ego override what you know to be the best parts of your lawsuit. The great trial lawyer knows where in the courtroom to move that spotlight around. It ought to be on whomever is important. They [jurors] want to hear the story. That's why they watch afternoon TV.
>
> **—Joe Jamail**

Although these men have great self-confidence and huge egos at one level, they never allow themselves to appear egocentric before jurors. They cannot become so wrapped up in themselves that they fail to look at the world through a juror's eyes.

Charisma

The image of a great trial lawyer as charismatic is a common one. Charisma was listed second most frequently in the Profession Survey. It was described variously as persona, presence, confidence, credibility, relating well to people, dominance in the courtroom, personal appeal, rapport, and the X-factor ("The difference between Ryne Sandberg and just another second baseman"). Many believed it to be an innate quality and fairly immutable.

> There is something and I'm not sure what it is, but it is called presence. I'm not sure how you get it because some people have it who are tall and big and some people who have it are little bitty. Joe Jamail is like that. Joe has a presence in a courtroom. He is a little bitty guy. He begins performing and he begins carrying on and joking with the jury and about the case and about everything, smart alecking. He has a kind of presence about him. People listen to him.
>
> **—Steve Susman**

The ancient Greeks gave us the word charisma, meaning divine gift. It was believed that leaders were imbued with a magical quality that inspired their followers to act. These qualities make others listen to them, and want to be persuaded by them. The concept of charisma may be difficult to define and measure, but the concept of leadership has generated a great deal of research in social psychology. The definition of a good leader comes close to describing the elusive aspect of charisma. By defining charisma in this way, we can understand what it is when we say the great lawyers "have it." The lawyer's role in the courtroom is a leader's role. Their followers are the jurors. Lawyers attempt, through their argument, to lead jurors to accept their theory of the case.

Leadership probably consists of all the traits discussed here: intelligence, charisma, love of competition, judgment, emotional maturity, and self-discipline. It is interesting that our fourteen lawyers do not tend to view themselves as leaders. When rating work values (see Appendix 4), authority over others was rated next to last in importance. This is in contrast with its importance to lawyers in the general population, who rated it much more highly on the Neo-Personality Inventory.

Even so, it has been seen that the fourteen lawyers' standings on the personality measures indicate that they do in fact possess leadership qualities. When in a group, they are more apt to take charge or to be outspoken in their views. On the confidential questionnaires, one lawyer lamented that he really did not want to dominate a group, but since no one else offered opinions he might as well continue expressing his.

One aspect of their leadership acumen is to avoid flaunting their intellectual ability. As one of the lawyers commented, jurors *expected* him to be better educated, to speak better, and to be more refined, and so consequently he does not disappoint them. Research has indicated that a good leader is generally perceived by his followers as more intelligent, but not perceived as disproportionately higher in intelligence. This narrow gap allows for confidence in the leader's judgment, but at the same time allows for accessibility to him as a person. If an individual is perceived as too intelligent, he is also seen as too different from his followers and therefore not as someone in whom to place allegiance.

Honesty

In the answer to the question, "What are the traits you most admire in others?" honesty was mentioned again and again by the group of fourteen as an important quality for all people to possess, not just attorneys. (See Figures 2-2 and 2-3). One lawyer responded, "There is no one on earth important enough to cause you to lie." It is difficult to know whether their strong sense of integrity contributed to their prominent status as trial lawyers, or whether their prominent status allowed them the freedom to maintain an uncompromising moral position. It is interesting to note that on the instrumental values or modes of behavior on the Rokeach Value Inventory (see Appendix 4), honesty was valued more highly than self-control. These attorneys would rather be truthful in their expressions than restrained.

The fourteen lawyers in this study make the claim that they operate within a strict code regarding their own ethics and honesty. More similar to a samurai than a "hired gun," they do whatever they consider necessary to win for the client within the guidelines of legal ethics and standards. As Bob Fiske says, "I want to win at all costs, short of doing something unfair." For them, a strict adherence to a set of legal ethics is important, not only for professional credibility, but also to avoid being judged as hypocritical by others.

Trait	Number of Lawyers Who Listed Trait
1. Honesty	11
2. Loyalty	6
3. Hard-work	5
4. Courage	5
5. Intelligence	2
6. Independence	2
7. Articulate	1
8. Humor	1
9. Lack of pomposity	1
10. Compassion	1

figure 2-2

Important Values for Children

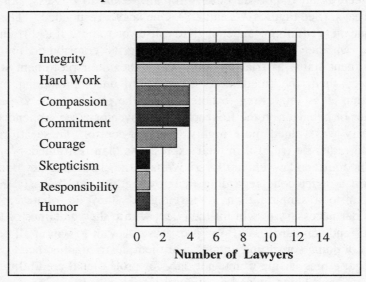

figure 2-3

Love of Competition

You've got to like competition. This guy's trying to beat you. What can I tell you? If you don't like competition, you can't possibly do this. For one thing, if you lose, it will destroy you.

—Jim Brosnahan

In our society, attitudes toward competition vary. Some people are uncomfortable with competition, become easily frustrated and discouraged in competitive situations, and avoid them when possible. In our culture, competition is often taken to an extreme. Frequently, competition leads to ill-timed outbursts of hostility and anger. Competitive behavior can also manifest into symbolic acting out, in which a person tilts with windmills, authority figures, a surrogate sibling, or a business rival.

Both Arthur Liman and David Boies argue that the competitive drive in a trial lawyer comes largely from an identification with the client. The capacity to associate and yet remain objective is a characteristic that surfaces again and again in these men. It may be that in trial practice for most people doing one or the other is routinely easy. Sustaining both the keen identification and clear-headed objectivity at a high level is undoubtedly much more difficult. To identify, to remain objective, and to relate to jurors, all at the same time, requires a unique individual.

> Competitive. Very competitive. [One] has to have healthy skepticism, has to be able to identify with the client but not identify to the point where he's blind-sided. But identification is very important. You can't try a case well if you hate your client or aren't comfortable with what he stands for.
> **—Arthur Liman**

These men are too skillful to fall into any of the above pitfalls. There is a clean, chiseled character to how they compete. There is respect for the opponent and for the rules of the game. They fight hard, accept the decision, and move on to the next challenge. These lawyers have the capacity for staying the course in long, drawn-out competitions. And they do not react to competitive pressure the way ordinary people do. They dig in and almost relish hardship as the going gets tough. It is unusual to see them become hostile, maintain anger, or lose perspective. By remaining calm and focused, they and others can rely on their judgment and decisions.

The psychological profiles obtained from the Rokeach Value Inventory reveal that these fourteen prefer competition over cooperation. During the personal interviews, they were asked to speculate upon whether the tendency to be competitive and aggressive is common among successful trial lawyers. The responses were mixed.

Bob Fiske suggests that different as these men might be in some respects they all must be aggressive, "Everybody has to have this thing flowing through their blood that says, 'I want to win this at all costs,' short of doing something unfair. Everybody has got to have that. You've got to have that aggressiveness when you're in court cross-examining a hostile witness."

Joe Jamail, on the other hand, finds it difficult to recognize a common trait, such as aggressiveness, in the trial lawyer's personality. "There are guys like me who are gregarious and love it. But I've seen some very quiet 'laid-back' people, who don't appear aggressive at all but who are very, very effective."

When the history, background, and present practice of these attorneys is examined however, it is clear that competitiveness is a focal consideration. These men would not readily give up trial law to pursue another career in law such as judging. (Asked on the questionnaire if they would ever like to be a judge, twelve said "no," and two said "maybe.") All the interviewees indicated that they would probably miss the "action" and find the bench confining.

Competitiveness for Jim Neal is not limited to his professional life. He says that although he enjoys playing golf, he couldn't play for relaxation because, "I go at golf like I go at the practice of law. I hope I practice law better but I put the same amount of intensity into it." Most of the lawyers have, over the years, held an active interest in competitive sports that they felt prepared them for the courtroom workout. Jim Brosnahan says, "I was very competitive in the athletic field in high school and in college. I think that's been a tremendous help [in preparation for trial law]. I won, I lost, I performed in front of people."

Several lawyers feel that the experiences of competing in athletics throughout high school and college were important lessons for competing in the courtroom arena.

Sports teach valuable lessons. They teach you how to win and how to lose. You can be an athlete and do a fabulous job and lose and you don't kill yourself. It hurts, but you don't kill yourself. A lot of people don't win in law because they're afraid to try because they're afraid to lose. And sports

teach you to try your damnedest. If you fail, guess
what? You didn't die.

—Fred Bartlit

David Boies remarks that the courtroom is "... like war. At least it
is a bloodless war. You can't get hurt unless the charts fall on you."

Hand in hand with competitiveness is the performance characteristic of assertiveness. In the responses from the Profession Survey,
assertiveness was one of the most pronounced traits of a good trial
lawyer. Assertive individuals, for example, prefer to be group leaders
rather than followers. They see themselves as dominant and forceful,
tend to take charge of situations, and assert themselves and their views
on others. Assertiveness neatly describes the concept of adversarial
style. This characteristic however is not restricted to the work place,
but is an integral part of their overall personalities. Possessing this
quality does not imply our fourteen are not cordial or polite in their
dealings with other people. On the contrary, I have found them
remarkably affable in their interpersonal relationships. However, just
as in the courtroom, they tend in all interpersonal encounters to
maintain a stance of analysis and interpretation.

Love of competition and assertiveness combine to produce an
individual who is a natural fighter. In another era he might have been a
samurai or knight. In our era, he is a trial lawyer.

Drive

When the fourteen lawyers were asked to describe the personal
qualities of an exceptional trial lawyer, *drive* was the most frequently
mentioned quality. Aspects of drive include self-discipline, hard work,
emotional intensity, and enthusiasm. Intrinsic motivation is also a
component of drive. Drive is one of the most salient traits displayed by
the fourteen lawyers. In the study for this book, this quality is
documented in both the personality measures and by the lawyers' own
self-reports. Achievement gives pragmatic meaning to their love of
competition, their tireless energy levels, and their thoroughness when
preparing for trial. However, it is their own definition of what
constitutes achievement upon which they rely during the tedium of
protracted discovery or in the heat of battle. They do not gain their
sense of self-satisfaction solely from external rewards, such as money
or notoriety. Social psychologists have documented that when an

individual attributes his reasons for engaging in an activity to external motivations, such as money, he begins to devalue and actually dislike the activity itself. The pleasure they glean from their own achievements is far more internalized. It is the satisfaction of knowing that they are doing a good job and fighting for the client. However, when it is all over, the notoriety, recognition, and money are burdens easily borne.

These men exhibit enormous energy levels when in trial. It is not uncommon for them to put in twelve to fifteen hour days for weeks or months at a time. (See Figures 2-4 and 2-5). They typically generate over 2,000 billable hours per year. Some have as many as 2,600 billable hours. They not only work actively at their immediate professional tasks, but as a group, they belong to an average of six different legal organizations and societies, some have memberships in as many as thirteen. They contribute an average of eight to twenty-five hours a month to these organizations. Ten of the fourteen manage to find the hours to serve on business or philanthropic boards. Eleven of the fourteen stated that they have an active interest in politics, serve on committees, or are involved in political fundraising efforts.

The activity level of these trial lawyers is not restricted to their work, but characterizes everything they do and have done. In high school, college, and law school, they were active in many organizations and extracurricular activities. One lawyer remarked that while in college, he had started his own business and made a great deal of money before he graduated. The pace of their lifestyles is more accelerated than the average person's.

In law school, when most serious law students have little time for anything other than studies, several of these men continued to participate in organized sports. Over half were involved in law review. Several held offices in fraternal organizations. Along with an active extracurricular life, they still managed to maintain excellent grades. At least five graduated first in their law school class and one lawyer proudly mentioned that his grades were the best in the history of his law school.

The enormous professional success of these men has occurred virtually as a by-product of their intense goal-orientation. (See Figures 2-6 and 2-7). Underlying their driven commitment is an intense desire to win. The great Earl Rogers once said, "People forgive everything but failure." Certainly winning is an obvious and clear demarcation

Hours Sleep Needed

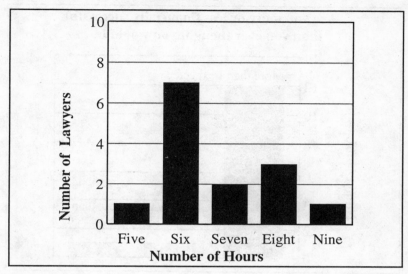

figure 2-4

Health & Work

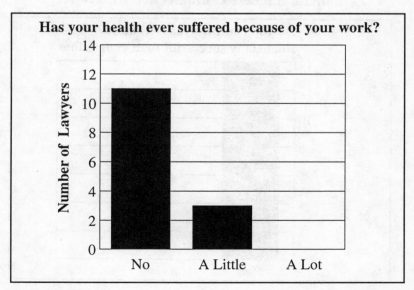

figure 2-5

Financial Success

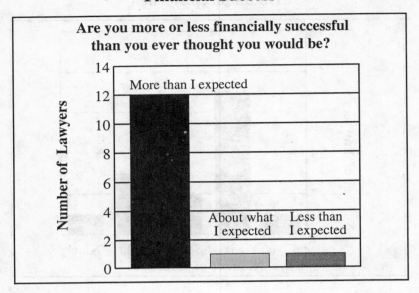

figure 2-6

Financial Success Compared With Father's

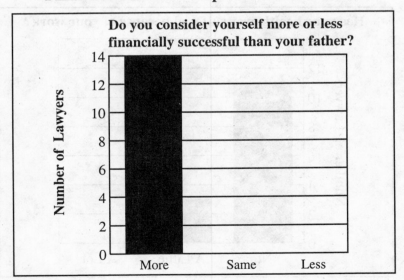

figure 2-7

between the successful and the unsuccessful trial lawyer. However, there is winning and there is winning. There is room in many legal disputes for each side to say it won—and lawyers are good at that. There are cases with undisputed winners. But there are many more cases where both sides can rightfully claim victory.

Success is primarily measured by financial accomplishment. Many people have heard about Joe Jamail, even though they may not know exactly how many trials he has "won." People remember his name because the media have emphasized that at one time he has made more money than any other lawyer who ever lived. Jamail received compensation of nearly $450 million for *Pennzoil v. Texaco*.

The fourteen lawyers did not attribute their reasons for practicing trial law to the money they make. In fact, when asked if they knew offhand what their income had been in the prior year, nine of the fourteen said "no." Nor was there a great amount of enjoyment in dealing with personal financial matters. They were asked when the last time was that they had bought themselves a gift. Four of the lawyers said that they had "never" bought a gift for themselves. Three said that it had been "years ago." When asked how often they flew first class only four said that they "always" flew first class. When asked how they viewed the role of money in their lives, the most frequent response was that it provided freedom.

It seems that the limits they place upon their own self-indulgence in their personal lives carries over into their professional lives as well. These fourteen men have every opportunity to be totally self-indulgent, yet they are not. Of course, the financial rewards of trial law practice are important for the lawyers in terms of how well they are able to provide for their families. However, most of them agreed that there are easier, less stressful means to make a lot of money. They practice trial law simply because they love it. (See, e.g., Figures 2-8 to 2-12). David Boies says, "I would practice law even if I inherited a hundred-million dollars. I like the excitement. I like the challenge. I like dealing with people. I like the working environment."

Work Enjoyment

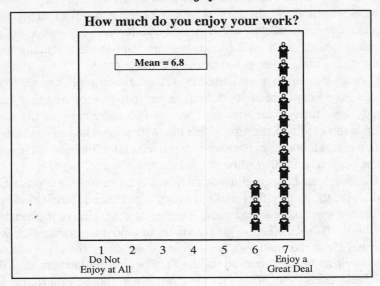

figure 2-8

Leisure Enjoyment

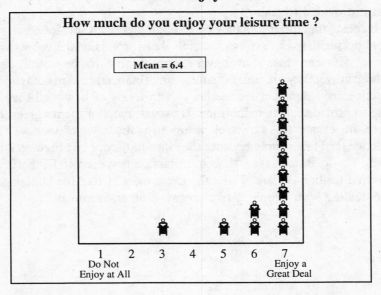

figure 2-9

Desire to be a Judge

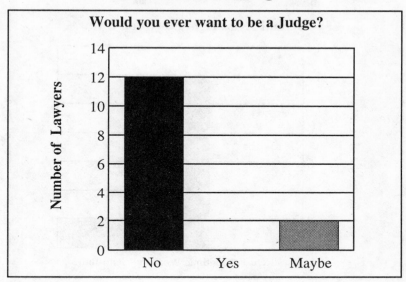

figure 2-10

Prefer Another Profession?

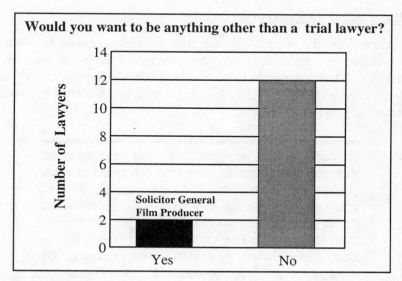

figure 2-11

Retirement

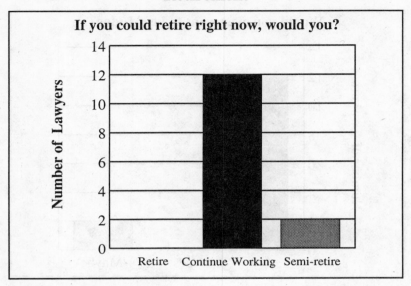

figure 2-12

Emotional Maturity

Underlying the intensity of their lifestyle and the enormity of their responsibilities, these men manifest an unusual degree of emotional stability. They do not become easily anxious, depressed, or particularly vulnerable to stress. In fact, they have an ability to handle stress very well.

I'm not a worrier. I believe that if you are convinced that you are prepared, that you are good at what you do, that nobody could do a better job, then all you can do is your best. And as long as you keep doing your best and don't slack off for something, then there is no reason to worry. I mean everybody feels anxiety. The stakes are high and you want to do well. It's the desire to do well and the ego that makes you go to court and [makes us]

put ourselves through those things when we don't
need the money. There's a difference between
being normally anxious like a quarterback is before a football game. That's normal anxiety and
worrying and I never take my problems home or
take them to bed.

—Fred Bartlit

When they suffer defeat, these men admit their role in the loss.
Regardless of how painful the disappointment, they do not wallow in
self-recrimination or alcohol. They learn from the experience and
actively do whatever is necessary to turn the loss into a win, to rectify
the situation. There is a tenacity in the use of the appeals process, in
seeking new trials when possible, and in pursuing every possible
remedy. After losing a case Phil Corboy,

> immediately filed a motion of retrial and didn't get it. I then
> filed the appeal and won and then settled the case. But
> during that time, I re-tooled. I started over on everything I
> did. I talked to jurors, tried to talk to find out what they
> thought, got some insights, got some answers, but re-tooled
> and rehashed and rejuvenated. And that's how I responded.
> I went into a blue fog with an absolute paranoid, completely
> suspicious attitude toward everything I did, and had to
> resurrect everything I did in the case to see where I had
> mistakes, where I could have done better.

This toughness and resiliency is characteristic of all fourteen
lawyers.

...losing is the scariest part about a [trial]. I don't
want to lose. The more visibility you have, the less
you want to lose. And, so that is very, very scary to
go to trial. And I should add that another characteristic of trial lawyers, a very, very, important
characteristic is the ability to get knocked down
and to stand right up. It's the ability to take a loss
because anyone who is a trial lawyer, if you try
enough cases, you're going to lose some... I'd
say a person who can suffer a real bad loss and

continue to function, that is, in my opinion, the
hallmark of a good trial lawyer.
—Steve Susman

On the Psychological Inventories the lawyers scored uniformly low
on overall neuroticism. Basically, they tend to be happy, well-adjusted
individuals. (See, e.g., Figure 2-13). However, there is one aspect of
emotional maturity that the fourteen lawyers did not characteristically
display. They tended to become frustrated easily, especially with other
people and other people's mistakes (as well as their own). The trait of
interpersonal impatience is one that is not generally associated with
leadership. This low tolerance for frustration might manifest itself in
an impatience with subordinates or an intolerance for tediousness in
another. Although this was not true for all, most shared this
temperament.

Years at Current Firm

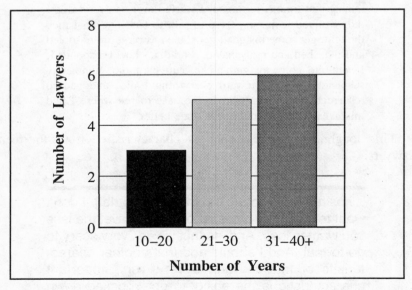

figure 2-13

Several of the lawyers are of the opinion that a lawyer does not
actually win the kind of cases in which they are routinely involved.

What happens instead, is that the other side loses it. They lose because they have been careless and because they have made a mistake. The fourteen lawyers have difficulty accepting mistakes in another or allowing themselves to make them. This intolerance is an important qualification for being an exceptional trial lawyer. They know that a single mistake may mean the difference between winning and losing.

Self-Discipline

The need for achievement spurs these men to rigorous self-discipline, although a number of them chide themselves for procrastination. Even though they are often engaged in a number of complex cases simultaneously, they are obsessive masters of time. They have an absolute horror of being unprepared. They follow a gospel of attention to detail. In fact, the image most frequently mentioned in the Profession Survey is the level of preparedness of a great trial lawyer. The respondents indicated that the professional gains made by the high-profile trial lawyers are primarily due to hard work and thorough trial preparation. As F. Lee Bailey once said, the winner is almost always the one who is better prepared. The image of a lawyer who is well prepared is consistent with the reality of the fourteen lawyers in this study. Their preparation begins months before trial. Joe Jamail commented that when trial begins, there should not be a single thing left to do. Every aspect of the case should be examined in detail weeks and months beforehand. Phil Corboy said the thing he likes least about being a trial lawyer is the preparation, but that it is an absolutely essential part of trial. He is not alone in his dislike for trial preparation. The other thirteen also prefer being in the courtroom, on their feet, competing. Their criterion for preparedness is undoubtedly more stringent than the average lawyer's. According to Susman: "[There is] a problem of remaining credible and believable if you don't know what the facts are."

When preparing for trial, ten of the fourteen need to become personally involved with every aspect of preliminary work. Four are able to delegate at least some of the responsibility. Bob Warren said that in one case, because the evidence represented four or five years of activity, there was no room for anything but his total absorption. Major personal distractions are just not practical during the preparation phase. These attorneys leave nothing uncovered in their search for important details. They generally need to conduct hands-on preparation for their trials, refusing to delegate responsibilities, for fear that they might miss knowing an important element of the case. Even those lawyers who tend to use large trial teams still see to it that they themselves know every aspect of the case.

These men intensely eschew any diffusion of their effort and energy. They have no time-consuming hobbies or serious avocations. Their vacations appear to be time stolen from trial law. Perhaps phrases such as "consumed by," or "obsessed by" overstate the extent of single-mindedness possessed by these men. But not when they are in a trial. During a trial, there is probably nothing, short of personal tragedy, which can deflect their attention from the business at hand. There are extensive demands made upon the trial lawyer's family time as a result of this preoccupation. Nine of the fourteen consistently remarked that the inordinate time away from their families has been an unfortunate by-product of their extremely thorough approach to trial preparation but essential to their professional success. Dispositionally the fourteen lawyers are unable to approach their profession in any other way.

The great trial lawyers are indefatigable advocates. Clearly these men are self-actualizing individuals who know how to use their potential, as well as other resources to their full advantage. They use trial consultants, jury research, and experts in demonstrative exhibits to give them an edge in understanding issues and in being more fully prepared than their opponents.

The lives of these lawyers have been dominated by an intense and at times, humorless, single-mindedness. When asked, for example, to relate the most humorous thing that had ever happened to them in the courtroom, none retold anything ordinary mortals would consider funny. They regard their profession with an almost austere seriousness. If they do or are involved in anything humorous in the course of their practice of the law it is apparently soon forgotten.

Objectivity

An important aspect of a trial lawyer's self-discipline is the ability to maintain necessary objectivity in trial law. According to David Boies, maintaining objectivity is one of the most difficult challenges to self-discipline any trial attorney faces. A lawyer cannot develop a personal stake in the ongoing process. If he or she becomes personally involved and invested in a particular approach or a particular theory, it is easy to become blind to other views. The fourteen lawyers constantly guard against becoming too personally embroiled in their cases.

Objectivity is also manifested in the practice of these fourteen lawyers insofar as they do not want their own desire to win to outweigh the client's best interest. The lawyers attempt to maintain an objectivity about what is ultimately the client's best interests, regardless of what they personally might like to see occur.

> You've got to have an ability to be very objective. That doesn't mean you're trying to decide whether your client is right or wrong. What it means is...looking at facts without preconceptions...keeping an open mind all the way through so that the day before the trial starts you get another piece of information, it may change the way you look at things. It is one of the most difficult things that we have to do.
>
> **—David Boies**

The ability to be objective is a prime directive, not just one among many points that need emphasis, but *the* point for Pat McCartan. A good trial lawyer maintains a sufficient distance from the case but that does not lessen his or her conviction of the case's merit. Objectivity makes for a much more effective presentation. The quality of objectivity is given particular emphasis by lawyers who are accustomed to being on the side of the defense. Defendants argue for objectivity, a cool head. A plaintiff, in contrast, must often be heated and disputatious.

Luck

Virtually all of these lawyers feel that luck has played a part in their success. (See Figure 2-14). Legend has it that great trial lawyers are self-made men who have molded their own destinies. Viewed historically as privileged individuals, they are nonetheless perceived as persons who have accomplished something rare and deserved. When the fourteen lawyers were asked, how much they believed in "luck," eleven said they believed in it a "great deal." Even more surprising, when they were asked if luck ever plays a role for them in the successful outcome of a verdict, all but one said "yes." Eight said that luck was "often" a factor. Five said that luck was "somewhat often" a factor. So, the lawyers did not only believe that luck was a factor in obtaining important cases, they also saw it as a factor in winning them. While the majority of this group of fourteen trial lawyers professes that luck has played a major role in their success, they do not deny the importance of their own hard work. Perhaps this explains the belief shared by several of them, that they in fact do not *win* the cases, the other guy *loses* them.

How Much Do You Believe in Luck?

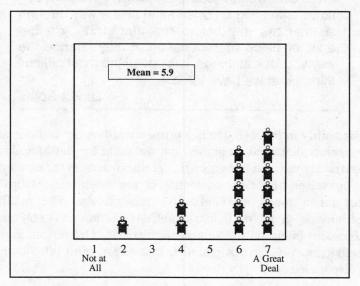

figure 2-14

Steve Susman, for one, has said that he has had some especially lucky breaks trying cases. These lucky breaks, plus the fact that he is a good trial lawyer, have helped him achieve his current status. In terms of actual talents and abilities, Susman felt that there were many lawyers with the necessary requisites to be called "great," but because of other factors involved (where they practice and the kinds of cases they got) they are not well known. Jim Neal went so far as to say that being in a position of national prominence was ninety percent luck. "I know the other ten percent is important...but it is purely luck in getting the right cases. If there had not been a Jimmy Hoffa, there wouldn't have been a Jimmy Neal."

In Reasoner's view, luck played a huge part in his success. He was lucky to begin with a great lawyer, David Searls, as a mentor. He also had many opportunities early in his career to go to trial. It was his good fortune that most of the cases that came his way did not settle before trial. He cites ETSI, the coal slurry pipeline case, "which was really one of the most satisfying experiences I could have had. In retrospect, I was lucky that Santa Fe wouldn't settle with me." David Boies also emphasizes luck in drawing a distinction between himself, for example, and the other 69,999 trial lawyers in America. "The CalComp case. That was an opportunity. Westmoreland was an opportunity. Those might not have come along. You can't create your opportunities." Once given an opportunity, a lawyer must make the most of it, so that it becomes a base for obtaining more opportunities. "Once you get a certain number of major victories under your belt," Boies observes, "you get a lot more opportunities. So it is the early opportunities that help."

The contribution of luck to success is something that is difficult to prove or disprove. People tend to embrace what is referred to by social psychologists as the "just-world hypothesis." In a just world, individuals are seen as deserving of their rewards as well as their punishments. It is difficult for most individuals to accept that someone may have achieved greatness by any means other than reliance upon his abilities. It is hard for many individuals to admit that something totally outside an individual's control, such as luck, may have influenced success or failure. The lawyers believe, however, that there are other individuals who have the same hard-work ethic, the same talents, and the same abilities. But those individuals have not had the same lucky breaks as they.

The Influence of Others

> I think I decided on being a lawyer by the process
> of exclusion. I came from a Jewish family so you
> either had to be a doctor or a lawyer. I couldn't
> stand the sight of blood and I didn't like science
> and math and I was fairly good with words. That
> left only being a lawyer.
>
> **—Max Blecher**

In all probability there is no trial lawyer "gene." Environment and learning play an integral role in enhancing and developing the abilities necessary to excel at trial law. However, there is one relevant dispositional trait that is undoubtedly present at birth, or shortly thereafter. It tends to remain fairly constant throughout life, barring major illness or personal catastrophe. This characteristic is a capacity for a high level of activity. This is a dispositional characteristic that cannot be learned.

Some people are simply more active than others. They have quicker reflexes, they think more quickly, they see things faster, they have more energy. Research in developmental psychology tends to support the position that we are born with certain dispositions, or genotypes. The environment then interacts on our individual genotypes to mold our individual personalities. In other words, an infant born with a high-energy level, and put into a sociopathic environment, might become a criminal. If put into an athletic environment, a child might become an athlete. If put into an environment that emphasizes education, hard work and honesty, that child might be inclined to pursue an academic career that makes the most of these values. It is the interplay between basic dispositional genotypes and environmental influences that determine who we are.

The personality traits common to these fourteen are primarily stable traits. Extroversion, intelligence, achievement orientation, and self-esteem are traits that usually appear before the age of five. They may vary slightly due to physical illness or catastrophic events, but they are, for the most part, with us throughout our lives.

This study did not seek to present an in-depth understanding of how these men developed in childhood. Although family backgrounds varied, there are common threads. (See Figures 2-15–2-17). Generally

Are There Other Lawyers In Your Family?

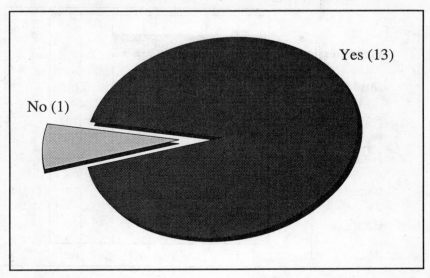

No (1)

Yes (13)

figure 2-15

Who Are the Lawyers in Your Family?

Son	7
Spouse	5
Daughter	4
Father	4
Brother	3
Brother-in-Law	3
Mother	2
Father-in-Law	2
Son-in-Law	2
Sister	1
Niece	1
Nephew	1

figure 2-16

Religious Orientation

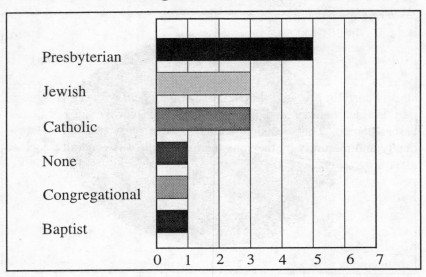

figure 2-17

Dominant Personality in Family When Growing Up

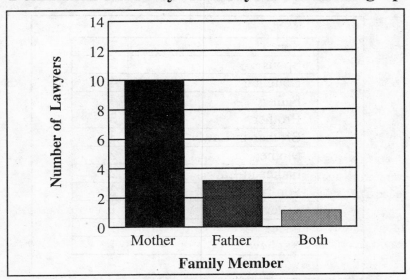

figure 2-18

there was at least one supportive adult in the lawyer's past. In most instances it was the mother. (See Figure 2-18). Additionally, the lawyers' families were very similar in their emphasis upon specific values: the importance of education, hard work, and honesty. Interestingly, a disproportionate number of the fourteen lawyers were first born or only children. (See Figure 2-19). They were given responsibility early in life, and they learned how to deal with it. As a result, they are autonomous and inner-directed. The family did not dictate career choice. That decision seems to have been reached independently and maturely by the sons themselves. It was generally decided after some positive experiences in school with forensics, debate, or with law in the military. (See Figure 2-20). They chose trial law while in their early twenties after they had enough experience to know what they were good at and what they genuinely enjoyed. (See Figure 2-21).

Most of the lawyers believed that law school did not prepare them for work as a trial lawyer. Upon graduation, they saw themselves as having some very basic, rudimentary skills for operating in the legal arena. Trial law, it was felt, was a whole different ball game. The training ground for trial law was the courtroom itself. Most of the lawyers agreed that what could be learned about trial law could only be obtained by the experience of trying cases. Of the fourteen lawyers in this study, ten worked as government lawyers in some capacity at one time or another. (See Figure 2-22). All but one of the lawyers believed that this kind of experience was beneficial for a young lawyer who wanted to obtain the skills necessary to try cases.

Along with gaining a wide range of experience trying cases, it was recommended that many of the necessary subtle skills could be learned from working with or against really good trial lawyers. This type of learning is called modeling or observational learning. It has been demonstrated to be one of the quickest and most efficient ways to learn new behavior. Watching successful trial lawyers in action, or competing against good trial lawyers, allows a young lawyer to model successful behaviors. A mentor relationship serves this same function. Ten of the fourteen stated that they had mentors, men whom they relied upon for advice, example, and encouragement. (See Figure 2-23). David Searls had an "enormous" impact on Harry Reasoner. Searls gave him a chance to make decisions on paper, so to speak, putting him in a simulated position from which he could "play the game of lawyer" until he was experienced enough to do it for real. Bob Warren

Eight Were First Born

Birth Order

Lawyer	None	Older		Younger	
		Brothers	Sisters	Brothers	Sisters
1				2	2
2		1			
3	0				
4				1	1
5				1	
6				1	3
7				2	
8			2	1	
9		1		2	1
10				1	1
11			1		
12	0				
13				1	
14				1	

The table displays the birth order of the fourteen lawyers. Two lawyers (#3 and #12) were only children. Only four lawyers have older brothers or sisters

figure 2-19

Military Service

Did You Serve in the Military?

Yes – 8			No – 6	
Branch	**Status**	**Induction**	**Condition**	**Duties**
Army	enlisted	drafted	peace	law/other
Army	enlisted	drafted	peace	law/other
Army	enlisted	drafted	war	other
Army	officer	volunteer	war	other
Marine Corps	—	volunteer	peace	other
Marine Corps	officer	volunteer	war	law
Marine Corps	enlisted	volunteer	war	other
Air Force	enlisted	volunteer	peace	other

■ How valuable, overall was the military to you? Mean = 5.75*

* 7-point scale (1= Not at all valuable, 7 = Extremely valuable)

figure 2-20

singles out Sherman J. Welpton, Jr. among the many "fine trial lawyers" from whom he gained valuable experience and benefits. "I got to see a lot of different styles and a lot of different characteristics all in action from backstage." One of his early role models was the famous Californian noted for his courtroom skills, Joe Ball, who later sponsored Warren for the American College of Trial Lawyers. For Phil Corboy, a Mr. Grossman, in the corporation counsel's office, (in Chicago) "taught me how to think as a lawyer, taught me how to get to the point, taught me to be terse, taught me to be factual, and gave me the ability to use my writing talents and channel them into legal writing. He also taught me [about] integrity."

Decision to Become a Lawyer: Age

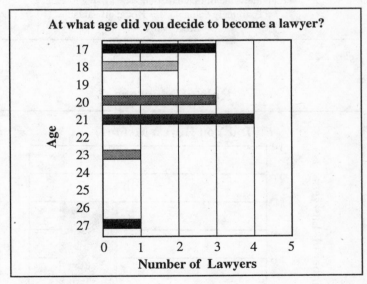

figure 2-21

117

Worked as Government Lawyer

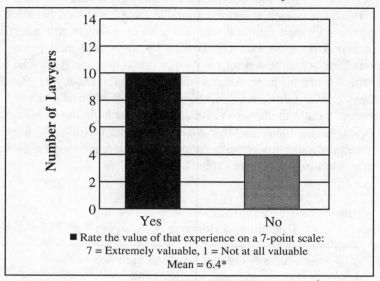

figure 2-22

Role of Mentors

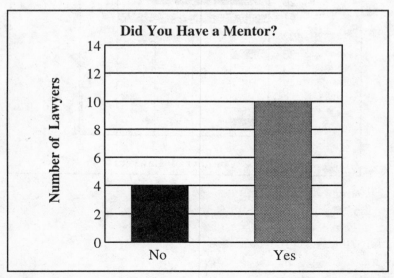

figure 2-23

Bruce Bromley, the late general counsel for IBM and partner at Cravath, was Tom Barr's mentor. Barr continued to seek advice from Bromley "until he died...He was really, far and away, the most significant influence. He had a very clean, clear mind." Case management was the most important lesson Barr learned from Bromley.

Max Wildman showed Bartlit what to do "when you get on your feet in court."

> Max was somebody who didn't have a lot of patience for detail so I learned that most of the time the unreasonable detail doesn't count. Max used to say, "Try cases. You'll never be any good unless you try cases. If you don't go to court, you won't be any good. Get in court and try cases." And I also learned that Max was himself in court. I learned that one of the secrets is to try to have exactly the same personality you have in court as you have dealing with people.

Bob Fiske points to a triumvirate of mentors: Judge J. Edward Lumbard, S. Hazard Gillespie, and Judge Lawrence Walsh. Lumbard advocated thoroughness, "He used to say, 'Never assume a God damn thing. Check every single thing.' Walsh was the same way—extraordinarily thorough."

> He really didn't want "yes men" around him, which I think is one of the things that gets so many public officials in trouble and can get a lawyer in trouble. I mean he wasn't going around, "Well, the vote is five to four so we'll do that." He would do what was in his instinct to do. And that, again, is something I've learned where you've got a sense in your stomach that is what you should do.

Conclusion: Personality in Action

The traits discussed in this chapter map a unique territory among human personality types. It is a territory inhabited by a small number, and only a few of these become great trial lawyers. Are the traits identified here actually crucial to greatness? How are they manifested in the courtroom? Can self-discipline, maturity, communication skills, and the rest of the identified traits make a difference between good and great? It will be apparent in the chapters to come that intense strategic planning is a vital component of courtroom confrontation. It will also be apparent that all phases of trial planning require judgment and intelligence of a special type. Objectivity comes into play, as does luck. In succeeding chapters, many courtroom tactics are discussed, including jury selection, the use of witnesses, documents, and exhibits, as well as the delivery of opening statements and closing arguments. In viewing these topics it will become clear that the communications skills possessed by these lawyers, in combination with their ability to self-monitor, and their competitive spirit, make them superb courtroom tacticians where it counts—with the jury.

A trial is often a protracted struggle. Fierce drive, combined with rigid self-discipline, enable a great trial lawyer to give a superhuman performance from start to finish. Finally, and above all, winning trial lawyers must have credibility. This, in part, is a function of their honesty and emotional maturity. Their effective and credible persona evolves from the nurturing influence of others, such as parents, mentors, and colleagues. Thus, the traits surveyed in this chapter are the DNA from which great reputations (and fortunes) have been made. In the following chapters, these personality traits are reflected in a rich variety of trial strategies and tactics.

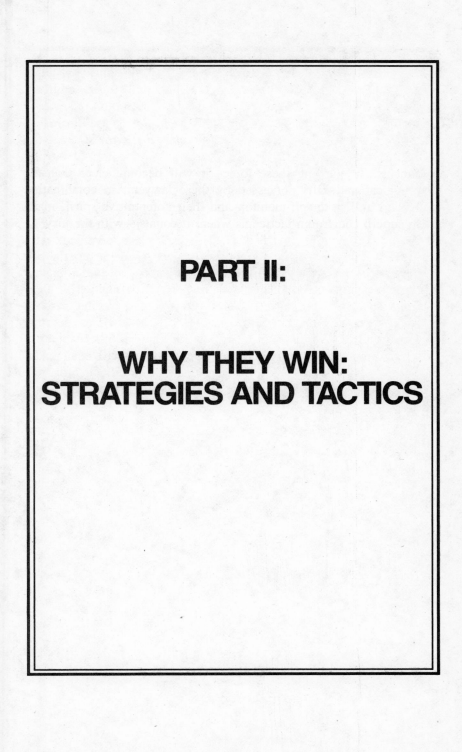

PART II:

WHY THEY WIN:
STRATEGIES AND TACTICS

CHAPTER 3 ▮▮▮▮▮▮▮▮▮▮▮▮▮▮

Evaluating the Engagement:
Pretrial Considerations

*Whether you want to let go of that gorilla or not, the
gorilla is not going to let go of you.*
—Pat McCartan

The first topics under consideration in this chapter are not,
strictly speaking, considered matters of strategy by trial lawyers. These include the decision to accept a case, reasons for
refusing an engagement, and decisions whether or not to practice in
certain parts of the country. The remaining topics, filing a case,
venue, and jurisdiction, do involve strategic considerations. How these
considerations come up and get resolved in the minds of these lawyers
is a fascinating process. They are by no means in agreement. The
nature and locale of their practice are two factors that account for the
rather wide spectrum of opinion.

Accepting a Case

The trial lawyers highlighted here are at the point in their careers
where they can easily afford to say no to a potential client. The
decision to take a client is not based entirely upon economics. The
nature of the case itself is important. Is it challenging? (See Figure
3-1). Is it interesting? Is it different? Is it something that will attract
media coverage? Is it a worthy encounter? Above all, is it winnable?

These lawyers are often offered the most difficult, high-risk, high-
stakes cases. They want to exceed past accomplishments in damages
awarded, in complexity, and in scope. There is also the lure of learning

something new. They welcome challenge and the clash of powerful interests. They take the chance of a big loss. Harry Reasoner addresses this:

> Clearly, I have no business handling a case like [Kidder] if I can't accept the possibility that we might take a hell of a hit in it. If I'm going to go into that fearing if we lose that it's going to taint me in some way, then I shouldn't be trying it. You see a lot of lawyers who avoid the hard cases.

There is contempt for those who take pushover cases. Personal-injury cases where, at the very least, compensatory damages will be recovered in settlement, and enough to yield a nice fee, hold little interest for these trial lawyers. Reasoner knows about a "prominent personal-injury trial lawyer that the only cases he tried were equivalent to walking in and pumping bullets into a quadriplegic." According to Reasoner, when some plaintiffs' lawyers encounter resistance they either settle the case or pass it off to someone else. A lawyer who never lost a case is incredibly lucky, settles too many cases, or avoids the hard ones.

Two criteria: Is the case winnable, and if winnable, will it be remunerative? That is, is the game worth the candle?

—Max Blecher

Few lawyers are willing to take a case they cannot win, although definitions of what it means to win will often surprise a lay person. Max Blecher assesses the prospects of winning a case in two ways. The case may pass muster in front of a jury, but appeals are almost inevitable. Therefore, it is important to evaluate the chances of a favorable verdict getting knocked down later on a legal point at the appellate level. The first question Blecher asks himself is, "If this body of facts is provable, how will it play out in the ninth circuit five years from now?" The second question he asks, "Can you win the case in front of a jury?" A case that plays well before a jury might not play well before a court of appeals and vice versa.

Will a single legal issue dispose of a case? If so, the opinion of a jury will not even be solicited. Blecher suggests that there is no point in enervating oneself for five years or having the client spend anywhere

Representation of Clients

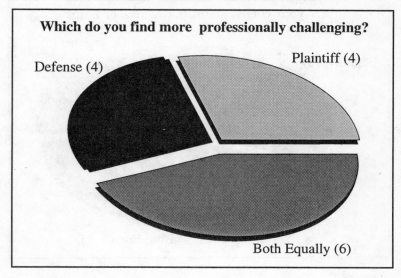

Which do you find more professionally challenging?

Defense (4)

Plaintiff (4)

Both Equally (6)

figure 3-1

from several thousand to a million dollars on a risky premise. Blecher's experience in representing a client against IBM underscored this point. The case was resolved in favor of the defendant on a directed verdict. It turned on the proof of a single legal fact. None of what the plaintiff brought before the jury had any bearing on the ultimate outcome of the case. Blecher suggests that this could have been anticipated with a huge savings of money and time.

> The clearest illustration of this, although there are many, is IBM. Umpteen millions of dollars were spent and I could have sat down with David Boies and said, "This case will turn on whether or not we have to prove IBM prices were below cost." Frame that issue and send it up for appellate decision without any evidence.

Clearly, the criteria that stand behind every decision to take a case are whether or not it can be won and whether or not it will be financially rewarding. Having passed that initial test, however, a case must be considered in view of other factors. (See Figures 3-2 and 3-3). However, before these points are addressed, it is interesting to ask: Is

Representation of Clients

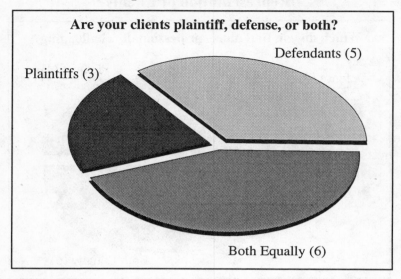

Are your clients plaintiff, defense, or both?

Defendants (5)

Plaintiffs (3)

Both Equally (6)

figure 3-2

Type of Clients Represented

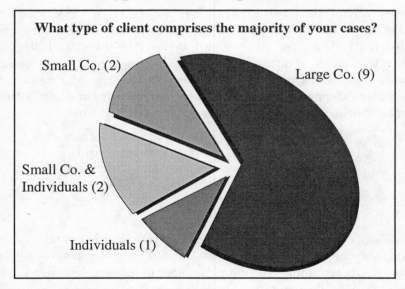

What type of client comprises the majority of your cases?

Small Co. (2)

Large Co. (9)

Small Co. & Individuals (2)

Individuals (1)

figure 3-3

there ever a time when a case is taken that might not be winnable or not make money? Max Blecher says yes.

> I'm influenced in marginal cases by the plight of a perspective plaintiff. If the plaintiff is well off and this is just a lark to him, I would be less moved to take it. If, on the other hand, this is the life blood of the plaintiff and he is facing some serious financial consequences, if he can't get help, I move in that direction.

How far any of these lawyers will go against their own financial interests in responding to such a call is unclear, but it happens with a fair amount of frequency.

Joe Jamail is often attracted to cases because of the people involved. Fighting for an injured party, a "little guy," has been a basic motivation for him. If the case is interesting, and he can help, he will probably become involved. The siren song of a good cause led Jamail recently to take on a personal-injury case.

> One of the girls in my office had a friend who was driving with her younger sister and her younger sister's infant. They got into a crash because of an ill-lit construction site. Kills the mother. Horribly injures the driver, the aunt of the infant. They [the defense] take the position of well, shit, give it up for adoption. Well, that's not my idea of justice. So I took the case. And I'll try that case. I may well take care of that little girl for the rest of her life, but she will live with some family member.

Another reason for taking a case is that a particular area of litigation might involve possible future rewards. A case might concern a new technology or a new industry where a trial lawyer can develop expertise and a reputation for specific legal knowledge. An antitrust specialist such as Max Blecher is always on the look out for potential areas of commercial activity. He considers health care in particular a fertile ground for litigation.

For Harry Reasoner, friendship and time are both factors of importance when considering whether or not to take a case.

> I don't have a precise formula. Often the determinant is how much time I have available. Today for instance, I declined to become personally involved in a matter that sounded very interesting and with substantial stakes simply because I'm preoccupied by the Kidder case being set for

trial. So to a degree, it's an accident of timing what you become involved in.

It also helps that Reasoner sets his fees at a level he refers to as "market-clearing rates." Close personal friends play a role too. He might take a case not otherwise considered in order to work with friends.

Phil Corboy presents several factors in accepting a case from the perspective of a personal-injury lawyer. First, he considers the source. If someone has been referring business for decades, and has a little case he wants the firm to handle, those years of faithful referrals are not going to be forgotten. Second, the size of the potential recovery is factored.

Mrs. Don Vinson wants us to handle a case for her. Twelve-hundred dollars has been paid by the insurance and the insurance company has a subrogation right to get it back. She is now working and she's well. "Look Mrs. Vinson, you don't really want to hire us because when we settle your case for five-thousand dollars, you are going to pay us seventeen-hundred dollars, and then you're going to pay twelve-hundred dollars back to the insurance company, and wait five years to acquire eleven-hundred dollars. Then you're going to record. Your name is going to be on an insurance company index that you've made a claim. And when you really injure your back ten years from now, you're going to be accused of trying to recover for the injury you had today. Do you really want us to do this? And, besides, it's against Prestige Insurance Company and they'll never settle it. You'll have to go to trial before you get it. And you're going to have to take a deposition...Oh, by the way, in addition to the seventeen-hundred dollars, you're probably going to spend six-hundred dollars in litigation expenses. So, go to the insurance company and use our name. Tell him you're going to hire Phil Corboy if

they don't settle your case and don't even call me
when you settle it."

And for this, Phil Corboy will not even send a bill.
—Phil Corboy

The decision whether or not to accept a case is made differently in
large firms than it is by attorneys who practice in small partnerships.
Large-firm lawyers such as Tom Barr, David Boies, Bob Fiske, Arthur
Liman, and Bob Warren consider a potential case in a different context
from the deeply personal set of considerations employed by Jamail or
Corboy.

David Boies talks about the "filters" a case must pass through in his
firm. The first filter is to make sure that there is no conflict with
another of the firm's clients. A recent illustration involved Boies who
represented the Baseball Owners Association in their defense of a suit
brought by Fay Vincent, the commissioner. The plaintiff, who Boies
was going to oppose, had ties with another client, Citibank.

> One of the things we had to face was whether Citibank, who
> we had represented in a multi-million dollar credit facility
> to organized baseball and who were depending on the
> ability of the commissioner to negotiate various things in
> terms of media contracts, was going to be affected ad-
> versely by kicking the commissioner out early.

The second filter is whether the firm is prepared to take on a
particular client. Although Boies has a good deal of latitude within his
firm, barring conflict, to represent the client he chooses, it must be the
kind of client the firm wants. And if it is, does he want to spend time
on the case? Or is it one of the rare instances when Boies feels he *ought*
to spend time on it. Whereas Jamail accepts a case through a
subjective pull, feeling the force of many "shoulds" and "oughts"
qualified by a number of pragmatic factors, it is somewhat the opposite
for Boies. He ponders the "shoulds" and the "oughts," not as primary
considerations, but as last qualifying criteria. "Every now and then for
some reason or another, you get a case that you might not particularly
want to do, but you feel for some reason you ought to take." Boies, for
example, took over a divorce case in which the children had been
kidnapped by their father. He was asked to help on the case by a fellow
attorney, and he elected to do so.

129

For Arthur Liman, who is in a large firm, the conflict factor is also important. Since he represents both plaintiffs and defendants, he carefully considers whether or not he can make a contribution. From a defense perspective this will usually be easier to evaluate, since the desired outcome is always the same: a successful defense against the charges of the plaintiff. The defendant is responsive and reactive. The plaintiff, however, is aggressive and initiatory. Plaintiffs may come forward with a variety of motives and potential claims. Deciding to become involved in a plaintiff's suit entails making an assessment of whether or not one wants to be a party to those motives and claims. And because the game is begun by the plaintiff, taking on a plaintiff's cause means deciding to start the game. Accepting a defendant is different. One wants to see the defendant weather the storm. Liman has given this considerable thought:

> Assuming you don't have a conflict, there are two factors that go into my way of thinking. One, is it interesting? Something that I'd want to do? And two, is it something that in effect, I can afford to do? Not every client can pay their way. There are some where you will do it even though the client can't pay the freight, and there are where the client has to be able to pay the freight. Third, I won't take a case if it's a hopeless case. If it's on the plaintiff's side, it's got to be a claim that I can work with. If it's on the defense side, it's got to be something where I can contribute. If all they want is for somebody to put up the white flag of surrender without even any negotiating leverage to get them a settlement, then I say, "You don't need me, go to somebody else."

Bob Warren's discussion of the matter demonstrates a clinical and pragmatic perspective.

> If I accept this business, which may be of middling size, am I going to make it so the firm is going to be unable to accept other major pieces of business coming down the pike? If so, it shouldn't be done. I have to think about the firm as a total business entity. Second, I've got to think about whether it is wise for me to invest a lot of time. If something is going to require a lot of my time and not use any other lawyers in this office, it's a losing piece of business. The firm doesn't charge enough money per hour for my time, even though I

don't come cheap, to pay the overhead of the case if I do it alone.

Obviously, one does not say no to regular clients. If a law firm is retained by a corporation, bank, or some other entity, it must be responsive to that entity. The lawyers in the firm may counsel a course of action that does not ultimately involve filing a lawsuit. That is what they are there for. With regard to what Bob Fiske calls "ad hoc, one-shot" litigation, he suggests the identity of the client is the major consideration.

> Who is the client? Is it a reputable organization? Are these good people, bad people? That's an important factor. Second, what's the nature of the matter? Is this something interesting? Where is it? I'm not in a big hurry to do another case out of town right now. How likely is it to go to trial? That's a factor for me. And then, of course, can they pay?

On the other hand, the economics of a smaller, newer firm dictate a somewhat different approach. Steve Susman makes it clear that economic considerations are paramount and his firm requires a deposit of $25,000 to take the risk out of the proposition.

When I began, partly because of cash flow, we had to be careful. Typically our client was not a Fortune 500 company, but rather the high-roller individual, here today and Chapter Eleven tomorrow...the developer, the guy who runs a savings and loan, the guy who has a small business. It has been my philosophy that I would rather go pick roses or smell them than work on a matter and not get paid.

—Steve Susman

Once it is clear that the cost-risk can be eliminated, Susman's group votes on whether or not to accept an engagement. In keeping with his desire to insure revenue for his firm, Susman looks for strong cases, even if the amount recovered is relatively small.

I've come around to believe that it's better to have a strong case with little damages than a weak case with huge damages. [At one] time I thought, "It's an iffy case, but God, if we hit, there are billions here." I've changed that view because in the first place, it is very difficult to estimate damages accurately during the case acceptance process. And in the second place, it is emotionally un-satisfying to work on a weak case, to work on a case that is really questionable where you feel like a blackmail artist, where you feel like you might hit but you're playing the odds.

The character of a client is sometimes a factor in deciding whether to accept a case. Jim Brosnahan, who admits to being a "case junky," nevertheless acknowledges that "you can't represent somebody if you can't control the case." He does not want a sycophant, but he is adamant about controlling strategy. According to Tom Barr, the freedom to make decisions is important, and can be compromised in certain instances:

Take something like representing the FDIC. There the questions were: could we limit the representation so that we only went after Drexel and Milken and not the financial community at large? Could we do things our way, as opposed to the government's way?

Refusing a Case

We were asked to represent the City of Tampa in connection with getting the Giants out of this area and my partner called me up and said, "What do you think about this?" I said, "If Athens was suing Sparta and you lived in Sparta, I don't think you'd represent Athens."

—Jim Brosnahan

Reasons for avoiding cases often turn upon the personality of the client, economic factors, moral qualms, and dubious legal standing. Most of the lawyers address the question of refusing a case from the point of view of moral scruples. Fred Bartlit makes a distinction between the white-collar criminal who "makes a mistake" and the child molester who acts out of an uncontrollable compulsion. "I don't want to be in the same room with the kind of person who would have sex with a ten-year old."

Jim Neal's perspective is considerably different, influenced by the theory in American law that any criminal defendant, no matter what the charge, is innocent until proven guilty and deserves the best available counsel. Neal seriously thought about representing John Gotti, the alleged godfather of one of New York's Mafia families, but he was too involved with Exxon to be able to take on Gotti's defense. Max Blecher on the other hand turned down representing the Marcoses. "I couldn't identify with them. There are some things that are so extreme that I could not bring myself to feel comfortable representing them."

In his best of all possible worlds, Steve Susman would only take contingency cases for plaintiffs. But economic necessity is such that the bottom line for him is that he will represent anybody who can pay.

> A big hourly case comes in from the worst villain in the world, the biggest security frauder and the biggest cheater, liar, stealer in the world, but they want to hire six lawyers here and put them to work giving them whatever weak defense there is going to be—I'd probably take that case if they can pay. It's not very rewarding work. It's not very satisfying work. It's going to end up on your loss column so you aren't going to be terribly happy about it. But, I'd probably do it. So, I can't think of anyone I wouldn't represent.

Another perspective is represented by Bob Warren. His credibility as a libel lawyer can only be maintained by refusing to take plaintiff's libel cases. He does not feel he can argue for a plaintiff and continue to be persuasive with juries when he defends a client against a libel charge. "It's very important from our standpoint to play only one side of the street. I won't take a plaintiff's libel case against a newspaper, because I would be arguing positions that would be antithetical to those I usually argue."

Contravening social policy that one supports through the prosecution of a law suit is not a factor mentioned by most of these men, but it is an undercurrent in some of their thinking, as when Jim Brosnahan refused to take the National Rifle Association as a client. Harry

Reasoner, although he mentions beyond-the-pale criminal defendants when he lists cases he would not take, also notes some social and political grounds for refusal.

> I would not participate in trying to overturn an FDA agency ruling on a drug that they felt was dangerous. I feel very strongly about environmental issues. I would, for example, not be comfortable in litigation that was designed to get a company to do things environmentally that I disagreed with.

Joe Jamail has turned down people on the basis of their personality. He also does not represent liars or bullies.

> I've turned down a lot of people just because of a person-ality clash. I just didn't need the money. Wouldn't if I did need it. Or somebody who I think is not being truthful. Ever since the first grade, I never liked bullies. I won't take either, as corporations or as individuals.

Phil Corboy who has his roots in the plaintiff's personal-injury bar, refuses cases when he does not sense a deep need on the part of the client. Once that criterion has been met, Corboy might be interested in considering the case, irrespective of who the client is.

> We have represented everybody from bank presidents to prostitutes, from insurance executives to pimps, to people who have been convicted of very bad crimes such as murder to people who are Boy Scouts. [But] I won't represent the person who lies, who tells me that they ran through a red light but they [the opponents] have a witness who was on the corner who will say the light was green.

Bob Fiske speaks to the care he takes in deciding to defend someone facing criminal charges.

> I do some white-collar criminal work and I am very careful about that. I wouldn't go near a drug dealer or I wouldn't go near an organized-crime figure and even in the kinds of cases that I get asked to take, nobody even asks me about those cases, but the ones I do get asked to take, white-collar crime, securities, fraud, or whatever I look very hard at it—who is the person, what is [his or her] reputation? He or she tells me they're innocent and I look at the facts and if I think there is a reasonable basis for that . . . I'll take it. But I

don't have much interest in defending somebody who I think is guilty.

The litmus test for Arthur Liman is whether or not he could explain his role as a defense attorney in a criminal case to his children. Although his basic values clash with those of his client, Bob Warren is involved in yet another libel suit, defending a person's right to free speech.

> I'm comfortable in defending that person's right to say what he said and not be sued for it or not to have to pay any money because of it. He has an absolute right to say whatever he damn pleases because it's a free country. And I intend to try to establish that, whether I agree with the agenda of this person or not.

Warren felt it necessary to clarify with one client the terms on which he was taking the case. He explained that he did not agree with or have much sympathy for the client's point of view and the client should take into account whether or not this was a problem.

Pat McCartan, a Democrat, defended a Republican president, and sued one from his own party.

> I got a big kick out of representing Ronald Reagan and right before that, I sued Jimmy Carter personally to invalidate his gasoline tax. I think those two matters reveal more than anything else that political preferences do not—and should not—influence client engagements.

Harry Reasoner also represents clients with whom he does not agree politically. This is consistent with the almost-virginal innocence these lawyers maintain in their legal practice with regard to political values. Reasoner has defended price-fixers although he does not approve of price-fixing.

> I've defended people who were guilty of it but it didn't bother me to attempt to keep them from being convicted or to attempt to minimize the damages that they were required to pay. Although frankly, most of the time you have the luxury of it being a sufficiently ambiguous conduct. It's not clear.

This is an interesting statement. Reasoner feels that if the conduct he defends is morally ambiguous rather than flatly wrong, he does not then have to feel guilty about making the decision to defend it. Clearly, the potential to feel guilty is there. At times, clashing values must be compartmentalized. Although in principle Reasoner disapproves of price-fixing, that disapproval does not have to flow consistently through everything he does. He will defend someone he believes is guilty of price-fixing. When he does this, one supposes a higher value takes control of the decision, the value of being a good lawyer. In this, Reasoner is probably quite typical of the group.

Apart from the refusal to defend heinous criminals, the refusal to take a case among these lawyers often turns upon occasional scruples regarding the values represented by the potential client. Left unsaid and largely taken for granted are the refusal of cases, however interesting, of clients who cannot pay, or clients whose cause, however noble, has no legal standing. *Pro bono* work, about which these men are modestly silent, can always be the exception to any rule.

Is It Important to Like the Client?

The lawyers agree that it is important to like the client, and even more important to give the *appearance* of liking the client. It is difficult to be an advocate in front of a jury if the jury perceives that the counsel dislikes the client. It is also important to like a client if one is going to generate the superhuman effort required in winning.

Frequently, the client for these men is another lawyer. Do lawyers like lawyers? They can, and often do. Although at times there is conflict, and probably even hostility, between a trial lawyer and a corporate client's in-house lawyers. But it is more likely to be the case that there is mutual respect, cooperation, and even affection.

Lawyers need to understand their clients, the client's motivation, the drive and personality traits that lead clients to behave as they do. It is necessary for finding empathy and identification so important for successful advocacy. Jim Neal looks for a way to understand why a wealthy man, for example, would steal. He tries to find redeeming virtues, and frequently finds them. This tends to make him more tolerant of his clients and therefore more likable. Even so, it is not always possible to like the client, or even have the client like him. An understanding however is sometimes possible. For Neal, "there have been a lot of cases I've tried where I have simply said to my client, 'You son of a bitch, you're not going to like me when this is over, but by God, you're [going] to respect me. Now let's get down here and get to work.'"

Clients lie. No doubt many criminal attorneys can tell a story like this one Neal relates:

> I remember the prime example of lying…an arson case. I really believed the client…I can't tell you for the life of me what triggered it, but towards the end of the trial I began to think, "That son of a bitch is lying to me. I believe he did this." He continued to lie. I tried the case. He was acquitted on all counts.

Neal finds a saving virtue in the fact that the man finally did admit he was lying. The admission could just as easily be considered a taunt as a virtue, but Neal, like all trial lawyers, has a strong compulsion to find something good in his clients. In the case of the arsonist who lied, Neal extracted a confession from the client, witnessed by someone else:

> I said, "You son of a bitch, you're off now, you're acquitted, you can never be tried again, but I believe you did this, I believe you've been lying to me." I guess the only saving virtue I can find in him is, he says, "You said they can't try me again?" "No." "And it won't ever get out of this room?" "Yeah," I said. He said, "Yeah, I lied to you. I did it."

Neal now protects himself against this sort of thing by postponing getting the client's story until he has heard it from a number of other voices. He will not interview the client in detail until he has learned everything possible he can learn about the case from other sources:

> I've seen it happen that if you start too early with your client, you talk about pieces of the case or show him pieces of the documents, you can get an actually faulty recollection or a lack of memory that when you lay it all out for him, it becomes something else.

Harry Reasoner believes that to represent a client effectively it is important to develop considerable empathy for the client. Reasoner has had his problems with in-house counsel. He comments on what must be a frequent occurrence: a CEO will either deliberately or inadvertently play general counsel against the trial lawyer. This can obviously be a complicated dynamic, especially where in-house counsel are jockeying for position among themselves and within the corporation. Frequently, they will have a history with the top executives in the company unknown to the trial counsel, and to a degree spill over into the dynamic among the players. Professional rivalry is not unknown. As Reasoner notes, getting too close to the CEO will earn the enmity of the in-house lawyers, who will then try to cut out the trial lawyer as much as possible.

> It's a dangerous thing, from a professional standpoint in the sense that I represented one company, achieved great results, and the CEO said in the presence of his legal staff, "Now by God, next time we have a problem like this...." He wouldn't deal with anyone who didn't bring me in immediately.

At that point corporate counsel set out to do everything they could to keep Reasoner from being involved in any further litigation involving the company.

Max Blecher is pretty candid on the subject of whether or not he likes his clients. He does not like them all, but he maintains that even when he does not like them he will still be their strong advocate in a particular case. It is more fun to like the clients, and it does help. Still, the main difference, Blecher insists, is the lack of gratification in working for someone he does not like. He says he can still win, but liking the client:

> Helps a lot. I mean, it makes you more comfortable, but is it important? No. I can represent a client I don't particularly like and have won. But it's less gratifying, let's put it that way. You don't feel as good at the end of the whole process as you do for someone who is really a decent person and, in your view, victimized.

The question of gratification is important to Bob Warren. Cool and objective as he is, Warren displays feelings toward his clients, without a doubt, and he values having his expertise appreciated. It is important to him to get a word of appreciation from people he helps in addition to his fee. When he says not getting the word of appreciation is "discouraging," he is clearly suggesting that he has other motives beside money for doing this work. And in that he surely speaks for all the lawyers.

Steve Susman at first avoids answering the question about whether it is important to like one's client, mentioning a number of important qualities he expects in his relationship with someone he represents.

> It is important that they not drive you crazy, that they not get in fights with you. It's important that they respect your judgment...listen to your advice...level with you. There are a lot of important things about the relationship, and I have had some clients who I feel extremely close to and friendly with and like a lot.

Then Susman reveals that important or not, it almost always happens that he does like his clients, and that liking them is both a cause and a result of the intense devotion he gives to the case.

> After a complete trial, you end up loving the clients. During a long trial where the client is with you and watching you and seeing what you do at night, at two or three in the morning, and how you are devoted to their case, they usually end up liking you and you usually end up liking them. It's hard not to with that kind of team work.

Phil Corboy likes to be needed, he is even a godfather to a small boy whose father whom he helped was badly hurt. Most clients he helps are grateful, a few are not.

> I've had clients bitch about the expenses, bitch about the fee they've agreed to pay, bitch about the jury result, bitch about the settlement even though it's the absolute dollar of an insurance coverage. Most of my clients are very brave people who, when everything is said and everything is done and the whole thing is over, are reasonably grateful because without us they recognize they would either not have gotten anything or much less than they got.

Joe Jamail, brusque as usual talks about what he did to a client he did not like.

> I told him, "Everybody hates you. Nobody likes you. Do you know why? It's because you're an asshole. You run around here looking like you just stepped out of a smelly toilet." I said, "Now, I want to tell you something. I've done all I can for your case. You're going on the stand in the morning. And the first time I see any of that arrogance, I'm going to be angry. And you can tell if I'm angry when you see me get up and leave." He got on that stand full of humility, and made a hell of a witness.

Jamail feels it is very important to like the client and that it will show in court.

If you like somebody, it's going to show. If you don't, that will show also. The client can't talk. You're the client's voice. And you can't fake that. You've got to get to know the client. How are you going to project the client's personality? The jury sees that client through the lawyer. And if I don't like him, they're not going to like him.

All right, face up to it. Why is it that you planned working on this matter Saturday from nine to one, but when you got in the office, you didn't do it? And maybe the answer is you don't like this person. Because we represent some pretty bad characters. I have my own set of values.

—Jim Brosnahan

Brosnahan admits he does not work as hard for somebody he dislikes. And Brosnahan knows that the jury will see immediately whether or not a lawyer feels good about his or her client. If you do not genuinely like your client, you have got to put on a good act. Brosnahan suggests you must do it through tone of voice when referring to the client and by letting the jury see you relate sincerely to the client. "If you don't like your client, which is entirely possible, then you have to discipline yourself to do a number of things to try to put as good a complexion upon the relationship as you can."

Trying a Case Away from Home

There is a great deal of opinion in the legal community and among jury consultants about the wisdom and advisability of trial lawyers practicing in parts of the country where their speech and personal style might be out of synchronization with prevailing customs. Some of these men feel confident that they can overcome such barriers if in fact they exist. Other lawyers respect them. Still others have additional factors besides speech and mannerisms that they consider when trying a case away from home.

Awkward logistics concern Max Blecher. The situation gets progressively worse the further he gets from his base in Los Angeles. He does not think it is a good idea to try and become nationwide in one's practice. In Georgia for instance he considers himself a "fish out of water." But by the time he gets to cosmopolitan New York he is fitting in again. Texas is a place he would rather avoid. "I think it's stupid for somebody to take a Los Angeles lawyer to Texas where they are very provincial. Who would trust you?" But even in his home state the practical nut-and-bolt problems are very real: finding a place to live and work, commuting home on the weekends, and staying in touch with the office.

As a young attorney, Phil Corboy was a "have gun will travel" type. It was good for business. He was bucking for a national reputation as a personal-injury lawyer.

> When I was younger, I did it for the purpose of building up a business. I did it because I tried every case I could get my hands on. I did it because I wanted to become well-known. I did it because I was gratified and I was excited about being called into another jurisdiction. None of those things appeal to me any more.

Corboy has not been outside of his hometown to try a case for over ten years. "I believe that there are lots of good lawyers in the world. Ordinarily New York doesn't need Corboy. California doesn't need Corboy."

Bob Fiske is not afraid of how he will play on the road, but he does recognize the dislocation to his family life as a major factor. Although recently successful on a number of out-of-town cases, he regrets being away from home. At this stage of his career it may be that personal factors weigh more heavily than they once did. But there is the advantage in being away from the office. "Somehow, when you get out of town, people assume you are just unavailable. You're not, it's just a different area code. But you can concentrate on a case much better." Fiske does not feel at any disadvantage because of his personal style or speech when he is conducting a trial away from home. But this may only pertain to large cities.

> I found in the major metropolitan cities that it is not a disadvantage to be from New York. In Miami, it makes absolutely no difference whatsoever. There wasn't a single Southern accent in the whole courtroom. Now, would I want to try a case against Joe Jamail in the Texas State Court? No, I wouldn't. I'd get a local lawyer to do that. I think New York lawyers probably are not regarded highly there, or in a lot of other places.

As for a man who is clearly one of the finest in the Lone Star state, Joe Jamail, the road holds no terrors. Jamail rubbed his hands together as he expressed himself on the subject. "I like it everywhere. I really don't see any difference. I have handled cases in Illinois, Michigan, New York, California, Arizona, Oklahoma, Louisiana, New Mexico; a lot of places." But even for Jamail it is easier to be within range of home despite his now owning an airplane.

Arthur Liman thinks discretion is the better part of valor for a New York lawyer in small towns, or even medium-size towns. He is sympathetic, but candid in his opinion of Vince Fuller defending Mike Tyson in Indiana.

> There are certain parts of the country in which a New York lawyer or Washington lawyer is at a disadvantage. To give an example: There is no better lawyer than Vince Fuller [who won the Hinckley case in Washington] but, it is clear that even so talented a lawyer should not have tried the *Tyson* case in Indiana. Southern Indiana has too much of a country-boy environment for a lawyer from a big city in the East. I won't try cases in a xenophobic forum where the jury's prejudice against New York lawyers may hurt my client.

In general, Liman advocates the use of local counsel in regions where the jury pool tends to be parochial. "I think it's dangerous in Texas unless you have local counsel like Harry [Reasoner] or Joe [Jamail]. On the other hand, I'm comfortable in the more cosmopolitan areas trying cases."

Pat McCartan is somewhat more confident about Texas, perhaps because of his positive experiences in the state. "Good judges always welcome good lawyers." McCartan has encountered occasional hostility in several jurisdications, but has managed to defuse much of it by using local co-counsel.

Finally, Jim Brosnahan suggests there is a sort of zone in which one might be all right, but beyond that there is the possibility of trouble. Brosnahan argues that attorneys place an undue burden upon themselves when they try a case in another community. They do not know the judges or the towns. He recounts an experience he had outside San Diego when he confused two demographically disparate towns with similar names.

> When you go to pick the jury, you don't know the difference between Oceanside and Ocean Beach in San Diego, as I learned. One has the last few remaining hippies and the other has a lot of retired Marine people, which is quite a difference. You have to blend in. You must do that and that takes a lot of work.

Now Brosnahan does research into a strange venue by subscribing to a local newspaper for at least six months in advance of trial.

Let us assume that the engagement has been accepted. What comes next for these attorneys? What are their basic pretrial considerations? The first line of strategic issues that must be assessed in the pretrial period are filing a case, settlement, venue, and jurisdiction.

Filing a Lawsuit

It is not a virtual certainty that once a client has been accepted a law suit will follow as night follows day. A cost-benefit analysis might be undertaken. The client's most fundamental interests need to be fathomed and taken into account. Perhaps most of all, the factors of anger, legal standing, possible return, and downside risk should be carefully assessed.

Harry Reasoner does not file a law suit precipitously. He is an advocate of a cost-benefit analysis whenever filing is contemplated. He asks himself, "How likely is it that the law will provide a benefit to them that will be worth the cost of the litigation?" When people sue for personal grievances or for damages, Reasoner thinks it is generally a mistake to litigate on the basis of principle.

I've had many people say they don't care what it costs, it's a matter of principle. I generally find it very healthy in those instances to say, "Well, fine. I want a million-dollar retainer."

—Harry Reasoner

Anger runs its course; and it is sometimes embarrassing to be involved in a costly and protracted lawsuit whose premise seems empty at the end. Reasoner feels that many litigants, after the initial catharsis, decide the principle is not so important after all. A carefully considered decision must be made early about filing a case. Once the process is begun it tends to take on a life of its own. There are few easy ways to terminate a lawsuit once underway.

Bob Warren, before filing a case for a plaintiff, to cite a typical example, wants to be certain that damage or injury has actually occurred. "The first issue in whether or not to file a lawsuit is: *has the person that's going to bring this lawsuit really suffered some significant damage?* In other words, you may have all sorts of swell legal points, but there's really nothing to be gained out of pursuing it." Also, there is nothing admirable or productive about having a disappointed client at the end of a case who has won two-hundred and fifty thousand dollars and spent seven-hundred and fifty-thousand dollars in legal fees. The second criterion to be applied by Warren:

> Do you have a case that's going to get by the pleading stage?
> There's no point in filing lawsuits that are going to get
> knocked out at the first crack out of the box. And finally, is
> it a case that can be won in front of a jury?

Doubts about the latter should not, in Warren's view, prevent an attorney from moving forward, absent a suitable settlement, if the other characteristics are present, namely genuine substantial damage and a legally viable claim.

Pat McCartan comes back to a point made earlier: It is much more difficult to initiate a plaintiff's case than it is to accept a defendant's. If the cost-recovery equation is favorable, McCartan suggests, consider the client's objectives and willingness to see the matter through. Once the train of events has begun, McCartan and others warn, it is war. Money and time will be committed and put at risk before the final outcome. There will be distractions for others in the firm. And it is far too easy to underestimate the required resources.

Arthur Liman favors a "cooling-off period" before filing a lawsuit. He tries to impress upon his client the difficulty of getting out of a lawsuit. Does the client have the stomach to stay the course?

When people come to see me, they are angry. I say, "Come back in three months." Or "There's a reason that there is a year's statute of limitations for libel actions because it is easier to start them than [it is] to end them. So see whether you feel as aggrieved in three months as you do today. If you don't, then don't bring the lawsuit because it will be like getting out of Vietnam."

—Arthur Liman

A lawyer must not lead a client to suppose there is a road from point A to point B when in fact no road exists. Liman is adamant on this point.

> One of the cardinal sins for a lawyer is to lead a client to believe that you can obtain a certain result and it turns out that it is unobtainable because the law requires a writing and you don't have a writing, or because the story is just inherently implausible, or it won't go down with a jury, or that the climate in this area is running very much in a different direction—it's dicey.

David Boies' approach to filing a lawsuit is as cautious or more so. He feels that it is part of a lawyer's function to seek ways of resolving a conflict other than filing a lawsuit. "See if there isn't some relatively simple solution that can be worked out that doesn't involve starting everybody's litigation engines running." He also stresses the downside risk, the possibility that there will be counterclaims with which his client may not be able to deal. Once it can be determined that there is a "serious, substantial lawsuit," the factors of the risk of counterclaims and seeking alternative resolutions come into play. At the beginning, a good attorney makes sure that there is not something else the lawsuit will generate in terms of counterclaims, disclosures, or discovery down the road that the client might not be able to fight.

Obtaining expert opinion where possible is an excellent tool for decision making. Jim Brosnahan prefers to have an expert's affidavit that warrants that in his or her opinion there is a course of action, evidence of guilt, or that some form of liability exists. This confirmation is Brosnahan's green light.

Steve Susman takes a much more aggressive approach to filing. He's proud of his reputation as a lawyer who is, as he puts it, always "headed for the courthouse."

> I'm a great believer in file your lawsuit first, negotiate second. So I am quick on the trigger when it comes to filing a lawsuit. When someone comes to me with a problem, I tell them, "Look, the minute that you disclose my name as your lawyer, we are headed for the courthouse, so let's not

play games." I want to try the lawsuit. I'm not a negotiator.

A more cautious Fred Bartlit does not want to spend two or three years of his or his client's life on an unpleasant experience. He has filed fewer cases than people have wanted him to file.

Max Blecher's work as a plaintiff's antitrust lawyer leads him to emphasize once again the hazards of the appellate process when deciding whether or not to file a lawsuit. He relies on his experience to tell him what is likely to evolve in the way of proof and how the case is likely to shape up. When he combines this with an assessment of the appellate climate, he is close to making his decision about filing. He considers the likelihood that in discovery he might find a bonus, a smoking gun, something unexpected; or the chance that something expected may not materialize. It is a no-go if there is any chance of a hole showing up that will cause a favorable jury verdict to be overturned on appeal. Blecher tries to anticipate if the appellate court will require some element of proof that the jury did not regard highly, one that is impossible to provide.

And then I ask myself, here it is in the ninth circuit, is there a hole in it? You might be able to persuade a jury or trial judge on this, but is there a hole in it, I mean, an IBM-type hole, that says, "You've got to prove lower cost pricing or you've got to prove that somebody stood on their head and spit wooden nickels."

—Max Blecher

The jury verdict is only the beginning, and the law in this case may be somewhat unstable. It could change during the time it takes for an appeal to be heard. What are the trends in the law? In short, the case must be a winner in two domains: before a jury and before a circuit court of appeals. Does it have a chance of survival based on the direction or trend in the present law? Five years from now is it likely to be winner? And, if this test can be passed, back up and consider: Can this case be won before a jury?

Turning to another page in the art of filing, Joe Jamail looks closely at how the grounds for negligence issues fall out.

First thing a lawyer ought to look at is whether or not there is a legal cause of action. You can't file everything in the world just because somebody got done some wrong to him. OK, so this person got hurt, where is the negligence? If there are three or four grounds of negligence, I discard all of them except the strongest.

Finding legal grounds is the first test, then he makes a subjective assessment, the way he always does.

> If you've got these three ingredients: negligence, proximate cause or product-defect cause, and damages, that's the first test. Arthur [Liman] uses something he calls a smell test. If he doesn't like the way the facts look or smell, he's gone. That's a good test. I incorporate that in my discounting.
>
> **—Joe Jamail**

For Phil Corboy, the smell of green is pretty important. Supposing his client was hurt in an accident in which the other driver had a twenty-five thousand dollar insurance policy.

You say, "You're going to have to go through all this, one-hundred thousand dollars, and I'm telling you it's not worth it. You got a bad break." I'm almost one-hundred percent successful with them. When I tell them don't do it, they're grateful.

To file or not to file, that is the question. In terms of pretrial strategy, filing a lawsuit starts a chain of events and counter events not easy to control and difficult to stop. As much as possible needs to be anticipated before the action is initiated. When it comes to filing a lawsuit, each lawyer approaches the matter in his own way, but there is a pretty clear consensus in favor of caution.

Settlement

> I've never been afraid to show cards, because no one's going to take those cards away from me.
>
> **—Arthur Liman**

Settlement to a trial lawyer is like rain to a ball player. But the game is not merely postponed, it is canceled. The lawyers in this study feel considerable ambivalence about settlement. Most of them feel a keen sense of disappointment when last-minute settlements prevent a case from going to trial after months or even years of preparation. Yet, they know that their job is to resolve disputes in favor of their client, and settlement occurs in over ninety percent of their cases.

The principal reasons behind settlement in most civil matters concern the cost of going to trial and the risk involved. Settlement is cheaper, and it allows more control over the outcome, which is the result of a mutual decision of the litigants, rather than the will of judge and/or jury.

The climate has changed quite a bit in the last few years. The major corporations have really tied the purse strings. Lawyers used to travel like nuns in pairs of two to everything. During the eighties you found that talking settlement got to be almost futile. Nobody wanted to settle because they all thought they were going to win.

—Max Blecher

Lawyers sometimes suggest that a case that was settled should not have been, implying that more could have been gained by going to trial. This is never a certainty, but they are accustomed to dealing in probabilities, and making decisions on that basis. Harry Reasoner feels that more cases should and could be settled. If there are good lawyers on both sides a higher percentage of cases will settle. He believes some cases go to trial because of the inability of one or both of the lawyers to evaluate the case properly.

Even after a careful evaluation suggests that settlement is a prudent course, there are many reasons why lawyers do not seek a pretrial resolution. At times they are afraid of appearing weak. (Pat McCartan sees this as a more prevalent factor than the cynic's view that an attorney wants to milk the case.) At other times lawyers are afraid to disclose elements of their case in settlement negotiations, fearing that if the case does not settle they have revealed something that will make it more difficult to win in court. Objectivity suggests that these factors will be overcome in good faith efforts to settle, but lawyers never have enough information to reduce calculations to purely objective terms. No one can be sure what will happen in a jury trial. Fear of the unknown undoubtedly results in settlement on many occasions, but the desire to roll the dice is also compelling given the size of judgments in many well-publicized cases.

The price of settling with Joe Jamail is always high, yet it may be cheap compared to what could come later. Ninety-five out of a hundred times, Jamail's adversaries avoid the courthouse. Jamail does not suppose it is because he is well-liked.

> Ninety-five percent of my cases settle. They have for years . . . I'm talking about only five percent going to trial in the last twenty years. I don't think they do it because I'm a good guy. And everybody will tell you that I don't settle too cheap.

And an offer once refused may not continue to be on the table. Liman has a rule that if settlement fails he does not feel bound by that proposal, "don't expect that it will be there next time. It may be, it may not be."

It is no surprise that Jim Brosnahan enjoys poker. It is closely related to what can go on in pretrial negotiations. And it is not just the cards, it is the player. According to Brosnahan,

> If Phil Corboy calls us and says, "I think it would be good for the clients on both sides here if instead of doing three years of litigation, why don't we get somebody to listen to us for a day or so and we'll kind of hammer this out. We'll see if we can settle it." I don't think anybody's going to say, "Phil Corboy's really afraid."

Tom Barr's mentor, Bruce Bromley used to say, "if you're weak you're weak," implying that the other side knows it, and there's no point in trying to pretend otherwise. All of this decrees, as Harry Reasoner suggests, that the client be given a "calm, objective appraisal of the situation, one that cuts through the emotional tensions and hostility that tend to arise in lawsuits." This entails looking at all the ramifications of a trial, including those that involve precedents that may be harmful later in other cases at other times. Putting too much stock in this kind of risk, however, can lead to an unsatisfactory settlement. David Boies was involved in a lawsuit in which many lawyers with whom he was associated perceived a prohibitive downside risk if the suit went forward. In this case, Boies nevertheless urged the client to go into court, with favorable results.

> I remember one of the early cases I had for CBS. Reagan barred all television cameras from the White House because there was dispute among the networks and CNN as to rotation. So he just banned them all. On behalf of CBS, we sued, and NBC and ABC also sued, to get that enjoined...I was very candid with CBS about what the risks were, what the opportunities were...We ultimately went to hearing and won and got the preliminary injunction.

In the final analysis, a palpable threat of a trial is what leads to real negotiations.

There are studies done by sociologists...[regarding] who gets the best deal in war, union negotiations, courtroom negotiations. The person who gets the worst deal is a reasonable, thoughtful person who sees both sides and is fair. The person who gets the best deal is somebody who is viewed as rash, unreasonable, confident, unpredictable in any negotiating context...the threat of a nuclear bomb is what gives you a good settlement, not the threat of sitting around a table negotiating.

—Fred Bartlit

The approach to settlement is largely strategic for these men. They want to try cases, that is what they love to do. But they roundly disapprove of allowing their desire for battle to interfere with a rational assessment of their client's interests. By and large, attorneys are willing to disclose telling elements of their case in settlement negotiations, and do not accept the notion that bluff and concealment is generally useful or appropriate. Most cases will be settled, and that is because the cost and risk of going to trial is unconscionably high.

Venue

Once an engagement has been accepted, however, evaluations must be made concerning judges and juries in various venues. (Note: In this section and the next, on jurisdiction, the attorneys will not be referred to by name because they make observations and comparisons that they would rather not have on the record. Hence, recourse to anonymity at this point is necessary.)

In the words of one lawyer, venue is about judges and juries, everything else is a distant second. He is surprised when a discussion of venue arises, and judges and juries are not considered. Venue should be chosen so that the jury identifies with the client. As a plaintiff's lawyer, he thus considers: How close are we going to be to where the plaintiff is? It is an advantage if the jury can occasionally see the plaintiff's logo on trucks or advertisements. If the plaintiff can be perceived as local and not an outsider, it will result in a hometown edge. Another reason for being close to the office and the plaintiff's place of business is to reduce the cost of the lawsuit.

Another attorney will choose a city where he thinks the judges are most likely to recognize the validity of his client's case. He tends to choose the federal bench in a particular circuit because in his view there are fewer ideologues. He avoids the state court because of the quality of the procedures, which he thinks are a "jungle" and where the judges are inferior to the federal bench.

One attorney considers venue so important *it determines outcome*. He believes that it is possible to demonstrate statistical variances in jury awards for certain types of injuries in various venues. In this, he is not willing to rely upon what he calls "general anecdotal mythology" but instead, relies on jury consultants.

Another lawyer gives an excellent illustration of how considering the judicial bench plays a part in venue decisions. On the federal bench, the seventh circuit is dominated by judges under the influence of the conservative, free-market University of Chicago schools of law and economics that formed such influential Nobel prize-winning economists as Milton Friedman and George J. Stigler. The wisdom among attorneys is to stay out of the seventh with antitrust claims that involve the concept of predatory pricing. Appellate review is the reason for staying out, not juries. Reference is made to a recent antitrust case:

> In this predatory-price litigation suit in Chicago, my suspicion is that they chose Chicago because the seventh circuit, dominated by Chicago School judges, doesn't

151

believe in predatory pricing. So they were picking venue,
not because of a jury pool, but because of appellate review
involved.

The case was moved to another city because it is near the plaintiff's
headquarters and because there is a judge there who moves the docket
quickly. Hence, it is anticipated that the plaintiff will receive a speedy
trial, and it is hoped, a favorable verdict.

At times the relative novelty of a case in a given venue might insure
a more advantageous climate in the view of one attorney. "In New
York they are bored with takeover cases, they'd throw them out.
Whereas you bring one up in Portland, Oregon, the judge gets
excited."

Somewhat different issues are raised by an attorney who argues that
the law, as well as the judge, jury, and counsel, vary from venue to
venue. He sees three basic kinds of issues: First, the law varies from
state to state, or if in federal court, from circuit to circuit; second,
juries are different in different parts of the country, and counsel should
figure out where a jury is more likely to be partial to the client; third,
venue strategy involves the consideration of which attorneys will be
involved in the trial. This means determining who the local co-counsel
will be if the lead attorney is coming in from elsewhere, as well as who
is on the opponent's team. Other basic logistical questions involve the
distance between the trial site and the sources of clerical support. "All
other things being equal, you're better off closer to home just because
your supply lines are shorter."

It is also possible, and at times necessary, to avoid large metropolitan areas where it is impossible to predict who the judge will be. It
is useful to try and target a small county where there is more
likelihood of determining who will be the judge. From a personal-
injury perspective, fine shades of difference can exist with regard to
venue as one moves from county to county. Verdict history is an
important set of tea leaves in such cases.

> If an accident happened in [county X], and the defendant
> lives in [county Y] that's no choice. [County X] is so
> conservative that there is no way that I would try a case
> there. If I did, I ought to be sued for malpractice. If you
> have a choice, you're going to pick the venue generally
> where you have a history of favorable verdicts.

This attorney feels confident with his efforts to assess a community based on the commercial infrastructure and the nature of the labor force.

It's easy to pick up a telephone directory to see what kind of industry they have. Do they have working people here? Is this a banking community? Is this a farming community? What kind of plaintiff have you got? You can lose your case picking the wrong venue, if you have a choice.

Another lawyer looks at the verdicts around his state and concludes that it is always best, when possible, to stay at home. In his state there are a few counties with a history of favorable verdicts, but most of his cases are filed in the circuit court of his home county. Most cases happen in this venue, and if not, he usually has the ability to keep them there.

The speed with which a case can be brought to trial is also frequently a venue issue. Still, for the attorney who raises this point, such an issue must remain secondary to the matter of choosing a jury. Depending on who the client is, who the defendant is, and what the nature of the case is, where will a jury be most receptive?

The availability of witnesses should be a principal consideration according to another attorney. Controlling the witnesses is critical, particularly since in his view the best proof in a case always comes in the form of testimony from the witnesses for the other side. This means one should sue "in the other guy's backyard."

> Most people look at it backwards. If they're suing a company, they want to sue in their own backyard, which is superficially right, but in my view, is almost always wrong. You should always sue in the other guy's backyard. And the reason is that you've got to have witnesses. If the case isn't being tried where the witnesses live, you've got to read depositions and show videos that are absolutely useless.

Reading depositions in court and viewing videotapes, in this lawyer's view, are not effective. Even so, they must be used in order to get a semblance of what proof the witnesses can offer before the court. From a plaintiff's standpoint, getting the adverse witnesses who can be impeached or who indict themselves is a problem that can be addressed as a strategy in venue.

> In my business the best and maybe only real proof normally comes from the other side. So I'm looking to use adverse witnesses and one question is, which ones are available to you? This is frequently a problem because if you're suing an out-of-state corporation in your own backyard, maybe most of your key people who made the decisions and the subject of litigation are not available to you. You may have to use depositions.

This often entails fights with judges over calling witnesses the other side wants to use to defend the case. If this fight is lost, an attorney will have to put on some of his best evidence by deposition, punch this in narrowly, and wait until the opposing lawyers bring out their witnesses. At that point he will have to use cross-examination to reinforce what has come before.

In summary, the key questions in venue for these lawyers involve juries, judges, and the historical disposition in a given venue. The speed with which a case can be brought to trial and the availability of witnesses, are important but lesser considerations.

Jurisdiction

In considering jurisdiction, the issue of the judge becomes virtually paramount, along with a variety of procedural considerations that often center on the importance of the uniform rules that govern the selection of jurors and the way in which the jurors' verdict is determined (must be unanimous in federal court). Some of the attorneys are direct about their preference for one jurisdiction over another. One of them says that, in general, in his home jurisdiction, he does not like the Republican judges who have been appointed in federal court. He argues that they are arbitrary and make status calls he does not agree with.

Procedural jury issues are of strategic importance. The broad jury pool in federal court makes it more difficult to evaluate the jurors, a matter exacerbated by limited voir dire. In general, federal judges conduct voir dire impatiently and feel that *any* six jurors will do. "Is anyone prejudiced? If so, raise your hand." According to these attorneys, this is the process by which federal judges often approach jury selection. In a state jury system, lawyers are able to establish a rapport with prospective jurors and this allows them a shot at an impartial jury. A number of the lawyers believe that federal court judges are also impatient with opening statements and impose limits on them by placing a narrow construction on what is non-argumentative. In addition, the lawyers feel that federal judges are more arbitrary in their rulings than state court judges.

One attorney dissents quite strongly from this point of view. But he would not go so far as to consider the state courts inferior to the federal courts. Basically, he sees little difference in the state and federal courts.

> Some of the best judges I've seen are state court judges [who] have been trial judges for a long time and maybe have more trial experience than some of the federal judges. There are also a lot of good federal judges. I don't see a difference to tell you the truth.

Looking at the matter from the corporate-defense perspective, this lawyer is not even afraid of the state courts of California.

People call California "The People's Republic of California," and stay out of the state courts. But I've been in state courts in San Diego and Sacramento. You hear horror stories. But people seem about the same to me. The judges seem about the same. The juries are the same people. I think there is a lot of mythology.

Another lawyer who used to prefer the federal courts now finds himself in basic agreement with the above. He sees a number of tradeoffs in moving from one court to the other. In his state there are interlocutory appeals that can stop a case in mid-passage until a ruling is forthcoming. This can slow the progress of a case considerably. On the other hand there is more limited discovery in the state courts, which can be an advantage. "I used to have a preference for federal courts, but they've gotten so jammed up with drug cases, and state courts have gotten better in [his state], so that I'm willing to consider state." Historically, he feels, the federal courts have had better judges, but that judges in state courts are improving. The fact that cases can be delayed through interlocutory appeals stands a disadvantage in state court, according to this attorney, who prefers a system in which only the final judgment can be appealed, just as in federal court. On the other hand, he points out, there is more liberal discovery in the federal court. Thus, in state court one pays the price of having the risk of interlocutory appeals, but on the hand, there is the advantage of more limited discovery.

Another attorney, who practices in another part of the country, and looks at matters from the plaintiff's point of view for the most part, prefers state courts. When he chooses for the plaintiff he takes the state court because the reputation of the courts in his state can be intimidating to the defendant. The myth about state court juries is that they award wildly irresponsible judgments to plaintiffs. This attorney feels that is not true, and that juries are quite conservative. He favors state courts, however, for other reasons. The split verdict (ten out of twelve creates a verdict) and wide-open voir dire are two enticements found in state courts. Also, the courts do not grant summary judgment. For this attorney, the speed of the docket is also a factor in choosing a jurisdiction.

> I prefer to be in a place that moves its docket very quickly. Where can I get to trial quickest? Then, where can I get a judge who will not grant summary judgment, will push this thing to trial and give us a fair trial?

Considerations of jurisdiction, combined with venue issues, lead to a salubrious climate for attorneys in certain parts of the country. One interesting phenomenon of this sort is the clustering of financially successful personal-injury lawyers around the Gulf Coast of Texas. It is possible to hypothesize that the state court jurisdiction in this area, for a variety of reasons, favors large judgments to plaintiffs. Further, the jury pools in some of the smaller counties outside of the large metropolitan areas have made these communities promising places for plaintiffs to bring lawsuits. Jury demographic studies have shown that the jury pools in these areas of Texas are generally pro-union and anti-corporation, particularly along the coast.

On the whole, the lawyers point to the rules in the federal system as a distinct advantage. Staying within federal jurisdiction, even moving from circuit to circuit, one finds a reliable playing field, with the goal posts in the same place, the dimensions of the field the same, and the referees employing the same rules.

> There are standard rules of procedure in the federal system. So that wherever I go the only variations I have are the personnel's idiosyncrasies and some limited number of local rules. I know the rules of procedure and evidence that will be applied.

Yet this attorney is less certain about the imputed superiority of the federal judges. If there was a gap at one time in the past, he suggests, it is narrowing.

> I used to think that the federal judges were of higher caliber. Some of them still are, but in my judgment, that's changed drastically so that now you get about the same competence in the state judge as you get in federal judges.

A colleague agrees that there has been an important shift over time. There was once a period when one always wanted to be in federal court. Now, there are cases in which a federal court judge's superiority is outweighed by the limitations of voir dire. He makes his decision with regard to jurisdiction on the basis of the judge and the jury pool.

> It depends on where you are. There are some cases where if it is a jury trial, and because of the restriction of voir dire examination in federal court, I may want to be in a state court and get that first opportunity to try my case to the jury. Generally, I will decide, assuming you have jurisdiction, based upon the quality of the judges and the jury pool, as to where I want to be.

Federal jurisdiction is clearly the first choice for one of the large firm lawyers. The matter of the judges involved is not a critical factor in his mind. Rather, he sees the issue in terms of the appellate process. He has an enthusiastic respect for the federal circuit courts of appeals, and would rather see a court in his circuit render a final verdict than any other court in the United States.

> Unless my local counsel has a particularly close relationship with the local judiciary, I would rather be in federal court than state court. That has at least as much to do with a court of appeals as it does anything else. There are some very good state court trial judges and some not so good federal court trial judges, but the federal circuit courts of appeals

are the best courts in the country. They are more dependable than any trial court, state or federal, more dependable
than state supreme courts and more dependable than the
United States Supreme Court, which has got so many
ideological agendas that it has ceased to be a dependable
court for the resolution of normal disputes.

Still another lawyer, who has exhibited the same mastery of the
federal courts as those of the state in which he practices, argues for the
relative superiority of the state courts. They are particularly suited to
clients of modest means because the conditions are generally more
open, the dockets less crowded, and the procedures less pretentious
and full of drill. Procedurally, he does not see much to choose between
federal and state jurisdictions. If anything, he feels procedure in state
courts is more realistic in many instances. He argues that discovery is
about the same for each and that the state courts have a refreshing lack
of "pomp and circumstance." He is put off by what he sees as a
numbers game in federal court.

Some federal judges attempt to equate justice
with numbers. "I move so many cases." Well,
what's that mean? If you've got two thousand
cases a year of injustice, I'd rather have one case
of justice.

On the other hand, another retains a preference for federal court
because of what he argues are the superior rules and enforcement of
rules for discovery.

As a defendant, I think a general preference would be for
federal court because it generally does a better job of
enforcing discovery. If you have a complex case, it seems to
me one of the things the defendant wants to try to do is to
eliminate inappropriate issues, to narrow and focus the
case, to knock out theories, that's more than likely to occur
in federal court.

The narrowing of issues is good for the defense, but plaintiffs,
according to this lawyer might well prefer the state courts.

> A strong ideological bent has been exercised in appointing circuit judges, some of the federal courts can be quite hostile to plaintiffs. A plaintiff might have a better shot at attaining and sustaining a verdict in a state court system.

The differences are so great in this regard, that this lawyer is ready to put forth the general proposition that most defendants regard federal court as being more favorable. Plaintiffs, as noted, would probably prefer state courts.

To attorneys who have a big commercial practice, jurisdiction is relevant to case management. For example, in federal court the same judge looks at the case each time it comes under review. In state court, unless an exception is made, the case bounces from judge to judge, something that is not desirable in a commercial case. In these large cases, the vast number of documents and witnesses involved make it difficult to move the litigation readily from one court to another. It is far better, from a case-management perspective, to set up for one judge and stay there for the duration of the case. Beyond this, in order to insure that the judge is completely familiar with all the elements of the case, documents, exhibits, and the like, attorneys must "re-educate the judge." In short, they must go over old ground, each time the case moves.

Of great concern to this lawyer, are the split juror verdicts in the courts in his home state.

> The big thing is the size of the jury, state or federal. In federal you're probably going to get eight jurors. You can use six to twelve, but they seem to be using eight and it has to be unanimous; whereas, state is still twelve and you only need nine. That's something to think about in the course of where you want your case to go.

Another lawyer, who defends white-collar criminals, points to the jury verdict issue as well. "In some states you don't have to get a majority verdict. And that is a factor that would levitate towards state court for some cases." Beyond this, in his view, it is back to basics. What are judges like? Where does the jury pool come from? He also feels that the quality of the judges is a major factor. Unlike one of his colleagues in the same state, he feels that the federal docket, drug cases notwithstanding, is better than the state docket, a reason for the plaintiff to bring a case to federal court, as well as a reason for the defendant to leave it there. In short, he likes the federal court in his state because he believes it is a more pleasant place to be, more organized, with nicer courtrooms, and better judges.

The traditional evaluation of federal versus state courts is advanced by the last attorney who is often involved in cases as a defendant in commercial disputes. He prefers the federal court because in his cases discovery issues are important, and the way discovery breaks in state court tends to favor plaintiffs. He likes the mechanical character of the federal courts. State courts can get bogged down with interlocutory appeals and other delaying tactics.

> I find that in the state court cases there are little tricks that people can pull within the rules that sort of foreclose some of your rights, such as forgetting document requests. Goofy little things. Quirks in their rules that I don't think really work right. In the federal system, the judge is going to say, "You filed an amended complaint." So what does it change? It doesn't affect my trial. In the state court, if you do that you can get set back a year just because you decided to adopt a new theory or some new idea.

Conclusion

Attorney strategies in the area of filing a lawsuit, settlement, venue, and jurisdiction encompass a combination of substantive, personal, and procedural issues. Where settlement is concerned, a number of human elements are at play, including gamesmanship and bluffing. In the remaining areas, venue and jurisdiction, strategy focuses on rules and procedures that are analyzed according to the interests of the client in a fairly cut-and-dried manner. Strategies in venue and jurisdiction are among the most objectively determined in all of pretrial preparations, particularly when jury specialists are involved.

Matters of personal style and temperament are also significant. There is, however, a surprising amount of accord, for example, on the subject of settlement strategy. There is also little disagreement about the importance of judges and jury pools in venue strategies, although the conclusions drawn are varied. Perhaps the greatest areas of difference occur in strategies involving jurisdiction. Preferences between state and federal courts vary considerably. Much of this variation is closely related to the region in which the attorney practices, his litigation specialty, and his kind of advocacy—plaintiff or defendant.

CHAPTER 4 ▇▇▇▇▇▇▇▇▇▇▇▇▇▇▇▇

Structuring the Case

*"I'm involved in a chess game the whole time when
I'm thinking of my witnesses."*
—Phil Corboy

In this chapter, our focus shifts to areas of pretrial strategy that
pertain to building the case. Each of these fourteen lawyers has
developed a personal strategy relevant to the substantive preparation of the case file. Nevertheless, there are striking similarities for
selecting witnesses, using discovery, depositions and interrogatories,
and formulating the theory of the case. This process, however, is not
necessarily in the same sequence or accomplished with the same
emphasis by the various attorneys.

Laying the Foundation

From the beginning, Jim Brosnahan acts as if the case is going to
trial. It does not matter that there may be a settlement. He knows, as
all trial lawyers do, that the motive for settlement is the prospect of
losing at trial, or not getting as much as one hoped. It is important to
give the impression that one is always ready to take the case to trial in
order to keep pressure on the other side. This cannot be mere bluff.

Brosnahan, whose background is in criminal prosecution, emphasizes physical evidence. It is important to get a feel for what has
actually happened, whether on the street or in corporate headquarters.
His first instinct is to go, take a look, interview witnesses. He will
spend time talking with each of the important participants. When he
completes these dialogues, he is satisfied that he will have a fairly
clear picture of what occurred. This phase of investigation is followed
by a round of activity in the office.

> There is the usual stuff: the exhibits, the law, the research
> on our opponent; which is very important. Who is this guy?
> How many trials has this person had? What are they like?
> What are their weaknesses? What are their strengths? Who
> is the judge?

At about this juncture, the problem list goes up on the wall. "I make a big list of the problems...the downside scenario. What are we going to do about this? What are we going to do about that?"

It is extremely important to come to terms early on in the case with the client and the likely witnesses. Any problems left untended will only worsen. A client with an unattractive personality is a critical liability, and this must be addressed. The client should understand that his behavior is an important factor at the trial. It may be necessary to work with him to insure his credibility with the jury, especially, as Brosnahan suggests, if the "client is an overbearing egomaniacal, crazy critter." Only through repeated exposure can an attorney gain a sense of who the people are on his side and how vulnerable they may be to attack.

> In the defense of corporate cases sometimes the client is a
> collection of people, and you have to deal with the weakest
> one because the plaintiff is always looking for the weakest
> one. And talk to them more than one time.

Then there is the question of the specialized knowledge involved. The attorneys in this study have not been johnny-one-notes, narrow specialists. They love challenge. Brosnahan, a voracious reader, relishes getting the information he needs for a case.

> I had a case involving lasers for a launch radiation lab and I
> bought a Goddamn book, nine hundred pages on lasers. I
> read the first one hundred seventy-five pages, which was the
> most basic stuff on lasers. I, at least, [got] superficially
> knowledgeable about the terminology and what the hell it
> is.

Attention to ancillary personnel is also extremely important. These include expert witnesses, and the people behind the scenes associated with the trial team.

> We want our experts early, although that is an economic
> factor. And I have good people. You always want to have a
> good accountant. You want to have a good investigator. You

want to have good people, get them in there, and find out what they think about this.

By now, what Brosnahan calls the sequence, the order of events in the trial, is in place, with a few blank spots yet to be filled in. He runs it back and forth in his mind like a film until every piece is in place.

I never handle a document in a courtroom that I haven't read carefully. I've seen too many lawyers have things blow up in their faces because they didn't read the document.

—Pat McCartan

For Max Blecher the first priority in trial preparation is to come to terms with the documents, "the single most important thing in my life as a trial lawyer." As a plaintiff's antitrust specialist, the written record, the paper trail, is paramount. Blecher goes from the documents to the depositions, which are somewhat less important.

> I read all the documents... because they are the hardest for anybody to explain. I then move to the next level of preparation in which [I] view all of the depositions taken, at least any of them that seem to be candidates for use at the trial, either as a live witness or under deposition form. My experience over the years is that depositions produce very little useful evidence, so I am very much wired into the documents.

The documents provide the skeleton of proof Blecher seeks to establish, while the depositions may add a little flesh to the frame. His cases often center around one to six documents that he uses to tell the story. This story is supplemented with material from depositions. Relatively early in the preparation, having selected his key documents, he then finds the visual aids to illustrate it, "I'm really big on visual aids."

The attorneys in this book use a variety of effective visual aids, ranging from poster-board illustrations created by artists or psychologists (who use principles of visual learning), to such high-tech items as laser-disc displays controlled by bar code readers and computer-animated simulations or event reconstructions. These are prepared by jury consultants with expertise in the area of gestalt and perception psychology and computer animation.

It is clear from Blecher's approach to the documents, the depositions, and the visual exhibits that he is looking for a thread to hold the case together. "What small segment from this huge body of facts can I take out to present to the jury in a story form? This is what happened. This is the case. This is why my client has been wronged."

Bob Fiske begins his process of "total immersion" with the summation—what do I want to be able to say to the jury at the end of the case? Once an outline for the summation is in place, he works backwards and constructs an edifice of proof which will be the basis for the summation.

Strategy from that point on depends upon whether one is a plaintiff or a defendant. Witnesses, documents, and depositions must be dealt with. He reads the depositions and organizes the documents, then gets ready to examine the witnesses on direct or cross. Fiske then prepares witness sheets (lists of points to be covered) for direct examination.

Arthur Liman concentrates on his opening, studies his witness folders, and makes sure he has the exhibits he wants. He then runs over direct and cross-examinations in his mind until he knows exactly what he wants to do. "I'm trying to figure it out from beginning to end. I've got to work on an opening...I run through the trial in my mind and I do it at home every waking hour." Liman reads every deposition, every document, and when

> I hear a witness say something inconsistent on the stand, I will remember that and be able to say, "Get me that document," and be able to bang the witness with it. So I cannot operate by not having read, touched, felt, everything in the case.

The method Liman employs tends to become problematic with a large discovery. It is not humanly possible to master the details in depositions, which would be the equivalent of *War and Peace* seventy-five times over.

> That's one of the problems with discovery. Obviously, if you have a seventy-five thousand page record of depositions, you can't do that. I'll still have to read every page of a transcript of a witness who I'm going to be examining, and I will, even if there's a digest, make notes of things that are important.

But because he "cannot delegate," he must reduce the entire mass of paper to a coherent set of notes with which he can work.

Phil Corboy knows in advance that he will not read every page of paper produced by discovery, but he will pay special attention to the depositions of fact and expert witnesses he knows are going to be important.

> I read the correspondence section in the file to give me an idea what has happened between the clients and our office, what's happened between the lawyers and the office. I then read the discovery. I do not read all the discovery. I know, by smell or by education, or by somebody whom I rely on, telling me that this deposition is useless or nothing was obtained. But I'll certainly read the depositions of all those people I know are important. All factual witnesses, all experts.

Corboy goes from reading the file to putting his team together, then drafting the instructions to the jury. Harry Reasoner proceeds in much the same way, devising a preliminary version of what he expects to prove in the trial, then drafts the instructions.

> One of the most important things is to develop a preliminary version of what the charge to the jury will look like so you will have in mind what questions that jury is ultimately going to be asked. All of your trial should be focused to when they come to answering the questions—you can show them that everything you've been doing relates to their responsibility.

Reasoner makes outlines for witness examination, but does not work from lists of questions. Instead he works from a "picture of the points" he wants each witness to make.

> I go through the depositions of the witnesses who I'm going to handle on cross and make outlines. I don't believe in writing out questions and answers because I think it is deadly if juries or anybody ever thinks you're reading or working from a script. Then I try to refine the points. These are the ten points that we want to make from this witness, how we want to reinforce them, and to reduce it to the simplest level possible.

165

Reasoner expects that the associates who help him on the case will devote their efforts to develop the points he wants to prove, provide documents to that end, and help with witnesses.

Tom Barr tends to view trials as a battle. He works with armies of assistants. It is his view that "more trials are lost than won." And the focus of any trial lawyer is

> never make any mistake—*never make a mistake*. You can make a misjudgment. That's different than a mistake. But mistakes are all the kinds of things that lawyers do because of lack of care, because of lack of discipline, because they haven't organized things properly, failed to take everything into consideration.

As a key part of his substantive preparation for trial, Barr compiles what he calls an "order of proof." Whether as a plaintiff or defendant he lists all of the factual and legal propositions to be presented, and when and how they are to be supported. Barr collates documents and depositions by witness and prepares outlines for direct examination. Procedural rules and rules of evidence supply criteria built into the order of proof. Within the order of proof, there are questions about the admissibility of certain kinds of evidence that he has to resolve through *in limine* motions of various kinds.

In long cases, in which counsel and associates may come and go, it is useful to develop pedagogical tools. "The Fact Book" Barr and his colleagues prepared for the defense of IBM is a good example. A virtual "course" in IBM litigation was compiled. New people who came on the case started with "The Fact Book." "By the time that case had gone on five or six years, I didn't really need much time to make an argument about this or that." (Barr produced 66 million pages of documents, took 2,500 depositions, and deposed Frank T. Cary, an IBM chairman, for almost fifty days.)

Substantive preparation involves finding a framework on which to hang witnesses and exhibits. Pat McCartan, like the other lawyers, makes an assessment of the trends in the courts with regard to issues germane to the case. The framework is developed "pretty far" in advance of the trial. McCartan places a lot of emphasis on the cases cited in the brief, which is prepared by someone else. He wants a case book compiled from the brief's citations. (A casebook is a compilation of photocopied cases cited in the brief.) The most important parts are highlighted. "If I have the time, I'll read the entire case. If I don't, I'll read the highlighting and anything it may lead me to read." McCartan desires, and gets, the same sense of control the other lawyers need over the case. It is a matter of having complete confidence during the trial. For this reason he reads as much of the depositions as he can, particularly those of the opposing parties and experts. McCartan abhors specialization, and considers himself the master of all skills involved in his work.

> In a major case on a fast track, like the Mobil Marathon case, where I am taking and defending depositions in a sixteen-day period, trying to establish the framework of our proofs and then going into court and handling the witnesses, I was being briefed by other lawyers and functioning in the courtroom like a barrister, which only heightened the excitement of that whole process. But if I have the time, I view my preparation as a very personal, intimate undertaking.

From the side of substantial preparation, all the lawyers devise a spine of proof early on which integrates documents, witnesses and exhibits. Finally, they all attempt in one way or another, to master the details.

There are a number of additional broad strategic domains that are worked on extensively before the actual trip to the courthouse. The first domain is discovery. Most of these men disdain the length and complexity of discovery, not to mention the deception and lack of comity sometimes displayed. Nevertheless, they are wily and artful in this critical pretrial phase. A second important domain is the consideration of witnesses. A great deal of time is devoted to deciding which witnesses to use, preparing one's own, taking depositions from the opponent's witnesses, defending depositions, finding and drilling experts, and so forth. The third domain is the area of depositions. These lawyers apply a number of sophisticated ideas to the use of interrogatories and depositions. As the documents are sifted through, the witnesses assessed, each attorney begins to nail down the theory of the case. A fascinating aspect of trial strategy is the circumstances in which the theory of the case is developed.

Discovery

In civil litigation there are widely different rules for discovery depending on the jurisdiction, and judges have some latitude within jurisdictions with regard to granting motions made during discovery. Discovery is supposed to be the complete disclosure of documents and data a litigant expects to introduce in the course of a trial. Lawyers know that discovery rules are designed to limit the contest to pertinent issues, to level the playing field, and to insure that one side is not talking about oranges while the other is talking about pears. It does not always work that way, though, because some lawyers use discovery to gain an advantage over their opponents.

There are a variety of strategies that can be pursued in discovery. Many are dubious from an ethical and/or legal standpoint. Hence, the purposes of discovery will not be served if one side or the other is not forthcoming. But it is not easy to cheat and get away with it, especially when confronted with these trial-savvy attorneys. Tom Barr talks about dealing with dishonesty in discovery.

> Discovery will not work if the other side is dishonest and sufficiently good at it. The thing that usually trips them up in a major corporation, or in most situations, is they try to destroy documents or hold something back. If you dig hard enough, you'll find something that tells you there is something else, and you'll be able to use it in some way.

Like so many things in the trial, the "devil lies in the details," and the details must be attended to directly if the devil is to be driven out. When the other side has turned over to the client a request for documents in discovery it is important to review the results with a skeptical eye. Many lawyers, on the other side, do not go personally and look for the documents. Instead, they will hand the discovery demand to the client and tell the client to collect the documents. It must be established immediately who is responsible for gathering the opposition's documents. This should be pursued tenaciously if the important documents or data are going to be revealed. Barr will question this in court.

> Then you make him take you through all the files he looked at. You ask whether the documents were produced from those files. Then you establish whether there are any other files, and did he look at those. You can beat that [cheating] if it's deliberate.

David Boies is alert to the possibility of the other side hiding documents.

> There are people who hide documents. The case I'm going
> to try on Monday, they hid documents on us. We caught
> them. They sat around, talked about it, and hid them.

Barr suggests that the search must continue, even when a brick wall is
encountered. This is because documents often exist in places that have
been forgotten or overlooked. "There is a tendency for bad documents
to exist in more than one copy. Even if one, two, or five [have been
destroyed] there will be another."

It is easy for patterns of harassment to develop in discovery. When
one side feels abused by the other, they want to retaliate. Protracted
discovery, in Arthur Liman's view, is a waste of time and money. He
feels that for the most part discovery is overdone.

> You try to figure out what witnesses you really need, but
> sometimes you have to persuade the client that it's not
> necessary to take as many witnesses as they want. Some-
> times if a client has been tortured in discovery, they want to
> torture everyone else and they forget that that's very costly. I
> try to be economical on discovery and not waste a lot of
> time. Get to it, get what you want.

If Corboy began his career today, he is unsure whether he would
handle pretrial business. He does not involve himself in pretrial
discovery and considers himself neither emotionally or physically
capable of doing it. Most of discovery is a waste of time and requires
him to be around people with whom he would rather not associate.

Overzealous young attorneys often string out discovery beyond
reason. According to Liman, "They keep searching and searching and
searching, hoping that they'll find some penny in the straw." David
Boies makes a similar point. He feels that dancing around a party or
witness with endless requests for documents and data is often just a
way of avoiding the inevitable confrontation when the witness is asked
about important events and actions point blank. Too many small-fry
are deposed. There are too many interrogatories and requests for
admissions. The discovery wars have become too expensive for nearly
everyone in Boies' view. "Battles about interrogatories and requests for
admissions are pretty well going by the board. Nobody can afford to
pay for it."

"Discovery rules are insane," comments Tom Barr, "developed in
the thirties for the purpose of preventing one side from being able to

hide the facts from the other. They did not contemplate the copy machine, the computer, the fax machine, none of that."

Pat McCartan attributes the stringing out of discovery to "insecurity on the part of the lawyers." It takes courage to terminate the process and go to trial. Lawyers often think there is something that somebody is hiding or that if they look longer something will surface before trial. It is not "like the medical profession where they have to run every test because they are afraid of malpractice. It's just an inability to draw the line on where they think they have an opportunity to prepare and try that case."

The Aristotelian, Harry Reasoner, talks about finding a golden mean in discovery, a line between being broad enough to "prevent evasion," and focused enough to attempt flooding the other side in a mass of paper. In a world in which everything exists in multiples, filed everywhere, it is almost impossible to destroy every copy of a document. That in itself is often a basis for obtaining electronically stored documents that can be combed for copies of letters, contracts, and so forth.

> I find it is increasingly important to focus on the retrieval of electronic data. What you don't want are printouts. If you can get it in disk form where your experts can [evaluate] it, it is immensely more efficient and it's the way that the company really answers questions for itself. If you have a judge who is sophisticated enough to make them give you that, then I think it can be enormously beneficial.

Reasoner also sees a cogent rationale for limiting discovery in certain kinds of cases. If the case is simple enough, good-faith undertakings to share the small number of relevant documents can be sufficient. In many tort cases, the number of legitimate documents of interest is a narrow universe if the other side cooperates in good faith. This will not work, however, in complicated conspiracy cases, in which one cannot expect the defendant's counsel to turn over documents that prove conspiracy. Sometimes, Reasoner suggests, such proof will come inadvertently—some unintended piece of incrimination will surface.

> I've never been satisfied that you don't need fairly massive discovery in conspiracy cases. Often the best evidence I've obtained was inadvertently produced when people flood you with hundreds of thousands of pages of documents

being reviewed by paralegals. Almost inevitably you'll find
in there some document they would have claimed privilege
on if they'd noticed it.

The proof might come in the form of a logical gap, or in the form of
a reference to some other incriminating document, such as a letter, that
can subsequently be obtained. Or subjects are mentioned, but no
correspondence exists pertaining to them. "In really hard-core cases,
you may want to depose their record administrators or secretaries
because in today's world, once documents exist, they're virtually
immortal."

Reasoner gives a fascinating example of how documents came to
light in a case involving Rio Tinto, a member of a uranium cartel.

One of the most dramatic illustrations of the difficulty of
the process is what broke the uranium cartel case. The
Friends of the Earth in Australia broke into the offices of
Rio Tinto, stole cartel minutes, and delivered them to the
California Public Utilities Commission. Up to that point,
you had a federal grand jury investigating Gulf. You had
massive discovery demands by Westinghouse and other
plaintiffs. Never surfaced. These people stole them and
produced them. Turned out that then when we knew who to
go after and what to go after, that the others did have copies
of it.

The theft of minutes enabled the lawyers to focus the discovery
demands in a way that was not previously possible.

The fact that unintentional proof can be transmitted in discovery is
why Bob Warren considers it a mistake to try and "drown the other
side in paper." Warren observes that it is never a matter of

"Open the door, come on in and take a look." Discovery
involves making a judgment as to which documents to turn
over. That doesn't mean that if you have a bad document,
you don't turn it over. If you have to turn over something,
you turn it over, but it's a matter of doing so *consciously*.

The abuse of hiding documents or lying on depositions, is one for
which there really are no reasonable enforceable legal sanctions. And,
according to Reasoner, "You'll get a judge who will dismiss a case over
what may well have been an inadvertent technical or arguable
violation, which is just as bad as the judge who does nothing."

For Joe Jamail and Bob Fiske, discovery represents, as the word suggests, a chance to discover where to attack a witness—a chance to discover areas of vulnerability. Jamail is always probing for weaknesses, like a boxer with a quick jab, looking for chances to soften up a witness and have him or her look the other way when the sucker punch lands.

> First, get the records, whatever they are. Then somebody will go through those religiously several times, making notes, showing me discrepancies, of one thing or another, and then I'll go over it. Mostly what I'm doing in discovery is looking at the witness by way of deposition and I'm not that interested in what he says because I already know what he has been paid to say. But I want his personality and I want to see how to pull his chain and what buttons I push, what nerves I touch, and make him commit. Totally, completely box him.

Once Jamail has a witness from the other side who has the profile he is looking for, a profile that suggests vulnerability, he finds out what there is in the deposition and records that can be used to tear that witness apart.

> And when that is done, I've got the personality profile that I want. I take what he is committed to and I get the best expert in the field I can find and say, "Shoot some holes in this for me. Tell me how this is wrong." Then when I get him subpoenaed and bring his ass to trial, I riddle him with it. Generally they will admit that my postulate is correct because it comes at them from a scientific point of view, not from me. Then I impeach him in what he had said in his deposition. This is what discovery does for me.

Refraining from cross-examination when taking a deposition in order to set up a witness for later attack is often a useful strategy in discovery. Bob Fiske used this in the Three Mile Island case. As Fiske relates below, he saw the moment come and go in the deposition, but let it pass, not wanting to blow the opportunity by alerting the witness. He passed over the point he intended to come back to during the trial, and continued on with an innocuous line of questions.

> We had a situation with one of the key operators, where he explained in his deposition what his reaction was to a certain reading of a certain gauge at a certain point in time.

> We had a prior interview that he had done at the very beginning, that he had forgotten about and the other side had not found. The Nuclear Regulatory Commission [NRC] had come up the day after the accident and interviewed these guys. To save money, they didn't have a court reporter, they just had a tape recorder in the middle of the room, and those tapes had never been transcribed.

Fiske and his associates found the tapes of the witness's interview with the NRC, and transcribed them. Fiske had this prior to the deposition.

> We had this explanation about what that gauge said. He gave an exact one hundred-eighty degree different explanation in the deposition. And we deliberately said nothing about it. We just said, "Fine," and went on to the next point.

Fiske theorizes that if he had revealed to the witness that he had the tape prior to the trial, the effect would not have been nearly as dramatic, and might not have counted for much at all.

> When he testified at the trial he said the same thing. Then we said, "In fact, didn't you say something exactly the opposite the day after the accident?" and he said, "No." We actually had the tape and played the tape. Gave the judge a transcript. On the witness stand he just...plain went to pieces. So my strategy always is if we're going to trial is not to impeach the witness at all—just let him think he is blowing it right by you and put it all on the record and get it under oath—and then organize it and do the impeaching *at* the trial.

Interrogatories

I have never had one of my interrogatory answers read against me in court and I don't want it to start now. I've answered interrogatories for thirty years. It's never happened that the other side stood up and read to the jury my answer. It shows you their value.

—Fred Bartlit

Interrogatories are sometimes employed by lawyers who thrive on pushing paper as opposed to going to trial. As a part of discovery, used by the plaintiff, the defendant, or both, lawyers are familiar with these written questions submitted to the opposition for their response. In the current climate of intense adversarial engagement, most of the lawyers in this study see little use for interrogatories, or written questions submitted to the other side. Occasionally, a request for pure facts is made, but the way to gather substantive information is by talking to the witness directly, and not allowing the lawyer to answer in his or her stead. Bob Fiske makes this point forcefully when asked about the uses for interrogatories:

> Virtually none at all. Just for pure facts—give us an organization chart on everybody who worked in this division in 1987...Names and witnesses are very important things. Location of documents is important. But substantive information can be much more effectively obtained through a deposition. I would, ninety-nine times out of a one hundred, prefer to do it in the deposition where you get the witness, not the lawyer.

Harry Reasoner also considers interrogatories to be of limited utility. They may be helpful for an initial overview, getting the names and titles of the players. But answers to questions written by lawyers "tend to be argumentative," since lawyers try to limit the information they convey.

Reasoner feels that limiting interrogatories is a good idea, since they are now so easily produced out of lists of generic questions.

> One of the vices of computerized printing systems is that people have form interrogatories and serve them for purposes of harassment. The notion of limiting you to twenty interrogatories and have to get leave to file more, is probably not a bad idea. That's true in the Texas State Court system, true in many federal courts.

It is these rules, according to Bob Warren, which have lessened the effectiveness of interrogatories. He reiterates the points made earlier about their adversarial character and the need to exercise caution when responding to them.

> Interrogatories have lessened in effectiveness as the various jurisdictions have put in rules on their numbers. The only

thing I can say is, in responding to them, you certainly have to be careful because they have a pleading-like element, and if you make some concession in them, it's liable to be permanent. They can't be handled lightly, but most lawyers aren't likely to make a case out of them.

Jim Neal agrees that most interrogatories will be answered in a self-serving manner. He suggests that requests for admissions may be useful if the judge will support such a procedure. He does not completely rule out the possibility that interrogatories may have some utility.

> I think they are helpful. You give your opponent a chance to frame self-serving answers that may be better than taking the deposition. Requests for admissions may be better for interrogatories if you can frame them right and you've got a judge who will enforce them if you are being fair about it.

Fred Bartlit knew from the first day he joined the firm that he hated writing interrogatories.

> I knew from the first day that it was the stupidest thing in the world. I used to say, "Why in the world have a lawyer answer the questions and have days to think about them when you could sit the witness down and look him in the eye and get an answer right now?"

For the most part, however, the taking of depositions is of far greater value in the minds of these attorneys than the submission of interrogatories.

Depositions

It is not necessary nor desirable in the view of Bob Warren for the trial lawyer personally to defend the depositions of every witness who is deposed on his side. But there are cases in which "every word counts." These tend to be the depositions, for example, of the company officers in a trial involving a corporate client because this person speaks for the defendant, the company.

David Boies wants to insure that there is no poison pill in the depositions of his critical witnesses. "Fundamentally, defending depositions is more difficult and more important than the taking of the depositions." He accompanies critical witnesses so that their attention does not lapse; or if a mistake is made, it can be corrected quickly.

As for taking depositions, these men prefer to take the key depositions themselves so they can begin to get an idea of how to handle the witness in court. For David Boies, and the others, it is indispensable preparation. "I commit to a client that I will take the major depositions, and I think you should. I don't see how you can be removed from the depositions and be really ready for trial." Boies will sometimes use a deposition to catch a witness off guard by reversing the order of questions. Witnesses expect a string of innocuous questions about their identity and role in the case before anything confrontational comes up.

> I'll ask the crucial question first or second. Guy is sworn in. I say, "Why did you fire my client?" He'll say, "I didn't fire him." I say, "Fine." Because it was a lie, we had him in a lie. But usually it's, "Where were you born? Where do you go? What happened then?" and so the witness [is prepared].

One does not want to squander opportunities by not being prepared for a witness on deposition, or appear ignorant when deposing experts from the other side.

I'll know better how to examine the witness at trial if I've dealt with them, and it also forces me to learn the case. I've got a lot of pride and I'm not going to go in and take an expert dep with a smart statistician or economist without knowing the case as well as he does. It forces me to learn the case before trial. And also, cross-examination. I'm a good cross-examiner and I will get more from the guy than the young guy will. I will get more every time.

—Fred Bartlit

Harry Reasoner brings up a subtle point about the purpose of depositions. You need to be clear, he suggests, about whether the deposition is aimed at getting coherent testimony that can be presented to the jury at the trial. Or, is it merely an attempt to probe for information as a general part of the discovery process? If it is the former, care must be taken not to inoculate a witness against the likely line of cross-examination.

> You always have to make the decision on cross-examining experts: do you want to reveal any of the ways you will try to impeach them depending on their testimony or do you want to reserve it? Often I simply want to know everything they have to say.

The taking of depositions is an "efficient discipline" in his view and to be prepared to take a good deposition, one must be "up to speed on the case."

Pat McCartan is a little concerned about giving away too much about what he intends to do with a witness for the other side in court. When someone else is taking a deposition for him, he expects that the territory he wants to develop in cross-examination will remain uncharted.

> In a major case, when I'm not taking the experts' depositions, I tell our people, "You tee him up, I'll deal with him then at trial. I don't want you to cross-examine him, just tee him up." That's hard because they get right to their point and they want to go the other step. I say, "If you ask one question too many on deposition, I'll kill you. Just get him right to that point where I can knock him off." Generally that's what they do.

Max Blecher is probably not the only one of these lawyers who feels that stonewalling and even bald-faced lying goes on when witnesses are deposed. This has grown worse, in his view, since he began to practice law. He feels stonewalling has been elevated to the level of a science.

> I remember as a young lawyer taking depositions was useful. You would sit down with a guy and he would tell you things. Today it is Stonewalling 101. Practicing law institutes have a course on how to defend depositions. Isn't that interesting? How to deprive the other side from learning anything.

One way to deal with the problem is to obtain the documents written by or received by the witness and limit questioning to these documents and incidental facts connected with them, "because beyond that, you'll get nothing." That at least will position the document so that it will be useful at the trial. Blecher explains "the best you can hope for is that somebody will look at a document and acknowledge that [he] wrote it." The usual technique in stonewalling, according to Blecher is that "they lie by amnesia. That's the technique. They don't remember when, in fact, they do." Recently, Blecher encountered an amnesiac witness, who when deposed said, "I don't remember anything." But Blecher discovered that he could use the amnesia effectively in front of the jury. He ridiculed the failure of the witness to remember anything, and in essence impeached him *in absentia*.

> I said, "The two people we talked to about the subject, you don't see them here. They weren't in that chair, they didn't subject themselves to cross-examination. For whatever reasons, they haven't come here to say, 'This is what we did and why we did it.' All you've got is this record. Is the uncorroborated word of one person telling you what happened? There are other people involved and you should wonder why they are not here. You should wonder why there is nothing in writing."

But sometimes a witness will lie outright about things that are incapable of being proven by any objective fact. State of mind or motive are things that cannot be impeached by any kind of hard evidence. And there are no legal remedies. The only way to triumph over the situation is to catch the witness in a lie before the jury, as Blecher related above.

> There are no sanctions against lying in civil cases, so they lie with great frequency. There has never been a prosecution for perjury in a civil case that I'm aware of, ever. Perjury is hard to prove, period. No prosecutor would ever bother doing it in a civil case, so it's just a dead letter and people can lie with impunity. The only thing is, if you catch them, then obviously the jury is going to react.

Strategies in the use of depositions are both defensive and offensive. Most importantly, they are a chance for a trial attorney to find out about the opponent's witnesses, to see "how to pull their chain," as Joe Jamail puts it. There are times when something incriminating or culpable comes across in a deposition. Lawyers who defend depositions are careful to prevent this from happening. Anyone who watched Brendan Sullivan, for example, defend Oliver North from the thrusts of Arthur Liman during the Iran-Contra hearings saw how much protection a good attorney can offer a witness.

In a 1992 pollution case against Monsanto Co., Jamail had this exchange, first published in the *American Lawyer*, with defense attorney Edward Carstarphen:

Jamail: You don't run this deposition, you understand?

Carstarphen: Neither do you, Joe.

Jamail: You watch and see. You watch and see who does, big boy. And don't be telling other lawyers to shut up. That isn't your God–*damned job, fat boy*.

Carstarphen: Well, that's not your job, Mr. Hairpiece.

(The witness tried to speak, but could not make himself heard.)

Jamail: What do you want to do about it, (obscenity)?

Carstarphen: You're not going to bully this guy.

Jamail: Oh, you big (obscenity), sit down.

Carstarphen, reached by phone in Houston, said, "It was typical Joe," adding: "I'm not that fat."

(by Benjamin Weiser, excerpted from "Are Too! Am Not! Are Too! Am Not," *Washington Post*, March 10, 1994)

Common Mistakes Made in Discovery

What are some of the typical mistakes lawyers make in discovery? Pat McCartan believes that:

> The worst mistake is trying to win a case on discovery. There are some cases where you can do that and I've done it. I won a patent case with a deposition of the inventor. But once the inventor admits that his invention is obvious, there isn't much more that can happen. You can't change inventors, right?

The point being that the defense was stuck with the inventor as a witness. No other expert could be substituted. When the inventor admitted that his invention was obvious, and could have been developed by anyone, the case for the defense fell apart. This would not have been so, necessarily, in the case of an expert witness who had provided equally damaging testimony on a deposition.

179

> If you can tear apart an expert on deposition, one of two
> things is going to happen. Either he is going to be replaced,
> or he's going to be forewarned and find a way to deal with
> the admissions that you got from him on deposition.

Another frequent mistake identified by McCartan is "getting lost in
the woods," which in itself qualifies as an abuse of the process. By
this metaphor, McCartan refers to instances in which a great deal is
uncovered in discovery, but attorneys are unable to winnow out exactly
what they should present to the court from among all they have
discovered. Still, the biggest danger for McCartan is giving away too
much by trying for too much in the form of an admission. There are
just not many cases that are won or lost on the basis of an admission.

> I think the biggest danger is disclosing too much of your
> hand on deposition of the plaintiff and of the expert. It's a
> fine line that you want to walk because if it is the kind of
> case where you can win it on deposition, and you see the
> opportunity to do it on deposition, you should. But those
> are very limited situations. However, because most lawsuits
> are won and lost by admissions, if you get the right
> testimony out of the plaintiff, or out of an inventor, or out of
> a policy maker, you may be able to win the case on
> deposition.

Jim Neal notes that taking depositions is exacting work, particularly when the objective is to provide transcript material that can
later be introduced in court.

> When I was trying civil cases I learned to be very
> uncomfortable if somebody else is doing your discovery. A
> mistake that is sometimes made is the failure to pin down
> the witness. In the progress of the deposition, [because it is]
> getting late in the day or you're trying to ask too many
> questions, you're trying to cover too much, you realize
> when you get the transcript back, "My God, I've given him
> wiggle room when he gets to the courtroom."

It can be a real disaster when people other than trial lawyers become
involved with discovery. Time is wasted because these people do not
know what they are looking for. Tom Barr levels some pretty severe
strictures against this practice.

> The biggest mistake that lawyers make is that the people
> who conduct the discovery are not trial lawyers and,

therefore, they don't know what they're doing and what they're looking for. They waste an enormous amount of time. A lot of the questions they ask are not proper. They're not prepared. They let the record get so mucked up that the deposition can't be read, and can't be used for cross-examination.

Liman weighs in on the chimeras of discovery:

> A young lawyer can come up to me (and these things have happened) and will say, "I had a terrific deposition." And I'll say, "What happened?" He says, "Look at this line. Look at this admission I got." I read it and I can understand what he's talking about. Usually it's not as good as you remember it, but it's there. There's a sentence here and maybe there'll be a sentence there and a sentence somewhere else.

Then Liman looks at the deposition from the point of view of an attorney who will have to use the document as a basis for examining a witness in court.

> And then I'll take the transcript home and read it. And those three lines were there, but there were a thousand things that kill my client. And so when you read the whole thing in context, the deposition stinks from our point of view. When I take a deposition, I tend to take my depositions with a view to what they are going to play like at trial.

The way a trial lawyer takes a deposition differs from the way a litigator would do it.

> I mean, I may not want him to repeat just the poisonous stuff, or if I do, I'm going to do it in a way that it's going to be so punctuated in everything that it's not going to have the same impact at trial as it might otherwise have. So that everything that I am doing pretrial, I am doing with a view to the trial.

The basic objectives in discovery are focused on preventing damage to your witnesses in the trial and preparing to inflict damage on the opponent. As Tom Barr has said he does not win cases so much as his opponent loses them. David Boies adds fuel to this argument as he cautions against making a mistake in discovery "that is going to come back to haunt your witnesses when they are crossed."

Withholding information in discovery is a mistake according to Blecher. Sometimes withholding documents is done by the client without the lawyer's knowledge.

> Lots of times the client just cleans house. The guy thinks his ass is at stake and he goes through his drawers and says, "I better get this out of here." And you'll only learn about this sometimes because a copy happens to have gone to his superior who does not know he's destroyed them. They give it to the lawyer and the lawyer produces it and wonders where your copy is.

It is almost impossible to find out information without giving information up. This is why Blecher feels another common mistake in discovery is seeking too much information and alerting your opposition to things they would not have ordinarily thought of. *Every question asked reveals something.* If a witness is asked, "Do you know Mr. X," when Mr. X is someone no one has ever heard of or thought about before, a red flag goes up. "Who is Mr. X? Why should they care whether or not I know Mr. X?" These questions arise at once in the minds of the lawyer for the witness being deposed. Blecher notes that another common mistake is to take too many depositions. By doing so, the other side might find among the superfluous testimony some trail or line of inquiry that they had not been aware of. Witnesses, documents, or facts that would otherwise have been left to rest come to light. But the single largest mistake that the other side makes in discovery, according to Blecher, is to have everybody on their side know nothing. They fail to conceive of how deposed witnesses will look to the jury because they are not thinking about going to trial. Their only concern is thwarting the other side from developing a case. When the witness finally shows up at the trial, he or she has to live with "I can't remember a thing" testimony.

This brief discussion of discovery strategy has obviously just scratched the surface. Generally, the lawyers believe there is too much discovery, and that there are a good many mistakes made in this pretrial exercise. Furthermore, there are enough abuses and deceptions attempted so that a good deal of the strategy of discovery at the present time is devoted to dealing with these transgressions.

Witnesses

Strategic Use of Witnesses

There are a seemingly endless number of strategic considerations where witnesses are concerned. How many should be used? What specific points should they be asked to introduce, reinforce, or counter? What is the role of experts? Of special concern to all of these men is the fact that using witnesses always involves considerable risk. Many cases are won on cross-examination, if they have not been won already in the opening statements or voir dire. Any witness can become a loose cannon under the pressure of a skilled and ruthless cross-examiner. Thus, it is important to determine if a witness' testimony is the best way to present the evidence. Bob Warren makes this point, and calls attention to the risks involved in putting a witness at the disposal of one's opponent.

> This is very important. What does the witness know? What can the witness be asked about? A lot of people put on witnesses to establish some point that maybe could be done without altogether. [This] gives their opponent a shot at something the opponent would never otherwise have an opportunity for.

Arthur Liman, too, is concerned about the chance that cross-examination may boomerang. Will the witness relate well to the jury and be credible? The way in which gender and ethnicity play out can be important too. The bottom line for Liman is to use absolutely no more witnesses than necessary. Jim Brosnahan wants natural story tellers, someone who can tell the jury the complete story. He also suggests that the fewer witnesses the better. "For every witness you put up there for whom something can go wrong, something *will* go wrong." A potentially disastrous witness might be spotted from his or her deposition. If this is the case, the attorney must work hard to remedy this witness' liabilities. Brosnahan maintains that in most cases only about five people plus the experts are essential.

Fred Bartlit joins the others in advocating fewer witnesses rather than more. Direct, to-the-point testimony from a few is better than a parade of lackluster, forgettable drones.

> I'm a great believer in less. I duplicate witnesses only if their testimony is ten or fifteen minutes. In other words, if

you have an array of customers and you want to prove a point: the customer thought this, that, or the other thing about the product—you put on a certain number of customers because that needs to be repetitive.

When Bartlit is plaintiff's counsel, a number of witnesses for the defense can be made available for cross-examination. He will call from the defendant's camp the key decision makers in the action under dispute, and build his story by examining them directly. If this is the case, the number of witnesses he calls may be larger than usual.

Tactics will change depending on the availability of witnesses. If the people are pretty freely available to you or in the rare case where the defendant says, "Yeah, I'll bring them out for you," or the judge orders it, then I look to put the case on through the key decision makers.

The tactics change again if Bartlit is unable to examine directly adverse witnesses because they are out of his subpoena power range. He will present the essence of his case through the reading of depositions, then work hard cross-examining the defense witnesses when they are brought up in the second half of the trial.

I'll read deposition extracts, just get enough in to get by your motions for judgment, and then do the real case when they bring their witnesses up. I frequently do more damage on cross-examination of the defense case than I do to them.

In general, the theory that fewer witnesses are better than more is borne out by juror research, which demonstrates how difficult it is for jurors to remember witnesses and to discriminate clearly among them.

Witnesses and the Elements of Proof

Bob Fiske notes how important it is for fact witnesses to be assessed in terms of the specific points they are called upon to make. Is a particular witness the best way to slice this particular piece of the pie?

On fact witnesses: First of all, what are you trying to prove with this particular witness? How important is that particular piece of evidence to the case as a whole? Is there any other witness besides this one who can prove it? And most important of all . . . what are the downsides of putting this person on?

It may be, Fiske suggests, that thirty percent of what a witness will say will be important to the case, but the other seventy percent might contain information that will prove damaging on cross-examination. A frequent mistake inexperienced trial lawyers make is putting a witness on without thinking about this risk.

It is a rare luxury to be able to choose among potential witnesses according to Tom Barr. Sometimes there simply is no choice. Sometimes a person is the only witness to a particular event or a person is so implicated by the opposing testimony that he or she must take the stand. If however, there is a choice, pick the witness who will be the most "convincing, persuasive, and will hold up on cross-examination...the most important criterion in the selection of an expert witness." There are two principal qualifications for allowing a witness to testify: intelligence and a straight-forward manner and attitude. The rest Barr feels, can be taught, although there are some people who, by their nature, will always appear not credible.

Witness Credibility

Part of the strategy of choosing witnesses is to determine if they will have jury credibility. This will even play a part in jury selection. What kind of jurors will find a key witness credible? The fact that a witness has something in common with the jurors will enhance credibility, according to Phil Corboy. He sometimes tries to match a witness to a particular juror, knowing that this juror might become an advocate for the witness during deliberation.

> Number one, are witnesses believable? Do they share something in common with the jurors? Are they superfluous? In picking the jury, we have to know who our witnesses are. If I have an Italian lady who speaks with a broken accent, I want an Italian with a broken accent on that jury. So I pick the jury with an awareness of who my witnesses are.

Corboy uses his knowledge of who his witnesses are going to be during voir dire. Alternative witnesses will be on hand in case juror selection does not yield a jury that matches well with the people who have originally been chosen to testify. In many cases, Corboy will have selected a number of witnesses, deciding at the last minute which ones to use.

> I want to know everything about my witnesses while I'm
> picking the jury, or de-picking. I'm involved in a chess
> game the whole time when I'm thinking of my witnesses.
> Let's assume I've got the jury and there are jurors on there I
> know won't like this witness, but I've got an alternative
> witness. I make a decision which witness to use.

Harry Reasoner makes credibility the "primary criterion" in
selecting witnesses. If the jury believes the witness, then the witness
has served his or her purpose. In addition, can the witness present the
facts clearly? Is the witness strong-willed? How will the witness hold
up under a withering cross? Reasoner considers the following factors:

> You see good witnesses who get their story out in a credible
> and sincere fashion, but then do great damage because
> either they are not alert or strong enough and they're led
> into damaging facts [on cross-examination], led into state-
> ments that they would never make sitting in a neutral
> context, being asked the question without pressure.

Arthur Liman makes an interesting observation about witness
credibility.

> There are some witnesses who can't answer a question
> directly. They tend not to be credible with a jury, if the cross
> examiner knows what he is doing. He can make [the
> witness] look . . . evasive.

For all the above reasons, letting a personal attachment interfere
with one's judgment about using a witness can be a critical error. For
Fred Bartlit it is important that a witness comports well with the jury's
notion of what that witness should be like.

> If you're going to pick an accountant, you want the
> accountant to be what the jury thinks an accountant is. The
> average juror thinks an accountant is a slender little guy
> with a green eye shade who is real serious and not a big
> salesman. [But] what most people do is get the head of the
> accounting firm whose job is selling. He's been to Andover
> and Harvard, Yale. He's real smooth. He plays golf with
> everybody, but he doesn't look like an accountant.

Credibility is then the deciding factor in calling a witness. This is
particularly true in the case of experts.

Expert Witnesses

> I've seen a lot of lawyers retain an expert and have him talk about everything from A to Z. Nobody believes that. Nobody is an expert on everything—except a guy drunk on martinis—he's got a PhD in the world.
>
> **—Joe Jamail**

Expert witnesses obviously need to be effective communicators who can impart the basic knowledge of their subject to the jurors quickly and convincingly, as well as survive a tough cross-examination. Professional witnesses have built-in credibility problems because the jury knows they have been paid to testify. This is why so many of these attorneys tend to think "experts cancel each other out." Then why use them? Because, as Arthur Liman suggests, it is sometimes possible to find experts who have not testified much in court and who will come across as impartial observers who simply want to lend their expertise to the cause of justice.

> If the witness is seen as a professional witness, juries tend to discount that witness' testimony. People from universities tend to have some credibility. A doctor who has been head of a department at one of the hospitals that everyone knows and who hasn't testified a lot will tend to have a lot of credibility. But it's how the expert testifies, not just the credentials.

The testimony that works according to Harry Reasoner is one that "reduces their specialty to a language the jurors understand." Reasoner also likes to stay away from "professional witnesses." Condescension and arrogance are the cardinal sins for any expert. An expert who commits these sins in pretrial review should not be used. Reasoner prefers either "academics or people who actually work in an industry as opposed to someone who is a professional witness."

Jim Brosnahan warns a case might be lost because of an expert, but rarely will an expert win a case. "Basically, the experts don't have to be great, but you don't want them to be terrible." The expert must teach the jurors without really appearing to do so. Unfortunately most experts want to lecture. "Everyone of them wants a pointer. So you narrow him, you put on the blinders," suggests Joe Jamail. It is this tendency to ramble that Bob Warren fears. Experts might express an opinion on one thing favorable to your case on direct examination, but their intellectual arrogance and urge to display their knowledge might lead them to express damaging opinions on cross-examination. Warren insists that experts be prepared to talk about one thing and one thing only. Warren knows there are lawyers around like Fred Bartlit, who present the guts of their case on cross-examination, and that this can involve getting the other side's expert into deep water.

Expert witnesses are extremely dangerous witnesses. They are extraordinarily dangerous because the range of cross-examination is limitless, and it's an opportunity for somebody to present an entire final argument in the guise of cross-examining the expert witness, not giving a damn what the expert witness says. I consider expert witnesses absolute time bombs.

—Bob Warren

Time bombs? Or essential components of the case? That has to be decided in the instance of every expert witness. Tom Barr gives an account of how bad things can get. He and David Boies represented IBM in one of their antitrust cases.

> There were two local witnesses used in the case. One was an accountant and one was an economist. David destroyed both of them and I'm not exaggerating—he destroyed them. The accountant almost lost his mind. He [got] so nervous, he began to laugh. The judge finally said, "Look, Mr. Witness, I don't know what you're laughing at. I think there is a serious question as to whether you're telling the truth or not."

The economist was even worse.

> The other was a so-called economist who was just an utter fool and didn't know what the hell he was talking about. The lawyer had tried to prepare him, but the lawyer didn't know what the hell he was talking about either.

Sometimes problems with an expert can be uncovered in pretrial research. David Boies gives an example in which an expert played so badly in a mock trial that it was decided not to use him at all.

> I was in a big antitrust case we inherited. The other firm got clobbered and... they wanted us to re-try it for them. But they had already picked this expert...a Nobel Prize winner. He had no personality. He was an egomaniac...We did a mock trial and we stuck him in. They hated him. They absolutely hated him. So the audience is everything.

When it comes to the matter of choosing expert witnesses Max Blecher would rather do away with them altogether. He feels they are of little value except in scientific cases.

> Most of them are whores. They will go from one side to the other, and you pay them off and they twist and distort things. It's a sad process. I would like to re-write the experts rules because I don't think you need them in most of these cases. Sure you need an expert in an eminent domain case. How are you going to put a value on the land unless somebody explains a reasonable way to do it? Maybe you need it if you're dealing with some scientific formulas or a patent case. There are certain areas where they are helpful.
>
> **—Max Blecher**

The experts in the cases in which Blecher is involved are clearly employed as touts for the attorney's side of the case, and jurors usually find this a kind of *pro forma* exercise which adds little. Most of the time they simply articulate the lawyer's view of the case in the form of testimony. But this can be accomplished through direct testimony. Instead, Blecher favors a wide array of industry experts who have direct, practical experience that lends credibility to their testimony. But far more important than their credentials in Blecher's view:

> Can they explain what they are talking about in the English language without talking about the square root of the hypotenuse and drawing silly little charts that only other

economists understand? Can they communicate? Are they salable? Are they people who the jury thinks are knowledgeable enough, have enough experience to be believed? Experience is an important thing and that's where the credentials become important. "What have you done in your life, sir?"

Witness Matchups: Joe Jamail

There is no better way to conclude this subject than Joe Jamail's discourse on his theory of witness matchups. The manner in which he used witnesses in the Pennzoil case could serve as a clinical study in the subject.

> One of the first things I do is to make myself a drawing of twelve boxes. As I go along taking depositions of the witnesses and of the defendant and the plaintiff, I start making matchups between the plaintiff and the defendant. I do this in pencil. Between this witness and this witness, between this expert and this expert. What traits does this defense expert have? What does mine have? I make notes in these boxes about what kind of juror I think would be most receptive to these kinds of traits that I am finding as I do the discovery. I've been doing this a long, long time. It's no guarantee, but it reduces the risk. When I am there, I am not looking at a tie or a shirt. I'm looking at some traits in these jurors that I want. It works for me.

In a personal-injury case, Jamail suggests, the key witnesses must be matched well with the jury.

> The key witnesses are the plaintiff, the defendant, and the expert...If there are eyewitnesses, yes. But usually in these catastrophes I'm dealing with, there are usually no eyewitnesses. These are usually plant explosions...the Phillips plant, the Arco plant, the Delta airplane crashes.

By this, Jamail means that the witnesses are determined by the character of the event itself. There is no choice of witnesses. Thus, the question of matchups becomes one of selecting a jury that will be more responsive to the traits of your witnesses than to the traits of witnesses on the other side. In Pennzoil, Jamail was able to think in terms of matching witnesses for his side to witnesses for the other side, selecting from a number of possibilities.

> Pennzoil, I knew, was going to be a contest of truth, of will, of personalities, and whom to believe. So I made matchups. I

decided which witnesses we were going to use after I knew which one of their witnesses were coming, and which ones I was going to use adversely. Then I began to try my case. The plaintiff has this advantage, he puts his case on first. So I can call all their witnesses in my case, if I so choose, which I did.

Jamail puts on the principal defense witnesses and forces the jury to see these witnesses through the plaintiff's prism first.

Every witness they had on but four or five, I put on. I was letting that jury see them through Joe's eyes, not through those friendly little hoops and jumps their lawyers were [putting] them through. So the matchups I made, because I took Kinnear's deposition, I knew DeCrane, his deposition had been taken. And our counterpart was Baine Kerr. Now, Baine is as tough as a spike, but very mild and soft-spoken, a small man. So I decided we'd lead off with Baine Kerr and let them contrast him with Kinnear. Made my argument easy. Just matchups, folks. Arthur Liman against Marty Lipton. That was a fucking mismatch. The two lawyers that were on the scene. Anybody who saw this or read the record would tell you that I eviscerated Lipton.

The most intense and important matchup was between the Chairman of the Board of Texaco, John K. McKinley, against the plaintiff, William Liedtke, Pennzoil's chairman. The defense, according to Jamail, had planned to show this man off, but not really demand any proof from him. Jamail subpoenaed him when he showed up for the trial.

The real matchup...I had taken McKinley's deposition, the Chairman of the Board of Texaco. He looks like a fox—has these sharp features and I was going to compare him to Liedtke. So I subpoenaed him when he showed up for the voir dire. I knew they weren't going to bring him to the trial. They were going to hide him out. I subpoenaed him, so I stuck him on. I put him on the stand. He made so many errors I was able to get to him real bad.

Once Jamail had McKinley set up as an untrustworthy city slicker who was pretending to be a good old boy, he delivered the coup de grace. The moment depended upon all that had come before, hours of hard work.

So I asked him if he knew what "bird in the hand" meant, after he had been a good old boy up there on that stand for about four hours. He said, "No, I don't rightly think I do." I could

191

> hear the jury groan, ahhh... But then I put Liedtke on. He was
> straight forward, angry at times... The jury needed to see... I
> put them on one after the other.

Jamail had worked on these matchups secretly, not even
sharing what he was thinking with his own people. He wanted
jurors to make a direct comparison between Liedtke, his witness,
and McKinley, the witness for the other side. He could thus directly
demonstrate his man's superior credibility. He wrote the names
across from each other, and then went over each point in the proof
with regard to how each witness would testify on a particular point.
Knowing the personalities is critical. That is why Jamail is so
interested in depositions, they are an opportunity to gather critical
information about personalities that can be used in devising
witness matchups.

> I've never told anybody this. But this is what I do. You've got
> to know your case, you've got to be willing to know the
> personalities you're dealing with and try to assess the
> personalities of the other side whose depositions you take,
> and make your matchups. Discard witnesses, bring in others.
> It isn't just guesswork. The Holy Ghost isn't going to descend
> on you when you walk over there. You've got to get ready
> before you ever walk in there.

Jamail's expertise and virtuosity in this area is worthy of a
closer study.

Developing the Grand Theory

> I never know exactly what people mean by the
> theory of the case. My theory of the case is,
> "We're right and the other guy's wrong. We're
> going to win and the other guy is going to lose."
> **—Tom Barr**

The idea behind the phrase "theory of the case" is fairly simple.
Something has happened about which there is a dispute. Side A puts
forth a theory of what happened and why it happened that exculpates
Side A from any blame. Side B puts forth a counter theory that places

all the blame on Side A, or at the very least exculpates side B from any blame. Theories, such as these, incorporate proof as well as statements of fact. They interpret fact, they attribute motive, and they tell a story in terms of a few key points. Most trial lawyers devise their theory or story of the case well in advance of the trial.

> Experience and the logic leads you to the point of seeing the heart of the case and saying, "there, that's what matters. That's where we'll stand," and, "We'll make our fight right here." That ability is very important. Part of that is decisiveness...and intellectual curiosity. A trial lawyer is a good life for the life of the mind.
>
> **—Jim Brosnahan**

Each lawyer takes a different approach to finding his case theory. For some it will come like a bolt from the blue; for others, the theory will fall out of a discussion with other lawyers. Often the discussion will not be directed at finding the theory as such. It may be a discussion of other subjects. It may be anything, in fact. There is frequently an element of serendipity.

It is most interesting and instructive to consider what some of the lawyers mean when they talk about the theory of the case. Tom Barr says it is a linear, chronological account of events. "If they fit that way, that's the way they happened. That's the way they are best explained." Barr notes that his best ideas about the case do not grow out of a planned procedure. "The light dawns, if you will, on a number of things, a lot of it early in the morning...often out running or riding or swimming or something. Sometimes in the office, sometimes because something somebody says triggers something in my head."

For Fred Bartlit, the theory of the case is a story in three or four sentences. If the story plays well in a bar then he will win (that is, if the patrons of the establishment are demographically matched to the jury). Quite astutely, Bartlit realizes that a lawyer cannot simply and arbitrarily characterize a case a certain way and expect to be convincing. By theorizing about the case in productive ways, and coming up with sound ideas about how to present his client's side in court, the odds of winning increase. Bartlit says he gets his best ideas under pressure, often when just kicking the case around with others.

> You don't sit down and say, "Now I've got to think of the
> thing." You're working on the case, and you're talking,
> you're kicking it around, and you're up at the blackboard,
> and suddenly, usually [it comes] earlier rather than later. I
> work in absolute bursts of creativity. The best ideas I have,
> many times, are when I need to have an idea. When it's the
> day before an opening or in an hour. The urgency of the
> situation brings forth some of the best ideas I have, ideas I
> never thought of until I was looking at the witness, and like
> a wave approaching, it just came to me. Some of the very
> best ideas are totally spontaneous, in the heat of the battle.

Max Blecher thinks coming up with the theory of the case is an intuitive process, "You look at the facts and say what is it that they are going to believe about this case and identify with?" The car is a good place to think, as are the shower and the treadmill. Most lawyers get their best ideas when relaxed and alone. Then the mind lets go of preoccupations and is open to the kind of leaps and connections needed to generate original ideas. Blecher particularly likes the car, one of the few places in the world that he feels truly alone.

For Phil Corboy, the theory of the case can be reduced to a single theme. He recently had a case in which the theme was damages. There was no need to contest liability. It had been admitted. The case involved the United Airline DC-10 crash in Sioux City, Iowa. The wealthy widow of one of the passengers who died on flight 232 hired Corboy.

> The theme was: *the jury should not give us what we deserve,
> they should only give us what the law allows*. My client was
> a rich widow. She may not deserve becoming richer, but she
> was entitled to become richer. My theory and strategy was
> to try to get jurors to overcome the knowledge of her wealth
> and decide that here's a rich woman who is entitled to
> become richer.

In the Sioux City case, Corboy did not have to present his theme to the jury however; he settled the case for the largest wrongful-death settlement ever received—twenty-five million.

The theme is in place before the jury is selected, of course, and juror de-selection will depend on eliminating people who are not likely to be sympathetic to the theme. How does Corboy come up with such ideas? How long does it take him?

> Somebody asked me one time, "You gave a wonderful argument in the ARCO case. How long did it take you to prepare that argument?" I answered as honestly as I could. I said, "Thirty-eight years."

Once, Jim Brosnahan made the character of the defendant his theme. He foreclosed many of the reservations the jurors might have had about his client for having confessed to a crime by presenting him as strange and eccentric. This explained the central incriminating fact that he had moved into the Sierra Nevada mountains—not to evade California taxes, but to have his own place in Nevada. And the final theme emerged.

> *"He's a little crazy, but he's not crooked,"* I told the jury in final argument. He was sitting there. I said, "He's odd, eccentric, but he's not a criminal." He had confessed, which really had nothing to do with the crime. We explained that, "This is the issue (tax evasion) , this is not the issue (moving to the wilderness)." The jury saw the difference.

Brosnahan knows a theme like this does not come out of analysis of the legal problems involved. It is a product of the imagination. Part of what is being done in formulating a theory of the case is the reconstruction of another's motives. That requires empathy as well as imagination. If the right trail is marked out, according to Brosnahan, if the facts start to fit the fantasy, then the rest of the story falls into place.

The intensity of the process, the degree of concentration involved, is virtually a mode of existence in itself. Brosnahan says of the ideas he gets, "They come after periods of intense reading and thinking about the case. You look at two hundred documents and one hundred ninety-nine don't do anything to you, but one of them is the key." And it could happen at any time. A theory of a recent case came to Brosnahan through a close study and analysis of photographs. The defendant was accused of making a bomb.

> In the Psinakis case, a criminal case, we were going over the FBI's crime scene photographs. And they've got a photograph of these tools together in a bowl, glue and stuff; it looks very sinister—it looks like something you could make a bomb with.

Context is everything. And sometimes the context is a product of deception, cheating, moving things around.

> In the photo there is a cabinet and on the cabinet there is a glue bottle. And we looked back at...all these pictures taken within half an hour's time in the house by the FBI. Now we look back at the picture of the stuff in the bowl. There's a glue bottle. There's a glue bottle here, there's a glue bottle there. Is it the same? We can't quite tell, we need a magnifying glass. Oh yeah, it's the same glue bottle. You know what? They moved it.

And the admission was forthcoming in the trial. It was a real moment of triumph for Brosnahan:

> She [the FBI agent] admitted this on the stand. This was so much fun. They gathered together things from all over the room harmless in nature and put them in a bowl and made what she called a staged photograph out of it. We proved that in the court.

Jim Neal Defends Elvis Presley's Doctor

[*State of Tennessee v. Dr. George Nichopoulos*]

Dr. Nichopoulos had already been found guilty by the Tennessee Medical Society of violating all the guidelines in the *Physician's Desk Reference* for prescribing drugs. Neal did not believe that the doctor was a corrupt man who over-prescribed drugs to Presley for personal gain. He believed him to be an ordinary, hard-working, kind gentleman. He wanted to understand why the doctor had done what he had done, and in presenting his theory to a jury, not get charged out of court. After talking to his client and using other lawyers as sounding boards, he developed his theory. If there is a plausible medical reason to continue prescribing amphetamines and other drugs, the doctor may do so. This doctor's patients were addicted when they came to him. He believed that if he could get them to continue to come back to him, he could slowly wean them off the drugs. This theory was accepted by the jury. His client was acquitted.

Pat McCartan is another lawyer who often sees the theory of the case in terms of a theme, but for him the theme is subject to change as the trial evolves. "More often than not, however, my first impression is

my last impression because I trust that more than what develops later."
For McCartan, as for many other lawyers, the compelling ideas about
the case now become a preoccupation. He cannot put them out of his
mind.

> Once you start this process, no matter how far back you put
> that matter in your mind while you attend to other things
> such as showering, shaving, driving to work, and what-
> have-you, it just keeps coming forward. Some of the best
> ideas that I have had come to me in the middle of the
> night . . . or reading documents . . . Sometimes reading a de-
> position transcript, preparing to cross-examine the witness.

Still, there are limits to creativity. One cannot exceed what the facts
are. Jim Neal talks about this limitation.

> You're always circumscribed by the facts, by your informa-
> tion, by the documents, what the witness has told you, and
> you're circumscribed by the law. It doesn't do any good to
> come up with a theory if the judge is going to say, "That's
> no defense."

Unlike many attorneys, Neal does his best strategizing in the
presence of others. Particularly when faced with someone who
contradicts your ideas, he argues, are you driven to question them
yourself. This often leads to productive, original thinking.

> When I was prosecuting the big Watergate case, my first
> assistant was a guy in Washington, Richard Ben-Veniste.
> Goddamn, if I said, "Look at that sun up there, how bright
> it is." He would say, "Now, there's a little film across it. You
> just didn't see that." Or something or other. I would get so
> mad at him. But when we'd thrash things out, the chances
> were overwhelming that we were on the right course.

Reading principle cases and law review articles is where Harry
Reasoner begins. He then works on developing as good an understanding of the facts as he can muster. From there he synthesizes his theory.

> It's hard to be creative safely without having a pretty deep
> understanding of the applicable law in the area. I've seen
> lawyers who tried a great case on the facts in the sense that
> they had an appealing factual story, but it just didn't mesh
> very well with the controlling legal theory in the area. That
> is a real danger.

A good story that does not fit prevailing legal theory is useless. For him, the process of finding the "happy metaphor" for a case takes time and cannot be hurried. The road to lost trials is paved with a lot of overcooked and half-baked theories.

Bob Fiske often finds the theory of the case in the course of dialogue with other lawyers.

> As you go around the room three or four times, you'll end up with a composite of ideas. [One] came from one person, you take a little bit of that, and a little bit from something else, and you put them together and try it out on your mock juries. Then you see what they think, and then you go with it.

In this, as with so many things, Arthur Liman likes to cut the Gordian knot. He will find the evident theme, and develop it into a story that will work for a jury. "The theme may not work as you get further along, but I try to start with a theme right at the beginning and keep developing and developing and developing it."

For David Boies there will be a range of theories of the case, all of which might be brought into court in one way or another. It is important to present these theories in a way that does not foreclose, or render inconsistent, something you might wish to say later. Starting out with a range of theories is not something most lawyers could pull off. Boies feels it is a particularly good approach for the plaintiff, who wants an excuse to keep firing "theories of the case that will keep you in court. Avoid saying something inconsistent with what you're ultimately going to want to say in case you lose one." A good illustration is the CRS (Computer Reservation System) litigation.

> Max Blecher came in with an essential facility argument. I came with an essential facility argument, a traditional monopolization argument, and a RICO argument. The judge, to everybody's surprise, dismissed Max's essential facility argument, dismissed my essential facility argument, too, but left in my monopolization and my RICO claim and allowed Max to then amend his complaint to adopt my monopolization claim. As a plaintiff you want to have, until you get to trial, multiple arguments and not only multiple theories, but multiple arguments supporting each of those theories. Part of the defendant's job is to make you choose and part of the plaintiff's job is to avoid choosing.

> Then get down to trial and that's when you've got to develop
> your real theory of the case. You need to tell the jury as the
> plaintiff when you open what case you're going to close
> with and you may want to leave a few things open and you
> may want to leave a few things unspecified, but you have
> got to tell the jury why you ought to win and it's got to stay
> the same.

Boies starts to look for his ideas about the matter in the case law,
going through the records of rulings of the Supreme Court and the
court of appeals. "I will read them in chronological order," he says.
Then it is on to the facts. These may exist in multiple configurations.
There will be discontinuities, overlaying versions, contradictions:

> You want to keep as much of an open a mind as you can,
> and then you want to understand how the facts fit together,
> what the connections are, what the discontinuities are in the
> facts, in the cases. Always remember when you're talking
> about the facts to keep overlaying different versions of the
> facts because it's not chess, it's three- or four-dimensional
> chess, because you have various versions of what the facts
> are.

As the defendant, according to Boies, the idea is to force the plaintiff
to focus on a single target, so that the defense becomes more
concentrated and direct.

> Make the plaintiff pick his theory, pick his facts, and then
> you can attack it. At the same time, as the defendant, try to
> keep your flexibility. When we tried the Telex case, we
> emphasized the practices case, mostly, and ultimately won
> it on market structure emphasized in discovery. In the
> CalComp case, we emphasized an awful lot of market
> structure and then won it on practices.

Boies is not sure how all this thinking takes place. He discounts the
suggestion that it is inspiration, but does acknowledge that he cannot
predict when an idea will come. As with the other attorneys in this
study, it is often in a state of semi-relaxation, away from the office.
Like Fiske, and Liman, Boies keeps a pad and pencil next to his bed.
Talking about the case fertilizes the mind. Boies feels it is important to
explain the case to others as part of one's own understanding. Any kind
of reflective or pedagogical process forces one to extend the bound-
aries of thought.

When it comes to getting ideas about the theory of the case, Joe Jamail has the last word.

> I wake up in the morning and think about it and I make notes. Driving to work I think about it. Drinking in a bar I think about it. There's just no pattern with me. Something will happen. I read a great deal. I still read a lot of literature, great literature, and a whole bunch of mythology. And I can fantasize with anybody. I don't see that there is a lot of difference between fantasy and truth. I really don't. Everything I fantasize generally kind of happens in a way or I'll make myself think it has happened. If you fetter or put anchors on your thought processes, you might as well be a proctologist.

CHAPTER 5 ███████████████

Preparing for Trial: Mustering the Troops

*A lot of witnesses feel like they're just baggage.
They're brought in to do something and then get out. I
want them to feel like it's a good experience.*
            —Fred Bartlit

Preparing for trial is like preparing for war, and as in the case of war, a general needs a staff. No single attorney, no matter how energetic and skilled, can go it alone. The efforts of a great many people need to be coordinated. There are many tasks that must be attended to in minutest detail. Long before a trial begins, research is conducted into the issues that will decide the case, and into the composition of the jury pool. There will be a period of discovery in which each side exchanges their work product, documents, witness lists, exhibits, depositions and the like. Witnesses need to be coached and briefed. Exhibits must be prepared and brought up to a standard that will approximate that used in advertising. Sometimes computer animation will be used. Artists will be employed. The instructions to the jury must be written and prepared for presentation to the judge. A support staff of other attorneys, paralegals, and administrative personnel must be assembled. It is not quite like readying for D-day, but it sometimes feels close.

Trial Consultants

Virtually all of these trial lawyers have worked with trial consultants. (See Figure 5-1). The use of behavioral science experts is an essential and widely used resource in any high-stakes case. The field of trial consulting and jury research was really initiated when David Boies, Tom Barr, and Nicholas D.B. Katzenbach (then general counsel of IBM) enlisted my help in the CalComp antitrust case in the mid 1970's. Today, consciousness of the value of consultants has become widespread.

Use of Trial Consultants

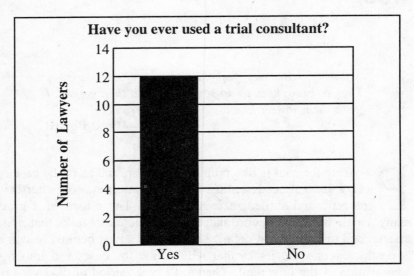

figure 5-1

It is not an exaggeration to say that consultants have brought about a basic change in how many lawyers prepare for trial. Trial consultants may do no more than confirm for a lawyer what he or she already intuitively knows, but that confirmation is extremely valuable if millions of dollars are riding on a "hunch." Routinely, and with increasing reliability and economy, consultants uncover problems with jurors, and discover global issues of concern to jurors often overlooked by the attorney. These services have been and can be expensive. Today there are effective, economical jury research techniques within the reach of most litigants.

The fourteen lawyers in this study have used a broad array of consulting services, from commonly used mock juries to the latest in the technology of demonstrative exhibits. (See Figure 5-2). Trial simulations, mock juries, and the use of focus groups are an important aspect of trial consultants' research techniques. And of course, jury research is something all but one of the 14 lawyers in this study frequently use. Phil Corboy, even has on occasion, hired a cab driver to advise him about certain neighborhoods in which potential jurors work and live.)

Use of Trial Consultants

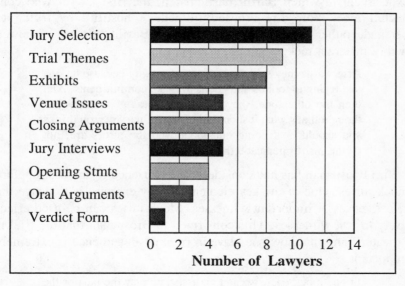

figure 5-2

Mock Juries

Mock juries are assembled to hear a simulated, stripped-down version of the case. They are chosen to match jurors who are likely to serve on the actual jury, and are presented with the principal elements of the case. Mock juries are then asked to render a verdict and to tell the consultants their view of the respective merits of either side. Mock juries can be used by both plaintiffs and defendants, and they can be used to test all or only a part of a case. They are the closest thing to a real trial, and, when used properly, they can afford incredible foresight into what might happen in the actual trial. One of the more interesting and novel uses of a mock jury concerns the testing of voir dire strategies. It is generally felt by consultants, as noted in the next chapter, that it is more important in voir dire to ferret out juror bias than to spend time pre-selling the case.

Fred Bartlit discovered how deep juror suspicions can become when an attorney tries to sell his case to prospective jurors rather than finding out about the jurors as human beings. In a jury research experiment in which Bartlit participated, the first lawyer who conducted mock voir dire aroused immediate hostility by trying to persuade rather than to seek information. Bartlit, himself, followed with a different tack.

> Afterwards they said we hated the first guy because he was just trying to fool us and get us to make commitments. And then the other one, they didn't say I was great, they just thought that's what it should be. The ordinary person thinks you should be finding out about who the jurors are, not trying just to persuade them.

Jim Brosnahan has had considerable experience trying cases before mock juries. One of the key elements in any exercise is to gauge the effectiveness of important witnesses. Mock juries can be used effectively to test witnesses. This confirmed to Brosnahan that the trial is "theater" and that how one plays in front of an audience is extremely important.

> In one mock trial, we had an associate play the part of the tax investigator and he was a real nice guy and very presentable and got up and gave his testimony. They hated him. Why did they hate him? They hate all tax collectors. We found that out. It was very, very valuable.

Phil Corboy was persuaded to change strategy in the Tylenol case after some work with a mock jury.

> Research gave us all the information we needed to settle the case. We knew what the problem was. The problem was proximate cause. The jurors did not think that the product was unreasonably dangerous. But they didn't mind our

204

using negligence. And by the way, we had already withdrawn our negligence counts and the defendants were coming in now to file completely new answers. When we got our mock jury, we withdrew our withdrawal and the negligence counts went back in because we had been informed, and we used it as reliably as we could, that the jury didn't mind having Johnson & Johnson tried on negligence. The jury didn't like them being charged with unreasonably dangerous conditions.

Shadow Juries

David Boies was involved in the first use of a shadow jury that I developed for him in the celebrated CalComp case. In this case, Boies defended IBM against antitrust charges brought by plaintiff, California Computer Products. A shadow jury is a group of people closely matched to the actual jury. This group goes into court each day and listens to the case. Each night their reactions are carefully studied, the hypothesis being that these reactions will be close to those of the actual juror. When undertaken correctly, we can then track how well the case is going, what aspects of the opponent's arguments, for example, are being well received and which are not.

Among other things, Boies learned something about the importance of dress in this instance. He learned that jurors pay attention to what lawyers wear, and that this can affect an attorney's credibility.

> One of the things I learned from the shadow jury reports in the CalComp case, and confirmed from the interviews with the jury afterwards, was that the jury, the women on the jury at least, were worried about the fact that I wore the same tie every day. They thought that maybe I was playing with them. Here I am representing IBM, and they had an image as to how somebody representing a big corporation would dress, and they thought that maybe I was dressing down for them. The CalComp case went over Christmas, and in early December, one of the women jurors asked the bailiff, "Does Mr. Boies really only wear one tie?" And the bailiff told me and I said, "No, I've got more than one tie, but every Christmas my mother gives me a tie and I wear it all year." The day after Christmas I came in with a new tie, and all the jurors were nudging each other and pointing at the tie.

Steve Susman, who has used consultants extensively, related a risky strategy he knows has been employed by another attorney with regard to shadow juries. The lawyer actually tells the real jurors he is using a shadow jury. He told Susman that,

> I tell the jury on voir dire that I am using a shadow jury. I tell them we have hired people to sit in the courtroom. I even introduce them if they are in the courtroom. "These are just average people like you are to give me feedback every evening on how well I'm doing; whether I am communicating because it's a problem during trial of my not being able to ask you questions."

This may be something to consider, but not for the faint of heart. Finally, Susman notes an important function of jury consultants. Their work in trial simulations can be a general learning experience as well as a specific one for attorneys. In Susman's opinion, "jury consultants teach you that what people say is not as important as they *way* they say it."

Focus Groups

Trial consultants often use focus groups to probe for global issues, that is, large overriding issues on which everything else is dependent in a forthcoming trial. Global issues can involve attributions of motivation, the interpretation of a particular event, or even the simple matter of liking or disliking one of the litigants. As an example, focus group research might reveal that jurors attribute the placement of a car's fuel tank to the manufacturer's excessive concerns about cost effectiveness and, hence, increased profitability rather than rational, engineering design implications. Discovering what the global issue or issues are likely to be can be done efficiently with focus group research. A device that began in the field of advertising, trial focus groups are asked to discuss and give opinions concerning a case or an element of a case. Out of such discussions a global issue may appear that the trial lawyer had not previously considered, thereby changing the tack of the case.

Jim Neal found focus groups of great utility in the Twilight Zone case.

> I have seen jury consulting work to be very valuable. In the Twilight Zone case we had a series of focus groups. Lost big in the first one, emphasized different facts in the second one, did better in the third.

The global issues revealed were not things that Neal, from a lawyer's perspective, would have been aware of.

> What emerged out of that are several things that I, as a lawyer, would never have thought important. One was to emphasize, and continue to emphasize, that the parents of these six-year-old children (who were killed on the movie set) were there. Well, that didn't impress me. They were Vietnamese, they could hardly speak English or understand it. They would not know what is going on in the making of the movie.

As it turned out, the fact that parents were on the movie set when a fatal accident occurred was important in the exculpation of the film's director. Their presence was interpreted by the jurors as a symbol of their consent to the children's participation and assumption of risk.

Demonstrative Exhibits

An area in which consultants have been used by virtually all the attorneys is that of demonstrative exhibits. (The pros and cons of their use will be discussed later in this chapter.) Bob Fiske sometimes has consultants prepare graphics for use in an opening statement.

> I think you have to be careful because it has to be, again, pretty short because the jury doesn't know much about the case. But I've done it. We've used consultants for that. I think that is a useful function that they provide.

Fiske is interested in the new technologies that are becoming available such as computer animation, and laser discs to handle unwieldy documents and depositions. He envisions an enhanced role for consultants as a result of these technologies.

> It is the next step in demonstrative evidence. I think it is going to require definite new techniques for lawyers to deal with this. I mean, if the guy who comes into the first trial where the other side is doing this and he isn't, that's bad. But even trying to learn how to do it, I'm sure the role of the consultants is going to be major.

Survey Research

The use of survey research as a guide to juror selection is something with which most trial lawyers are familiar. Sometimes referred to as "jury polling" by lawyers, it involves the use of sampling techniques and questionnaires to ascertain probable juror predispositions in a given venue. Survey research is frequently used to determine juror attitudes in a case, or to find evidence of bias, which can then be used as a basis for a change of venue motion. Information about bias is also used to "de-select" biased jurors, that is, eliminate them through peremptory strikes and challenges for cause.

These surveys primarily rely upon telephone questionnaires. Anyone can write a list of questions, but if meaningful answers and meaningful interpretations are desired, skilled psychologists must be involved. Groups of questions, called scales, are used to probe specific attitudes or to establish specific dimensions of juror personalities that will be relevant in the decision-making process.

One attorney works with trial specialists to consider venue issues. He recalls a survey done by the author of this book on attitudes toward nuclear power.

> It was fascinating and extremely useful to us in ultimately settling the case. [We] found out that while the jury pool the venue would hold our client in low regard, they held our opponent in as low or *lower* regard. This experience reinforces my belief that you need to look behind intuitive notions or general anecdotal advice.

What he learned from the survey was that he could settle from a position of strength rather than from a position of fear. The client was in far better shape in terms of potential juror bias than previously thought.

In a case in which Jim Brosnahan is involved, a relatively large sample is being tested.

> In the case I'm about to take to trial, preparing for voir dire, I've got jury research. They're going out and they're going to talk to six hundred people. They're going to come back with profiles and I'm going to make a decision. With that as a resource, I will make the decision what jurors to de-select.

Making recommendations about the de-selection of jurors, finding out which jurors might possibly hurt, is a basic objective of survey research. At times, it will also identify jurors who might support one's case.

Phil Corboy recently used survey research to ascertain what kind of damages a jury might award in a personal-injury case. The case was put through a simulated trial. "I used research to receive a recommendation about jurors [and] tried the case before a retired judge. After four or five days of trial, we were offered the coverage [of] $5.75 million."

Corboy is preparing to avail himself of consultants' recommendations about jurors in another case. A large survey will be completed and jurors will be ranked on a scale of one through nine for approval on his side. Dimensions such as gender, occupation, education, political orientation, and ethnicity will be used. Corboy gives an example of how these factors will be sifted through a computer and recommendations made.

> They will then give, for example, as a result of their computer check those factors which will bring a person up from a three to a five or down from an eight to a six. Maybe a college graduate black person, male, will be a bad juror unless he's under twenty-five thousand dollars a year. But if he's a thirty-five- or forty-five-year-old black college juror who's already been assimilated into society and has become part of society and part of the accepted establishment, he might not be a good juror for me.

This information can be used to assemble mock juries made up of people of varying degrees of favorability or receptiveness to the client's case, and to see how these individuals react according to who makes up the group.

> Then they're going to go out and get twenty-four people, two nines in this group, two ones in this group, a seven, a five, and three fours. And they're going to do the same thing with another group. They're going to put twenty people in a room and I'm going to put on a mock trial. And those twenty-four people are going to be put into separate rooms. [I'm] going to put on a truncated version including all the bad parts of my case and concentrate on the good things. They're going to get an analysis of what the law is. I'm told what their job is and I'm going to give very short final arguments and one of the other lawyers is going to be giving a short argument and then I'm going to give a very short rebuttal.

Each of the mock juries will be studied in order to affirm recommendations about certain types of jurors. Corboy will then evaluate what he has been given.

> I'm going to get a videotape of each jury, see where the differences are, see if there's any similarity between the nine that's here and the nine that's there, the one that's here and the one that's there. See if there was any legitimacy to the one that jumped from a one here to a three over here to see if it really does change and I'm going to come out with a resource that's going to give me some insight into what the research has developed.

Corboy knows that not every lawyer puts a lot of stock in this kind of research.

> It's a process that some lawyers think is ridiculous. They're very smart, they know how to pick jurors, I don't. They also think that it's an abnegation of their job. They don't understand what I'm using it for. They don't understand that I'm not bound by what I see. I'm only using it as someone else's thoughts that I can utilize and make a decision on.

Communication consultants have also proven to be valuable. Bob Warren relates an early instance of employing consultants to tailor his style of presentation to the needs of a case. On the space shuttle program, an employee had made allegations of mischarging against North American Rockwell. Warren was engaged to represent Rockwell in the issue of the employee's wrongful termination.

> We went to trial down in Norwalk (Los Angeles), and it was one where the opening statement was televised, which was by no means a common experience at that time. [The employee whistle blower] had been on "Sixty Minutes" to tell his story. One of his co-workers had been on "20/20" to make the same allegations.

Warren wanted to weigh in effectively against this media blitz.

> I had been appointed the Rockwell spokesperson because we couldn't have any of the senior executives do so—they were involved in the case. So, I received media training and learned how to talk in sound bites, which was a totally new experience for me.

Support Staff

Attention to ancillary personnel is critical to the success of a trial. These men work with a tried and trusted group of people. Other attorneys who serve as trial associates are experienced colleagues who often function as team leaders with a support staff beneath them. Each "team" is responsible for a part of the case, legal research, briefs, witnesses, documents, exhibits, or a specific area of proof. (See Figure 5-3). The support staff often drills witnesses, conducts and/or defends minor depositions, and collates and prepares documents. Often, one or more trial associates will appear in court. Although these attorneys could easily hire a large staff, ten of the fourteen revealed that they personally are involved in *every* aspect of trial preparation. Most expressed the preference to work with a small group in order to oversee and control all trial aspects. For David Boies, "everything that is happening has implications for what happens in the courtroom and I want to participate in that."

Legal Research

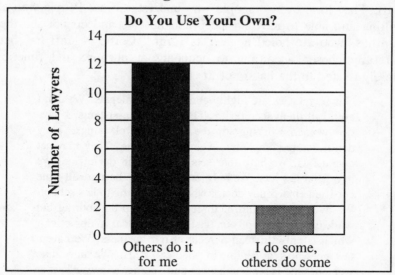

figure 5-3

Bob Fiske likes to see one person responsible for each particular witness "to do all the spade work." Where possible, the case is divided up by subject matter. A trial associate is put in charge of each subject area who reports directly to him.

Max Blecher's office can field about three teams of attorneys, and he might work with any one of the three. An advantage to a small or mid-size firm as opposed to one of the giants is that none of the counsel with whom he is associated are strangers. The attorneys are assigned early, and depending upon which case comes to trial, Blecher could work with the same people several times in a row.

Arthur Liman prefers to work with a small group, and stays closely in touch with the work, particularly as trial approaches. His recall of the paper trail sharpens as he gets into the trial, and he counts on his helpers to deliver documents to him as he calls for them. Even in large cases, there are only a handful of people who work right under him. But it has to be small because . . . "I cannot delegate responsibility for knowing the case."

Phil Corboy acknowledges that he makes terrific demands on his staff. They have to be "people who understand me. People who are willing and able to have no sleep and no eats and do not see their families, who are holed up just as I am." Corboy's staff has been carefully chosen according to economy of purpose and function, closely related to the nature of his business.

> Our secretaries are highly competent paralegals. We don't even call them secretaries. They're legal assistants. I have two women working for me that know pleadings. They don't dictate complaints. They may collate. They may get documents. We have four sets of people in our office. We have trial lawyers. We have preparers. We have a full-time certified emergency doctor who is now going to law school. We have a minimum of three people who do nothing but work on that part of our business, [medical malpractice], which is only thirteen percent of our business. We have a lawyer who's a genius in medical stuff. We have two women. One is a nurse lawyer and another a lawyer lawyer who do nothing but prepare cases for trial: depositions and discovery—medical aspects of the case. So, when I'm getting ready for trial, I have myself, I have the lawyer who has worked on the case to prepare me for it, I have my legal assistant, and I have a minimum of one more clerk who gets the legal file through the lawyers I'm working with ready for trial.

Fred Bartlit works with the same pyramid model favored by a number of others. There are "chiefs of staff," each responsible for an area of the case, who report directly to him. He meets with the people regularly during the trial, and feels strongly that the meetings should display an upbeat, positive tone.

> I've got several partners I like to work with who are sort of strategists and sort of chiefs of staff. In an ideal situation, I like to have a younger partner there for the trial to meet with the clients. I meet every day, maybe for an hour at the end.

Brosnahan's team is generally compact, one other attorney in court, several other attorneys on a background team. In a big case, the background team could be much larger. Brosnahan has had cases where he worked with twenty lawyers or more. Working out of a big firm with a large number of specialists, Brosnahan also often finds himself going to trial with different attorneys. This is not easy for him, he prefers always to work with the same group. Yet, it is important to Brosnahan to have a younger associate involved in every trial. He, like so many of these men, is conscious of the need to pass on the torch. (See Figure 5-4). It is part of his responsibility to the firm, and it is also a mission to insure that the art and folklore of trial lawyering remains alive and well. (See Figure 5-5). "I always want to take a young person out there to have some role in the trial because there is no other way for them to learn than to do. I sometimes have them sit second chair."

Exhibits

Where new technology is concerned, these lawyers seem to follow Pope's adage, "Be not the first by whom the new is tried, nor yet the last to lay the old aside." (See Figure 5-6). There is interest in such things as laser-disc technology and computer animation, and a willingness to take advantage of anything that is of real practical value. In the main, since they are usually involved in civil proceedings, their attention focuses upon demonstrative exhibits rather than tangible evidence frequently introduced as an element of proof in criminal trials.

Fred Bartlit puts the use of demonstrative graphic exhibits in an interesting context— his personality as a trial lawyer. He suggests that working without graphics is to depend upon the force of one's spoken

213

Role of Mentors

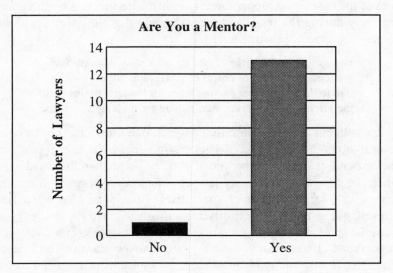

figure 5-4

Law Firm Management

Do you involve yourself with any aspect of a law firm's governance?

Type	Yes	No	Amount Liked*
Administration	13	1	2.8
Training	14	0	5.6
Recruiting	13	1	4.7
Compensation	13	1	2.6

(*7-point scale: 7 = Enjoy a Great Deal, 1 = Do Not Enjoy At All)

figure 5-5

Personal Computer
Used in Work

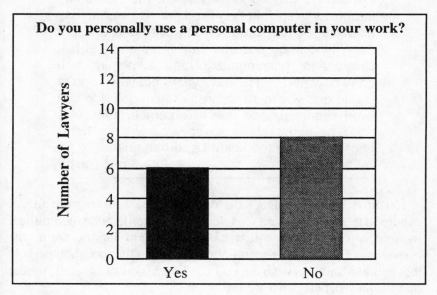

figure 5-6

word alone. This kind of reliance is not something he would advise for a younger attorney.

> I've always used a lot of visuals. I've had some jurors say lately that they liked the visuals but they also like it when I turn off the overhead and put everything away and stand up there and just talk slowly and meaningfully. That's something you can't do when you're thirty years old when you're young and you're immature... You're going to use overheads because they'll remember that. You don't have the ability to speak from the heart because you're too scared and nervous.
>
> **—Fred Bartlit**

Bartlit is not happy about the demise of the spoken word in our culture. He knows the reasons for it, the proliferation of political rhetoric and exaggeration that has scant regard for the truth, the corruption of language by sound-bite artists, and the foolish hyperbole that bombards us every day on radio and television. It is small wonder that we only believe what we see.

> Unfortunately, the spoken word is distrusted. Seeing is believing. So, you've got to show them something, number one. Number two, the average American is no longer able to take things in through their ears. Television has made them eye conscious.

Consequently, Bartlit uses a technique on cross-examination that integrates visual information with spoken information. He displays documents and depositions on a screen and goes through them with the witness. He makes this as theatrical as possible.

> If I were cross-examining you, I'll say, "Let's look at Paragraph four."...A big, key exhibit. [In the courtroom] the lights are up, (I'll know the marshall's name) and I'll say, "Sergeant Smith, would you mind cutting the lights?" So, it's just like TV.

Bartlit does not find laser-disc technology particularly beneficial for certain kinds of cases. "People are used to fabulous TV quality and document exhibit quality on TV is rotten." In addition, Bartlit likes to *appear* to run risks in court. Working without notes, grabbing documents out of a box as he needs them, gives a risky, hands-on character to his presentation that he thinks plays well with the jurors.

> These big-firm guys love sitting in the back of the court-room at their table bringing things up on the television monitor and asking questions, because they're safe. There is a big risk when I'm up here with no notes and out of my head, I've got to ask the right questions. It's much safer to sit back there, but you're not proving anything.

On the other hand, Bartlit is positive about computer animation. There is a multiplicity of applications for computer animation. For example, it is a superior way to show the way a human body moves in a car during a rollover. In the case of the pollution of ground water by a refuse company, computer animation can be devised to show the actual penetration of the water molecule by various toxic substances. In medical malpractice, computer animation can be used to show how a particular procedure was performed. In short, it is a powerful tool for getting the jury visually involved in the actual occurrence of an event that is the subject of dispute.

Max Blecher is a devotee of exhibits. He constantly accompanies the examination of witnesses with documents. It is a mistake not to display the relevant document when a witness is testifying about its content.

> My view is that you start with them (exhibits) in opening statement and never stop. Never examine a witness about an important document that isn't up on the screen for the jury to look at. Perfunctory documents you can do away with. But every important document should be up on the screen while you are examining. "Did you write this?" you ask. And the document is there to see.

For Bob Warren, one of the advantages of an exhibit is that it becomes etched in the memory of the jurors in a way that can rarely occur with the spoken word. Because visuals make such a strong impression it is important not to muddy the waters.

> An exhibit has a permanence about it. It's one that a jury can latch on to. It's determinative in some way, and it doesn't go away. So the knack on an exhibit, it seems to me,

is to pick out the ones that really count and not flood the jury with a lot of documents that don't count, and thereby dilute your exhibit presentation.

If an exhibit is made part of the trial record, Warren suggests its significance in context needs to be demonstrated. There is only one exception to that rule.

> Lots of lawyers mark things in evidence and the jury never has a clue of what's happening. If it's worth marking and putting into evidence, it's worth putting up on a screen and highlighting and pointing out the importance of that document through examination of a witness. There is only one exception to that and that is when you plan the exhibit to be a hidden bomb to be used only in final argument.
>
> **—Bob Warren**

Warren thinks laser discs are extremely valuable. However, he cautions, "if you are representing the economically superior party against the economically disadvantaged party, and you show everything on laser disc and it wasn't tremendously more impressive than if the same information had been put on butcher paper, you might pay for it."

David Boies is a strong proponent of the theory that the jury needs only a few cogent anchors to decide a case. He mentions two such exhibits in the Westmoreland case:

> I had a cable that Westmoreland had sent saying, "I am being successful in convincing people that there is light at the end of the tunnel." I also had an exhibit that showed if their estimates of troop strength in the beginning of 1967 were right and their estimates of the number killed in 1967 to 1968 were right, at the end of 1968, there was no more enemy, we'd won the war. Those were two powerful demonstrative exhibits.

Boies also follows Fred Bartlit's practice of using an overhead projector to display documents during witness examinations. During cross-examination he creates exhibits on the spot.

> [What] I like about the overheads is that I create exhibits
> while on cross. I'll take a sheet, put it up, and it will have a
> label on it, "Mr. X's testimony about Y." I'll have a series
> of questions, "Did you do this?" "Did you do that?" I'll fill
> those answers in as we go. Then I'll hand it to somebody,
> they'll run it through a Xerox machine on acetate and
> you've got a visual. I'll mark it as an exhibit, put it back up
> and say, "Now, you just said this, right?" "Yes." "Offer it
> in evidence."

Boies also likes to use exhibits in his opening statement. Since
there is such a heavy burden upon the defense to present the essence of
their case in its opening he believes the defense should use exhibits to
reinforce its principal points.

> Plaintiff's going to get a chance immediately to give the
> jury the verification for what is presented in the opening
> statement. Defendant isn't going to get that chance except
> during cross-examination, which is a very awkward and
> clumsy way to do it. As a result, you really want as a
> defendant to put those anchors in front of the jury in your
> opening statement so they have something to hold on to as
> they see all this other stuff parade in front of them.

There are two kinds of exhibits. For Bob Fiske "pre-existing
documents are the best. Documents don't lie. So, to the extent you
have those, you use them as much as possible." The other kind of
exhibit is the illustrative teaching device prepared expressly for the
trial. Often Fiske will incorporate these into his opening statement.

> I might want to use an organizational chart to explain,
> "Here are the people at Xerox who are going to be
> testifying. Here are the people I'm going to put on from
> Sunrise. I want you to understand what their positions are.
> He's the president, he reports to him, he reports to him." A
> simplified chronology of events, a story.

Jim Neal likes to use exhibits in his opening as well as in
summation. He points out that this should be cleared with the judge
first.

> You don't want to be stopped in the middle of an opening
> statement or summation by the judge saying that something
> is improper. You clear that. You have charts you want to use
> in opening statements...pre-made charts. Frequently, my

219

> charts are simply what I've written out by hand or on an
> overhead projector where I'll take a flimsy that my parale-
> gal has prepared, and while the jury is listening, I'll
> underline it. Also, depending on the confidence of your
> opponent, the opponent in the heat of battle may let you
> leave those charts out there while he is putting on his case.

In keeping with his aggressive style, Joe Jamail likes to use
documents to sandbag his opponents. He will pop up a document that
points out a glaring inconsistency in someone's testimony. He feels this
tactic is the most effective way a document can be employed.

> I just wait until he gets on the stand. I usually use the
> instrument itself. If I want it blown up, I'll have it blown up
> to reference an argument...I'll make copies of all my
> exhibits and have the bailiff pass them out to each juror as
> I'm using them so they can follow along.

The idea of giving each juror his or her own set of exhibits is a
technique that Jamail has practiced for some time. The device has
several virtues. It puts the jurors in possession of a permanent record
of what has been adduced as evidence by Jamail to which they can
refer during deliberations. It also draws them into the case as Jamail's
confederates. Although all lawyers want to do it, few have Jamail's
ability to recruit the jurors as allies.

> ...the court gives them a notebook. They don't know
> where it comes from. They have an exhibit notebook that
> they can take with them. Those exhibits have been admit-
> ted, there they are. Mr. Jamail said this here. Mr. Jamail
> said this there.

If Jamail wants to show an exhibit of an important locale, say the scene
of an accident, he will not necessarily produce a large blow-up placed
on an easel in the courtroom. Instead he might pass snapshots among
the jurors much like friends sharing Polaroids in a living room. It is
part of his strategy to bring the jurors out of their role as juror and into
a natural setting in which they will use common-sense reasoning to
which Jamail appeals for proof. If an accident had occurred on an
overpass for example, Jamail would

> ...bring in photographs of it. Usually small ones. If I want
> one big one, I bring it in sometimes. I just don't think that
> is necessary. I like to touch, OK? I like walking over and

handing it to the bailiff and standing in front of the jury and the jurors feeling what I am giving them. I don't know why. I just like that. They pass it, they are looking at me, and I give it to them, and I look at them.

Jamail says he has never used exhibits in his opening statements, but he will steal a march on his opponent by employing visuals in voir dire, such as a chart made to show the damages involved, or the charge to the jury.

> Let me give you an example of the use of exhibits in voir dire. I'll have a chart made, let's just say showing the damages written on chalkboard. It would be the exact jury charge that the judge is going to give to the jury on damages. When I come to the damage part of it, I pull it out and say, "I have presumed and believe that his Honor is going to submit this charge to you. Don't just consider his loss in earnings." And I go down these elements with them. "Is there anyone here who could not consider this element of damages? And if the proof shows it, write in five million dollars?" I've cleared it with the judge before.

Jim Brosnahan finds that exhibits are powerful teaching aids and can make a tedious subject lively.

> Videos are good. Hanley did the one in the MCI case in Chicago. It was very good. He got this folksy guy, "Hello. I'm going to go up and show you the connections." Couldn't be duller subject matter, but video made it a really interesting thing.

Arthur Liman is fairly conservative when it comes to the new technology. At times he has approached exhibits in a minimalist fashion, but doubts that that is really adequate.

> I have played it every which way. I have done my own drawing, but I don't think I can always get away with poor-boying it. But I think that you can overdo it in the sense of making it seem like it's too monied, particularly when you're representing people with money. I think it's important, though, and every case I have tried, the jury always wants them, even if the judge won't let them go in. They want them and I think they're very important. I think a lawyer is foolish not to take advantage of it.

Nevertheless, it is clear that Liman remains somewhat of a reluctant dragon. He is such a master of the spoken word that it is difficult for him to acknowledge the need for any other channel of communication. Not so with Harry Reasoner who states that he is visually oriented, and finds it easier to absorb a mass of material by reading than by listening. This holds true for jurors too.

> You don't have everybody's undivided attention for an hour. If a juror misses some of it, he can look over and see it as an established proposition. When you change exhibits it is a new opportunity to capture somebody's attention again.

Tom Barr, who has used graphics effectively in many of his cases, recalls an example of a graphic that became a point of derision.

> I've seen some used that backfired. [In] one case, the plaintiffs used with their first witness a kind of clumsy chart... It was an earnings chart and was colored in a rather disgusting shade of red. I called it the chart they spilled ketchup on. I said, "Now, let's talk about this chart you've spilled ketchup all over. That's what you did, didn't you?" Everybody laughed. I called it the ketchup chart. It happened to be a phony chart.

On the other hand, using exhibits that are visually striking but which cannot be easily plugged into a line of attack, or using so many the blitz dulls perception, are common problems. "You can't," Corboy says, "make the assumption that the jury knows what they're for. Using too many exhibits so that they're surfeited, so that they can't get it all in." Corboy looks with relish upon a potential mistake that his opponent may make in an upcoming trial in which he is involved. He believes that his opponents are going to introduce a number of videotaped depositions and that this will not be successful.

> Although they're not exhibits in the technical sense, they're going to offer into evidence depositions by videotape. I hope they use all ten of them. It's going to turn that jury off. "What, is he trying to fool us?" You can overuse exhibits, is what I'm saying.

Bob Fiske worries that the use of high-powered, slick exhibits might hinder credibility. Jurors sometimes find sympathy for the under-financed, well-meaning, everyday, garden variety litigant with their hand-drawn charts.

You have to be careful that it does not come across looking too glitzy and you're subject to the, "Look at this rich corporation, they had all this money to spend against my poor little guy with his black-and-white thing here." I think a lot depends on who the adversary is and what the adversary is doing. If they're doing it too, then fine. It is a trade-off. But even if they are not, then the question is, is the glossy color thing so much more convincing that it's worth the hits you take for looking like a Hollywood advertising agency?

—Bob Fiske

Jury research reveals that this can be a problem, however. Jurors consistently provide positive reactions to graphics that are consistent with the level of visual attractiveness and sophistication seen outside the courtroom.

Preparing Witnesses

Most trial witnesses have never been a witness before, let alone stepped into a courtroom. Often the issues are emotionally charged and a witness may have a personal stake in the trial's outcome. Furthermore, witnesses know that lawyers for the other side are going to try to tear them apart, pick them to pieces, or both. They are normally anxious; they may also be scared.

David Boies offers the view that fear may help concentration. As Samuel Johnson once said, "When a man knows he is going to be hanged in a fortnight it concentrates his mind most wonderfully." Boies suggests that anxious witnesses make fewer mistakes than those who are overconfident. Jim Brosnahan believes nervousness stems from their fear that during cross-examination the other attorney will find something. To relieve this anxiety, Max Blecher tries to convince the witness that he will protect him. Just tell the truth and let me, the lawyer, deal with the consequences.

By in large my preparation [of a witness] is, "Go to your deposition and tell them anything they want

223

> to know and admit to stuff freely. [Tell them you]
> once had a load of ice cream rejected because it
> had rat hair in it. If that gets into evidence it's my
> job to deal with that. Don't deny it because if they
> impeach you, you're not only stuck with the rat
> hair, but you're lying about rat hair. That's too much
> for me to deal with. I can explain the rat hair. I can't
> explain why you lied about it."
>
> **—Max Blecher**

By confessing, the witness at the very least will appear honest. If the witness succeeds in creating a neutral context, Blecher will have something to work with in presenting the testimony in the best possible light, and in a way, that will contribute to proving the case.

> Juries understand that people make mistakes in life. Some-
> times you make the wrong judgment and sometimes rat hair
> will get in the ice cream. But I think that the jury can focus
> on the real issues in the case and let that kind of dirt slide
> by. Frequently if you get enough dirt on the other side, you
> can trade dirt. "You drop the rat hair and I'll drop the fact
> that the president of your company was out with a hooker."

Jim Brosnahan takes a similar approach. He wants the witness to tell his or her story without fear of adverse consequences. If the witness knows what part of the testimony is key, and why it is key, then there is a framework. He or she has a mission that is well-defined, and this mitigates the fear. He tells them, "There is no reason for you to worry about this. It's simple. All you have to do is go in there and tell them what you saw, that's all. It's not like you have anything to fear. Just tell them what happened."

Joe Jamail impresses upon his witnesses that they have the best possible lawyer on their side, and that they will be protected by his expertise if they tell the truth. Jamail tells his witnesses not to worry about their ignorance. They should stick to the point they are on the stand to make. The only disgrace is to weaken with regard to conclusions.

> I don't just fling you up there and say, OK, you're an
> expert. The other side may bring in books. If you haven't
> heard of them, tell him you haven't heard of them, he can't

use them. If you disagree with them, be ready to say why you disagree. You disagree because your own training and education tell you that that's not so. Just because it's written doesn't make it true. [The jury knows] everything that is written in the newspaper is mostly bullshit. You build that witness's confidence. Hey, Joe is here. And the court is there. You will not be abused. What are you afraid of? The guy can't hit you, he can't kill you. It's your idea. These are your independent evaluations and conclusions. The only way that you can be disgraced is if you come off those conclusions.

Jim Neal helps his witnesses overcome fear by impressing them with the fact that they know more about what they are going to testify than anyone else. Hesitation destroys credibility faster than anything else. Constantly offering qualifiers to everything one says is also damaging. Answers should be given, but not explained.

> You let them see the courtroom, you let them sit in the chair, you tell them, "You know more about what you're going to testify than anybody, don't be concerned. You know what you're saying." Listen to the question, answer the question that is asked, and be sure to answer it directly. You warn them that if you get into explaining every answer, you're killing yourself.

Certain kinds of witness preparation can exacerbate fear however. Fred Bartlit feels that videotaping witnesses, for example, will make them more self-conscious than they would be otherwise. And a witness's demeanor cannot really be changed. "I never videotape witnesses. Never. I videotape myself all the time. [In order to test his delivery of an opening statement.] I'm not going to videotape you and then make you be better. All I'm going to do is make you worried." Bartlit believes in simulating the trial conditions as much as possible in order to rehearse a witness. He also believes that lengthy cram sessions are counter-productive. He suggests that three short, but intense periods are better than endless, exhausting rehearsals. If a witness is from a different city, and it is vital that he or she be present when called, and in good form to testify, measures must be taken to insure that this is so.

> All my cases are out of town... If the witness isn't the most sophisticated, I want them met at the plane. I want their bags put in the car. I want them taken to the hotel and checked in and taken upstairs. I want them to know where they're supposed to be and have somebody get them and bring them over. I want my chief of staff during the day to do all the run-throughs so that at night when I get out of court, I can take them through and they're pretty close. They feel part of the team. If we're having pizza, they're gonna have pizza.
>
> **—Fred Bartlit**

Bartlit thinks it is difficult to work with witnesses who are, as he puts it, "elite people." In the case of such witnesses, pretensions must be overcome.

> Most elite people make bad witnesses. That is, people who have grown up in an elite background, gone to elite schools, and consider themselves different from the people on the jury... Give me a man who started a company from scratch and built it up. Every time, he'll be a great witness. Give me a self-made man.

Although there are different approaches to witness preparation, all these lawyers agree that it should be taken seriously. The prevailing idea is that witnesses must be truthful and natural in their testimony. Jurors must like and identify with them. What are some of the specific techniques used to create at least the illusion of truthfulness? What can be done to make a witness appear credible and likable?

A basic tactic of witness preparation is to drill the witness enough so that she is confident, but not so much that she becomes stale. Spontaneity is important for credibility. For Bob Fiske, if a witness sounds rehearsed, credibility diminishes.

> I don't usually use questions and answers. All I need to know is what I want this person to say. So I have that in front of me and then I'll run through... at least once before they go on the stand. Ideally, it's a combination of making sure

the witness understands what he or she is going to be asked and what he or she is going to say, without losing the spontaneity that you hope will happen in the courtroom.

Over-rehearsed witness testimony will come across as bad acting.

> You can rehearse it to the point where you are sure from the transcript that it will come out looking beautiful, but in court it could come out as totally rehearsed and totally unpersuasive. One of the judgments you have to make is knowing when you have gotten to exactly that point, where you've gotten well enough prepared but you don't want to lose spontaneity.

It is also important, according to Fiske, to prepare the witness for cross-examination by using another attorney to play the part of the cross-examiner. The witness should get used to the difference between direct examination with a friendly attorney and a hostile cross-examination with the opposition. Removing the element of surprise is helpful. Witnesses have more confidence once they believe that nothing will pop up on cross-examination that they have not already dealt with or thought about before.

Thinking about cross-examination for Fiske corresponds to his strategy of using the witness on direct. "The side that calls them puts a lot on the line when they put that person up. This is the downside of calling witnesses." Often, for this reason, neither side wants to call an ambiguous witness, even when that witness's role in the matter is central. Fiske remembers such a case:

> The judge kept saying, "Why hasn't either side called this person?" The logical person. Everybody is talking about him, but neither side called him. The reason was they looked at it the same way we did. They call him and he's got all these bad things to say about them. And we call him, and he's got all these bad things to say about us. So neither side called him.

Witnesses themselves will sometimes opt out if they fear being embarrassed or harassed. These are usually witnesses tangentially involved, not in the employ of either of the litigants, and with no direct interest in the outcome.

> There are a lot of witnesses who think, "Why do I want to get involved in this? You're going to put me up there and

227

> somebody's going to cross-examine me, somebody's going
> to try to make me look like a jerk. The easiest thing for me
> to do is say I don't want to get involved in this. I don't want
> to testify. Forget it."

A reluctant witness must be made to feel reasonably comfortable and confident that he will not be embarrassed. Jim Brosnahan observes that witnesses like to know exactly what they will be doing in the trial. Knowing when and in what order they are going to appear is important. Removing as many unknown elements as possible will enhance a witness's confidence and willingness to testify. However, he cautions, that pressure builds for a witness when too much emphasis is put on preparation. Sometimes an overprepared witness falls apart. Brosnahan once encountered a witness who had appeared in previous trials and was so worked over during his testimony he was in a stupor; he would say anything no matter what the question or who was asking.

> When I was a prosecutor, I had a big bank case. The San
> Francisco National Bank went under and the bank examiner
> had examined the Goddamn bank four times and missed it.
> He'd been called up before a congressional committee,
> maybe two. He'd had to go into the comptroller's office and
> tell them all about it and he testified in about five places.
> By the time I got him, he was like a wet dishrag. So, I
> worked with him, and worked with him, and worked with
> him. There is a phenomenon . . . witness mesmerization. It's
> like a fugue state. I mean, they just don't care anymore.
> They just want to be out of there.

David Boies believes that there is no one way to prepare a witness. But one thing is basic: "Take them through the points that the other side will raise on cross-examination." He does not use a question-and-answer format. He would rather work through a narrative of the witness's story. Boies will do run-throughs and have others do run-throughs. Cross-examination will be simulated. Pains will be taken not to script the witness. It is also important that there be continuity in tone between direct examination and cross. Sometimes a witness will be confident and convincing on direct examination, then become tentative or defensive and testy on cross. Boies states that this must be avoided if possible.

I want it to come naturally. And I want the direct and the cross to sound alike. Sometimes I tell witnesses they are a little too smooth. Slow it down, break it up a little bit, because [when] you get to cross, you're going to want to be more deliberate. I don't want it to look like you're confident on direct and uncertain on cross.

—David Boies

Bob Warren feels that the witness should be made as attractive as possible to "the trier of fact." He goes so far as to suggest that the actual content of the testimony is not as important as whether or not the witness is liked. At least this is something he tells witnesses during preparation. "A witness needs to be prepared in the art of being a witness in the sense of being attractive. By attractive I don't mean physical beauty, I mean somebody who will be received well." Warren uses videotapes of other witnesses to illustrate positive examples of testimony. This also demystifies the process of appearing in court. Then he or someone else goes exhaustively over the facts. The object in this is to make sure the witness knows the plot so that an unanticipated or surprise question can be answered in such a way as to fit the story.

> The key thing from my standpoint is what the witness has in mind. This ought to be done on one page, the ultimate story that the witness is conveying—the plot. The witness ought to be able to figure out whether the answer [he is] giving to any question fits within that plot. If it jars and it's the truth they must say it.

It is important that the witness not be lured into some gratuitous digression, some tangent that might prove harmful. "For God's sake, don't reach out looking for the opportunity to volunteer some statement, something ill-considered that may be quite inaccurate that jars with the essential synopsis," Warren notes.

Pat McCartan wants a witness's confidence to build, particularly in cross-examination, and thinks this happens when the witness finds out that there are no surprises in store. "You want to hear at the end of the day, 'They didn't ask me anything I hadn't heard before.'" Because of the factor of mistrust inherent in litigation, witnesses may fear that they are being used or manipulated. It is a mistake to view the witness as some kind of trained seal to be put through its paces. "Witnesses will do their darndest if you develop a personal relationship with them."

Jim Neal feels that witness preparation should focus on the "critical, pivotal witnesses." The strain upon these people can be tremendous. John Landis, the movie director and co-defendant in the Twilight Zone trial was on the stand for eight days. The fact that Landis weathered this ordeal was due to extensive preparation.

> Pivotal witnesses, usually the defendant, win or lose the case. I will spend hours, days, weeks with them. I will go over every possible question. John Landis was on the stand for eight days. Finally about the eighth day, the dragon, Lea D'Agostino was getting irritated and said, "I've bet you've been asked all these questions." "Yes," Mr. Landis very calmly said, "oh, yes, I've been asked all the questions you've asked me and a whole lot more."

Neal was asked who should attend to the preparation of a critical witness:

> Me. Me, me, me, me, me. I think Oliver Wendell Holmes said regardless of how complicated a case is, there are only a few witnesses and a few documents that are going to decide the case. I'd rather understand a few documents and handle them well, than to have a lesser knowledge of a hundred thousand documents. I'd rather see my pivotal witnesses prepared than to worry about a lot of others who may come across.

One of the aspects of witness preparation upon which Neal particularly concentrates is the interaction between the witness and the examiner. A rhythm and synchronization must be established.

> I think the most overlooked part of a case and perhaps the most important, is how you, the examiner, and the pivotal witnesses interact. I spend time on that. I'll go over his testimony and I may say, "Wait a minute, that's the time for you to answer the question with a yes or no." Go to another question, "Now this is a question where you may want to carry on some." And you get a good rhythm. I know a newspaper reporter wrote on the [Governor Edwin] Edwards case that my direct examination of Edwards, if I may be a little bit immodest, helped his testimony substantially.

Steve Susman engages in much more crafting of the witness's testimony, using videotape and questions and answers. He feels he can shape their answers considerably without giving them the appearance of being a puppet.

> Primarily, one of the most important things to do is practice them on video over and over and over again. For cross, primarily. For direct of your own witness, I write a Q and A. For my own witness where I've got privilege, I write the question and answer. Then I give it to them and they change the answer and then we go over it again. I think the one opportunity you have during the trial to orchestrate absolutely what's going to be said is during your own witness's direct examination.

Susman feels the risk of having the witness go off track far outweighs the risk of appearing unnatural or scripted. He tells the witness to learn the answers, but not to memorize them. Susman concentrates on the "ten hardest questions" his witness will have to confront. Beyond these questions, Susman maintains, "everything else is peanuts." He is concerned that a large number of short prepping sessions is superior to a few long ones.

> I will not let them practice with a witness more than fifteen or twenty minutes at a time. We schedule sessions for several days at nine, eleven, two, four [o'clock]. You see improvement from session to session. It doesn't matter substantively what they are asked about—I don't really care. What I'm interested in is how they handle themselves.

There is obviously some consideration of content. Susman looks for problem areas in a witness's deposition and goes over these:

> I usually read their deposition myself and I will highlight or put a sticker on something that gives me real heartburn. There won't be much that gives me heartburn. Maybe I'll even write out a better answer than in the deposition. How are we going to respond? Or, write them a note, "When you're asked this question you ought to say, 'Yeah, that's how I answered but if you'll look over on the next page, there on three pages, I clarified that.'"

Susman relates a particularly effective tactic he uses with problem areas of a witness's deposition. He will put a change in the testimony on the trial record before the witness takes the stand for cross-examination.

> If in going through their deposition at the last minute I find
> any mistakes that they have made, that they are going to
> have a problem with, I'll write the other side a letter the day
> before they get on the stand and say, "I know he went
> through the deposition, I know he signed it, but we have
> been reading it and he's told me that this is not his
> testimony." He gets on the witness stand. The other lawyer
> is trying to impeach him with this testimony, "Well, this is
> your..." "Mr. Jones, I told my lawyer, Mr. Susman, to
> correct that history. I saw that for the first time, I made a
> mistake." Not much a lawyer can do about it. "Well, you
> testified under oath?" "Yes, I did." "And you signed it
> before a notary." "Yes, I did." "Well, you..." "I'm sorry,
> I made a mistake." Jurors tolerate that.

In Susman's view, witness preparation is often a matter of fine tuning
testimony and dealing with potential problems.

> So it's that process. Reading the deposition. Heartburn
> stuff, either correcting or modifying or cross-referencing;
> and then the video preparation sessions over and over again
> only on cross, not the direct.

Harry Reasoner is more cautious when it comes to preparing
witnesses for fear they will appear "coached and mechanical." He
indicates that there might be legal implications of having a witness
practice on video. "I'm dubious about it. I've always been suspicious
that it's probably discoverable, that you would be entitled to ask
whether they had practiced on video or not." Subtle credibility factors
are important for Reasoner. Naturalness, a sense of conviction,
accurate knowledge, all of this can be developed through making the
witness comfortable and able to present what they say in a context of
understanding. Reasoner fears a witness who seems to have memorized testimony.

> I try to get them as comfortable as possible with the process
> and to make them realize this is not a magic act... where if
> they say the wrong word the dove comes down and we lose.
> I try to give them a full understanding of how their
> testimony fits in context, and the implications of it, and just
> make them comfortable. Some lawyers try to get witnesses
> to memorize things... [but] the jury wants to see that this is

a witness talking about something the witness actually knows about in his own words.

Tom Barr tries to put himself in the position of the witness by "understanding all the facts that the witness understands." Barr then considers what all the other witnesses are going to testify, and decides with much deliberation the specific points he wants made by the witness. Once this decision is made, Barr works with the witness until the witness is comfortable with the testimony. From there, the work of preparation goes on to cross-examination "and [I] backhand the hell out of him and satisfy myself that he's going to stand up well on cross." Barr adds an interesting point that has not yet been noted. He does not want communication between his witnesses. He feels that this can "contaminate" the testimony. He does however want the jurors to see a relationship between the witnesses.

> I expect that relationship to be something that gets translated through the lawyers and I generally say to my witnesses, "I don't want you to talk to each other about what you're testifying," because sometimes they get asked that on cross-examination, "Well, what did you say and what did he say," and that often ends up with, "Are you sure?" "I'm not sure."

Fred Bartlit so values spontaneity in his witnesses that he does not tamper with it if it is there from the beginning. If on a simulated direct, his witness falters, he will write out an answer. He may also write answers if the witness starts to wander. Bartlit concentrates on only a few critical points in any case, and each witness should give testimony aimed at the proof of one or more of these points.

> The most you ought to have are three overall points in a case. It's nice if you have one. So I want what the witness says to be clearly going down in support of one of these points. Second, I want the jury to hear a conversation where he does not have to do or say anything that would make them dislike him.

Bartlit tries to present the witness in the most flattering light as subtley as possible.

> If there's a resumé to be presented, I don't say, "Now did you make all A's in school?" [Instead] I put the resume up on the screen and I ask him about everything on there

except about making all A's. I let the jury see that for
themselves. "And I was a fighter pilot in Vietnam, one
hundred thirty missions." That's up there. They get to read
it.

David Boies reminds us of the dangers of ill-prepared witnesses.
They are unaware of their own documents, and inadvertently and
unnecessarily say things that are inconsistent with what is in the
documents. Because of this ignorance, the witness may be impeached,
caught in a lie, or unwittingly give proof to the other side. Another
problem is going out on a limb and having it sawed off from behind.
"Witnesses can take positions that are too extreme. The lawyer knows
they're not going...to hold, but just the fact that they take them may
damage their credibility." Yet another error is failing to target the
important points in a witness's testimony in pretrial preparation.

> Not framing either document discovery or interrogatories
> precisely enough to be able to target key points in a
> witness's testimony. They take a shotgun approach, and get
> buried in paper. And they never find the stuff that is really
> critical.

Jim Brosnahan makes a similar point. If a lawyer fails to build into
a witness's deposition important testimony, trouble can ensue. This
can occur from an earlier bout of "amnesia."

> Lawyers coach their witnesses in depositions not to know
> anything, to be dumb at the deposition: "If we ever need
> you in trial, we'll make you smart." That is counter-
> productive. Screws them up frequently. Because you can't
> make a lot with witnesses who didn't know a damn thing at
> their deposition: "I don't recall." So we never coach our
> witnesses to be dumb.

Another significant problem regarding a witness's deposition is
failing to ask all the important questions. One cannot be one hundred
percent sure that the witness will be available for trial, so it is a good
idea to get the important points of the witness's testimony on the
record as soon as possible. It helps, Brosnahan points out, to have
given the deposition considerable thought beforehand.

> Deposition takes place, lawyers have come from out of town
> to depose the witness. It's Friday and everybody wants to
> get home, and the last cross examiner finishes. Now, so

many lawyers will say, if it's your own witness, your own
client, but particularly your own witness, "I'll reserve my
questions until the time of trial." Supposition has been that
you'll always have that person available to you at the trial.
That's usually right, not always right, but usually right. But
it is also a result of laziness—the time of day. You haven't
quite figured out what you want the witness to say; you
don't want to spend the time to do stuff; you haven't exactly
thought out your defense—how you're going to twist it. So
you leave that to another day.

But at the time of the trial it might be advantageous to have some key
testimony from a witness, but risky to bring an unprepared witness
into court to weather a dangerous cross-examination. If the testimony
is not in a deposition there is no choice but to omit it or risk putting the
witness on the stand.

Jury Instructions

Instructions to the jury, as trial attorneys know, may be of critical
importance to the outcome of a trial. When jurors are told at the
beginning or the end of a trial that they must come up with particular
findings, that certain issues need to be decided on the basis of
particular criteria, the die has been cast. Judges tend to want
instructions that make the case easy to review on appeal; that is,
instructions that closely parallel those in previous cases. Attorneys
want instructions that highlight issues important to them particularly
in areas in which they have strong proof.

Most of the lawyers begin work on instructions as soon as they think
there is a chance of a trial. Instructions are given by the judge to the
jury. They cover the elements of proof required for each charge, the
legal definition of the charges, and other points the jurors need to be
aware of during their deliberations. The compilation of these instructions is a joint undertaking of the judge and the attorneys party to the
case. The lawyers in this study give varying degrees of importance to
the task. For a number of these men, the instructions can serve as a
framework within which they operate. For the most part, plaintiffs
prefer simple instructions. But that entails running the risk that the
whole case will be lost on a global basis, that the case will be decided
on the basis of one broad, general matter.

There seems to be a consensus among the lawyers that jurors have difficulty interpreting and understanding instructions, and that one way to build error into a case is to give the jury a number of abstruse instructions so that they will make a mistake in disposing of their charge. Thus the door will then be open later to appeal. Clearly, there can be a good deal of strategy connected with instructions. This can become so tedious that lawyers like Pat McCartan have an aversion to doing them, while Steve Susman is convinced that they are of no importance whatsoever. Tom Barr opines that since juries do have difficulty understanding instructions, and particularly from a plaintiff's standpoint, it is important that they not be told too much.

> My belief about instructions is that most juries don't understand . . . them. I am prepared to argue for every single instruction our way. I don't want the jury to be told something they shouldn't be told. A lot of lawyers are not careful about that, they take the best instruction they can get and therefore, they've built an error into the case that will ultimately lose the case.

As a defendant, Barr believes that one way to keep the door open for reversal on appeal is to give the jury numerous chances to stumble.

As a defendant's lawyer I want the jury to have more hurdles to jump. The chances that they will do something wrong are increased by asking more questions and for more special verdicts. The more questions I can get them to answer, the better off I am.

—Tom Barr

Since jurors have a problem interpreting instructions, Barr prepares a jury by giving them "when it's important, a necessary slant to the instructions." This can be done as early as voir dire, in the opening statement or in the closing statement. If, for example, when representing the plaintiff, a particular instruction involves the defendant's knowledge of the contents of a letter, Barr can review for the jury the specific ways in which this knowledge could have been illegally gained.

Fred Bartlit does not find instructions of equal importance from one case to another. When they are important, he will often return to them in his summation and indicate how the instructions are keyed to what needs to be proved, or in the same context, what the other side failed to prove.

> It's very case specific. There are cases where one instruc-
> tion makes an enormous difference. What I like to do is put
> that up on the screen in final argument, then write under it
> the things that show that instruction is not satisfied.

As a plaintiff's antitrust lawyer, Max Blecher has had abundant experience writing jury instructions for the kind of cases he takes into court. He wants findings in the typical areas that come up in antitrust cases, areas that are well-defined and generally understood. The defendants he faces, however, abhor the kind of clarity he seeks. They want a finding on virtually every fact at issue. The result is a process of tedious negotiation.

> The problem is that the other side, instead of using standard
> or pattern instructions, will write up their own version.
> They recite all the facts, "And if you find that and then you
> vote for this ... " So the enervation process sets in, and
> always during trial we try to negotiate out a set of
> instructions that both sides can live with.

Bob Warren notes that instructions have the power to influence the tone of the proceedings. In the worst-case scenario, the instructions sound like a litany of one side's sins and the other side's virtues. Warren hopes for at least a balanced tone in the instructions, so that the jury perceives that the contest begins from a position of parity.

> I often think that instructions are most important from a
> standpoint of tone. When the instructions are read, you
> don't want there to be a tone that sounds adverse to you. I
> think a lot about how these things are going to look when
> they are all put together and read at once. Are they going to
> sound like screed for the other side or is it going to have
> stuff in there that sounds balanced?

David Boies is not so sure that the jury pays close attention to the instructions. But instructions are the law, and it is important to have them securely on the record. Bob Fiske is one who entrenches the instructions in his case proof, beginning with the opening statement.

He argues that a lawyer must conform the proof at the trial and in his opening statement to what he expects to be in the instructions.

Pat McCartan is an admitted procrastinator when it comes to instructions, which he will delegate early in his preparation and then try not to think about again.

> There is a theory that the best way to prepare a case is to sit down and draft the jury instructions first, then prepare your proofs. I will get somebody started on it early. Dealing with jury instructions is a thing I don't personally enjoy.

Jim Brosnahan also puts the matter on the desk of an associate. He believes, however, that instructions need to be discussed by everybody, and that they establish the main three or four elements that make up the essence of the proof.

> In the first two or three days I will usually say to an associate, "Give me a set of instructions in a case like this," or more specifically, "This is a civil case, it is a patent case, and there are going to be four elements that have to be proved. I want to see the instructions on it."

Jim Neal agrees with Brosnahan and Fiske that the instructions can delineate the structure of proof.

> It's like the opening statement. There will be three or four instructions you've got to win on in your typical case. I focus on those in the very beginning. I tried this big case in Chicago. We were charged on thirty-five counts of inter-state travel in aid of racketeering, i.e., bribery of state officials in Chicago. We gave the state officials the money, no question about it. My only limited defense was that it was not bribery because my man didn't have the requisite intent to bribe. He was reacting to extortion and fear. Reasonable fear of losing everything he had.

Here, Neal needed to limit the charge to the jury because he perceived that he could only mount a defense if the instructions focused on a specific finding, the "requisite intent to bribe."

In this, as in many areas, Steve Susman goes his own way. He does not attribute much importance to instructions. Although he acknowledges that instructions will, in a sense, incorporate the idea to be proved. His approach to proof is so focused on developing a story that reference to the instructions for him is completely superfluous.

> I don't think it makes a hell of a lot of difference. I know
> generally, for example, this is a breach of contract case and
> a tortious interference with this, I know what I've got
> basically to prove. I know the elements of both sides. So I
> don't worry about the instructions that much. You've got to
> figure out what your story is going to be, but instructions
> are a totally different thing. They are very detailed and very
> immaterial in my opinion in most cases.

Despite his down-playing of instructions, Susman does make sure he
has the questions he wants in the charge to the jury.

> If I know that I can submit a punitive damage theory, I want
> to make sure that I am going to get a question on punitive
> damages. I like to be sure I'm going to get a question on A's
> negligence and B's negligence and not just A's, so I begin
> thinking about things like that.

That having been done, at the end of the day, it does not really matter
anyway.

> I've never been in a case where I thought the instructions
> made any Goddamn difference...just a waste of everyone's
> energy. Unfortunately, in trials, instructions are required to
> be submitted right before you get ready to argue the case.

Arthur Liman views instructions in a somewhat different light. It is
important to Liman to get certain matters pinned down, such as what
constitutes a reasonable defense or what is the requirement for
damages.

> I start thinking about instructions fairly early. Not in terms
> of writing them early, but I start thinking about them in
> terms of what am I going to be encountering because the
> judge has the last word. There are places where the judge
> gives the instructions, then the lawyers sum. But in most
> courts, it doesn't work that way and you can get killed with
> the instructions.

In this as in all else, Harry Reasoner takes a meticulous approach.
As a defendant, he looks closely at the plaintiff's theories to see what
the jury is likely to be told in the form of instructions so that he can
start to muster proof within this framework. The recent Kidder case is
an illustration.

For Kidder, we did our first draft of instructions shortly after we were hired. We took the plaintiff's theories and said how would you instruct the jury on each of these? Because you ought to be thinking always [about] what the jury is going to be asked and what they going to be told is relevant. So you think, what evidence do I have that fits? What can I say?

For these trial attorneys, instructions are organic and germane to their conceptualization of the case. Devising instructions involves relating them to the proofs and arguments and insuring that they exemplify and incorporate the principal elements of the case.

The Client in the Courtroom

I had a client one time with bad brain damage on the left side of his head talking about the absence of ability in his right hand. I did not know it, but I dropped a coin during the trial. He picked it up with his right hand. It happened to be a quarter. Thank God it wasn't a dime. And thank God he had trouble picking it up. But the jurors noticed it. They noticed left-side damage. They noticed he picked it up.

—Phil Corboy

There are times when it is a good idea to have a client or representative of the client in the courtroom. It can humanize a case and create sympathy. It can put a human face on a corporate presence. A plaintiff's lawyer in personal-injury case might want the client in the courtroom to garner sympathy, particularly if there are visible signs of the injury.

Sometimes a client who wants to sit in court day after day can be a problem. Phil Corboy has the client in court for only certain aspects of the trial, "maybe in the beginning to testify and certainly at the end for final argument." In personal-injury cases the client is frequently unable to be in court.

First of all, if my client happens to be horribly injured, he can't or she can't sit around this courtroom for two weeks. Or, if he can, he's not as badly injured as I said, or if he can, he may give the wrong impression to the jury somewhere along the line.

Corboy feels that clients can be overexposed with bad results. "To know is to dislike...I don't want that widow of mine sitting in that courtroom with her two kids for three weeks." Arthur Liman has a somewhat different point of view. He sees value in having the client in court. He thinks it might give him a chance to show the bond between him and the client, which can be effective with juries.

> It's important to convey the impression that I think this is a
> serious process and I have a serious role to play and that,
> while I'm not stuffy, I'm behaving with appropriate dignity.
> They ought to perceive that I like and sympathize with my
> clients.

Thus, Liman will sometimes have the client sit at the counsel table. He thinks this tends to "humanize" the client. Particularly where someone can play the role of "designated" corporate representative and if this person is a good witness it might have a very positive impact.

Personal Preparation

The final topic in this discussion of strategies connected with trial preparation concerns the personal routines and disciplines these men adopt as they go to trial. The remarks that follow often illustrate a regimen that is described in connection with the period of the trial itself. As the trial date approaches they cut themselves off from social engagements, other work, and interaction with colleagues who are not directly involved in the case. For Bob Fiske, intense absorption in the trial squeezes out leisure time. All other activities contract. "I read less in the paper, skim it...take shorter lunch hours, and see less of people."

Occasionally there is a trip out of town in the immediate pretrial period for a concentrated shot at formulating strategy. Phil Corboy leaves his office and works out of his Chicago condominium.

> I isolate and absorb. I ingest everything that I'm going to
> need for the trial. I just become part of that file and I keep
> away from other people. I divorce myself from the outside
> world for a minimum of two weeks ahead of time and get
> ready...

I've got an office where you sit down and shoot the shit in and all that, but I've got a room I really work in. Nobody goes in there but me or whomever I take. I'll never have more than one file in that room. It's the one I'm going to try next. I try to spend a couple or three hours every fucking day in there honing it, polishing, thinking. I like to do that. To me it is like creating a novel almost. Here I am. I can put this witness on to stick it on this son of a bitch over here. Or this one is weak, I'm going to move him back over here. I may not even use him. You've got to think about it. And it all goes back to what kind of personality are you dealing with, because jurors are human.

—Joe Jamail

Arthur Liman is flexible in choosing a place to work. He will work at home or in a conference room at the office but insists on seclusion and freedom from the telephone. He cuts himself off from all obligations two weeks prior to trial. Harry Reasoner withdraws into the world of the case much as the other lawyers do. He comments wryly that he "might lose his sanity" if he tried to go in and out of his concentration once the thing starts. "I do better if I regard the trial as kind of a closed world and don't get out. I mean my sanity might return if I took too long a break from it."

Fred Bartlit gives some interesting tips on how he spends a typical trial day:

I get up at about four AM and I'm at my desk by four forty-five and that's when I do the heavy work. At the end of the day, I go to the gym for an hour and a half. If necessary, I meet with the client to tell them where we are and what we're going to do the next day. I work generally by myself for a couple of hours. I try to get a good night's sleep. I try to get in bed by ten.

Although he is a very early riser, Bartlit doesn't believe in work jags. He will not stay up all night to prepare for trial. "I do a lot of reading on the physiological aspects of trial work and stress. There are studies that show the ones who went to bed will do better the next day than the ones who crammed all night."

Pat McCartan undertakes significant lifestyle changes as part of his preparation for the trial. He recognizes that heightened demands are going to be made upon his physical and mental resources. His approach is something like that of a boxer training for a fight.

> First I change my living pattern. I do not drink. I will stop drinking as far in advance of the trial as possible. I don't drink a lot anyhow, but I think you're sharper when you don't have alcohol in your system. So I will generally shut that down sometime in advance of the trial. I will also start exercising more regularly...It is important when I'm in trial that I do get regular exercise and lots of sleep. I am a firm believer that you get ready for trial before trial.

CHAPTER 6 ▊

Facing the Jury

> *Anybody who picks a jury by (their) occupation is*
> *looking for a f-----g heartbreak.*
>
> **—Joe Jamail**

W hen a trial lawyer enters the courtroom for the beginning of trial, and faces the jury panel for the first time, emphasis shifts from strategy to tactics. Tactics are the means employed after the battle has been joined. They are the tools and techniques used to carry out strategic objectives. It may be a strategic consideration to get certain kinds of people eliminated from a jury, say Republican white males, therefore, certain tactics will be employed in voir dire to achieve this objective. It may also be a strategic objective to present a particular theory of the case, or particular elements of proof in a persuasive fashion, beginning with voir dire and continuing into the opening statement. Tactics are the means for carrying out such a strategy.

Great trial lawyers are great tacticians. They seize the moment, which is what tactics are all about. They think on their feet and do whatever necessary to assert their client's interest and maintain an advantage once won. The ability to function in a demanding and open situation, in which surprises occur and the unpredictable is often an opportunity, is a quality these fourteen men possess. They are always aware of how they and their case appear to the jury—from the earliest moment of voir dire to the final rebuttal at the close of trial. The tactics discussed in this chapter concern the dynamic between lawyer and jury. These include tactics in voir dire, jury selection, the opening statement, and tactics generally employed when communicating with jurors.

Voir Dire

Voir dire [from Old French, *voir* true, truly; and *dire* to say], as all lawyers know is the questioning of prospective jurors to determine their fitness to serve. A potential juror is not allowed to sit if he or she has a bias against the parties involved. Challenges on grounds of bias or inability to abide by the juror's oath are known as "for cause" challenges, which might be exercised as often as necessary. A certain number of peremptory challenges are allowed in order to keep someone off the jury. And no reason has to be given for these. Besides the obvious and important purpose of voir dire, "picking" a jury, a smart attorney will use voir dire strategically to persuade and assess jury dynamics. Since voir dire is the only opportunity counsel has for dialogue with members of the jury, many use it to condition the jurors to their cause. Sometimes the communication is subtle, simply getting the jury to like the attorney, or, at the very least *not* dislike him. Voir dire is sometimes used to calculate jury dynamics. For example, one might identify the foreman or some other strong opinion leader. Another tactic in voir dire is inoculation. This is the presentation of potentially damaging elements in a manner which will neutralize their effect.

There is some debate whether persuading a jury during voir dire is wise. As we shall see, opinion is divided; and much depends upon who is doing the persuading. One thing is clear, the primary purpose of voir dire must be the de-selection of biased jurors, and this in itself is a formidable challenge for a trial attorney. Biased jurors often conceal their bias. Sometimes they want to be on the jury in order to carry out their own agenda. Bias will be less of a problem for a plaintiff seeking damages for the victims of a plane crash than for a corporate defendant in an antitrust suit. On the other hand, the defendant in the plane crash will have to try and eliminate jurors who will want to give "blue sky" damages to any injured plaintiff.

Selection, Persuasion, Inoculation

Each court has rules for the selection of a jury. The first rule of jury selection is to know these rules. Bob Warren has learned this lesson well.

> From trying cases in other jurisdictions, I have become
> very sensitive to the fact that just the mechanics of picking a

jury are very, very different in different places, and if you don't understand those rules and figure out how to use them, you're going to be very badly treated.

The most important task, according to Warren, is to get rid of the juror who is "really hopeless." Steve Susman agrees.

You don't select jurors, you obviously get rid of them. If it's a twelve-person jury and you get six strikes, four of them may be fairly clear and you may have two that you're concerned about. So you want to find out about these people and what their attitudes are going to be on certain issues of the case.

Tactical mastery of voir dire for Susman is understanding when "I'm not going to relate to that person, and that person's not going to relate to me." But often it is an iffy process.

I think that we have butchered the concept of voir dire sufficiently around here so lawyers don't use it right and probably I don't use it right. We need to re-think the whole concept. I've conducted so many voir dires where I've sat down and said, "Well, I sure gave them a good argument, but I don't know anything about them..."

Phil Corboy also sees voir dire as a process of getting rid of those jurors who do not "come with an open mind." The lawyer's job then, is to de-select the jurors he feels incapable of persuading.

I cannot expect to pick twelve good jurors because I have an opponent and he's got some competency. He is going to have the ability to get rid of the jurors he doesn't want. So I can't really pick. All I can do is get rid of those who are hurtful.

Lawyers tend to view voir dire as a chance to persuade. Early in his career, Jim Neal used voir dire in this way. Not so much any more.

The old fashion way to conduct a voir dire was to argue your case, asking closed-in questions so that in effect you presented an argument in the form of the question. The juror is going to say the right thing, yes or no. I have been persuaded by jury consultants that that is probably counter-productive. More and more you're not going to get away with it; you're probably not getting the information you need.

Neal has learned that jurors frequently conceal their position when confronted with direct questions. More subtle techniques are required to uncover bias.

Harry Reasoner is still convinced that persuasion *and* selection can be pursued in parallel, particularly in the state courts where voir dire is more liberal.

> First try to identify those people who would not make fair or desirable jurors from your perspective. Second, in the state court practice where you are given the leeway to do it, particularly if you're a defendant, [it is] a valuable way to show the jury your side of the case. Give them a clue as to what is going to be involved and try to make them understand your side of it as the plaintiff's case unfolds.

Voir dire is one way for the defendant to overcome the disadvantage of following the plaintiff. As a defendant Reasoner sees voir dire, as well as the cross-examination of the plaintiff's witnesses, as opportunities early in the trial to give the defendant's side of the story.

> I do believe that the principle of primacy is of great advantage, getting to tell your story first. In fact, as a defendant, I look for as many opportunities as possible to tell my side of the story through cross-examination of their witnesses.

Jim Neal believes jurors can be conditioned to like the messenger, thereby smoothing the way for the message. Sometimes, conditioning involves making jurors familiar with the most favorable aspects of one's case, as well as telling them what they should not be thinking about. Again, this might involve helping jurors interpret instructions, the charge to them to make certain findings. Jim Brosnahan feels this is worth doing if the judge permits it. Restrictions on this vary a great deal from court to court. Some judges permit a fairly loose and open voir dire. Others do not. Voir dire can be used to give a case a particular subjective coloration. For example, it might be important to prove that nothing of any great consequence is at stake in a particular trial. This could be conveyed by moving quickly through juror selection. There is the added benefit of avoiding juror boredom. "I never want them to be thinking, 'He's wasting our time. Why is he doing this?'" Brosnahan suggests.

Fred Bartlit gives an example of how he uses voir dire to give a juror a sense of importance, a sense that he or she has special knowledge or qualifications useful to the deliberations.

My approach is, "Let's see. You're a school librarian?"
"Yes." "As librarian, do you have anything to do with
numbers or budgets?" "Why, yes I do." "What library do
you work at?" "Well, I work for four different libraries."
You make them feel good about themselves. You make them
feel that you have picked them, not because you can fool
them, but because they have skills that you can use.

Bartlit also puts himself in a position to demonstrate solicitude toward
jurors, another persuasive device. This involves:

Knowing the name of the juror on the left and the juror on
the right so that if a witness gets in the way, you can say,
"Excuse me, your Honor, I don't think Mrs. Knox can
see." Ever seen that done before? No, not often, I'm sure
Corboy does it.

Bartlit is not above flattering jurors, using knowledge that he has
picked up in his travels to establish a sense of co-orientation.

But you have to know enough about the world, for example,
you have a guy who is running a machine forming aluminum turkey pans. How do you make him look good? I read
a lot, I know about the world. I say, "Well now, this machine
that forms these turkey pans, what kind of speed do they
operate at?" "Well, three hundred a minute." "My God,
that is really fast. The setup for that must really be
something." He knows what the setup is and I know. Others
don't.

For Arthur Liman, the first order of business is to find out what
kind of attitudes the jurors hold. "What's the sense of conditioning a
jury if the attitude is against you to begin with and it's inflexible?" As
long as attitudes relevant to the trial are uncovered, he is definitely
interested in connecting with the jurors, made easier through dialogue.

Second...I want to develop a rapport with the jury. This is
the only time that I can have a conversation with the jury;
otherwise, they are just listening to me. But here, I can have
a conversation. I can ask them a question. They can answer
it. I can come back and ask the next question. We can have a
dialogue. We can decide whether we like each other. And
maybe I can establish a little credibility with that jury. A
third thing, is, if done well, for me to start my themes for
my opening.

Liman relates a fascinating ploy once used by F. Lee Bailey to influence jurors *before* he entered the courtroom.

> Bailey once did a voir dire on television that wasn't a voir dire, but it was brilliant...there was a famous doctor who [had an affair]. The doctor had been convicted in the press...Bailey was starting his career, but he was well-known at his beginning as a superstar. He was on all the local television stations, which was unusual in those days, and they kept saying to him, "What are you looking for in a jury?" Bailey said, "There's only one thing I'm looking for. I want an intelligent jury." He kept saying that, "I'm going to strike people who aren't intelligent and I'm just keeping the people who are intelligent." So when he went and he picked his jury, every person he left on felt complimented... because they were intelligent. It was all bs. I mean, that wasn't what he was doing.
>
> **—Arthur Liman**

The jurors will also note how an attorney behaves during voir dire. Those who remain on the jury will reflect on who was challenged and why. Liman feels that overall, voir dire is one of the most important elements in the trial. "The way in which you use your strikes is important. You want your jury to feel that you respect them."

Turning to the question of reading jury dynamics during voir dire, Liman believes it is sometimes possible in a court with an open voir dire to pick out the foreman of the jury and to use that information in the course of the trial. This cannot be done however when question-naires are used to pick the jury. "Unless you can do a voir dire yourself, it's impossible. The average federal judge today wants to engage in a contest to see who can pick a jury the fastest." But Bob Fiske notes that in the federal court in New York, juror number one is the foreman. Therefore you might "challenge the person who is sitting in the number one seat because you don't want him as foreman even though you'd be perfectly willing to have [him] sitting in the number five seat." Here Bob Fiske is acting on the assumption that a jury foreman must have leadership qualities, tenacity, and the ability to persuade others. We know from juror research that this is not necessarily the case. The foreman might be someone who is meek and mild, someone who plays a retiring role in the deliberations, but merely attends to certain housekeeping chores. The foreman need not be, and is not necessarily, an opinion leader on a jury.

> When I walk in that courtroom and they bring that jury panel in, I'm looking at them. And I'm seeing every move they make without them knowing that I'm staring. Every move they make. How they are dressed. How they line up, who pairs up. Strangers will pair up, kind of like birds, they really will. The walk from the jury assembly room to the courtroom makes new friends or acquaintances... It's kind of like in the Marine Corps. "I sure hope I get to be in the same tent with Sam." "I hope you get on this jury with me."
>
> **—Joe Jamail**

Jamail often eliminates one of two jurors who pair up in order to get two clearly independent jurors, instead of two minds thinking like one.

On the other hand, Harry Reasoner notes that at times trying to figure out how a jury will behave, or specific jurors behave, is an idle exercise.

> One of the most instructive exercises I had was in this *Dallas Morning News* case. The jury was out seven days. We were all speculating endlessly. My now partner, Bill Simms from Dallas, Jim Kronzer, John Hill, both of whom have been at the game for decades, eminent trial lawyers who have seen many juries, Wayne Fisher who is a great plaintiff's trial lawyer here, Frank Jones from Fulbright and Fellow of the American College, we were all guessing. We all had it totally wrong. The guy that we thought was our strong advocate, was really the one who was hanging in for the plaintiff. The guy we were worried about, thought was on their side, a young Chicano, flashy dresser, was strong for the defendants. Wound up ten to two. This black fellow

> who wore all this gold, looked like a drug dealer, and a
> Hispanic bank clerk, probably in her sixties, a diminutive
> looking little woman, she was adamant, never moved. But,
> we all mis-guessed it.

David Boies gives consideration to the subject of juror interaction
and dynamics, but like Reasoner, realizes the futility of relying on
something so problematic. One defense tactic that he employs is to
make sure there is an opposite pair of jurors on the jury to increase the
chances of a holdout for the defendant if all goes wrong and the verdict
is strongly pro-plaintiff. This only can be useful where the plaintiff
must have a unanimous verdict.

> I don't put a lot of weight on [predicting jury behavior]
> because I think it's so chancy. The one extent that I do, is if
> I'm in a defendant's mode [and I want to] guarantee a hung
> jury, I'll try to get two or more strong opposites on that jury
> in the hope that they will clash. That's about as far as I take it.

Virtually all trial attorneys agree that probably the most powerful
and useful persuasive tactic in voir dire is that of inoculation. After
eliminating bad jurors Steve Susman tries to take the sting out of a
potential bite. Sexual misconduct by a client or witness, a secret tape
recording, someone's drinking problem are examples of "the kinds of
things the judge has refused to allow you to *limine* out, so they are
coming in." Such elements can be broached and neutralized in voir
dire. Supposed clashes of regional style and values can also be
ventilated, and jurors can be bonded, so to speak, to the proposition
that they will not allow these differences to color their verdict.

> The fact that you're Texans and you're in trial in California,
> or that your clients are Japanese on trial in Houston. Those
> kinds of things, seems to me, are very effectively dealt with
> during voir dire. Talking to people, telling them, "This is
> going to happen during this case. I need to know how this is
> going to affect you?"

In order to use the tactic of inoculation in voir dire, the lawyer cannot
be afraid of the answers that might be forthcoming. Susman admits he
used to be afraid when introducing negative elements of his case into
voir dire.

> I really wasn't sure how to handle them. Scared that
> suppose the person says, "I mean, yeah, if he tape recorded

a conversation, that's fucking illegal and immoral. I don't like that one goddamn bit." So, you are worried about asking the question, "What do you think about someone who tape records conversations?" But you want to find out.

Pat McCartan, from the perspective of a corporate defendant, gives a classic example of inoculation. When representing his client, General Motors, in a product liability case, he expected the jurors to be so impressed with GM's deep pockets that awards would be astronomical no matter what the circumstances of the case. On voir dire examination, he told the jury how large, successful, and wealthy General Motors is. He emphasized that it was important for the sake of justice that a corporation get a fair trial just like an individual. Was GM's wealth going to influence them in deciding this case? He again raised this in connection with the burden of proof. "Are you going to hold this injured plaintiff who needs compensation desperately, who's going to be in pain for the rest of his life, to the burden of proof against a large corporation who can afford to pay him anything he wants?" McCartan recalls what happened on one occasion when he was using this tactic:

> I was going through this drill on the voir dire examination. I was on about juror number six or seven or eight and . . . one juror whom I had questioned earlier stands up, blurts out, "I can't do it." And the judge looks at him, and I looked at him and said, "Mr. Vinson, what's the matter? What can't you do?" "I can't be fair to a corporation like that in a situation like this."

McCartan used this piece of gratuitous good fortune to score points with the jury.

> It was the most riveting moment you can imagine. And I walked over and the judge was ready to excuse him and I said, "Excuse me, just a moment, Your Honor, please." I walked over and I said, "Mr. Vinson, I want to thank you for being so candid and forthright with us here today. This obviously is very important to this plaintiff." I said, "Your Honor I ask that he be excused." I thought I'd won the case, no matter what happened. There was no way anyone on that jury was going to say anything in the jury room about our ability to pay. We did win the case.

Juror Selection in Federal Court

It is interesting to note that the absence or limitations of lawyer-conducted voir dire in federal court were not strongly reflected in the lawyer's discussion of jurisdiction (see Chapter 3), in which a majority demonstrated a preference for federal courts over state courts, or at least an indifference between the two. At any rate, juror selection in federal courts with its limited voir dire poses special problems. Not only are there generally few opportunities to begin presenting the case in a persuasive manner, there are often limits to how effective an attorney can be in jury selection. Pat McCartan notes that attorneys are somewhat at the mercy of the judge.

> The terrible thing about jury trials in federal court anymore is that these judges conduct the voir dire. It's very cut and dried and routine. A judge will ask the question, "Will you give a corporation a fair trial?" Who's going to say no? Unless you have the jury service that you folks [the author and his colleagues] provide, you're going on stereotypes, hunches, and impressions. I always have an uneasy feeling at the conclusion of jury selection in federal court that I really don't know the jury, and I don't like that.

David Boies adds the point that there is no opportunity in federal court to establish a rapport with the jury. "You want to try to make friends with the jury, get to know them, understand them, test them, begin the process of persuasion. In federal court...if you try it, you'll probably get what limited chance there is to voir dire the jury cut off by the judge."

Voir dire has become such a lost art in federal court that on occasion when it is allowed the attorneys may not know how to conduct it. Arthur Liman encountered such a situation in a recent trial.

> Voir dire is disappearing more and more. In federal courts it has been gone for a long time. They've had experiments of re-introducing it. I found it interesting that when they had an experiment in the Southern District and I got up to do a voir dire, the lawyer on the other side didn't know how to voir dire a jury and so I used the voir dire and he didn't.

Who Makes a Good Juror?

I'll tell you the people who do the job, case in and case out, are those guys on the factory floor. They call a spade a spade. They have a different relationship with their employer. They bargain with the employer. They don't sit in silent resentment like many others do. They bring a different perspective and more importantly, they know where it's at. They know where the truth is and where it isn't. They've heard more lies in their lifetime than a lot of people. And they're going to call them lies. Truck drivers, lathe operators, crane operators, people like that. You've got to be careful with the executive types, certain level of executive personnel who want to be one of the boys, who don't want to go into the jury room and side with the defendant corporation.

—Pat McCartan

Among trial lawyers, there are considerable stereotypes about jurors. Every attorney has some idea about what kind of jurors are good for what kind of case. They know the right jury for any trial is case specific, but they cannot resist holding onto certain fixed notions. They obviously base these notions upon their vast experience. Pat McCartan, who often works for large corporate defendants such as General Motors, has some definite ideas about jurors he does not like.

I don't like bookkeepers. I don't like middle-management white-collar types. I don't like people who work for utilities. These people, I have found, over time, have a lot of frustration with their employer and their employment situation. So as irrational as it may seem, I generally will move them out. During the sixties and seventies, I was very leery of the flower children, even in their mature years, with long hair and what-have-you because there was a rebellious-type attitude there.

Steve Susman feels that he is more persuasive with men than with women. And since he admits that juror evaluation is not his long suit, he does well to rely upon consultants.

255

> I've made mistakes, put the wrong people on the jury. In this one case, what really got me in trouble, was that my opponent lives in River Oaks. A woman who was a librarian at a private school in River Oaks, I let her stay on the jury. I wasn't concerned enough. It turned out that she identified with this guy, although he didn't have anything to do with that school. He lives in River Oaks, a big home, big name in Houston. She just loved him.

Jim Brosnahan adamantly adheres to the position that every case is different and will require a new analysis of the jurors, even if some of the themes are familiar. On the defense side he usually does not want retirees, or divorced or unhappy people. In some cases, political party affiliation is important; in others, inconsequential. "Male/female differences—sometimes they're crucial, sometimes they're meaningless."

Jim Neal does not put much stock in stereotypes about who constitutes a good juror for a given type of case. However, he notes that when he was a prosecutor in Tennessee, he wanted Du Pont employees because they were steady hard-working family people who stayed with the company for over thirty years, "that kind of salt of the earth, blue-collar worker." But in terms of picking a jury based on ethnic origin, that is strictly case specific. In fact, for both the defendant and the plaintiff, every aspect of juror character and attitude must be assessed in the specific context of a given trial. Ethnic factors can be important, but they may not be, and if they are they will cut differently each time.

Joe Jamail denounces the idea of picking a jury by occupation, and makes it clear that he follows no rules for juror selection.

> Anybody who picks a jury by occupation is looking for a fucking heartbreak. For instance, some housewife that lives in a small house in the suburbs who has a one hundred dollar a week allowance, how is she going to think in terms of millions of dollars for somebody hurt? Now, that's a selling job...A banker dealing with millions of bucks is more likely to do it if you can convince him. He may be harder to convince of the injury. But what purpose is it in winning the goddamn battle and losing the war? Yeah, I found negligence, proximate cause, and they gave me eight bucks. Bullshit.

Max Blecher, stating his views of appropriate juror types, roundly denounces one common stereotype, that antitrust plaintiffs want minorities and the underprivileged on juries. He says that people who believe this

> ...are absolutely wrong. I know they think that we want minorities and the underprivileged class who will think about the case in a class sense. The little guy, the David against the Goliath. It might have been true before antitrust got complicated and before we injected the economists and the econometric studies, and the notions of below-cost pricing, and the whole host of complexities that have come with the development of antitrust law. Maybe it was true twenty-five or thirty years ago. They grew up thinking that because their mentors told them that. But I don't look for that at all today.

Blecher prefers jurors who can assimilate complex information.

> I like people with college degrees, if possible. I'd rather have somebody who works for General Motors or IBM than, for example, a government worker who is removed from the processes of business life. [A] person in a business environment understands some of the things we are talking about. "They did this vicious thing. They lowered the price and my client's sales dropped and that's the beginning and end of the story." But today, you've got to figure out was it above cost or below cost? Is it an average variable? What's an average variable? You're talking Greek to people.

Arthur Liman basically believes that whether or not a juror is acceptable depends on the case. However, there is one occupational group he definitely does not want on a jury: "Lawyers, because there is too much of a risk that they are going to engage in a game of matching wits with you."

Bob Fiske, like many of his colleagues, likes to find questions that will be good predictors of how jurors will view a case. Sometimes it is really a matter of making sure that jurors have adequate relevant life experience to understand the position the plaintiff or defendant is in.

> In this case we just tried, one of the important questions for us was, "Do you own a house? Did you buy it? Did you use a lawyer when you bought it? Did you get it appraised? Was there an appraisal on the house? Did you ever see the

> appraisal? Did you ask for the appraisal?" All of the things
> that were going to come up through the testimony of the
> purchasers that the government was going to call. We
> wanted to find out as much as possible what the juror's
> actual experience in a similar situation [was] to that of the
> witnesses that we were going to call.

Beyond this kind of highly focused juror selection, Fiske advocates
trying to line up general attitudes with verdict preferences.

> Depending on the case, you want to find out as much as you
> can about their general attitudes: are they conservative, are
> they social liberals, what is their economic condition, those
> kinds of things. Beyond that, it is more subtle. I mean they
> might not have a "bias," but they have attitudes towards
> things which may even turn out to be subconscious.

What kind of juror does Joe Jamail like? "Honest to God. I've got to
look at them, I've got to smell them, taste them, touch them, feel
them."

Questionnaires

An important method for dealing with a limited voir dire is the use
of questionnaires. Such questionnaires are case specific and are
usually composed by jury research specialists. They are based on
pretrial research into global issues and juror attitudes and beliefs.
They can offer an opportunity to obtain sensitive or potentially
embarrassing information from jurors. Questionnaires can help detect
juror bias obliquely, thus making it more difficult for jurors to conceal
how they really think about the parties or issues in a particular matter.
Most of these attorneys use questionnaires whenever the opportunity is
made available by the court. The advantage to questionnaires, according to Jim Neal, is that "you get more candor and you get more
answers than a judge is going to let you get in voir dire." Arthur
Liman is less sanguine. He feels that questionnaires leave him in a
position of having to exercise his strikes without really knowing very
much about the jurors.

> If they haven't filled out something that says that they read
> all about the case or that they formed an opinion, then the
> questions that the judge puts tend to be superficial. Unless
> the juror confesses prejudice, the next thing you're there

having to exercise your strikes and you know very little about those jurors.

Harry Reasoner believes that anything is better than nothing when it comes to basing juror evaluation on the available information. He tries to get judges to use questionnaires, and he will at times solicit the help of juror psychologists. But he feels the necessity to devote voir dire to "eliminating the obvious problems and wind up with a group who will give you a reasonably fair shake." David Boies also feels that questionnaires are valuable, in that they are the only way to refine the operation of voir dire in a federal court.

What you're primarily trying to do is to figure out what predilections exist that may not be obvious, and if you've got a questionnaire that the jury has already filled out, depending on the extensiveness of that questionnaire, you may be able to use voir dire to focus in on a few jurors and a few issues and it can be pretty effective. Without a questionnaire, voir dire in federal court is a pretty blunt instrument.

—David Boies

Joe Jamail agrees that questionnaires can be useful. He uses questionnaires even in a voir dire in which he has an opportunity to question the panel. He collects basic background that he does not want to get verbally. He can then use his standup voir dire to confront the jurors, almost as if he is cross-examining them.

They help both sides. It helps me mostly because it gives me all that mundane information that I don't have to stand there and do. I can hard impact my standup. With the right questionnaire, I can voir dire any jury that I know right now in about an hour and a half except in the most complicated of cases. I write out what I think is a fair, reasonable voir dire and I've never had a federal judge refuse to give it.

Max Blecher has definite opinions about questionnaires. He finds them harmful to the plaintiff. He believes that they frequently screen out the best jurors by getting too much information, particularly information that will provide a juror with a reason to be excused. The question, "How long can you devote to this case?" eliminates those with responsible jobs who might not be able to sit for a substantial period of time.

> So you lose that cream element you can really appeal to, who can understand a more complicated case. I am not a big fan of the jury-screening techniques because I think it distorts the process and, in the long run, is going to contribute to this idea that we should do away with the jury system.

However, Blecher allows that what he calls the Exeter-Williams-Brown crowd need to use questionnaires because they do not know how to evaluate jurors and could not possibly understand how a group of eight, ten, or twelve people from ordinary life think.

Opening Statements

Opening statements are probably the most compelling aspects of a trial. It is the occasion in which an attorney may address the jury directly to tell them what the case is about and what he intends to prove. In situations where the judge conducts the voir dire or the lawyer has only limited input in jury selection, the opening is the first real opportunity to establish a relationship with the jury. Opening statement is the first time he or she can build rapport and establish credibility. Although statements are not supposed to be argumentative, most judges permit a certain amount of subjective rhetoric, but will admonish those who go "beyond the pale."

First, you want to put in everything you need; second, you don't want to put in a lot of extraneous stuff that distracts, and third, you don't put in stuff that you can't sustain.

—David Boies

Current research indicates that jurors make up their minds early in the trial. This has been a rather bitter pill for many lawyers to swallow. They bridle at the implication that other elements of the trial, after voir dire and the opening statement, do not carry the same strategic weight. Other elements of the trial, however, are obviously important. The point is, that in many cases jurors develop a strong predisposition or verdict preference early on, and other things being equal, they will stick to that position until the final vote. Of course, it is always possible to lose a case that has been won. In addition to recognizing the importance of the opening statement, the majority of these lawyers believe what jury research has aptly demonstrated that relatively short openings tend to be more effective than long ones.

Max Blecher adheres to both doctrines that the opening is terribly important and that it should not be overly long. It is also important not to be timid or to engage in general platitudes. It was once believed unwise to discharge all the fireworks in a case at the beginning leaving nothing for later. Blecher notes that certain aspects of certain cases need to be explained and put on the table early. The opening statement is an important opportunity to teach the jurors about the relevant subject.

> You have to explain the industry. There are industries out there that I've never heard of. You've got to explain what the process is and you have to explain what a monopoly is. And in explaining that you have to explain why there is an antitrust law and why monopolies are bad. They know why dogs shouldn't bite the mailman in the ass and they know why you shouldn't go through a red light. They don't know what a monopoly is and they don't know why it's bad.
>
> **—Max Blecher**

Blecher argues that the opening statement is critical, and enough time must be taken to enable the jurors to understand the context of the case. Background must be filled in, and for this purpose, he suggests, that they "be shown a lot of pictures and charts." And Bob Fiske points out that, "You only get to talk to the jurors twice. In the summation you're going to be giving it everything you have. So to do anything less than that the first time, is a mistake."

Fred Bartlit recalls a bygone era when an opening statement was based on a recitation of the issues. No more. That would bore a jury to tears.

> If I say to you, "There are seven important issues in this case. The first issue is whether the stock issue on June 1973 by Mr. Jones was properly registered." You've already forgotten it.

Instead, the opening statement should tell a story.

> "The story begins three years ago today. Four men were sitting around a table. One of them is there. One of them is there. The other two wouldn't come to testify. They were discussing a new share of stock. The ownership of the company was at stake." You don't tell them what to decide. If you're really, really good at it, you tell a factual story. And as they hear the story, conclusions emerge in their minds. The story I tell is my road map for trial. Everything I tell them in the story I will prove. I don't say I'm going to make promises, I just do it.

Bartlit makes the interesting point that not a lot of passion or strong feeling is appropriate in the opening. Intense feeling can only come when the jury feels you've "earned the right" to be passionate. Harry Reasoner agrees that it is not a good idea to be too heated in the opening. Other common mistakes are including too much detail, slipping into legal jargon or bombastic oratory, making arguments that nobody could possibly understand at the beginning of the case, and orating at, rather than talking to, the jury. Further, the attorney should play the role jurors think he ought to play. This, and making the salient points about the case, are the most important objectives of the opening in Reasoner's view.

> My hope is that the jury, from the tone and the way I conduct myself in the opening statement, will come away with the impression that I'm a person [who is] credible, somebody who is playing an appropriate role in the process, treating them with respect, somebody whom they feel they should listen to in trying to sort out the truth of the matter.

Bob Fiske, understanding that jurors make up their minds early, feels that the opening and closing statements should thematically bracket the case. Granted the judge may not allow the same degree of argumentation, but within that limit, Fiske believes the same powerful arguments should be presented on both occasions.

Jurors tend to make up their minds early in the case. So, in my mind, the opening statement, within the limits that the judge allows, ought to be as close to the summation as it can be. In other words, there is no reason to hold anything back. You should take your best shot; subject only to this obvious point; that you don't want to overstate it and leave yourself vulnerable to the other side coming back in summation saying, "He said he'd do this and he didn't," kind of thing.

—Bob Fiske

Getting too passionate can lead to a kind of advocacy that is not credible, and there is the further problem of promising more than can be delivered. There are not many cases in which one side will totally dominate another. Lawyers are so adept at countering each other's moves that a jury will rarely find a trial a convincing demonstration of a lawyer's claim that he is going to demolish the opponent. That is almost never what happens in a trial, and it is not credible to pretend that it will.

Joe Jamail is not sure that jurors wait until opening statements to make up their mind. He feels that many of them have committed to his side during voir dire—at least, his opponents have made that claim. Jamail takes the occasion of voir dire to use more persuasive and emotional tactics than he does in the opening statement. Openings for him tend to be brief and factual.

I've been accused of committing people on voir dire and the case is over when Joe is through voir diring them. When J.J. does that shit, you go home. I don't believe that. I have done all I need to do by way of opening statement in my voir dire. But in opening statement, I stay extremely factual. A lot of friends have said that Joe uses a voir dire like an opening statement and an opening statement like a voir dire. But it isn't quite true.

Voir dire is the time to throw down the gauntlet. It is during voir dire that Jamail asks the jury if they will accept certain proofs and "have the courage" to make certain decisions. By drawing a line in voir dire, which says "you are either with me or against me," Jamail has focused attention upon himself as a leader and a moral force. This is a difficult tactic for other lawyers to overcome. It is also a very difficult tactic to pull off, and few can do it.

> I am more emotional on the voir dire than I am on the opening statement. "It's now hurting time, folks. You either have the courage to put the money down on these bastards that hurt this person, or I made a mistake. This is what the proof is going to be. You told me you were big enough to do it, now let's see."

Jim Brosnahan emphasizes the importance of the opening statement. "Absolutely crucial. So important it's kind of scary. You've got to get off on the right foot and they've got to understand the basic issues, your side of it." Brosnahan sees problems in the opening when counsel promises more than it should. Burdens are shouldered unnecessarily when an attorney undertakes to prove something that he does not have to. "They will use words that can be quoted later against them. That's a strong rhetorical point, 'My adversary said this and I quote...and now you've seen the evidence and it's this.'" Overaggression (a problem throughout a trial) and being "too warm too fast" with the jury are other mistakes made in opening.

Brosnahan makes notes for his opening but never reads from a written text. None of these men read from a text during the opening statement. There will be enough of that, too much in fact, when they are introducing documents and depositions later. Brosnahan wants to be conversational, somewhat familiar in the opening, perhaps even understated.

> I did get a jury, a couple of them, to cry at the end of one opening statement, which I thought was very good for us. We were the plaintiff and we were seeking insurance proceeds for a widower whose wife had died and the insurance company was claiming she committed suicide, but it was an accident. So I described this young lady, a young socialite in San Francisco [who] died in her sleep. A couple of them cried...The husband was right there. So the opportunities are very real for opening statement.

Brosnahan believes in testing opening statements. A mock trial is a good place to debut an opening statement, to test lines of attack, to see what works. It is also an opportunity to determine how strong certain issues are and at what point to "surface" them. "You're not going to put it all in the opening statement. Some of it you're going to let develop."

Pat McCartan talks about setting up "flags" in the opening. These are the themes the jury is to watch for. At closing he will note how he has touched all the flags he has set out, while the opponent has not fulfilled his opening statement promises. Promising too much and attacking too early are typical mistakes. If the case is going to turn on who is telling the truth it is important not to impugn the opponent's veracity too early, before proof has been presented.

Steve Susman will be as aggressive as he can without being so argumentive that the judge intervenes. He tries to get in as much as possible without overstatement. "There is no question how successful I am depends on how much the judge will give me. I try, very carefully, not to overstate anything. I think that is death." Susman sometimes feels at a disadvantage in giving his opening because he often comes to the case late. He is frequently engaged only when it has become clear after a protracted period of litigation and negotiation that a case is going to trial, and that a real trial attorney must be given command. In such instances, he learns as the trial proceeds details that would have been effective when he delivered his opening statement. But sometimes *not* knowing can be an advantage, it keeps him from getting bogged down.

During opening, Arthur Liman emphasizes the importance of repeating the central theme; another is inoculating the jury from becoming "ill" over some highly negative piece of information. "And, I want the jury to have some confidence in me that I'm not there as an orator. I don't want a Fourth of July speech because those don't work anymore."

According to David Boies, as plaintiff, the two most important rules in opening statement are simply to tell the jury the case; and second, do so clearly. "There is no excuse for not having an absolutely dynamite plaintiff's opening statement." And if done correctly, he maintains, the jury could decide then and there for his client.

An opening has a special significance for the defendant. To Bob Warren's thinking, defense will not have another opportunity to present the case for a long time. The only exception to this will be the chances on cross-examination. But these are limited opportunities at best.

> The defendant is going to have to be there for a very long
> time having to endure witnesses in whatever order the
> plaintiff cares to put them forward, and not be able to do
> anything but knick knack points with cross-examination,
> unless the plaintiff makes an error in terms of who they put
> on the stand.

Warren got a break in the Ramada case when the plaintiff put on a
knowledgeable witness. Warren cross-examined him for six days.
Barring such unforeseen good luck, in the opening statement "the
defense had better offer a pretty compelling view of the essence of the
defense because it's going to be much too late otherwise."

In this, as in so many of the aspects of the trial, Phil Corboy
approaches the opening statement with the elegance of a Zen master.

> Tell a story. That's all I do. I no longer use: "I want you to
> assume," "the evidence will show" because it might not. I
> also don't flatter the other lawyer—they might think I
> mean it. I try not to be too long. A mistake I've made is to
> be too long. I try to tell a story. "On July 19th, nineteen
> hundred and eighty-nine, Flight Two-Thirty-Two left Sioux
> City, Iowa with Boston its destination. It was destined to
> stop in Chicago, Illinois. It never got there. Over Sioux
> City, Iowa, the plane fell out of the sky." That's going to be
> my story.

The lawyers have all gotten religion on the length of the opening
statement. The preponderance of evidence from our jury research
studies is that "less is more." The juror quotient for boredom is high,
their attention span less than most people suppose. The days when an
attorney spent a whole trial day or more on an opening statement are
buried in the dust bin of litigation antiquity. When asked how long the
opening statements should be, the fourteen were surprisingly precise.
Harry Reasoner likes to make his opening statements even shorter
than they are.

> I'm generally of the school that few are saved after twenty
> minutes. If the judge will give you thirty, the judge gives
> you an hour, I don't have enough discipline not to use more
> than twenty minutes. But I have become a great believer in
> visual aids and I try never to talk for more than a few
> minutes without giving the jury something to look at.

Phil Corboy might go as long as an hour on opening. Judges, he notes, rarely limit time on an opening, but will do so on summation. If this is the case, he incorporates closing arguments into his opening. "I use catch words in my opening statement. 'A plane fell out of the sky. Forty-four minutes of terror. Forty-four minutes of knowing he was going to die.'"

As a plaintiff, David Boies is aware of the impact of the opening to the defendant. With this in mind, he will seek an agreement to impose limits on the opening statement.

> If I can get a defendant to agree that we'll have half-hour statements, that's what I'll do. If I can convince a defendant to have ten-minute opening statements, that's what I'll do. Although an opening statement is critical for the plaintiff, I can give my opening statement with my first witness. I'll select my witness so that my witness gives my opening statement for me and does it, maybe, in a little question-answer forum.

Unless the plaintiff gets careless and offers the defense a witness susceptible to open-ended cross-examination, the defendant will not get such an opportunity.

> He won't ever get a chance to because two months later the jury will be so educated, in my way, that he'll never be able to undo that. As a plaintiff, I will take as little time as I can convince the defendant to take because I think he needs the time more than I do.

Conversely, when Boies is the defendant, he will go for a longer opening, because it might be his last chance to present his case for a long while.

> I will err on the side of having longer opening statements than shorter opening statements. The jury will tend to get a little bored but no more bored than listening to witnesses basically. You can liven it up with exhibits and films and clips.

Fred Bartlit strives for economy, the elimination of the inessential. He suggests opening statements should be, "Forty minutes, max, usually thirty." Bob Fiske thinks it is hard to keep the jury's attention span if it goes longer than forty-five minutes. The unfamiliarity of the material makes special demands upon jurors. They might be able to absorb more in summation after they know what the case is about and do not need to work quite as hard to process information. Joe Jamail wastes no words, "No longer than about fifteen fucking minutes. Depending on the case. I did Pennzoil in twenty minutes." But like God, when he created the universe and all that was in it, Jamail spent seven days on voir dire.

However, Jim Brosnahan thinks there are occasions when one might go up to two hours, two and a half in a complicated case. He says that opening statements should be "as long as necessary. I don't think there is any limit." For Pat McCartan it will vary with the case. "As we know, there have been all-day opening statements. I personally like to stay around an hour or forty-five minutes." The optimal length for an opening statement, according to Jim Neal, is about thirty to forty minutes, although he has presented openings up to three hours because the case was complicated. "But boy, when you get beyond an hour in an opening statement, you're risking being counter-productive." Warren's rule of thumb is forty-five minutes, but that can vary. "You run a risk at longer than forty-five minutes to an hour." Arthur Liman believes that openings over forty-five minutes tax the patience of the jury. He suggests that even in complicated cases an opening of fifteen or twenty minutes may be enough.

Attorney and Jury Dynamics

> Don't let anybody ever tell you that a lawyer is not a big, big part of a jury verdict. It's bullshit. If that wasn't so, I wouldn't be here.
>
> **—Joe Jamail**

Attorney/jury dynamics is basically a matter of credibility—which lawyer is to be believed. This is a subtle and often elusive aspect of any trial. In case after case, credibility is seen to be closely linked to how well the communicator is liked. In the view of social psychologists, this is necessary, but not a sufficient component of credibility. It is also important to display expertise, factual command and knowledge of the subject. We tend to believe someone we like, and we may distrust someone who is unlikable. Attorneys understand these dynamics well, and have interesting views on the matter of being liked by the jury.

Is It Important for the Attorney to be Liked?

Tom Barr does not think it is absolutely essential for jurors to like an attorney in order to believe him. He suggests that most jurors can rise above a simple subjective gut reaction to a lawyer and decide to trust or not to trust an attorney based on other factors. "I think most people have enough decency and integrity within them that when they're told they have to act like honest forthright people, they will try to do that." Max Blecher is one who argues that it is important that jurors not dislike you. He does not want the jurors to have to overcome any personality obstacle in choosing his side. He wants jurors to be at least neutral.

Being liked as a prosecutor was not essential in order to be effective with jurors according to Bob Fiske. On the other hand, as a defendant, it is important to be likable.

> When I was prosecutor...I was a dedicated public servant on the side of justice and truth and all of that. For a defense lawyer, it is very important that you're a friend and nice guy. In a criminal case, I think it is much more important for the defense lawyer to be liked than the prosecutor. In a civil case where things are more equal on both sides, generally speaking, I'd rather be liked than be aloof.

According to Pat McCartan, credibility is only a "short step" away from being liked. "You're the one telling them what the case is all about and why it should be decided in favor of your client, and if you don't have credibility with the jury it isn't going to work." For Harry Reasoner the importance of being liked is not always the same from one case to another.

> If you have a case with a quadriplegic and the judge lets it go to the jury, it's hard to lose. It's a question of how big you win. Representing a corporation, my suspicion is that it matters a lot more whether the jury comes to like you or dislike you.

Bob Warren knows that even though jurors might like you, it is no guarantee you will win the case. And Fred Bartlit thinks clarity is more important than being liked.

> Most lawyers think that liking is a big thing, but I've seen too many cases where a guy was a complete asshole, who was boring, and ran on and on and on, but he had a good

story and the jury went with it. I've seen it happen too many times. Clarity, understanding. Those things are more important than being liked.

But Phil Corboy would argue being liked is even better than being right. "Of course the jury's got to like you. We're not talking about the fairness or the unfairness but that's a fact. Of course they do. They may not know it, but they do."

Talking to the Jury

I don't use highway, I use street. I'm not in a motor vehicle, I'm in a car. I'm not a plaintiff, I've got a name, although the defendant's a defendant.

—Phil Corboy

Corboy advocates a natural, spontaneous style of communication and believes in using his skill in communication to gain feedback from the jurors and to address problems he detects.

I'm quite a believer in eye contact with the jury. During opening statement and summation you look at each one in turn and you get a sense of, by doing that, who is getting it and who isn't. You can tell who is relating to you and if there are people who aren't, then you try to deal with that situation by talking more directly to them.

In order to use such tactics, Corboy studies the jury intently.

I watch jurors. I take important things down. By the way, in our jurisdiction, jurors can take notes. So I watch to see what they're taking notes about or to see if the note-taking dies out. Note-taking is a spirited activity at the beginning.

Since the jurors quickly become disillusioned with note-taking, Corboy watches to see if later they take notes at key points in his case. Also, he never drinks water in front of a jury. "They can't drink it. I say put it on the defense counsel's table to drink. Give them all the water they want." And, he says adamantly, you must play straight with the jury and respect their intelligence.

I never tell the jury I'm going to ask some questions which are not personal, then ask them what their middle name is.

270

If I am going to ask them personal questions, I tell them I'm going to ask personal questions. I never try to get away with something in front of the jury. You've got to be very, very careful that you don't insult their intelligence.

Jim Brosnahan suggests that the mood communicated to the jurors is important. Then he likes to use language rich in visual imagery.

I'm a believer in moods, not just when you're speaking, but in everything else, too. It's how you look, and how you're responding, and how you're acting. Try to look relaxed, confident, polite. Then, in terms of communication, you need word pictures. It's just like art. It's a description, for example, like saying that this little town in Nevada is part old and part new. There is a fish hatchery there, a couple of restaurants. There's an inn. It's the kind of small town a lot of people want to move to.

Number one is having a theme the jury believes. The second thing is, with clarity, showing that the theme is, indeed, supported by the evidence. And the third thing is a thousand different things you do to enhance your credibility and not fit the stereotype of the asshole lawyer.

—Max Blecher

Juries change, and what works with one will not work with another. There are no norms for persuading juries, according to Joe Jamail, "Before we ever get to the courthouse, after the voir dire and the questionnaires, I think I know as much as I can about the personality traits of the juror." Direct communication with each juror is essential to Jamail's style.

I immediately take that badge off of [the jurors]. Most lawyers don't. They tell them how wonderful they are— judges of the fact, and all that shit. I don't do that. I start to humanize them. I want them to hear this case like somebody came to them in their living room and told them this tragic story...I try to insert something that would appeal to each juror's personality. I think that's advocacy. Advocacy means to win them over. That's how I approach it.

Very personal. And with a sense of morality because without any morality there is no law. Law is bullshit without morality.

"A lot of lawyers go through tremendous effort in selecting a jury, then they go about trying a case without ever looking at them," says Pat McCartan who spends a lot of time looking at the jury. Every time there is a side-bar conference he looks at the jury to determine who the strong jurors are, who is with him. But in the end, in Fred Bartlit's view, it is the lawyer who "got right to it," did not waste the jury's time, and was prepared.

Tactical Errors

Ass kissers never win in front of a large group. You can only effectively kiss ass in private.

—**Tom Barr**

There are many ways in which lawyers can go wrong in trying to influence jurors. Most mistakes follow from making a faulty assessment of who jurors are and what they expect. Trying to flatter jurors is a mistake, trying to dictate to them and tell them what they should do is another. Underestimating the intelligence of jurors and dealing with them in a condescending manner is an irretrievable disaster. Adopting the wrong emotional tone is a mistake. Being arrogant, being too contentious and thereby obnoxious, making too many objections, are self-inflicted wounds. Behaving discourteously toward judge and jury is also an obvious error but not infrequently observed.

Max Blecher adds his voice to those who warn against condescension. Jurors cannot be bullied or fooled. Common mistakes in communicating with jurors include, "telling them what they ought to do. Believing that jurors are dumb. Throwing a bunch of crap on the wall that nobody can understand." Coming back to one of his themes, the bumbling prep-school lawyer, Blecher warns against trying to bamboozle jurors.

Many prep-school type lawyers don't understand how juries think and so they appeal to them with the wrong facts. [They] think that juries are dumb, they look down on them, not necessarily consciously, but subconsciously. So they make arguments that either are condescending and dis-

272

cerned as such by the jury or which no reasonable person would accept. An elephant is the same as a giraffe. Why not? They're both big and have big necks.

Blecher thinks the same kind of lawyers frequently make the mistake of being dispassionate and blasé. Getting emotional is an anathema. "If the jury sits through an hour and a half of a guy reading out of a notebook or speaking to them in a soporific monotone, the jurors are either sleeping or thinking, 'What am I going to do for dinner tonight?' They just tune out."

Bob Fiske advises, "make it very simple, very colloquial, at their level. One or two syllable words. I think jurors like logical common sense more than they do rhetoric." Jurors feel their time is being wasted by self-indulgent attorneys. They dislike lawyers who are arrogant and impatient, who make them wait. Jamail thinks jurors are turned off by:

> Lawyers who object for no reason. Repetition. If they perceive their time to be wasted. A witness who is evasive. They begin to take sides. They've got likes and dislikes. I have seen the jurors get so angry and hateful. You can see body language.

Susman has seen a number of situations in which jurors are turned off. What is it that lawyers do that makes this happen? According to Susman, by:

> Being obnoxious. Being arrogant. Being impolite. Making jurors wait, being made to wait while injunctions are ruled on. Being made to wait sitting around the hall or in the jury room while the court is doing something else—they hate it. Not hearing side-bars. Having to sit over there, leave the room when something comes up. Little things can distract. The clothes you wear, biting on a rubber band, playing with a toothpick, things that they watch. You never know what it is, but I'll tell you one thing, they sure do watch a lot more than I ever thought. Sometimes I think they don't listen at all because they are watching too carefully.

Jim Neal relates a situation in which a lawyer pandered to the jury with disastrous results.

> I tried a case a year ago, and this lawyer was so obsequious, so overly sweet. For the first day or two, that wasn't bad.

273

Such things as, "May it please the court, I suspect the jury would like a break to go to the bathroom." All of that stuff. After the first couple of days it was clearly annoying to everybody in the jury. He didn't know when to stop.

Phil Corboy suspects some attorneys think jurors are stupid, and act accordingly. He suggests they have no business being trial lawyers. "How can they have such disdain for the jury if they're in a system where their job is to persuade the jury?" Lawyers who think jurors are stupid have essentially abandoned their responsibility to persuade.

If that's what they think, they should be shooting craps, they shouldn't be in there trying to persuade jurors. If that's what they believe, then they have no respect for their title. It's like lawyers who argue and get into court and insult judges at pretrial and scream and argue with the judge. How can they be in this milieu and have such little respect for it?

The essence of juror persuasion lies in treating jurors with respect and dignity. Overdone attempts to flatter or cajole a jury are invariably disastrous. Direct communication is primary. When these men face a jury they are in a concentrated mode of scoring points and marginal advantages at every turn. This is done subtly and with conviction.

CHAPTER 7 ███████████████

Putting On the Case

If the judge is difficult, that's my fault. If the judge is dumb, I can only hope to educate him. Do I always win? Of course not. You can't win an argument with a judge.

—Phil Corboy

The spine of proof in a case will come out of the examination of witnesses, the presentation of key documents, exhibits, and on occasion an important deposition. Putting on a case is an art form similar to a director shooting a film or staging a play. Some cases are extremely technical. These cases are difficult to understand and tend be boring. Sometimes judges are hostile and that hostility must be overcome. Above all, the road to effective persuasion of judge and jury must be found.

The Trial as Theater

The lawyers eschew the idea that they are actors in the courtroom. The reason they do not accept this characterization is obvious. The very notion of "acting" or playing a part does not comport with the attributes of sincerity and credibility so important to these advocates. In fact, the notion of acting reinforces a negative stereotype of a lawyer who pretends to believe whatever is useful or convenient for the moment. But, at times, he is an actor. There can be little doubt of that. Not only is he at times an actor, but he is often so thoroughly convincing that he warrants the highest accolade an actor can earn: he appears sincere, and the audience forgets or never perceives that he is acting.

275

Instead of perceiving their role as an actor, however, these men display their tendency to lead by viewing themselves as producers and directors. Tom Barr feels that "trial is like the production and direction of a play."

Arthur Liman makes some similar observations about trials as theater:

> I've had people talk about trial lawyers as actors. I don't think of it that way. I think a great trial lawyer is more like a director, if I was to look for an analogy to Hollywood or to the stage, and what a director does. In the first place, a director has got to have a story. You're going to have to have a story which involves themes. You've got to have the capacity to tell a story. Not everyone has that capacity to tell a story. They can bore people and they may miss parts of the story. [We] all know people who tell jokes and they somehow have left out something so it's not funny.

Putting on a case is something like casting a play.

> You've got to be able to cast it well—who your witnesses are going to be. You've got to have the right sets. Those are your demonstrative exhibits, your other aids. It's got to be told in a way in which you evoke the emotion you want and that means a verdict in favor of your client.

Bob Fiske says, "You've got the audience sitting there, you've got to put it on in a way that maximizes their attention and their ability to keep interested in what you're doing." Bob Warren echoes the comparison of trial lawyer is to the work of a director, "the ultimate preparation for trial the same way that a producer and director might set a stage show."

Bob Fiske gives a marvelous example of trial as theater from his prosecution of Nicky Barnes:

> I think more and more the theatricality is very impor-tant...When we had the [Nicky] Barnes case, just the way we started the case, the first witness we called was the superintendent of a condominium complex across the river in Fort Lee, New Jersey...

This was where Nicky Barnes lived, under the assumed name of Wally Rice. Fiske shaped the testimony of this witness in a way that developed very graphic and dramatic word pictures. He asked the superintendent to

> "Describe your building," and this is the first witness and the jury is wondering what this is all about. "Describe your building." "Well, it's a thirteen-floor building." "Do you have apartments on every floor?" "Yes." "Do you have a penthouse?" "Yes, we have a penthouse." "Describe the penthouse." He describes this luxurious thing.

The owner of the penthouse was Barnes, a.k.a. "Wally Rice." Fiske inquired about Mr. Rice, about his cars, for example:

> "Tell us a little bit about the owner of the penthouse. How long has he had it?" "Oh, he's had it about two years." "Does he have any cars? Do you have a parking garage?" "Oh, yes." "Does the tenant have a car?" "Oh, he has three." "What are they?" "Oh, he has a Ferrari and a Mercedes and a BMW." Then I said, "Oh by the way, what's the name of this tenant?" and he said, "Wally Rice."

Then Fiske identified Barnes as the one who lived in all this splendor under a false name.

> I said, "Do you see Mr. Rice in the courtroom?" "Yes, he's right over there," pointing at Nicky Barnes. So, right away, you get the picture of this opulence and the guy living there under a false name and we did that *twice* with superintendents from both apartments where he had used a false name. Then we put in his tax return which showed four hundred fifty thousand dollars a year of miscellaneous income...and we had the case ninety percent won right there.

The image of Barnes living in luxury is what gave the drug dealers who testified against him credibility.

> Because the actual witnesses we had to testify against him were real unsavory people. I mean they were just awful people: drug dealers who...we'd had to make all sorts of deals with them to get them to testify. If we put them up first, their testimony would have been very shaky, but starting out with this kind of stuff, we had this very solid

proof right at the beginning that got the jury very excited
and built up this enormous aura of wealth and cover-up and
so forth.

The theatrical juxtaposition of Barnes' opulence and the sleaze balls
who testified against him won Fiske's case in the early rounds.

Direct Examination of Witnesses

Direct examination is considered the most difficult task in the trial.
Because it is non-confrontational, and the witness takes the stand for
long periods of time, direct in a question-and-answer format can be
deadly dull. Using visual props is one way to energize direct
examinations. Different witnesses can also be positioned to tell
different parts of the story. This enlivens testimony and addresses the
jurors' relatively short-attention span. Just as they tune out one person,
an astute lawyer puts a new witness on the stand to perk up the jurors'
interest. Multiple witnesses also mean that the credibility of the entire
case is not dependent upon the credibility of a single person, which is
always a risk.

Trial attorneys frequently face the challenge of examining difficult
witnesses, or who pose other special problems because of their power,
wealth, and personality. The jury does not expect to see a powerful
CEO, a self-made billionaire, or the head of a media empire led around
like a puppy dog. Such witnesses are people who are used to getting
their own way in life. In general, this kind of witness knows what he
wants to say with or without the lawyer's questions. This is a potential
problem in a jury trial since people of enormous wealth and power are
often viewed unsympathetically. Therefore, it is important that these
witnesses be likable and credible, that their testimony be focused and
to the point. In other words, these witnesses need to be controlled like
any other witness.

Tom Barr had two cases with Ross Perot in which he had to use
specific techniques of direct examination because of Perot's character
as a witness. In one, Perot was sued by his former company, EDS, in
Virginia where his new company, Perot Systems is located. In the
other suit, Perot counter-sued in Texas.

There was a lot of tension in the Perot litigation—a lot of
real emotion. When Perot left General Motors, he entered
into an agreement, a buy-back agreement. That agreement
provided that for a period of two years he could not engage

in business for profit that was in competition with EDS. And that thereafter it could be for a profit and, he could for an unspecified period, hire employees of EDS to engage in that business.

In Barr's judgment the agreement had been a bad business decision on the part of General Motors, drawn up carelessly and made under extreme pressure.

It was an incredible agreement. It was a piece of incredible stupidity on behalf of General Motors. It was a contract that was almost too good to be true because it gave Perot the right to go into EDS and say, "Joe, Bill, Ed, follow me."

Perot boasted that he had taken the heart out of EDS.

He'd cut, as he put it, "The ten best regimental commanders at EDS, the guys who were not fat, dumb, and happy yet, who were still looking for promotion and to make a lot of money." He hired them all, the best ones. And they formed a new company.

Perot tapped the management level in EDS just below the highest level in the chain of command.

The trial was Ross and the regimental commanders against the old division commanders. The EDS people, the guys who ran EDS, had been Ross Perot's division commanders. Now Ross, the general of the army, and the best regimental commanders were all on the other side. So EDS sued Ross, Ross sued EDS. We sued in Texas, they sued in Virginia.

The circumstances of the case with Perot were such that only Perot could lose. Barr did not have to worry about protecting the interest of anyone else on his side. No one else on his side had a financial interest in the outcome. Thus the whole context of the trial dictated the tactics Barr employed with Perot. This made Barr willing to let Perot do whatever he wanted to do as a witness. Barr reasoned that it was better to let Perot go his own way as a witness, rather than try to direct his testimony.

Ross Perot was very difficult to control. And in a sense, when I put Ross on the stand, rather than try to control him, I tried to pitch it. I tried to throw pitches I knew he'd like to hit. But it was very different in his case because we were playing entirely with his money and if he wanted to do it any

279

particular way, as long as I did whatever I thought I should do, it was his money.

Arthur Liman recalls his early days as a prosecutor in the criminal division of the US Attorney's office in New York where he learned about handling witnesses.

> I remember that we had a system that in your first trial you had to bring something called a trial book to the head of the Criminal Division. [I had] a lousy little drug case. You could have tried that sleepwalking. And I had my questions and he looked at them and said, "There isn't one good question here. They're all leading. Can't ask one of them."

Liman found this exasperating. He did not really believe there was any such thing as a non-leading question:

> He said,"You've got to say, 'Where were you on this night?' to the agent and, 'What did you see?' and 'What happened?' and 'What happened next?' and 'What happened after that?'" We went through this a little and then I said, "I didn't come to the US Attorney's office in order to say, 'What happened? What happened next? What happened after that? What happened afterwards? What happened next?'" I said, "I'll try not to lead too much, but I can't just simply have letter-perfect questions." And, of course you learned.

Liman emphasizes how important it is to ask non-leading questions.

> The reason for non-leading questions was to make sure that in a direct examination, you had a good witness, the jury focused on your witness and it was the witness' story, not yours. Whereas, on a cross-examination, you want the jury to focus on you and not pay any attention to the witness basically. You want your questions to be suggestive and, hopefully, effective—to be the things that leave an imprint in the jury's mind.

There is some variation in the tactics attorneys employ in questioning a witness on direct examination. Principally, a choice is usually made in favor of either letting the witness tell a story in a relatively unbroken narrative form, or answer pointed questions briefly and directly. Jim Brosnahan wants his witness on direct to tell a story. He believes, however, that the pace should vary. He also advocates a means of displaying related exhibits to the jury in the course of the testimony.

> Maintain interest. Move quickly. Have a good method to display exhibits for the jury. Concentrate on sequence, both of sequence of the questions to the individual witnesses one after the other so you are telling, really telling a story. It's really clear and interesting what happened here...developing a little bit like the play.

Direct examination should also look ahead to cross-examination by inoculating the jury against the worst things that can come out on cross. "Deal with negative stuff...get it out so that it doesn't hurt so much on cross. That's a big item." Brosnahan's preference is to let the witness talk. But not every witness can be given free rein to carry on an answer in a narrative stream. "The witness who is nervous or voluble—people start to talk, they don't want to stop, they're just going to go forever. So you've got to say, 'Excuse me, let's change the subject.'" Developing fluent direct testimony is an art wherein the attorney must watch the speech pattern of the witness and interject enough and yet not too much.

> Listen to somebody talk. When you ask "Did you see the nuclear explosion?" Some people, say, "Yup" like Gary Cooper. Well, we're going to need more than that.
> **—Jim Brosnahan**

Joe Jamail takes a somewhat different approach to direct examination. He feels that the jurors have an attention span of about six or seven minutes per witness, and are probably never as attentive during the cross-examination of a witness as they are on direct. As plaintiff Jamail counts on conducting a pointed direct examination, then watches the defense bore the jury with a tedious cross-examination. Jamail plays to the jury at this time, making eye contact, sharing their boredom, establishing a bond.

> Juries don't want to hear a lot of long-winded bullshit. I got the first shot at it and if I'm going to squander that, I'm a fool. Invariably, what happens is the defense will spend

hours fiddling around with it. I'm over here watching, I'm looking at that jury. Jurors don't like to feel their time is being wasted.

Phil Corboy talks about introducing the overall theme of the case into direct examination. Every witness on direct examination contributes to the theme, supplies some relevant fact. Each witness plays a role in providing proof. Each witness should know what his or her purpose is, and be prepared to carry it out.

> So when I put a witness on, it's going to be for a specific purpose. The brother is going to go on to show how this guy started from nothing and built this company up. That's going to be the brother's role. I'm not going to talk about his athletics. I'm just going to talk about how he built this company up. Another witness is going to talk about the man's community affairs.

Corboy suggests that witnesses need to be "goal-oriented" and need to be aware of the limitations of their role.

> I don't want the brother of this dead man showing that he's going to lose thirty million dollars in the future. That's a role he cannot satisfy. I want him, if he doesn't know an answer to a question, to say so. That's tactics. I don't want him to assume responsibilities that he has no ability nor sense in assuming.

Witnesses are given limited assignments. "Don't give him a job to do that he can't handle on cross." Corboy will not try to insulate a witness from harm after the witness has been prepared to testify.

How do I protect them on direct? I don't. That witness is going to be well prepared to sit down and answer my questions directly. When he's up for cross too, I have to let him be vulnerable. I can't prevent cross-examination [from] being really devastating. If it is, you can't change facts. All you can do is prepare him for cross in a way that you think cross is going to come out.

—Phil Corboy

Corboy will develop points on direct that he expects to constitute areas of attack during cross-examination. This is so the jury won't be surprised by things the opponents bring up.

> They're going to ask you if you've talked with me about a difficult issue or point. Well, I'm going to ask you about it. "Really?" You mean, you're going to tell me?" Of course I am, I'm not going to put you on the stand without talking with you. I will ask you on direct examination, "Have I talked with you?"

Typically an attorney, like Corboy, will strike certain agreements with the other side, such as "you don't ask my experts how much they're being paid, and I won't ask yours." These are what he calls ground rules.

> We won't bullshit ourselves about asking experts are they paid or how much they've been paid. Of course experts get paid. What difference does it make? Number two, you don't ask each other's witnesses [did] they talk to Corboy? Of course they talk to me and your witnesses talk to you. If they [are] people that I trust and have confidence in, we sit down and say, "Look. Here's some ground rules. Do we agree on it? If we don't agree, fine."

David Boies does not like long-winded, unbroken storytelling on direct examination except in rare cases in which the narrative can be used to make connections between exhibits. The tactic he favors on direct is to have the witness give an answer in the form of a paragraph that he will follow with a precise question. "'Let me try to understand, are you saying X?' You give it to them a little slowly so that those who are sort of coming along can get a sense of it and then you restate it and bring it home."

Bob Warren feels that direct examination is one of the more difficult aspects of the trial. This is so because the witness must create meaning, and the attorney must ask questions in such a way that coherent meaning evolves in the testimony. Cross-examination can be incoherent to a point. It may not matter what the answers are, the question is the critical point. Cross-examination floats and probes until a question hits home and a point of significance is reached. Direct does not work that way.

> Direct examination is hard. It's hard unless you have a very lax court [permitting leading questions], because your witness has to carry the day. There are many cross-examinations that you can conduct that what the witness answers almost doesn't make any difference. That's certainly not true on direct examination.
>
> **—Bob Warren**

Jurors evaluate the witness' testimony beyond the actual words used. Demeanor, style, perceived levels of comfort, honesty, and credibility will actually be part of the juror's decision-making process rather than the mere words in the trial record. Warren advocates something like the following:

> "This is who the witness is. This witness is a person, you're getting to know this person, you're getting to have a judgment about this person. Now the witness is going to tell you what we want you to accept and believe in this case." But if you just put a witness up there and have him say that without establishing himself as a person to be paid attention to, I don't think it accomplishes anything except makes you a record on appeal.

Pat McCartan agrees and calls direct the most challenging aspect of trial practice. Judges sometimes will make it difficult by cautioning against redundancy and using other means of speeding along the testimony by demanding proofs of relevancy and noting that others have testified on similar grounds. But the hardest part of direct is overcoming boredom.

> Cross-examination is a lark, but direct examination, can either be the driest, most boring thing in the world, because of the way [lawyers] go about questioning the witness, or it can be the telling of the story with some life and some excitement. With the limits on direct examination, it's not all that easy to do and, you have to get yourself out of the mold of, "What happened next," into, "As you turned the corner and he approached you, did he say anything?" Those are two different ways of saying the same thing.

McCartan frequently feels his side is in such a strong position as defendant after the plaintiff has finished its case that he dreads having to put on his own witnesses. "They're going to be cross-examined so at least let's get them out there with a head start with the jury, with something that has some life and color to it before they're cross-examined." And, he maintains, few lawyers do this competently. McCartan favors short-answer questions. In order to avoid leading, he wants each question to work off a previous answer.

> It really is a, "what happened next question," but it's dressed a lot differently. There will be some interest. Like the witness coming around the corner, you're going to get to the point of the examination which is what he said to him at that point, which is the important thing. You may as well put some suspense into it. They're going to remember it, it's going to be more dramatic.

Jim Neal does not have a rule regarding narrative versus short answers. He believes it will depend on the nature of the testimony and the personality of the witness. But witnesses need to know when a short, direct answer is called for, as opposed to a rambling response.

> You want the witness (if he's the kind of witness you like) talking to the jury, not you interjecting all the time. Yet, there are other questions where you simply want a yes or no. You ought to develop your witnesses so that he will know when it is a direct yes or no question that is being asked, or you want the witness to know where he can expand.

Neal also believes that witnesses should rotate to whom they speak, some of the time to the jury, some of the time to the attorney asking questions. It is awkward for a witness to face the jury just to fire off a short answer, and then turn away again to face the one asking questions. "But," Neal suggests, "if it is a question that he wants to expand upon, it is good for him to look over there casually and talk, and then look back at me. All that makes for believability."

From what Steve Susman has said about how he prepares a witness for direct, it is clear that the tactic he favors is a question-and-answer format with short questions and short answers. "The jury wants to hear the witness, not you, point one. But point two, is that the jury is not interested in hearing speeches from the witnesses." Since Susman wants the witness to be disciplined, it is important that the witness not be asked to learn long answers, this will make the witness apprehensive, something that must be avoided. Since open-ended questions produce nerves, Susman does not have the confidence in the witness' ability to handle an unscripted situation.

> If you ask him, "Tell me what happened on the day in question?" he's going to be very nervous about remembering all that. Basically, I begin by constructing it with a short question and a short answer where they have to list something in the answer. The questions are, "Why did you do this?" And I'll put a number one, so they will remember that there are three things. "My wife went hunting that day." "My secretary was sick." And something else.

Susman recognizes that this can get choppy. He will occasionally urge the witness to open up a little bit. The script is only a guide, not to be slavishly followed. Susman wants naturalness, and will work in court to create this.

> So then I'll open the witness up a little bit more. "Well, tell us, in your own words." Now, the witness is getting comfortable with it at that point and we might come back to the planned format. I script it very carefully. But when I actually get into court, I don't follow the script very well, but I have scripted it.

Arthur Liman wants the witnesses on direct examination to talk to the jury, to develop a sympathetic connection with the jurors. He struggles with the problem posed by direct, of getting the witness to tell a fluent, interesting story. He feels he cannot give the witness free rein just to tell the jury what happened, tempting as that may be, but must add a certain amount of structure.

> I may be wrong, but I prefer to let them talk to the jury because I think it gives them a chance to develop a rapport with the jury. Everything is relative. When I say let them talk to the jury, I have never done what I sometimes have been tempted to try which is to say, "You've been sitting here and you've heard all this testimony. Tell us what *really* happened."
>
> **—Arthur Liman**

Liman suggests, astutely, that questions should highlight points in the narrative, and mark places to come back to.

> You have to structure it, and you also want to be sure that they get the high points, and one thing that a question does is it stresses the high points so that you can let them have some narrative but then you have to come back and pick it up and highlight.

Harry Reasoner does not want to appear to be leading the witness, but would rather have witnesses give the impression that they are doing their best to tell the truth in their own words. "You must gear it very much to the witness. It is very difficult to get a coherent story out of some witnesses without leading or bordering on leading them constantly." Reasoner prefers broader rather than more pointed questions for fear of looking too rehearsed. "But with some witnesses you can't afford to do that. You have to ask very specific questions. I'm always fearful, if it is too tight, the jury gets kind of a puppet-on-a-string impression."

Tom Barr is also concerned that the witness be prepared as a result of what is said in direct to withstand cross-examination. Barr would not really do it, but he sometimes tells the witness that he may leave when the witness is being questioned by the other side. Barr knows that one of the most important points in the preparation of a witness for direct examination is to anticipate possible lines of cross-examination and to insure that the witness will not waver. He wants his witness to be secure and self-reliant.

> I tell the witnesses that I may get up and walk out of the room while they're being cross-examined. They have to learn to follow my rules. I give them the usual rules about understanding the question and being sure they understand it. Answering the question and not volunteering and so forth.

Barr expects his witnesses to face tough questioning from the other side because he will be tough on the opponent's witnesses, forcing a lot of objections. He expects opposing counsel to retaliate. If his witnesses can take care of themselves without Barr objecting a lot, he will make a point of this in summation.

> I want to be able to tell the jury, "You saw what happened when I cross-examined the witnesses. My opponent, Mr. Jones, was all over the place. I had difficulty getting my

questions answered. They had a lot of trouble telling the truth. On the other hand, with the witnesses that they put on, what did I do, object once or twice?"

Max Blecher wants his witnesses on direct to give short, punchy answers. Frequently, the plaintiff will be a key witness. This is important, Blecher thinks, for several reasons. If the plaintiff does not appear, the jury may think he is disinterested. Also, Blecher would like the jury to identify with the plaintiff, which is much easier if they meet and hear him. The plaintiff will testify about how he has been injured, while other witnesses will focus on the behavior of the defendant that resulted in injury.

> I put my own witness on mainly as a showcase. Mainly because a jury has to see this plaintiff and they have to identify with him or at least be neutral about him, but they must see him. If he isn't there and he isn't interested, he isn't a part of the proceeding, it's really hard to persuade that he should get anything. In most of our cases, the plaintiff doesn't know a whole lot. He can only explain how he got injured. The key to our cases is the inner-workings of the defendant.

Since the plaintiff is only being showcased, the questions asked should be direct and short.

Most of the time he's window dressing. You say, "Here's the plaintiff...He's going to tell you how he had a nice business and then one day came to work and he didn't have any raw material and he had to close the door and sixty-seven people got laid off and he went from making two hundred thousand dollars a year to zero and he's now in a bread line down there on Spring Street," and sit down. What does he know? I mean, that's it.

—Max Blecher

The plaintiff does not really know how or why any of this happened. "Let the jury see and observe him. He's a nice person, he looks like a decent American citizen, why should this have happened to him?"

Bob Fiske prefers the control afforded on direct examination by a short question-and-answer format. He tells a witness ahead of time that he should be prepared to "run with" a particular question. "Again, it depends on how articulate the witness is. If you get a few witnesses who can be really articulate, then you give them more latitude." Fiske comes back to the key problem on direct—creating interest. He likens the trial attorney to a television interviewer. The same guest can be more or less interesting depending on who is interviewing. "The way the lawyer asks the questions on direct is a very important part of keeping the jury's attention and bringing out the story." Fiske makes the additional point that there are often ways to use transitional questions with witnesses or questions that refer to another witness' testimony. This is a valuable means of weaving together the testimony of different witnesses. Effective direct examination relies on organization. Witness organization and the manner in which questions are asked are key elements. Build into the question either subtly or directly something that refers back to other testimony. Direct examination is not simply putting on a witness and letting him or her tell the story.

Fred Bartlit is of the school that wants to see the testimony on direct be like a "conversation in a bar," a real-life event. In addition, he notes that there are a number of mistakes that can be made in direct examination.

> Trying to cover too much ground. Saying to witnesses, "If he asks you this, you say this," and assuming they're going to say it. The direct examiner is a director of the symphony. If the symphony plays a false note, it's the director's fault. Common faults are writing out questions and turning the pages and looking at the next question, or walking around while the witness is talking.

Generally, the lawyers fall into two groups when it comes to direct examination. One group prefers the degree of control over the witness that can be obtained through the use of short questions and crisp answers. A second group prefers that the witness develop a more continuous narrative than the short question/answer format allows. All agree that the interaction between the witness and the examining attorney is critical. It is the art of the attorney to assist the witness to appear credible and likeable to the jury. Knowing when to interrupt, to ask for more information, to steer the witness away from a dangerous reef, are all part of the job.

Creative Use of Depositions

There are a number of clever and effective tactics to make the presentation of depositions something more than the routinely boring event it can be in the hands of lesser trial lawyers. Overall, these tactics involve making the deposition as lifelike as possible and building into the presentation as many attention-getting devices as possible. Actors might be hired, or appropriate people on the trial team will be asked to pose as the person whose deposition is presented.

For a change of pace, Max Blecher once switched places with his client. Blecher played the part of the witness, and his client took his role. At other times, when it is necessary to read a deposition, Blecher puts the document on an overhead screen; and if possible, puts the deponent on the stand, and simultaneously shows and reads it.

> If I'm reading a deposition and you are sitting at the witness stand, I'll put the document on the screen and I'll go over and I'll say, "Now, Mr. Vinson, you see this?" I'm reading from the dep but I am re-creating what happened in the deposition. I'm using the document. I have never spent two hours reading a deposition and never will. I've never spent a whole day reading deps and never will. I've got ways figured out to get around that.

Phil Corboy enjoys casting surrogate witnesses to read depositions. The object is to strive for verisimilitude and credibility.

If I'm taking the deposition of a nun, I'm going to have a nice, sweet, young girl take the part of the nun. If I've got a neurosurgeon, I'm going to have a dignified fifty-five-year old man who looks like a neurosurgeon read the deposition.

—Phil Corboy

More and more frequently, depositions are being videotaped. Production quality, however, of these videos is generally not consistent with television broadcast standards. And too often little thought is given to how they will be effectively used during trial or the impact they are likely to have on jurors. In too many cases, the final product is a tedious presentation of "talking heads." In actuality, these depositions are usually less effective than the admittedly mind-numbing exercise of reading long passages from paper depositions. Blecher is negative about the use of these video depositions. He would rather have a surrogate on the witness stand because a better pace is maintained and it is more effective for him to play the examiner. "I have a good voice and I can change the pace. Depositions weren't made to be shown. There are long pauses. It's boring. [You have] a higher quality product with a live witness reading it than showing some guy sitting there endlessly droning on late in the afternoon." Videotapes are only effective in Corboy's view if the witness is sellable, and if he is sellable, it might be better to have that witness in person.

Bob Fiske wants videos if there is a heavy load of depositions in a case, but only if the witness comes across well. If the case has many depositions it is wise to use videotape. If for some reason video depositions were not produced, the next best thing he advises to do is to trim the depositions to a minimum and carefully choose people to read them. When Fiske has a choice, he has criteria for using a surrogate witness or a video. "If you have a very presentable witness, you'd clearly go with the video."

If Joe Jamail has a great number of depositions he will spend the time to pick the shortest statements out of the best two or three. He will present those "in about fifteen or twenty minutes in a video or otherwise. And you can count on it—the defense is going to come back and try to play all that shit and it's going to piss off the jurors." He gives copies of depositions to the jury. Although they might not be able to take them into the jury room, at least "they've seen what they want to see, and then they're going to listen for four or five hours." Jamail likes to use videos to embarrass a witness whose demeanor and pattern of speech underscore the negative aspects he wants to impress upon jurors. For example, he will show a deposition of an exceptionally evasive witness so that jury "sees him hemming and hawing on the record." Jamail does not, however, want the jury to see a witness *he* is making squirm. He fears the sight of discomfort might make the witness sympathetic.

Pat McCartan also believes in whittling down a large number of depositions to the essential few. "And you've got to change the people. You can't just put a paralegal up there or a secretary and let him or her be three witnesses." He recommends continually changing the channel, breaking up the stream of depositions with other trial activities.

> You've got to separate them, if you can, with some live testimony, or argument or recesses or lunches or something. And I have found that separating it, and occasionally asking somebody on the other side if they'd take the stand and read the answers for the opponent. Generally, if it's one of their people, I like to do that.

McCartan is wary but respectful when it comes to using video depositions in conjunction with other new technologies. He believes that videos in combination with laser-disc technology can be formidable, but that there can be times when the medium overwhelms the message. He cites the Maxus case (*Maxus Corporation Co. v. Kidder Peabody & Co., Inc. Martin A. Siegel and Ivan S. Boesky*) as an example in which electronic depositions were used.

> Did you read where they settled that case for one hundred sixty-five million dollars? The boys down in Dallas represented Maxus on that. They made very effective use of videotape depositions and the laser disc, and at the opening they had a "Hollywood-Squares" type box arrangement that came up on laser disc progressively, which had Boesky not remembering this, Siegel not remembering that. It was devastating. It was pretty powerful stuff.

Harry Reasoner tries to videotape depositions, limits and tightly edits them. If the judge allows, when a witness is interrogated about a document, he puts the document on the screen, and uses a pointer when he asks about various lines. This helps to hold the jury's attention. "Reading depositions to a jury is deadly, there is just no question, it is deadly." Reasoner will sometimes try to reinforce valuable parts of a deposition by reading them to another witness and saying, "Now, did you know so-and-so said such and such?" He suggests that this may raise questions of what is proper for a procedural point of view, but they are generally overcome.

Steve Susman does not feel that using depositions as proof is ever that valuable, except on rare occasions. "So why the hell are you doing it for the record? The only testimony in a deposition that is going to impact a juror is if it is such a zinger you just want to blow it up, put it on, stand by, and brag about it." Often, in Susman's view, no one, not even the lawyers, knows what the deposition is really about.

I sit there as a lawyer and listen to someone read depositions that I didn't attend or take, and I have no idea what they stand for, either on my side or the other side, how is the juror going to know? I think it is a total waste.

—Steve Susman

Presenting a Technical Case

Not a large number of technical cases go to trial. But if they do, they are often among the most important high-stakes trials in US courts. And one of the most difficult challenges faced by any trial lawyer is to try a case that is, by its very nature, tedious. Patent cases, many antitrust actions, or white-collar criminal cases in the banking and securities industry are so loaded with abstruse technical issues that it is a Herculean effort to bring them alive. One way to tackle such a case is to assume that there are interesting issues involved or the case would not be coming before a jury in the first place. It is the responsibility of the attorney to find the drama. Complicated, dry, issues can be made accessible and everyone can regard the case as a learning experience. Max Blecher takes just such a positive attitude.

> I love it when there's something that was complicated I didn't understand and I learn what it means. I feel so good about myself. The average juror is that way and more so. If there is something they originally thought, "Oh my God, this is beyond me," and suddenly they understand it, they feel good. It is a wonderful feeling.

It can be exciting and interesting to learn, but there is boredom in every trial. Blecher has almost unlimited confidence in his ability to instruct jurors. He believes that jurors find complicated issues of greater interest than self-evident issues.

The acquisition of knowledge is one of the most happy events in the world. If you've got a case involving a complicated patent but you make the patent issue understandable, the jury likes that better than a case involving a traffic accident in an

> intersection because they walk out and say, "I understand all about diodes."
> **—Max Blecher**

There is never enough time to make *everything* understandable. So Blecher suggests instead to make just one thing comprehensible. In most cases, there is always one transcendent issue on which to hang the case's theme.

Bob Fiske considers himself fortunate insofar as the Three Mile Island case was not tried in front of a jury. Making aspects of that case interesting to jurors would have been arduous. As it was, he used a large number of visual aids for the judge. "We would have used far more with the jury. I think that would be true of any technical case. This is where you'd really have to have a lot of demonstrative evidence."

The tactics employed by Joe Jamail in dealing with a difficult technical case are similar to his approach to any other trial.

> You've got to humanize it. I might say, "Accounting is an honorable profession. Cheating people is wrong. And more than that, a guy who would do that is somebody different from you and me. You really need to see how his mind works, and how a person like this can come up with alibis and justify cheating, lying, and stealing. And we're going to bring you such a person." Then it's no longer a case about arithmetic. It's a case about the son of a bitch who did it.

Pat McCartan suggests that some of the new technology, such as computer animation, can be helpful in making a dry case more entertaining and salient, "it's the only way to dress it up. You can't even do it with an animated witness that much. You try to, but you just can't."

Harry Reasoner also points to graphics as a large part of the solution to boring witness testimony.

> In a technical case, particularly, visual aids can be of enormous importance. I've seen the jury become fascinated with a model. They might find a witness boring as hell, but they could become very intrigued with how the model worked. They can also focus on the graphics where the drone of the witness is mere background to understand-

ing and help them to understand the graphics with questions.

When an attorney is able to master the facts and information in a technical case to a point where he can make them interesting for a jury, the case turns a corner. Arthur Liman looks for analogies and everyday language to explain hard concepts.

> I have some bright people who help me and by the time they are able to make me understand it, I can make a jury understand it. I insist that they keep simplifying it and simplifying it and simplifying it and then through analogies, ultimately get it down to the point to where not only can I understand it, but I can explain it to anybody. I might say "I'm still having trouble understanding how a photovolt tag cell works, explain it to me again."

But a lawyer must guard against being perceived as someone who has a technical grasp that sets him apart from the jurors. Liman feels he can learn without pretension. "If they want to use their language, let them use their language, but then I'll restate it in my language so that the jury will understand it."

Difficult or Hostile Judges

Judges can be hostile or biased. Sometimes a judge will be unreceptive to an out-of-town attorney. At other times, a judge will not want to make the effort to hear a long or complicated case. The lawyers in this study, for the most part, trust judges and consider them colleagues. Some of the worst disappointments these men have experienced in their careers involved judges who did not, in their view, treat them fairly. All the lawyers are prepared to deal with such a situation if it should arise. They will try hard, however, to know the judge before going into a given venue so that there will be no nasty surprises. Harry Reasoner notes that there are judges antagonistic to the case, surly, "impatient or bored or who want to get out of there." Reasoner always tries to remember to use the same degree of advocacy and effort for a judge he uses for a jury.

According to Joe Jamail, lawyers are in court to plead a case, and judges are there to make rulings. "I will not argue his ruling because that's unprofessional. When he rules, that's it. You've got a job to do, he's got a job to do, the jury's got a job to do. All of our jobs are equal." Part of being professional for an attorney is making certain he is not perceived as a wimp, allowing himself to be pushed around or intimidated by a hostile judge. On the other hand, he is determined not to be disrespectful. He lets the juror know that they are as independent as the judge is. "I don't say anything about the judge to the jurors. They pick it up. They're not stupid." Hold your ground, but do not challenge the judge. That is Jamail's axiom. "A good, skilled lawyer can make the judge fall into error every time. And they know it."

Phil Corboy thinks the lawyer is to blame if the judge is difficult, at least he says so, referring to himself.

If the judge is difficult, that's my fault. First of all, I give them all the law ahead of time. I give them all the issues ahead of time. I give them the instructions ahead of time. I give them the statement that he has to give to the jury. I make everything as easy as I can for him. I give the judge the instructions on the first day of trial. I give the judge a list of the exhibits that I'm either going to use for offering or for identification and I give them to the other side. I do everything to make the judge's job easier and I do everything to make the other lawyer's job easier. Therefore, when he becomes a complete jerk, that difficult judge isn't difficult with me. If the judge is difficult, that's my fault. If the judge is dumb, I can only hope to educate him. Do I always win? Of course not. You can't win an argument with a judge.

—Phil Corboy

Pat McCartan makes several observations about the importance of how the jury perceives a lawyer's relationship with a judge, particularly if the judge is difficult or hostile. "The worst thing you can do is roll over in front of the jury, and it's obviously the worst thing you can do in terms of protecting your record." One must be firm but polite in front of the jury. The jury might wonder why the judge has it in for the lawyer. He advises to get everything on the record. "You can sometimes say within earshot of the jury, 'I'm sorry, but again I must ask you to permit me to make my record on this.' Jurors, you've got to give them credit, they're listening to what's happening. They know what's up in many instances."

Make sure that reporters are there for everything, even for conferences in chambers. "Then [the judge will] know that you know what's going on. You'll come out as well as you can in front of the jury and then take your chances on appeal."

Judges have tremendous power and can stop a case cold in its tracks. Defense attorneys, according to Blecher, gear their whole effort toward getting the judge to render a summary judgment in their favor.

> Judges definitely have a marked effect on the outcome. In today's world, where a summary judgment is a real way of losing the case, just to get by summary judgment is an achievement. So, you have to have the right judge even to get to the trial. Most of the defense bar are litigators whose function is to set up the case for summary judgment. That's the reason they won't let the witnesses tell you anything. They feel that the witnesses tell you something, then you can get over summary judgment. Their goal in life is to avoid trial, to gear it for summary judgment. Then they can come in and say, "There's a total absence of evidence. The plaintiff hasn't produced a single witness that knows anything about this." Summary judgment.

Judges play to the jury, just as lawyers do, Blecher notes, and can influence the outcome of a trial. "If the jury likes the judge, and most the time the judge tries to ingratiate himself to the jury for public relations purposes, it can influence them." Blecher argues that whether a lawyer is able to get the whole story to the jury, or the lawyer can only manage to get a truncated version that does not help the jury fully understand the case and decide it properly, depends partly on the judge. Judges will also try to intimidate attorneys, particularly younger, less-experienced counsel. Blecher dealt in an effective manner with a judge who intimidated a younger associate. "I said, 'Judge, pick on me. This woman is but two years out of law school. We're doing the best we can. Pick on me.' The judge was pissed, but quit picking."

Bob Fiske has never experienced an all-out antagonistic judge. He has had some, however, who were prejudiced in favor of the opposition. He thinks it can be hazardous to take on such a judge in front of a jury. One is reminded of what Jamail has said about the need to find subtle ways of telling the jury it is independent of the judge. The last resort is to take on the judge in front of the jury because juries are enormously responsive to the judge. Juries think the judge is neutral, and a good judge can, even if they are hostile to one side, perpetuate that belief. The lawyer who is confronted with a hostile judge has to be careful not to clash with the bench too much in front of the jury. The jury's natural instinct is to side completely with the judge and the lawyer takes a beating. "In most cases, you just have to eat it. And then you put it on the record, outside the presence of the jury, so you preserve the record for appeal."

Fred Bartlit argues that lawyers get from a judge what they make the judge into. If they are difficult, the judge becomes difficult. He too, does many things to try and make a judge well-disposed toward him.

Make the judge's job easy. Don't make frivolous arguments, drop points when you know you're losing them, don't file long briefs, don't attack the other side. You make deposits in the bank. Never ask for delays. Never ask for extensions. Never ask for breaks. As soon as the judge says a break, say, "Yes, sir, this is a good time." Never stall.

—Fred Bartlit

Bartlit believes that just acting decently in front of a judge will score points. "It's been at least twenty years since I had a trial where at the end of it the judge didn't genuinely say, 'Mr. Bartlit, I've really enjoyed this trial.'"

Are There Cases a Jury Should Not Hear?

What is the proper scope of juries as triers of fact in the legal system? The scope of jury competence is a vital aspect of putting on a case. Do these lawyers believe, in thinking about putting on their case, that it might be better to see the matter tried before a judge or panel of judges, or some appointed commission? Periodically, the American jury system comes in for a good deal of criticism, even hand-wringing despair. It is seen as cumbersome by critics, or as ignorant, unfair, and anachronistic. It is occasionally argued that cases are now too complex for a jury to understand, that trials are inefficient and expensive, a luxury we can no longer afford. (The total daily cost of a civil jury trial is $2,549, exclusive of attorneys' fees.[1]) Arguments on all sides of the issue are put forth about the quality of juror decision-making, and the continued availability of people to serve on long trials. The United States is unique in the wide use of juries. Other industrialized, advanced nations do without juries. In this country, at present, certain cases such as the political districting cases involving constitutional issues ultimately to be decided by the Supreme Court are heard in front of a judge or a panel of judges. What other kinds of cases are better disposed of in this manner? Should there be more of this, or none at all?

Phil Corboy is a strong proponent of the jury system. His belief in the capability of jurors is deep, and he feels the onus is always upon the attorney to present the case in an understandable form. The values of ordinary men and women, the basic rules and precepts we live by, must be used to settle disputes, no matter how complex. This can only be possible if lawyers are able to frame these disputes so that they can be understood by ordinary people, who can then apply the basic thinking that governs our social arrangements to make a specific decision. It is an imperfect process, but nothing else is as good. Corboy suggests there is no case a jury should not hear, but there "are only cases that certain lawyers should not try." If the lawyer is not competent enough to communicate the facts with the jury, then he shouldn't be a trial lawyer. Corboy points to *Pennzoil v. Texaco* as a case in point. Corboy credits Joe Jamail with being able to put the case in comprehensible terms. The basic point at dispute was the honesty of one company in dealing with another.

> Look at what Joe Jamail did in that case. Is Joe Jamail a dummy? Or was he smart when he got that verdict? Joe Jamail broke that down into the simplest of terms. It was an honesty case. *Did they or did they not make a contract?* That's how he tried it. Now the other lawyers probably tried it on some complex theory with pieces of paper and everything all over the place. Joe broke it down so billions

---

[1]Administrative Office of the US Courts, Budget Branch, *Daily Cost of a Civil Jury Trial*, Feb. 19, 1991.

of dollars were understandable to people. Why can't twelve jurors do it and learn about it and comprehend and understand as well as one judge?

One of the beauties of the jury system is the disinterest of the jurors. Jurors can judge an honesty issue very well.

Jurors are as capable as any judge or magistrate of knowing whether a person is lying, fudging, exaggerating, exhorting. Jurors are just as capable of looking you in the eye and seeing whether you're telling the truth or not. Jurors are just as capable of adding and subtracting. Jurors are just as susceptible to persuasion, just as capable of being won over. I have no hesitancy in concluding that there is no case in the world that jurors are less capable of handling than a judge.

—Phil Corboy

Joe Jamail takes issue with the argument that jurors are ill-equipped to understand a case, "I suppose then if we carry that to its logical termination, a rapist should have nothing but a panel of rapists on his jury because they know more about rape than anybody else."

If one goes for specialized knowledge as qualification for triers of fact, we lose the broad human perspective. Jamail is persuasive in this regard.

We're not talking about technical. We're talking about human beings. Property rights and human rights. And that takes humans to do, not technocrats. If that's the case, why don't we just get a computer and stuff it with the facts and get our answer. The practice of law is not a cold, cold, hard, rigid thing.

The mistakes jurors make are in their perception of the gravamen of the evidence. They are not deliberate mistakes, and they are often traceable to deficiencies in the way the attorneys have presented the evidence. Jamail comments on so-called juror mistakes:

I think most the time they are not premeditated mistakes. I think at the time jurors do things, they've done it based on what they perceive the preponderance of the evidence to have been. I really do. I've lost some cases. I was so angered by it and frustrated. But I look back at it and think I should have lost every one I lost.

Max Blecher has a number of thoughtful insights about juries. To begin with, he realizes that while there are many brilliant judges, he has been impressed with the insight jurors bring to a case.

I am struck by something that I can't believe is true for every judge, that is they [jurors] understand the cases, despite what Chief Justice Burger and other people have said. It's remarkable to me, not only how they understand it, but in some instances, I've been astounded to have them make connections between things and reach conclusions that I never even thought about. That's happened on more than one occasion and I walk away scratching my head, "Jesus, why didn't I think of that?" So they have a perspective that is really remarkable and I really have an enormous amount of respect for the way the process works.

Of course, according to Blecher, elitists will always take a different view based on their inexperience and naivete. Those who criticize it usually do not trust the common people to make important decisions. "If a jury doesn't understand the case, it's not their fault. It's the lawyer's fault."

The standing instructions to the trial lawyers in Pat McCartan's office are never to give up a jury in a case where one is entitled to have one. McCartan prefers the odds in a jury trial over those with a judge. It is a greater risk to depend upon a judge than upon a jury for a fair hearing.

I think it comes down to as simple a proposition as six or eight or twelve minds are better than one. Your odds are much better. Judges have become calloused. They've heard too much, seen too much, and if they have their own agenda, you're done. With a jury, you've got a shot, and I don't think anything is too complicated for a jury to understand if presented properly.

—Pat McCartan

Harry Reasoner, however, does see difficulties in presenting cases with highly technical components, such as patent litigation, to juries. "How does one communicate to a jury on the question of whether a computer-chip technology infringes another? You have to wonder what drives the ultimate jury decision." But if a jury trial is not the best forum for resolving such issues, what is? Reasoner is not sure. Appointed government bodies, such as the Federal Trade Commission or the Patent Office, are not promising in this regard.

> My only hesitation in saying that you ought to take it away
> from juries, is that it's not clear to me who you give it to.
> The Federal Trade Commission was created to deal with
> economic issues. They would do better than the courts,
> they would be experts, etc. Many would argue that that has
> been a miserable failure. Look at the Patent Office. It
> doesn't seem to me that's anything to be proud of and, by in
> large, the courts have done a better job than the Patent
> Office.

To find or establish a body of impartial decision-makers with the expertise to make the kind of determinations in a technical area that might be necessary to render justice, is a conundrum. "If you created a computer commission and then let the political process work its will, you wonder what kind of people would be up there making those decisions and where their biases would lie." Reasoner ultimately supports the jury system when he reviews the alternatives. This seems to be because the issues involved can almost always be reduced to a question of credibility. Reasoner brackets the issue of whether or not credibility can be ascertained without comparing what someone says to a set of actual facts. If the facts are hard to determine because they involve specialized domains of knowledge and descriptions, then juries need to depend upon attorneys to simplify and explain these facts. Thus, as we have seen so often, whether or not an attorney is believed is critical.

> Juries decide as much on their notions of who is credible
> and who is not. It does force settlement which, probably
> most of the time, is a reasonable solution. And at the end of
> the day, is a decision by jury better or worse than a decision
> by some type of specialized commission you create? I guess
> if I had to pick right now, I'd pick juries.

Steve Susman agrees that barring the invention of some "super great decision-making computer," some Wizard of Oz of jurisprudence, juries are the best game in town. He states that a judge is basically just like other people on the jury, "except he has a law degree which doesn't qualify him for anything, it just means he knows how to read cases, it doesn't mean he knows how to find facts . . . I don't think there are any cases that the jury ought to not hear." Susman refuses to accept the notion that some cases are too complicated for a jury to hear. Most cases are simple; and if complicated, the themes are simple. "I'd rather have the judgment of twelve people in the community than a single judge, no matter what the complexity."

Arthur Liman believes in the jury system because it is generally too dangerous to let one person make the decision rather than a group. In a group, individual biases and prejudices can cancel each other out. In an individual they go unchecked. "And there is nothing worse than having a judge who's against you from day one and has the ability to make the decision. So, I start with the proposition that juries should hear all cases." Liman does recognize the need for some exceptions. These include situations in which a flood of claims come into courts, automobile accidents, for example. Sheer volume will make it necessary to dispose of these cases in another way. "We will end up with no-fault. It's going to take a long time, but it will happen." The same is true, Liman argues, for giant product-liability cases, asbestos litigation is a good example, in which there are literally thousands of plaintiffs. There will be other products that will have caused an injury or created health problems, and there will have to be a system to deal with them. The real challenge, Liman believes, is the economic impact of runaway judgments "because we really could put American industry out of business if we were to say that any punitive damage verdict or any kind of compensatory verdict, no matter how unfounded on the evidence, goes." Liman believes safeguards are available, even in part, if judges will use them. But, subject to these caveats, the bottom line, for Liman, is that the jury system works.

> And there are enough safeguards. The Supreme Court came up with Haslip and the courts apply those factors and there's no reason in the world why our system can't work. It's got the flexibility to work. It's going to be up to the quality of judges to make it function. So, I'm comfortable with juries.

> I believe in the jury system and I think that it provides
> better justice than one man or one woman rule.

David Boies allows that he is probably a less strong proponent of the jury system than many of his colleagues. He agrees that juries have a good track record in determining credibility. The problem he perceives is that jurors often focus on issues that the law does not consider important. In other words, the problem for Boies is that jurors do not think like lawyers. Consequently, they are inclined to use general moral precepts and values along with relevant social attitudes, rather than rules of law in making decisions. Behavior scientists who have studied this completely agree. Salient issues for jurors are often not the legal issues lawyers like to emphasize. As a juror consultant, I have been involved in many such cases in which an element of subjective motivation, liking or disliking a litigant, for example, or some symbolic event of no real legal consequence, was far more important to the jurors than many lawyers were aware of or were prepared to deal with.

There are some things that juries do very well. They do a pretty good job of telling when a witness is lying, when a witness is comfortable or uncomfortable, a pretty good job of telling whether a lawyer is being natural or not, particularly in a long trial. They pay a lot of attention. They try hard. But fundamentally, they will more often than not in difficult complex cases, focus on and decide on issues other than the issue the law says they ought to decide on.

—David Boies

Boies does not explicitly embrace the concept, but he suggests that it would be a "good test" to see how many times both sides would like to have a jury decide a case. He guesses that in the majority of cases one side would want a jury and another not. He suggests that this is because both sides recognize that a jury would favor one side more than a judge. Clearly this is another way of making the same point, that juries tend to decide cases on something besides legal issues. Judges obviously take a more legalistic approach to a case. The side that wanted the case decided on legal issues rather than broader moral precepts or values, or prevailing social attitudes, would favor a judge. Boies has some interesting ideas about making juries work better.

> We've got to give juries more help. We've got to think about allowing juries to ask questions. We've got to think about giving juries .some kind of written statement from the parties. None of that is without its problems, but we've got to look at the jury system and how it operates and how it relates to the function of judges. We have to do this with an open mind. A lot has changed in the last couple hundred years and we've got to be prepared to examine that.

It is interesting to note that when discussing the ability of juries to "get it right" most of the members of the judiciary with whom I have talked have a healthy respect for juries. In fact, in an informal survey of more than twenty judges, all concluded that they agreed with the jury's ultimate decision regarding guilt, or liability in more than ninety-five percent of the cases they tried. My experience in having personally conducted hundreds of post-trial juror interviews in a wide variety of cases throughout the country, confirms the belief that juries try exceptionally hard to get it right and do a good job. Generally, when I hear lawyers complain about juries, it is because they are unhappy with the verdict. Talk to jurors in the same case and it is clear the lawyers who lost did not do a particularly good job. Skilled trial lawyers are disappointed when they lose, but rarely have I heard them blame the jury.

CHAPTER 8 ▬▬▬▬▬▬

Confronting the Opposition: Cross-Examination

"I'm not a good old boy, I'm not a buddy. I'm the lawyer."

—Joe Jamail

Cross-examination is one of the most adversarial elements in a jury trial. Lawyers are frequently aggressive, witnesses defensive. Encounters between hostile witnesses and attorneys out to drive home key issues of fact and credibility make for potentially volatile moments. Jurors savor the chance to see this and are usually the most alert and expectant during cross-examination. Cross-examination presents opportunities for counsel to use many rhetorical tactics. Objectives are defined. Should a certain witness be destroyed on cross-examination? Should another be treated with respect and consideration? There can be real surprises here. An adroit lawyer must be prepared either to take advantage of the unexpected or to engage in rapid damage control, as the case may be.

I like doing it after I'm in it. I don't like preparing for it. Yeah, cross-examination is fun. Sure, you have to make sure you don't appear like a bully...you have to make sure that you're not being a smart ass. You can't get up and say, "I've got a few things to ask you," and then ask thirty-five questions.

—Phil Corboy

Demolishing a Witness: Joe Jamail and Pennzoil v. Texaco

Earlier we became acquainted with one of the most high-profile commercial cases in legal history *Pennzoil v. Texaco* (see Chapter 1). It will be recalled that Pennzoil engaged in protracted negotiations to buy Getty Oil. Texaco, which later purchased Getty Oil, was then subject to a lawsuit brought by Pennzoil, represented by Joe Jamail. Jamail conducted the cross-examination of two witnesses for Getty Oil, Marty Lipton and Lawrence Tisch. The case turned on two principal issues: Did Pennzoil have a deal with Getty? And did Texaco tortiously interfere with that deal? Both Lipton and Tisch were brought by Texaco to argue that there had been no deal between Getty and Pennzoil. Marty Lipton testified at length that there had been no agreement to sell Getty stock to Pennzoil. Jamail prepared for his cross-examination of Lipton by using impressions obtained from friends, which he says were useful in destroying Lipton's credibility in two and a half days of cross-examination. Jamail did not depose Lipton. "I had a little background on the guy's personality and I had refused to take his deposition because I wanted to force them to bring him." Jamail wanted to know why Lipton wanted Texaco to guarantee him personally from liability if he was not worried about a deal being broken with Pennzoil.

> So I asked him, "If there was no deal, why did you insist that Texaco give you a complete indemnity, as well as the Getty Museum, if you abandoned the Pennzoil so-called agreement in principle?" "Well, that's just normal." I said, "Oh, no, Mr. Lipton, it's not normal that the buyer gives the seller an indemnity. Anybody who has bought a washing machine knows that."

Typically, Jamail reduced a business transaction of immense scope to the level of buying a washing machine, bringing the matter down to a level the jurors can relate to. He goes on:

> I finally made him admit...he knew I had him...He got to where he couldn't even look at me. So he made an off-the-cuff statement that was not good and I said, "Well, what you're really saying, I take it, Mr. Lipton, is that if this Pennzoil agreement were between ordinary people and for not as much money as this agreement and not in New York, that you would consider that to be a contract."

Again, Jamail frames the issue in common-sense terms, creating a barrier between jurors who are the "ordinary people" in question and the city slicker, wheeler-dealer, New Yorkers. For the jurors it would have been a done deal. Lipton was forced to agree with the proposition Jamail had advanced.

> He said, "Yeah, I guess you could put it that way." He was dead then. He knew what he said. Right then and there I knew. And I carved him up. I was so hard on him. Some people thought I was too hard on him. But you can't be too hard on a guy who is as successful as that and who looked like he did and is as smart as he is...

The fact that Lipton was an attorney himself precluded much sympathy, it was suggested. Jamail agreed.

> Juries are not going to get down on you if you're right. If you can prove your point. And I was gambling. But I knew I could. I felt like I could. You've got to take chances. That cross has been cited more than any cross done in a civil case in this century.

Lipton left the witness stand embarrassed and angry. As for Lipton's attorneys, "they didn't like it, but they were always acting like somebody in the last stages of syphilis." For Jamail, "everything was euphoric." The tactical devices employed in the Pennzoil case are vintage Jamail. Early on, he learns personality traits that he can play upon to make the witness vulnerable. He then establishes an "us versus them" constellation by bonding himself to the jury, and demonstrates that the witness is, in essence, not "one of our kind." There are a number of ingredients. One is to establish that "we" have different values than "they." Another is to paint the witness as arrogant, as if he is beyond the rules that "we" play by. Finally, Jamail can embarrass and ridicule his witness with withering sarcasm. He times this so skillfully that jurors accept it and even root for him. These elements were also present in the cross-examination of Lawrence Tisch in the same case.

Tisch, the billionaire president of CBS and a Getty Oil board member, was another witness who testified that there never was a deal between Getty and Pennzoil. Jamail had a document, an important element in the proof that there had been a deal, but Jamail was saving it. He wanted to destroy Tisch's testimony at the same time he introduced the document. The jury was asked to consider why a man like Tisch, worth so much money, would be interested in breaking a deal with Pennzoil so the deal could be made again for a few dollars a share more. Jamail recounts his cross of Tisch:

> They brought Tisch to prove that he was worth two billion dollars. Now here I am trying a case with a jury that, you know, billions of dollars were unheard of. And they are proving this one witness had two billion and he was on Getty's board.

Jamail immediately started to create his "we versus they" constellation.

I asked, "You are a friend of Mr. Getty?" He said, "Well, I don't know how you define friend." I said, "Well, I don't know the New York definition of it, but I know the Texas definition of it." And he looked at me with such hatred.

—Joe Jamail

Given his age and appearance, Tisch was potentially sympathetic. Having eviscerated Lipton, Jamail saw the need to treat Tisch with a certain amount of deference.

> He was kind of a grandfather-looking guy and they wanted to like him. So I decided I'm not going to jump him because I had just left Lipton's blood, liver, and kidneys all over the courtroom.

Jamail had the exhibit he wanted to use in his pocket, a little time bomb waiting to go off.

> There was a little bitty exhibit that nobody had paid any attention to. And when it went in, I had a copy made of it and I carried it in my briefcase all the time at that trial until he got on the stand. That morning I had taken it out and put it in my coat pocket.

Jamail laid the ground work carefully for the use of the exhibit. At the same time he baited and mocked Tisch until he became testy under the Jamail needle.

And I said, "Mr. Tisch, your lawyers have gone to great pains to tell this jury how wealthy you are. Two billion dollars? Well, you didn't get that by accident. You worked for it, yeah? You probably know more about investment banking and investment bankers than anybody in the world." "Well, I don't know about that. I know about them. Obviously, I know more about them than you do, Mr. Jamail." Very shitty. "I accept that, sir, I accept it."

Tisch was pushed further on his knowledge of how investment bankers work.

Have you had occasion, sir, to have retained them on one or more occasion?" "Many times." "Worked with them?" "Yes, many times. I told you that." Real shitty and the worse he is the easier I am. The grandfather I wanted the jury to see was a shitass. And I was real nice.

By now Jamail had Tisch moving the way he wanted, in the direction of attacking Jamail.

I said, "Well now, I'm concerned about something. How are they paid?" He said, "Just like you, on a contingent fee, only they don't charge a third." Of course that is grounds to have him reprimanded. I didn't say anything. "Very well, very well. But you don't know what my fees are, do you?" "No, I don't, but I assume..." I said, "Well, what do you mean, contingency?" "Well, if they make the deal, they get a part of what the deal is sold for or acquired for. For instance, if it's a billion-dollar deal, he'll probably get a one and one-half percent commission or maybe five percent over, whatever..."

Jamail gave the jury a moment to digest this and then asked Tisch a key question.

"Well, when do they get paid?" He said, "They get paid after the deal is done." I said, "Well, you must be mistaken there." "Don't tell me I'm mistaken." I said, "You mean, they don't get paid unless the deal is done?" "That's right." I said, "When do they submit a bill? Do they submit the bill before the deal is done?" He said, "That's stupid. You're asking stupid questions. Of course they don't. They wouldn't be in business. They have to wait until the deal is done before they submit the bill."

The moment had come for Jamail to produce his document.

> "Take a look at this, will you Mr. Tisch? What is that?" It
> was a bill from Goldman Sachs to Getty, dated January the
> third when we said the deal took place the night of the
> second for services done on the Pennzoil deal. I said,
> "What does that look like to you, Mr. Tisch?" He looked at
> me with such hatred. "Mr. Tisch, does that look like a done
> deal or at least the investment bankers thought it was." He
> said, "Yeah, it does." "Thank you for coming, Mr. Tisch."

More euphoria for Joe Jamail. "Shit," Jamail chortled, "I had that son
of a bitch blown up the size of that wall when we got to arguing it. But
that's what you do in a case."

Cross-Examination Tactics

Preparing Witnesses for Cross-Examination

Careful preparation before the trial helps an expert witness defend
his or her credibility under cross-examination. When Pat McCartan
prepares his witnesses for cross-examination he puts himself in the
position of his rival. He considers where he might attack the witness if
he were conducting the cross. McCartan looks at the deposition and
considers it in the light of relevant documents. "You've read their
deposition. You know where they've left a few openings here or there,
or something they have said that is going to, perhaps, give them some
trouble or confinement." After he has identified trouble spots,
McCartan goes over the questions he thinks will be asked. He
evaluates the witness' answers. He does not instruct the witness to lie
or shade the truth, but he carefully formulates answers that tell the
truth without hurting the case.

> I cross-examine them and say, "Look, here's the kind of
> question you're going to be asked. Here's the way it's going
> to be asked," and listen to their answer and tell them
> whether I think that's a good answer or not. I'm telling
> them there are ways to answer questions that are truthful
> and which are more effective than other ways.

McCartan sees a close connection between preparing a witness for
direct and for cross. It involves mastery on the part of the witness of
the same areas of the case, the same documents, the same elements in

the story. "You say, 'Now look, here is where you're going to be saying this or getting into this area. You've got to keep in mind these three documents. They're going to be coming back at you.'" Witness preparation, according to McCartan, is the most difficult part of the trial. A nervous witness must be calmed. If the witness is going to supply important facts and is a relative newcomer to the case, the problem may be exacerbated. They have not lived with the case long enough to gain a reassuring familiarity. On the other hand, a witness steeped in the details who knows a great deal about the case might fear making a mistake in part because he feels his testimony is so critical. The attorney's task is to put witnesses in a positive, stress-free state of mind, to give them confidence. One way to do this is to impress upon them that they have sufficient in-depth knowledge of the matter to protect themselves against attack in cross-examination.

> I put them at ease if they are a professional or an expert and even someone within an organization or corporation by telling them, "Look, you know more about this subject than that lawyer. All that lawyer knows is what somebody poured into his ear the day before he's going to cross-examine you...he doesn't know half of what you know about this area and you just make sure that you remember that."

Preparing witnesses for cross-examination works best according to Bob Warren when someone on the lawyer's team imitates the style the opposing attorney is likely to employ. This is done on videotape.

> One thing you have to watch out for nowadays is this business about what can be asked on cross-examination, what preparation have you had and not had. Something that seems as if somebody was being primped up or taught to mislead.

Witnesses who appear to be talking parrots or who have memorized "a story," are not credible. They may be "primped up" to sound and look pretty, but they will not be effective.

Fred Bartlit advises attorneys to warn their witnesses not to argue with the trial attorney because the attorney is highly skilled in argumentation and knows the case better than any witness.

> A witness who tries to wrestle or spar with a very experienced trial lawyer who knows the case is going to get murdered...it's like me playing basketball against Michael Jordan. I'm not going to say, "In your face, Michael."
>
> **—Fred Bartlit**

The Expert Witness

The use of expert witnesses is a subject of considerable controversy among trial lawyers. Experts are used in almost every case in present-day litigation, so much so that the expert-witness business has become a cottage industry. There are experts of all stripes, specialists for plaintiffs or specialists for defendants, and they can cost a fortune. Many "experts" are actually professional witnesses.

In the opinion of the attorneys here, given good lawyering on both sides, experts tend to cancel each other out. Jim Brosnahan agrees with the proposition that jurors feel the same way. At times it is easy, and even fun, to destroy the credibility of an expert witness. The jury often discounts expert testimony unless the expert has tremendous credentials.

> But one of the most fun things you can have is to discover that the expert on the other side has done so much work for that lawyer that the income over the last five years has probably been about a million and a half dollars. And then it doesn't matter what they've said.

Experts who have been highly paid by a number of litigants over a considerable period of time will not be believed no matter what their testimony.

Jamail believes that one of the reasons expert witnesses are frequently subject to aggressive cross-examination is that many are not honest and credible. Too many are, as he puts it, "bought and paid for."

> Usually, in the field of engineering, there are certain "consultants," they call themselves. They've been with a governmental agency or an engineering agency somewhere and then they become a club cadet [Jamail's euphemism for a testifier]. And then on the plaintiff's side, too. They send out brochures every day.

Max Blecher recalls a recent example in which an expert had testified in an earlier trial contrary testimony. The witness was also vulnerable on the basis of the conceptual framework within which he operated, which was out of synchronization with prevailing academic wisdom.

> I had a guy last week who came and criticized our definition of relevant market and he had testified in an earlier case on a market in the same general area for the plaintiff that was even narrower than the one we picked. He was really embarrassed. It was hard for him to explain that. His definition was at odds with the academic literature. So he was vulnerable on his basic concepts and qualifications.

But that was a rare opportunity, Blecher points out. Nevertheless, even when an expert is not vulnerable, cross-examination is still an opportunity to reinforce one's case. This can be done by getting in more references to important exhibits.

> "Doctor Smith, I know you've taken the position that thus and so is your view. Have you looked at Exhibits forty-two, sixty, and seventy-seven?" And frequently, the answer is no.

The other side will have committed a characteristic mistake—failure to show all the relevant exhibits to the witness.

> I have frequently seen the guys almost blanched-looking, "No, I haven't." "Well, does this give you any cause for concern?" And sometimes they will say, "Well, a little bit." If they say no, it's not convincing. But I don't really care what they say, because I get a chance, once again, to put forty-two, sixty, and seventy-seven up on the screen.

The fact that the expert is unfamiliar with these exhibits will be a point against his credibility with the jurors.

> Let the jury see this guy studying this for the first time and what are they saying to themselves? "This guy didn't even see the other side's case. What the hell does this opinion mean? It's a one-sided opinion."

And Blecher will continue to drive home the point.

> "So, doctor you haven't seen all the documents in this case? You've only seen what counsel has elected to show you."
> "Well, I guess so, because I only got a package of

documents." So, that's the approach I use with the experts.
I lay out my case again. Everytime they put a witness on, I
want to put my case back.

One of the most important issues in cross-examination is how
aggressive a lawyer should be with a witness. Making this decision
entails an assessment of how the witness has come across to the jury on
direct. If the jury likes a witness it is clearly a mistake to treat this
witness roughly. There are other, subtle ways to undermine the
credibility of such a witness. In addition, the jury must understand the
purpose of cross-examination of a particular witness. If the point of a
cross-examination is to impeach a segment of testimony, it is important to frame that point. And once the witness is impeached this must
register loudly and clearly with the jurors.

Jim Brosnahan addresses both issues. He feels that a nonaggressive
style can be effective. "Many times you can get good things from a
witness if you're not too aggressive. If you work with them and ask
them things, they will tell you, if you ask it the right way." Brosnahan
also raises the possibility that he may want to surprise a witness on
cross. Although, in general, he cautions against being overly aggressive. Under the right circumstances however, he will go at a witness
with hammer and tongs. If there is a way radically to undermine a
witness' testimony, the lawyer should take that route and make sure the
jurors know what happened.

> I've heard a lot of trial lawyers say, "You know, you
> never destroy the witness. It never happens—
> only on TV." I don't agree with that. I've destroyed
> many witnesses. I think you've got to think that
> way. If there's a way just to totally undermine their
> testimony, you've got to do that.
>
> **—Jim Brosnahan**

Setting Objectives

Joe Jamail's primary theory of cross-examination is to go immediately to the point. Jamail believes that jurors feel imposed upon by
the onus of jury duty and are impatient with anyone who wastes their
time. He scores points with the jury by coming quickly to the heart of
the issues in cross.

> I'm pretty good at cross, OK? I go right to the jugu-
> lar...juries appreciate that. They're imposed on, first off.
> And that little civic speech the judge gives is meaningless to
> them. They've been sitting on those hard benches and
> you're giving them five bucks a day and it costs twelve
> bucks to park. So you have got to do something with that
> jury. You have got to show that you are bingo, bango. And
> the other side is fucking around with you.

Phil Corboy does not really believe that there are rules for cross. Being good at it is instinctive. But he does identify three basic objectives in cross-examination, and it is usually necessary to do one of the three. One, "shore up and adapt," that is, reinforce points made on direct and address points made by the other side; two, destroy the witness; or, three, question the witness in such a way that gaps in the case are filled. Attempting one or more of these will depend upon the witness. An effective tactic is to develop a piece of information from one witness on cross that undermines or contradicts the forthcoming testimony of another witness.

> Let's assume the issue is present cash value. And one of
> their witnesses is going to devastate you or at least
> contradict what the system should be and you want to get
> from this witness something which is going to be contradic-
> tory to their next witness. Maybe so much so where they
> won't even use him, [and this] certainly puts his credibility
> at issue. Or, I'll get this witness to agree to certain facts,
> certain systems, certain theories which are contradictory to
> some other portion of their case. I'm not going to destroy
> an expert witness unless I've got contradictory testimony
> statements. I'm not going to do it. You can, but it's not
> likely. So, what you want to do is get from cross-examina-
> tion that which will shore up your case or your examination
> of another witness.

Most of the time it will not be possible to destroy a witness. Both sides will have had too much time to prepare for this to be possible. Consequently, cross-examination needs to be patient and methodical. "You've got to pick and choose. Cross-examination is really an art in today's world with discovery being what it is," (protracted, highly adversarial, and a contentious phase of litigation). Corboy's preparation for cross-examination is worth noting. In this, as in everything, he is meticulous and thorough. He familiarizes himself with everything

317

the witness has said and done. His objective is to discover where he or she is vulnerable. Sometimes a personal characteristic is important.

> I have been told that the witness [who] I'm going to be cross-examining in this case tires late in the day. If I get her late in the day and it's accurate, I'll test it out. She may get testy with me. She's kept this jury here four hours, now it's my turn to cross-exam and all of a sudden, she's looking at her watch or she's playing with herself or twiddling . . . she might have some hackneyed answers. It might become easier than I know. I get lucky in cross-examination.

In preparing himself for cross, Pat McCartan decides what he wants to get out of a witness from the depositions and documents. He knows with some certainty what the other witnesses will say and through the use of a document or deposition he will outline his particular line of inquiry. Although cross-examination is far more flexible and open than direct, it is important to have objectives well-defined. Be prepared to take advantage of opportunities as they arise but adhere to the plan, McCartan suggests.

> Cross-examination is free-wheeling, but it has to be disciplined. You should have no more than four or five goals, admissions, or testimony that you want to elicit. The art comes into play when you see a crack, a fissure, open up somewhere. Go in, but don't lose your way; come back and stick to your road map.

Cross-examining witnesses is like fencing. When there is an opening, the thrust must be executed. McCartan made masterful use of an opportunity in the *Mobil v. Marathon* case. His goals were well-defined, and in the course of pursuing them he had a bonus fall into his lap.

> I'll never forget the cross-examination of a witness in the *Mobil v. Marathon* case. I had several goals that I wanted to accomplish with this witness. One of them was to show that up until this time, when the oil industry was being deregulated, while you had giants in this industry, they were very tightly constrained and the industry was structured by regulation. Now the federal government was going to peel away all that regulation, and I was contending those companies that had the resources were going to dominate the industry.

The witness was a world-renowned economist, whose area of expertise was the operation of markets and the forces that determine price and competition. With the relaxation of government regulation, it was expected that giants such as Mobil would become even more dominant. McCartan wanted to establish this fact.

> This examination started out with the history of regulation. He waxed eloquently on it, on the way the industry was tightly regulated, right from the wellhead to the gasoline pump. And then, we were there. And I said, "All right, what are the market forces going to do now?" I knew he was a free-market economist. He said, "Well, the end of this regulation, the market's going to control." And I said, "And the strong will soon dominate the market?" He had to say yes.

McCartan brought this witness to admit that market forces were not perfect, that it was difficult for perfect competition to prevail so that there would be no price differentials within a given market. Judicial intervention was necessary for smaller, independent companies, such as Marathon, to survive and compete for the benefit of the consumer. Mobil was contending that the appropriate market was the nation as a whole. Their contention was that the same market price prevailed everywhere, that the playing field was even. McCartan led the witness into coining an image that was amusing and rather ludicrous.

> Mobil's economist was maintaining that the market for gasoline extended nationally, from coast to coast and border to border. I was cross-examining him about the pipeline system in the United States and asking him in effect how crude oil from a tanker arriving from Saudi Arabia and unloaded in Louisiana was going to be refined, shipped to Massachusetts, and sold for the same price that would prevail in New Orleans when there wasn't even a pipeline connecting New Orleans to Massachusetts. He was becoming very exasperated, and I kept pressing the point. Finally, he said, "I don't care if a magic fairy takes the oil from Louisiana to Boston." Well, we quickly adopted his contemptuous words as our label for Mobil's economic thesis, we hammered home the point that our opponents were relying on the agency of a "magic fairy" to support their theory of a national market.

McCartan found this a marvelous piece of serendipity.

> Oh, it was a bonus. I mean, I'd like to think it was effective cross-examination. It wasn't. It was really a product of his frustration. And we closed up the cross-examination by impeaching him on the first edition of his treatise. The magic fairy was a bonus. I knew he couldn't get the pipeline to connect these markets, but he had to get it up there some way. I never thought he'd say it would be with a magic fairy.

McCartan reviews the goals of this cross-examination, a real masterpiece of tactical expertise. He set out to develop the following points:

> Release of controls made it more important than ever that the court protect the consuming public and not let the last independent fully integrated oil company be swallowed up, point number one. Point number two, if it is a national market, how does oil flow on a refined basis throughout the United States at the same price, when you have all these transportation costs? Final point, impeach him on his treatise. Three very important goals for cross-examination, but with a lot of bonuses in between.

David Boies puts a strong emphasis on preparing for cross-examination. He makes a file by topic of those portions of a witness's deposition that he wants to explore during cross. He then adds related documents to that file under the relevant topic. This stack of folders is his ammunition for cross-examination.

> I will sit down and read the guy's deposition all the way through. I will mark the portions I'm interested in by drawing a square around it. I'll put those pages in a series of manila folders that I have labeled by topic. And in those folders I will have some documents, too, that people will have gathered for me. That's what I will cross from. Generally, I will have done this the night before.

Harry Reasoner subscribes to the idea that cross-examination should attempt to develop a limited number of pointed objectives. What these will be depends upon the witness. "If there is an opportunity to impeach the witness through documents or contradictions in testimony and to damage the credibility of the witness, I give high priority to that." Reasoner notes that credibility points made on cross-examination score high with the jury. In order to take full advantage of this possibility he modulates his aggressiveness. More aggression will be tolerated by the jurors when it is leveled at highly paid experts than against other, more sympathetic, witnesses. "I try to make a judgment as to how much aggressiveness the jury will think is appropriate. For highly compensated professional experts, my general notion is the jury will feel I'm entitled to beat up on them to whatever extent I can."

Jim Neal has two principal goals in cross-examination: to make an immediate impact on the jury and to nail down points for summation. A major problem in cross is trying to get too much. "You've got to know what you can safely get out of the witness on cross." Courts will not always allow Neal to do what he wants on cross-examination.

> If a witness says, "X happened," I'd like to say, "Mr. Jones, you heard Mr. Y testify that that didn't happen, didn't you? Is he lying [or] telling the truth?" Of course that's probably inappropriate, but some courts will let you do that. Particularly if it is the defendant who is being cross-examined.

Fred Bartlit agrees with others who say cross-examination is a question of developing a series of points. It is a good tactic to arrange the points in order, with the most important coming last, but that may not be possible. Depending upon the way the cross-examination evolves, counsel takes what comes. "Makes sense to start strong, finish with a good point, and if you're going to take any chances, take them in between." During cross, Bartlit likes to have a steno pad handy on which he has written information. This, he feels, lends him credibility, demonstrating that he does not rely on his memory for detailed facts, particularly numbers. The only time Bartlit writes out a question in advance is in a case in which impeachment is at stake. "I'll show the jury I'm using notes and I'll make sure that I am being precise when it counts." Appearing to depend upon notes, even if it is not strictly necessary, makes Bartlit appear like an ordinary mortal.

> I used to have it all in my head. And some juror said he couldn't believe I was getting it right because I had no note paper. So now I use paper where you would be expected to use paper. It's not a tour de force where I'm trying to show people I'm smarter than they are.

Bartlit rarely adopts an accusatory style in cross-examination.

> I ask cross-examination questions differently from anybody
> else. Most people say in cross, "Isn't it a fact that...? Isn't
> it true that...? That's correct, isn't it?" I think with that
> accusatory style of cross you don't get as much with the
> witness. The jury thinks that that should be saved for
> specific situations.

Bartlit tends to lower the barrier between himself and the witness on cross, muting their adversarial status.

> My style is, "Were you there? Was Smith there? Did you
> say so-and-so? Did he say so-and-so? Did you talk about
> this?" See what I mean? It looks more like an impartial
> search for the truth than an accusatory kind of thing.

Bartlit has several objectives in cross. Among other things, he wants to use cross-examination to find support through the opponent's witnesses for the story presented in his opening statement. "Because what I get out of their witnesses will be more believed than what I get out of my witnesses."

Impeaching the Witness

Attacks on credibility are de rigueur for all cross-examination. The only sure-fire way to assault credibility is to catch the witness in a contradiction or a factual error that can sometimes be branded as a lie, but indirectly, in order not to create sympathy for the witness. If Bartlit intends to work closely with depositions in order to impeach the witnesses from the other side, he establishes the groundwork for this in his opening statement.

> If there's going to be a lot of impeaching I say in my
> opening statement, "Now, there's something in this case
> called depositions." (And you always know the court
> reporter's name.) You say, "Mrs. Jean Jones over here is our
> court reporter and those of you who haven't been in court
> before are going to be surprised to know that she is getting
> every single word now as we say it. She can write as fast as I
> can speak. To save time, we've asked all these questions of
> witnesses before, etc."

Bartlit goes on to relate the use of the ominous "red-backed" deposition.

So, we've asked them about the case and we do that so we can only go to the important points. I'll say to the jurors, "When you see me pick up a document with a red back, that's a deposition. That means that I've got with me the testimony of this same witness on another occasion. Now, sometimes people say one thing before trial and sometimes they change their testimony at trial and the judge will tell you the meaning of that. But when I pick up this deposition with the red back, that means I think the witness has said something different."

Bartlit leads the jury by hand through the impeachment process.

What I do is point out to the witness what he said today and what he said on another occasion. So the jury gets trained when they see that, and when the witness says something, I say now, "You just said blank. On a previous occasion under oath, did you say something different?" ... The red thing gets picked up so much. Then in the final argument you say, "Remember in the beginning I said sometimes people change their story? Well, every time I've picked up that red thing, that meant I thought he changed his story. And if he hadn't changed his story, Mr. Vinson could have objected. He didn't object once. I picked up that book one hundred twenty-six times in the trial. One hundred twenty-six times they changed their story."

A visual cue is a compelling technique. Perceptions that come through multiple channels, the spoken word reinforced with a visual stimulus, are forceful and easy to remember. For such a device to work and not be viewed as a sleazy ploy, Bartlit knows he must have the right kind of jurors who will not be offended by his red-backed depositions. For Bartlit, the right kind of jurors are those who will appreciate theatricality in the courtroom.

A feel for the ambience of the courtroom is important in deciding whether or not to be aggressive.

After you get into it for a while, then you can get rough. Then you can say, "Oh, come on, Mr. Smith." If you do that early on, you get hammered ... the judge gets irked. So you have to have enough feel and control of the ambience of the courtroom so that you're not overbearing, you're not mean. But when a guy says, "I wasn't there," you say, "Are you kidding?" It gets real quiet.

Everything is done to make the witness look evasive. It has to be demonstrated rather than observed.

> In other words, if you ask a guy a question and he doesn't answer it, you say, "OK, for the second time..." He doesn't answer. You say, "Now, Mr. Smith, for the third time..." He doesn't answer. "Should we try again for the fourth time?" You don't care how much he talks. But you want the jury to see that he's being evasive.

The time to become overbearing is when the jury is fed up with the witness, and wants you to do something.

> You say, "Now, Mr. Smith, yes or no?" And if you've been a craftsman and you've set it all up, you get a win. The judge will say, "Yes, answer the questions." See? You've created a vignette that will be remembered.

Max Blecher, as plaintiff, has maximum opportunity to make points with the jurors early in the trial on direct, still values cross as a chance to prove his case.

> When you are cross-examining the other side, this is your only opportunity to get into the inner-workings of the decision-making process of the defendant. Your only opportunity to confront them with the documentary evidence, which I consider to be the cornerstone of every case.

Cross is a wonderful opportunity to hammer a witness with a document.

> "Now in this document you say the plaintiff was a nuisance. Why?" You develop that. "What was the nuisance about him? And did you talk about that further? How come there are no documents following this one? Did you have a staff meeting about it? What did you...?" And you just develop your case, quickly and get out.

Blecher also believes that one must come to the point quickly in cross-examination. For example, if the witness wrote a number of documents, the trial lawyer should exhibit them. In this manner, the witness can be used to re-focus the case. Sometimes it is possible for a plaintiff to re-focus his or her case during the cross-examination of an expert witness, particularly if the defense is careless in whom it picks as an expert.

For Bob Fiske cross-examination is the hardest part of the case. And it is "interestingly the one area where day in and day out the experience of the prosecutor's office is less of an advantage because in many of these cases, whether it is a US Attorney or a district attorney, frequently the key witness, the defendant, does not testify." Or, the defense may call few witnesses or no witnesses at all. As plaintiff, the government calls witnesses who testify against the defendant. These witnesses will be cross-examined by the defense attorney. The prosecutors, who do not do much cross-examination, are really specialists in presenting a direct case.

> You put it on the direct case and that's where the defense attorney gets up and attacks the credibility of the witnesses and talks about a reasonable doubt, but doesn't put the defendant on and doesn't call any witnesses. So the ability to develop cross-examination skills is less than if you were working for a legal aid agency.

Fiske also notes, as others have observed, that cross-examination is the most spontaneous and improvisational part of the trial. Less of it can be rehearsed, there will be more surprises, and there is less ability to control what the witness says.

In the opening, you know what you're going to say; summation, you know what you're going to say; the direct, you've rehearsed that. The one thing that is really spontaneous in the trial is the cross-examination. You think you know what you're going to do, but you never know exactly what the answer is going to be and then you have to formulate the next question right on the spot.
—Bob Fiske

Because cross-examination is a kind of free for all, Fiske is in favor of limited objectives. Like others before him, Fiske sees both the possibilities of getting something favorable for the case out of cross and of perhaps destroying the witness. At times it might be a combination of both.

Fiske suggests further that an attorney may need to change affect in the course of cross. Getting favorable information out of a witness may require being nice, and this can often occur at the beginning of the examination. When these possibilities have been exhausted one can sometimes shift to a more combative tone.

> My feeling is you're always going to get the favorable stuff out first. You're nice, you get up and smile, da, da, da. You get all that out. Then you say now about the rest of the stuff and then you really go after it. But you don't antagonize him by doing that first and then try to get the favorable stuff later.

Impeaching a witness may be easy, difficult, or impossible. Easiest is the case of a prior inconsistent statement, often in a deposition, or in a document such as a letter or memorandum.

> But other than that, you can either ignore it and then try to deal with it in summation later and explain it away, which is what you do if you don't really think you can impeach it, or you can suggest either the person was mistaken—it happened very quickly, things on their mind, a long time ago, they can't remember...Or, you could just come out and say you're a no-good liar. And that's when you really push all the chips out in the middle of the table because then it's a personal confrontation. If you don't pull that off, then you really hurt yourself with the jury. It is a critical judgment call. A mistake may have dire consequences.

One tactic employed in the impeachment of a witness is to keep the witness on a tight leash. That is, narrow the options for the witness down to yes and no responses. Do not permit the witness to explain his or her way out of a tight spot, a contradiction, or a lie. "I think an extremely important part of this," Fiske says, "is maintaining control of the witness, the leading question answered yes or no." It will probably be necessary to take a tougher tone than before, to interrupt any attempt to divert the direct question. "Don't let the witness make a speech. Cut him off. 'That's not my question, my question is this, answer it yes or no. Can't you answer it yes or no? Isn't that clear enough for you?'" *Maintain control.*

> And no matter what the answer is, you've got to make the jury think you're in control. Whatever it is. You can't look like, oh wow, I just took one on the chin. And that's the hardest thing for lawyers who are starting, the ability to, number one, control a witness in the first place, and then,

number two, act as if you're in control even in situations
where it may be getting away from you.

At times one gets a chance to ask a "heads I win, tails you lose,"
kind of question. Fiske gives an intriguing example in a criminal case
in which the defense had put on an expert witness to support the idea
that an alleged bank robber was insane. In this instance, the criminal
prosecutor did get a chance to engage in cross-examination. The
psychiatrist was asked if the escaping thief had thrown his gun into the
river.

> I remember John Keenan [US Federal District Court Judge,
> Southern District of New York] when he came to lecture to
> the assistants when I was US Attorney because he was an
> excellent cross-examiner. He gave this example of a defen-
> dant who robbed a bank and claimed he was insane. The
> question was [to the psychiatrist testifying that the defen-
> dant is insane] "Did you take into consideration the fact that
> after the bank robbery, the defendant threw the gun into the
> river?" You don't really care what the answer is because if
> he says no then obviously that impeaches him and if he says
> yes that impeaches him also. Either way, you can't lose.

Steve Susman also comments on the chance that the answer helps,
no matter what the question.

> If you can't score, at least get in a few good arguments.
> "Isn't it true that you didn't call my client because you
> didn't have anything to tell him? Isn't that the truth?" If
> you ask a question the right way, the jury believes you,
> whatever the answer the witness gives. You made your
> point. The jury understands it's the truth and it doesn't
> make any difference what he says. There are a huge number
> of opportunities like that during cross-examination.

In his general remarks on cross-examination, Arthur Liman notes
with others that a game plan is vital. A lawyer may want to milk a
witness or discredit a witness—sometimes both. But if both are to be
done, in which order? One kind of cross-examination is useful if the
aim is simply to give the jury a general impression of the witness. If
the desire is to make points with the jury, the cross-examination must
be organized in a way in which the jury can follow closely. Liman also
notes that the cross-examiner has the advantage because jurors are
particularly alert during cross.

> Cross-examination is the one time when a jury really pays enormous attention to the lawyer. That jury watches, they understand, and if you're good at it they look forward to that moment when you get up because you are going to be bringing out things that did not come out before. That's when you get your fan club on a jury. You can just see the jurors who are waiting for you to do something that didn't happen before. And they look forward to it.
>
> **—Arthur Liman**

Does one ever confront a lying witness? Joe Jamail responds:

> Oh, yeah. I've done it many times. "There is no nice word for this, sir. You have just lied to this jury." But I will have certain proof of it. They will have testified to something and will have a prior statement. This happens. I don't know how they think they will get away with it.

Bob Warren believes that cross-examination for the defense is as important as the opening statement. Often, however, the opportunity to make points on cross is limited by the fact that the plaintiff's witnesses testify to matters of minimal importance and scope. This was so, Warren relates, in a recent case in which he represented the defense. In a San Jose, California bond case, plaintiff gave Warren witnesses for a period of time for which opportunities to cross-examine were limited because the testimony they gave on direct was not of overwhelming importance, and they did not know enough to be made to appear important or interesting to jurors. Clearly, if cross is not interesting it should not be prolonged.

Asking Questions Without Knowing the Answer

One adage in cross-examination is that a question should *never* be asked without knowing the answer. The general idea is that counsel should be in control and not vulnerable to a nasty surprise. Not all the lawyers accept this notion and have some interesting ideas about its applicability. Jim Brosnahan accepts the rule with two exceptions. "One is you've thought about it. You don't know the answer, but you figured out what's likely. And even then, you approach it with caution with preliminary questions that will illuminate the situation a little bit." The other exception occurs when an answer is of such importance that an all-or-nothing risk must be taken.

> I did this in a case in San Diego. If we're going to win this case, we've got to get this answer. It was that stark. And so, I tried to figure out how to ask the question and I worked up to it and I got the answer. I was lucky. I did get the answer. So there are times when you have to do it.

Joe Jamail has also taken the risk. At times the tactic is employed because of a stubborn expert witness. The expert witness who has become an advocate for the opposing side is a typical example. Jamail will ask a question, the answer to which he does not know, when he considers an expert vulnerable, and will take considerable risks in questioning him. The hope is that the expert will ultimately contradict himself, sound foolish or "over-educated."

> If you've got a witness who is being obstinate just because he's been paid or for whatever reason he has chosen a side. That is the worst kind of witness. To let a jury think he has become an advocate. Now, an expert is supposed to come give his opinion and that's it and, you know, let the chips fall. Now a lot of them become advocates and that is horrible. They are easy meat.

Only an experienced attorney should ask blind questions, David Boies suggests, and it is a good rule for an inexperienced trial lawyer to bear in mind. When the answer is to be a yes or no, a virtuoso has the confidence and expertise to respond appropriately to either answer. Boies suggests that it can happen with a document or testimony from a deposition.

> There are a lot of times when you ask a question that you don't know the answer to. Sometimes it is because there are either [one of two likely answers] you can take apart. Sometimes you're in a position with documents, or with deposition testimony and the like, so that either answer you can take apart.

At other times, an attorney has pushed to a point where it is impossible not to continue even though one cannot quite predict the outcome. One suspects that if the witness goes on it will be good, and if the witness refuses to go further it will still score points. "If he goes the next step, you have a chance at making him look absurd. If he refuses to go to the next step, maybe the jury will be uncomfortable with whether he really believed what he said before." Sometimes, Boies tells us, intuition simply decrees that one must take a chance. There is an element of predictability in the first two general examples he gives. There may be instances when a gut feeling tells one to plunge ahead blindly. "The third situation is where there is an answer you really want and an answer you don't want, and you don't know which one you're going to get." It may occur when there is reason to believe that a witness is not completely loyal to the other side. Or, perhaps the witness can be intimidated or lulled into giving something away unwittingly.

> You may have a witness who, although the other side has called him, is not really necessarily in their pocket and you may feel you can develop something with him. You may have a witness who is in their pocket, but you think you can get something out of him before he understands what is happening, or maybe you've got him to a point where you think you've got him intimidated.

Bob Fiske, who is as respectful of the difficulties inherent in cross-examination as any of the other lawyers, if not more so, still feels "the rule" unrealistic. Far too much in cross-examination would simply remain inaccessible if one followed such a restriction. Fiske sees cross as a chess game in which one narrows the possibilities for a response the way a chess master forces an opponent into a restricted number of moves until there is really nothing left to do. When asked about the rule, he expressed skepticism that many subscribe to it. "To say I'm not going to ask a question because I don't know what the answer is going to be is confining the cross-examination much too much."

Phil Corboy also argues that it is a mistake not to take chances. One must run risks in cross-examination. It is a mistake to think there is an answer to every question. An attorney has to have the guts to ask a question without knowing the answer, and then know how to handle the consequences. Obviously the questions are key. Getting an answer that does not completely comport with his theory of the case, in Corboy's view, is not necessarily bad. In framing questions one needs to watch inflections for hints to where the witness is headed.

I don't believe just because a witness says something
different from my theory of the case that he or she is a liar
and therefore, if I get them to say something that agrees
with me, that doesn't mean they're telling the truth or not
telling it. It's the jury who makes the decision as to whether
it's true or not true.

Bob Warren offers a somewhat contrary point of view. He feels the
classic mistake on cross is to get unexpected answers. His solution is
interesting. It is not necessary to ask only questions to which the
answer is known, but ask questions when you do not *care* what the
answer is. "That's why my cross-examinations are almost always ones
where it almost makes no difference what the witness says because all I
really want to do is get a document up and highlight the good parts of
it."

Hostile or Sarcastic Witnesses

An attribute of all these men is that they know how to deal with the
small annoyances and aberrations one encounters in a jury trial. Very
little surprises them. Phil Corboy acknowledged that it is not always
easy to deal with a hostile witness, but that the thing to do is to force
the witness to exaggerate his or her hostile traits even further. "Make
him more snotty. Make him appear to be a smartass. I do as much as I
can to make him that way, and in addition to that, show he's biased."

It was seen earlier in Joe Jamail's cross-examination of Lawrence
Tisch that this can work very well. Jamail echoes Corboy's point:

Encourage them to be more sarcastic and more uncoopera-
tive. Just do everything you can to let the jury see it.
Everything. Just keep encouraging it. You can beat up on
anybody too much. But you know when to stop and the best
way is to let him beat up on himself. Your object is to win
this case for your client. If he is sarcastic and you're not, the
jury is going to say, "Well, he shouldn't treat Joe that way."

Pat McCartan takes the same tack with a hostile witness. One baits
the witness, driving the hostile behavior to excessive levels, but the
jury must not see that the witness is being provoked. "Maybe the most
effective thing you do on cross-examination is to get that hostility out
in the open," he suggests. McCartan had such a witness in the *Mobil v.
Marathon* case. He had a document showing that internally Mobil had
valued Marathon at about a third more than they were offering for the

company, although the relevant information was blacked out. In cross-examining Mobil's CEO, McCartan turned an antagonistic witness white hot.

> He's a character [the CEO]. He testified in both the antitrust and the securities cases. When he was testifying in the antitrust case, I went after him pretty hard. One, I had a document that showed they had valued Marathon on a per barrel basis internally at about a third more than they were offering. Of course, that was all redacted, and I insisted that he tell us what that valuation was. He was just dodging and weaving and going crazy and finally the judge said, "Answer the question." So he had to tell. When that was out, all hell broke loose.

It is important to gauge the jury carefully in dealing with a sarcastic or hostile witness according to Jim Neal. Juries will roundly approve of beating up certain witnesses. Sometimes a neutral witness will become unsympathetic.

If not initially, it may come to the point where they want to see you beat on the witness. It's dangerous, but I've seen occasions where I know damn well the jury has wanted me to beat up on a witness as much as I could.

—Pat McCartan

Common Mistakes

Failure to go for the jugular is a common error in cross—just "paddling around the edges," as Jamail puts it. Failing to focus on key points is another related error. You can also "beat a dead horse," according to Pat McCartan, and go wrong "asking questions in the blind," warns Bob Warren. There are all kinds of elementary mistakes. Joe Jamail mentions that it is always a mistake not to focus on the crucial part of a witness's testimony. Another particularly egregious faux pas is to repeat the witness's answers. Too much repetition is deadly. It is also a mistake to permit a witness to avoid a question. Phil Corboy mentions ways of effectively dealing with such a witness:

They say, "Well, I can't answer that in general terms." "Well, how about answering it in particular terms?" "I can't answer that yes or no." "Perhaps you can answer it yes first and then no at another time?" You watch for idiosyncrasies, subtleties which will give you an opportunity to gain and then you go after him or her.

David Boies says the first common mistake on cross is to allow oneself to become too diffuse in dealing with everything the witness has said. Since the witness has been put on the stand for the other side this means that most of what is said will be favorable to the opposition. "You ought to get what you can from this witness and get the witness off the stand because unless the other side has made a mistake, this witness is going to exploit open-ended opportunities in a way that will hurt you." The only time to refer directly to something the witness has said, according to Boies, is when there is a direct contradiction, "an absolute, positive winner."

It is generally not a good idea to begin a cross-examination by saying, "Now, on direct examination you said X," and then you repeat the bad thing he said. The only time you want to do that is when you have an absolute winner and what you are trying to do is damage this guy's credibility and you say, "You said this. That really isn't true, is it?" Now he's got to say, "Well, yes it is." "Are you sure that's true? You're telling me you're absolutely confident of that? Do you want this jury to evaluate your general credibility . . . on whether or not this statement is true?"

At this point the witness has been backed into a corner, hard to emerge with credibility intact. "Usually, you don't want to repeat their direct examination. Get the points that you can make, damage his credibility, and get him off." Damaging credibility is the name of the game. And in order to achieve this it is not necessary to prove the witness is lying. Demonstrating uncertainty, vacillation, and a willingness to backtrack are also convincing to jurors.

Your job is to damage his credibility if you can, not necessarily by making people think he's a liar, maybe just by making people think he is a little out of touch or does not understand or didn't say what they think you heard him say or didn't have a basis

> for saying it. This will give the jury some sense
> that this is somebody they ought not to rely on.
> **—David Boies**

Do not try to do too much, Boies recommends. "We've all been guilty of that because we all like cross-examination, and we all think if we can just have enough time with somebody, we can break him down."

Jim Neal comments that it is a mistake not to have well-defined objectives in cross-examination, both principal objectives and lesser objectives. "Lesser objectives should be something that you know by reason of the deposition or a document that you can establish. It may not be dynamite, but it is something so you can end the examination at least looking satisfied, making the jury think you've accomplished something in the cross-examination." In summary, the principal objectives in cross-examination are the impeachment of major points in the witness' testimony or reinforcing major points of proof in one's own theory of the case.

Picking up on Neal's point about objectives, David Boies suggests that a lawyer should set up the good points and frame the context before they are sprung on the witness. This essentially involves setting a trap.

> The second most common mistake is when you do have
> something that is really good, springing it before you've got
> the witness nailed down so that you spring something on
> him and then he walks away from it because he walks
> around it, he sees where the trap is. What you want to do, if
> you really want to hit his credibility, is you've got to nail
> him down. You've got to get in the jury's mind exactly what
> he is saying and phrase it exactly contrary to what your
> evidence is and then spring it on him.

Joe Jamail's interrogation of Lawrence Tisch is an excellent example of setting and then springing the trap. Jim Neal adds that the impeachment of a witness must then be etched in the jurors' minds.

> And if you impeach a man on a prior inconsistent state-
> ment, you want that jury to understand what he said on the
> stand. You want that drilled in, re-emphasized by that
> witness, and then you want to pull it out and say, "Mr.
> Jones, you gave a statement to the FBI at a certain time and
> in that statement you said..." or "Mr. Jones, you were

> before the grand jury and you were asked the following
> question and you gave the following answer." That has to be
> set up so it has some impact.

Another mistake, and the hardest to avoid, according to David Boies, is adopting the wrong tone "and attitude with a witness, beating up on a witness too much or too little. Beating up on the witness too much so the jury feels sorry for him, beating up on him too little so the jury doesn't think that you've damaged his credibility."

Besides beating a dead horse, Pat McCartan believes another error on cross is the lack of preparation and structure. This often leads to a dangerous shotgun approach, questions asked indiscriminately, no apparent line of thought. The impatience of the jury or judge may be incurred and the judge asks, "What the hell is the point of this exercise? Where are you going?"

Jim Neal notes the old chestnut of asking one question too many. In addition, he has a catalog of other errors. When cross-examining a witness about a document, that document should be exhibited, so "you're not fumbling around for a document, and you lose the moment." Another tactical error on cross-examination is to object too much when your witness is cross-examined. He observes that there are good reasons for objecting, but that a price is paid each time one does.

> Every time you object, you sustain a little nick. Now that
> nick may be worth it and the nick won't be great if you're
> sustained and if it's an important area, and the nick will be
> worth it if this guy is killing you and you've got to stop this
> flow.

The jury wants to hear the cross-examination and will quickly become impatient with an attorney who objects too much during cross.

> I don't think they mind some objections, I don't mean that.
> But boy, I hate to see a case where a lawyer objects again,
> again, again, again. He pounds in the answer. He frequently
> is going to be overruled. It seems like you're hiding
> something and you don't want the jury to hear [it].

In order to keep from having to register a large number of objections, Neal suggests pursuing a specific strategy at the beginning of the trial, dealing with critical issues by getting rulings from the judge behind the scenes through *in limine* motions.

I'm not a big objector. I'll tell you why I'm not. I will file a mass of motions *in limine* asking for pretrial rulings on issues that I think are critical and if I keep them out, rather than objecting in front of the jury, I'd rather the court rule. So I am a big motion *in limine* man. I think of every possible issue that may come up in the trial that I arguably have a right to or arguably have a right to keep out and I put them to the judge in advance.

—Jim Neal

Steve Susman agrees with others who have suggested that a common mistake in cross-examination is to carry on too long, chasing after a kill that can never be achieved. Another mistake is "being too damn subtle, where the jury really doesn't understand the point you're making." Failing to underscore adequately the significance of what has transpired is another. Susman, because of the nature of the kind of trials in which he is involved, is not usually presented with a witness he can carve up.

One of the problems of being a commercial litigator as opposed to a great personal-injury lawyer or a criminal lawyer, is that I'm dealing with very, very smart witnesses all the time. They've got more degrees than I've got, and they're making more money than I'm making. They are top executives, vice presidents. These people are good and they have rehearsed long and hard with their lawyers just like I've rehearsed with mine.

You cannot usually score big with such people (although Jamail and McCartan might argue that the bigger they are the harder they fall). Susman believes that you need to chip away at these cagey witnesses. But he cautions that it is necessary to guard against making the mistake of going on and on with questions trying to score a kill that cannot be bagged. "So you keep saying, 'If I go a little more, maybe I'll score a few more points.'"

According to Tom Barr, "you've got to take what they'll give you and stay away from what you can't get." Attorneys need to learn that there are times to talk and times

...when they should keep their mouth shut, asking questions that they don't know the answer to, being smart-alecky...If you can only hit a few short passes, you keep throwing short passes. If you can only run up the middle, you run up the middle. But don't go for the bomb if they're going to pick it off.

Barr, the quarterback, gives an example of misplaced tenacity on cross-examination that was completely out of order and counter-productive. By harassing a witness, the examiner forced the witness to become more credible than he had been when he gave his initial answer.

I once saw a wonderful example out in federal court in San Jose. A drug case. The prosecution witness had testified that he met the defendant and sold him some kind of drug. Very simple, direct testimony. And then the defendant got on the witness stand and testified he didn't meet him and didn't buy the drug.

The green prosecutor decided that something could be gotten from assailing this to-be-expected blanket denial.

The prosecutor, a young kid, jumped up and said, "Did you meet so-and-so?" Snarling, caustic voice. "No, I did not." "Isn't it a fact that you bought drugs?" "No, I did not." The defendant's lawyer gets up and asks the questions again. The kid prosecutor jumps up and he asks the question on cross-examination. By this time, the defendant, who had been obviously lying the first time, has now gotten mad because he's being asked over and over again the same questions and he's really giving the answers with some vigor and some fire.

By now the witness is beginning to sound almost believable.

The defendant's counsel gets up for the third time and asks him the same questions. The prosecutor jumps up, now for the third time. The judge says, "Wait a minute. Enough. Stop. Sit down."

The cross-examination had been a disaster for the prosecution.

The net result of all of that was that the testimony of the defendant was about ten times as strong as it would have been if the prosecutor had just gotten up and said, "No questions."

The case should have been set up as a simple matter of the defendant's credibility versus that of the authorities who charged him with the crime.

> You can believe the FBI agent or the DEA agent, or you can believe this guy. You can argue that to the jury. He really didn't have anything to ask, but he felt like he had to cross-examine. He didn't have to cross-examine and he shouldn't have cross-examined. I didn't stay to see what the jury did.

One would expect that the team of Reasoner and Jamail to be up for any challenge on cross-examination. Not so. Reasoner recounts an incident where he found himself faced with an extremely sympathetic witness on cross. Reasoner, in retrospect, realizes it was a mistake to cross-examine this witness in the first place.

> Jamail and I were trying a case together where we were representing a guy who manufactured trailer homes and sold them on lots, had a savings and loan that financed them, and had gotten an insane insurance company to give him mortgage insurance.

The litigants were both rather unsavory, the product of greed and the lax loan policies of that place and time.

> They wrote a mortgage on a trailer home for any deadbeat who walked by, and then when the guy couldn't pay they claimed the insurance. These two were suing each other, the trailer guy and the insurance guy, so not terribly attractive. The other lawyer brilliantly put on this poor black lady who is trying to raise her grandson. Her trailer fell apart, she walks down the street five miles to find the salesman who won't answer his calls. She said there he was, sitting in his office.

When it came time to cross-examine this woman Jamail decided that discretion was the better part of valor. He passed the ball to Reasoner.

> Jamail who is supposed to cross her, says, "Here, you take this one" and walks out of the courtroom, leaves me there. I stand up, which was the first mistake I made. This black lady is sitting there with tears streaming down her face. I try to ask her a few innocuous questions. She just sobs. And so finally I said, "Ma'am, I wish you to know that my client thinks you've been treated terribly. We're going to fix your

trailer for you." Of course, I'm lucky the judge didn't throw me in jail.

Reasoner knows what he should have done. "If I had been quicker, I would have just said, 'I pass, Your Honor, we have nothing to say to this lovely lady.'" In general, Reasoner argues, cross is the time to be forceful and to make the big points with dispatch. "You probably have maximum command of the jury's attention when you first begin."

Bob Fiske comes back to points made before about cross-examiners who have no purpose or organization in what they are doing. At times, lawyers seem to take for granted that if they merely repeat the direct the jurors will see the point they wish to make. This recalls Steve Susman's observations about being too subtle. The point must be driven home. Lawyers must not give the impression, according to Fiske, that:

> They don't know where they are going. You have to figure, what is my objective with this witness? What is the point I want to make? And there are a lot of lawyers who just get up and they already know what the point is and the witness sits down and you really wonder why did they even do this cross-examination? Sometimes it just repeats, in one way or another, the direct.

Fiske reinforces the observation that was demonstrated so vividly by Tom Barr in the example of the inexperienced prosecutor. What was stilted testimony on direct can be carelessly converted into words with conviction on cross.

> I've seen this happen a lot. A witness will get up on direct and no matter how spontaneous the lawyer tries to make it on direct, it always tends to come out a little bit (witness is nervous) stilted. Then the other lawyer gets up and starts cross-examining and now it's spontaneous and all of a sudden, the witness comes to life. The same answers are coming back, only with emotion and conviction. What was pabulum on direct becomes very vibrant, vital, believable testimony on cross-examination.

A common error Fiske says, "is to bring a witness to life on cross-examination, repeating all the bad stuff."

One final note on cross-examining belongs here. The doomsday scenario. What do you do if the case is going baldly? Jim Neal has been there.

I've taken chances. Shit, I've violated every rule you can violate. But if I do, the case has gone to hell already and I'm going to have to have lightning strike.

—**Jim Neal**

Dealing With Opposing Counsel

As with all else in the trial, relationships with opposing counsel are seen as an opportunity to score persuasive points with the jury. The jury pays close attention to interactions between the lawyers for each side. It is not helpful for the jury to perceive that you consider the lawyer on the other side your buddy. They then assume you are a weak advocate or unsure of your grounds. Anger toward the other side sometimes will impress a jury if it is controlled and apparently justified. If it is too intense, jurors will be alienated.

Bob Warren never gets mad in court, but rather displays controlled, deliberate anger.

> There is no such thing as getting mad or losing control. That doesn't mean there isn't a place for anger, but only if there's a place for it. You do not have the luxury of any kind of unrestrained emotions that do not contribute to the end [of winning the case]. With the opposing lawyer, let's say you have somebody who is personally insulting and so forth, you may do something like bear it with great dignity for awhile, and then "the line is crossed." Then comes anger, but only at a time when the jurors would expect anger and think it appropriate.

Warren recalls a courtroom incident wherein he induced anger in an opponent to gain an important tactical advantage:

Early in my career I represented the Irvine Company. A mega-billion dollar issue. I remember the opponent was a guy who was President of the Sierra Club and I didn't think he wrote very good briefs but he sure as hell was a terrific oral advocate. But I remember one time during the course of the trial we were having a long argument before the court, the day it was devoted to argument, and during the morning, I included in my stuff something that was a needle to him. It wasn't an apparent needle, but I knew it would rankle. And I was on the floor all morning. And there were news media always in the courtroom. Well, in the afternoon...my opponent got up and began to argue and he went on for about half an hour and then, this obviously had eaten at him, his voice began to rise and he just lashed out into this tirade—a denunciation of me for no "apparent" reason and the judge is looking at him like what is going wrong with your head. The newspapers wrote up the next day that Mr. so-and-so had launched into this inexplicable tirade. But, if he had immediately stood up and screamed [when I initially threw him the barb]...but he sat there and he let it stew on him all during lunch and then he lost control of himself and permitted himself to be angry. Well, he never should have done that.

Steve Susman notes that jurors expect to see attorneys in an adversarial role. Credibility depends upon giving them what they expect.

I'm never friendly with the other side during trial because I think the jury does not understand that. I think juries anticipate the lawyers are going to be adversaries and they're going to be at each other's throat and be mean to each other. At the same time, I don't go out of my way to be obnoxious to the other person. But my experience tells me juries expect lawyers to object, they expect lawyers to fight, they expect lawyers to be adversaries. There's no use in disappointing that expectation by being the nice guy, cavorting with the enemy.

—Steve Susman

Arthur Liman emphasizes treating the opposition with respect, but he will display indignation if he is confident he will not be viewed as superior or holier-than-thou. "If they behave in a manner that permits me to be righteously indignant without being sanctimonious, I do so."

If Pat McCartan gets the opportunity to show up the opposition in a bad light he allows the jury to see his indignation. Never stoop to the opposition's level, and never let the jury assume that opposing counsel are friends.

> Generally, I want them to think that there is a distant professional relationship, no matter what my opponent is doing. Many lawyers give you the opportunity, which you should never pass up, gradually to build indignation through the course of the trial towards their conduct. And, I think it's the most effective defensive technique there is because a lot of lawyers will overstate, over-try, over-plead, overdo their case and try to take advantage of every opportunity.

And even when a lawyer's conduct is most grievous and it is obvious to the jury that the line of civility and courtroom manners has been trespassed, McCartan advocates acting direct and professional when responding, and not trading insult for insult.

Phil Corboy wants to make a specific impression upon the jurors by the way in which he relates to opposing counsel. He is annoyed with himself when he goes against his rule in this matter. He wants jurors to think

> ...that I'm a courteous observer of the rules. That I am their [opposing counsel's] antagonist, but I'm not antagonistic. I am professional at all times. That's why I get mad at me when I violate this...I do not flatter the opposition. Again, the jury may believe it. I do not call them by their first names even though they may call me by my first name. I am not overly friendly, but I'm courteous and any time they ask me for something, I'm quick to help them. I don't fawn over them but I'm not discourteous to them. If they say, "Judge, rather than go through this witness' qualifications, is it all right if I put into evidence this resumé of his qualifications?" I say, "Of course, your Honor." Or they start laying a foundation for something, "Your Honor, I have no objection to this." I try to make it as easy for them as I want it done for me and if they've pissed all over me, I'm going to be even nicer to them. I am not going to retaliate with urine.

Jim Brosnahan does not think jurors place much weight on relationships between the lawyers, but feels being acrimonious toward the other side accomplishes little.

I assume that juries are good enough to think that that relationship is one of the least important issues in the case. But, if your opponent cheats, what are you to do? Not overreact. Deal with it in some way that gets that across. I think jurors like the most professional straight-forward development of testimony, no rancor between the two sides. In civil cases, certainly, it's not good to be fighting with the other side.

Joe Jamail presents some interesting views on dealing with a team of opposition counsel who are resolved to maintain a unified front against him. Frequently in a case where there are multiple defendants, a corporation or several, an insurance company or several, and they will have Jamail as plaintiff. Jamail is adept at getting close to one of the lawyers and cutting a deal at the expense of the others. By picking the lawyers off one by one Jamail insures that since they do not hang together, they will hang separately. He can see their resolve.

"Boy, that Jamail ain't going to split us off this time and pick us off one by one." Usually it takes me about a day and half to make the motherfuckers go at each other's jugular. It's easy. Just pick on one of them for a full day. His response will be, "Well, he [his colleague] did it, too." It just happens. They can't handle it. Human nature will not allow them to sit there and get hit on in that fashion.

Jamail remains cool toward his rivals. He describes the relationship as

Very distant. I don't do that buddy, buddy act. You never see me touch one of them in the courtroom. You see them sometimes huddle? I stand aloof. When they approach the bench, I never go up there until the judge tells me to come up. The system is adversarial. My client sits back there and I want them to see me with that client as being understanding and sympathetic but not maudlin. I'm not a good old boy, I'm not a buddy. I'm the lawyer.

Bob Fiske feels it may be in the defendant's interest to appear to be friendly with plaintiff's counsel in order to downplay the seriousness of the dispute. It is different for the plaintiff.

> If you are the defendant, you want to cultivate, "Well, we're good buddies here, we're good friends, there is not much to this, this isn't that serious." If you're the plaintiff's lawyer or if you're the government prosecutor, you don't want that. Particularly in a criminal case, I think the last thing the prosecutors want is to be seen as fraternizing with the defense lawyers in front of the jury.
>
> **—Bob Fiske**

Fiske also believes this to be true to a major degree with a plaintiff in a personal-injury matter in which punitive damages against the defendant are being sought because of some purportedly reprehensible, outrageous, willful, wanton conduct. He argues that there is a sense of moral outrage that goes with being the plaintiff, and to the extent that the plaintiff's lawyer is joking with the defense lawyer in front of the jury, the outrage fades.

Tom Barr has met acrimonious types in the courtroom, and suggests that they are quickly brought into line by most judges. Lawyers who misbehave in the courtroom act unacceptably because they have been trained in depositions and not trained in court. Hostility and acrimony is a result of incompetence. Lawyers who are mean-spirited and obnoxious do not know the difference between "being tough and being nasty. They don't have any confidence in themselves." Abrasive tactics are not effective in court, and Barr almost welcomes abrasive behavior on the part of the opposing attorney because he is confident that he can find ways during the trial to make him pay. "You have to stop him. If he doesn't know what he is doing, it's quickly going to turn into a mess."

Fiske tries to react to hostility and obnoxious behavior with equanimity, but it is not always easy.

> You try not to let it affect you. You try not to react the same way. That's very hard. And it's like a hockey game. You know, you've got an elbow and you know you're not supposed to hit back but after a couple of elbows, you do hit back.

Fiske, like Barr, sees acrimony on the part of an opponent as a gift in the courtroom, because it is such a self-destructive tactic. "Clearly it is folly in the courtroom. If it happens in the courtroom, then you just sit there, the voice of reason [while] the other one is the wild, screaming idiot."

Hostility and obnoxious behavior is also, Brosnahan suggests, a result of faulty understanding of how to win, and how to pursue an adversarial relationship within rules. Some lawyers think that advocacy has to do with denying somebody an extension of time, and similar marginal annoyances It is a lack of vision, according to Brosnahan. "Their idea is that they'll just wear you down and you'll settle. You won't want to do it anymore. There are some really bad tigers out there in the jungle."

Closing Arguments

Many lawyers feel that a case can be won or lost with the closing argument. I disagree. By the end of the trial, jurors have already made up their minds. However, if it is a short case, a day or two, the closing argument can be very persuasive since it closely follows the presentation of witnesses and major issues. If it is a long case the most one can accomplish is a buttressing of position for those who are already won over. It is hoped during closing that counsel might be able to influence those who are neutral or wavering. Those who are adamant at this point will not be moved. There is considerable folklore and mythology about dynamite closing arguments—verdicts "stolen" by wily advocates. However, the preponderance of evidence shows that the summation is overvalued. Be that as it may, these lawyers take it very seriously.

Harry Reasoner draws upon a "jury argument file" compiled from the beginning of his preparation to create his closing argument. He composes an outline to be used for addressing the jury. "I may write out something, thinking it through, but I never have more than an outline when I actually argue. I just think you gain so much from the jury if you speak to them rather than reading." Reasoner thinks the importance of the closing argument varies immensely, but he dissents strongly from those who maintain that the trial is virtually over by the time summations are given.

> That may be true in simple cases, but I think, particularly in complex cases where there are instructions and legal theories that are not commonsensical, that the jury is going to have to try to understand if they are conscientious.

345

Reasoner takes the instructions up to the jury during his closing and explains to them how he thinks they fit the evidence and how the jury should respond. When one moves beyond these objectives, Reasoner is less certain about the impact of a closing statement.

> How much juries are swayed by passion or beautiful rhetoric, I think is much more speculative. They all tell you they're not, but that's obviously what you would expect them to say
> **—Harry Reasoner**

Tom Barr's perspective is probably closer to that of the behavioral science experts. He has moved away from the more dramatic implications lawyers read into closing. In Barr's mind, the summation is

> ...probably overrated by lawyers. Probably everybody thinks of themselves as getting up and giving a closing argument that pulls disaster out of the fire, turns it around, sends the jury away in tears, they come in and say, "Kill the bastards on the other side."

Nevertheless, his skepticism not withstanding, Barr says "I think that you want to pound the evidence" one last time.

Fred Bartlit uses the closing argument to summarize his case, and to woo the jurors once again.

> Tell them once, it happened. Tell them twice, it happened. Tell them three times, it happened. You're echoing the themes in your opening. I do it different ways. Sometimes I start off by saying, "You know, it's been a long trial and you've kept notes . . . " And tell them how attentive they are and all that.

Bartlit thanks the jurors and pays them compliments, clearly a tactic requiring skill.

> For example, if there have been jurors who fought to get off because of hardships, I may say, "I know this has not been a picnic. There are jurors with huge family responsibilities and this is the last place you wanted to be. But you sat there and went through this expert testimony and watched it like

hawks..." You may look at the juror, but it's not an ass-kissing thing. It's got to be true, because if it's not true....

Bartlit reviews the evidence, and points to the flaws and weakness in the opponent's case.

> Then you talk about the evidence and if you can tie it into the structure, you try to make it obvious. Jurors like "one and one equals two," so you try to be as absolutely specific as you can. Four things. The third thing is if the other guy has been a schlemiel, you say so. Witnesses have lied and changed their story and you say, "Let's get to brass tacks. You're supposed to bring your common sense. You know that if people have a good case, they don't have to keep changing their story. So that tells you immediately everything you need to know."

Bob Warren sees the summation as a chance to pull everything together into a coherent whole. It is also an opportunity to pull a rabbit out of hat, if any rabbits are available. Warren came up with one in the Ramada case.

> The claim was that our reporter wrote all these typewritten notes about conversations with people and confidential sources and so forth, that he had phonied up those notes, that this was a practice of his. Well, as we prepared for final argument, fortunately we had been given about three to four days to do it, it began to click that you could take from unimpeachable evidence, such as from adverse witnesses, from third-party witnesses, from other documents, that you could find indicia that would support each and every sentence in those notes, that the reporter couldn't have known if he was just sitting down there making them up.

Hence, Warren's closing argument was to demonstrate this with the use of the projector. Warren puts a note up on the projector, and went over a particular sentence.

> "Maybe you remember the testimony of Mr. so-and-so," and then put up the transcript page. "And lo and behold, there is something that matches. How could that be if this was phoney. How did he dream this up? How could he?" And so in the closing statement there was a great coming together of evidence.

Although for David Boies winning a case in summation is almost impossible, he argues, "If you're behind, the most you can try to do is get somebody to hang the jury. Realistically, I don't think you can turn a case around in a closing argument, particularly on a long case."

For Phil Corboy, closing arguments offer a tactical possibility for pinning down the overall picture. It is déja vu all over again.

> The job of a closing argument is directly related to your overall theme. My overall theme has got to be convincing the jury that the rich widow is entitled, not deserving. We're going to accept that she isn't deserving, nobody is deserving of all this money, but she's entitled as a matter of law. I've got to be careful of being crass. I can't let the discussion degenerate into just dollars for a widow.

Arthur Liman is another who respects the power of summation. "I try that case to a view to what I am going to do on summation because I can get killed on summation or I can come out ahead on summation." There is more than one way to get murdered on summation. One is the notorious bad document, the bomb shell that opposing counsel held throughout the trial, so lethal that trying to inoculate the jury against it was too great a risk. Arthur Liman worries about this.

> Suppose there is a document which, because it came in quickly the other side didn't make much out of. But it's a bad document for me. I know it's going to get blown up in summation. I know that if I haven't dealt with it, I'm going to be badly hurt. I know that if I state a fact one way and there is a document that just proves the opposite, that I'm going to be destroyed in summation.

Consequently, Liman looks at the case as the trial proceeds not just in terms of his own summation, but also in terms of what the other side is likely to do in closing.

There can be these time bombs that have been planted. You've got a whole field of them and they're all going to go off at one time in summation. You've got to focus on it.

—Arthur Liman

One trick Liman remembers from his days as a prosecutor involves holding back something on summation that can be used on rebuttal. Liman says a good prosecutor

> holds back on his opening statement something. He knows what you're going to do in your summation and then he finds something that he's held back which he can use to just sort of to puncture a hole in something you've said that makes you sort of want to slink under the table. Prosecutors who were trained to use rebuttal to do that, which is opening summation, make it flat, let the defense lawyer have his opportunity and fly high, and then you go ahead and puncture him.

Liman advocates foreclosing this tactic with a tactic of his own and a plea to the judge. First he can say to the jurors on his summation:

> "I'm not going to have the opportunity to answer the rebuttal, but you can be sure that there is nothing that he will say that I would not be able to answer on the basis of the evidence here." You've got to have your credibility. And then the other thing that you have a right to insist (not every judge will enforce it) that the judge restrict the rebuttal to new things that you raised and not just simply doing things that could sandbag you.

If Liman as defendant did not cover a point in his summation, even a point in the prosecutor's direct examination, then the prosecutor has no right to raise that point in rebuttal.

> It's where most of the prosecution cases in the white-collar area are won or lost, in that summation area. It's neglected, it's not understood, but everybody who tries white-collar cases knows that the summations are the lethal part of the case.

Steve Susman buys the assertion that jurors have decided the case by summation, but he thinks that closings are an important chance to give jurors ammunition to use in their deliberations. Also, it is extremely important to answer the other person's allegations tit for tat. "I think what you're really doing is giving the people who are already on your side the backbone never to change and persuade others."

"Very important," is how Jim Brosnahan rates the closing argument, partly because of the need to define a case according to what it is not, and to foreclose certain interpretations by the jury that are irrelevant and harmful to your side. Brosnahan registers a strong dissent when anyone suggests summation is not important. He lists what needs to be done:

> To define again what the case is not, "It's not this, not that, not something else, it's this." To marshall the evidence on certain points. "This number of days have to be accounted for. These are accounted for. Here's the reason, there is a question about, here's the answer. You see how we got it." Very, very important. I guess Lee Bailey in the seventies suggested final argument is not important, but I don't agree with that at all.

There is a direct relationship between openings and summations. "The themes in the opening should be very much like the themes in closing. Maybe incorporating a new way of saying it, an additional way to keep up the interest, but there should be a strong relationship between the two." And Brosnahan thinks it is important to develop a personal style of argument.

> The argument is very much a question of style. Final argument is a personal thing. That is why it is hard to teach it. And you change it a little bit from case to case but not a whole lot. That's really you out there when you are giving that final argument.

Bob Fiske thinks closing arguments are more important the longer the trial. Presumably this is because of a diffusion that takes place, a blurring in the minds of jurors. This phenomenon certainly exists, even to the point, studies have shown, where jurors cannot remember which side a particular witness is on. "In a short trial, in many ways, the opening statement could be more important."

Even so, Max Blecher asserts, no matter what the length of the trial, by the time summations are reached, the "jury is largely there." But he also agrees with the other lawyers who have suggested that important reinforcement can take place.

> It is reinforcing to the people who believe in it. It obviously could move a few of the people who may be on the fence or don't quite understand the evidence or what its significance is or how to go about even thinking about putting all these facts into some orderly pattern.

As in openings, making grandiose claims is a mistake. A particular danger is to make statements about conclusions reached from evidence that are contrary to the jurors' impressions. (Using a shadow jury could be a major advantage.) Bob Warren issues several additional cautions, "excess vituperation, demanding that they find more wrong with the other party than is supported by the evidence. And third, sometimes just absolutely having the dead-wrong theme. Just picking a story that doesn't have any compelling selling power."

Phil Corboy gives a nice, succinct litany of mistakes often perpetrated in summation:

Crassness, discourtesies, personal attacks when they're not justified, snottiness, looking down at jurors, taking the jurors for granted, overstating the case, overemphasizing something, concentrating on minutia, going on too long, being repetitive, mistaking the law, arguing something which you've been told not to argue.

—Phil Corboy

CHAPTER 9 ▮▮▮▮▮▮▮▮▮▮▮▮▮▮

Winning, Losing, and In Between

> *It ain't like baseball..statistics are much harder to
> keep.*
>
> **—Pat McCartan**

If strategies are to be evaluated in terms of outcomes, then a
definition of what it means to win must be in place. There are ways
of defining a win for a defendant, and ways of defining a win for a
plaintiff. These men have clear-headed ideas about how winning is
defined, and they do not delude themselves with bogus, self-aggran-
dizing definitions. Bob Fiske quotes former Senator Aiken of Vermont
on the subject of Vietnam with tongue-in-cheek: "Senator Aiken once
said about Vietnam, 'Let's just get out of there and say we won.'" But
that is not really good enough when keeping score on the outcome of
lawsuits.

Defining a Win

Tom Barr, looking at a win from the plaintiff's point of view, bases
his definition on the amount of money recovered. Even if the client is a
corporation seeking to obtain an injunction or some other legal relief,
the question can still be seen as one of money. "A win for a
corporation is measured almost invariably in financial terms, whether
directly or indirectly. I have never been involved in a grudge match
between individuals."

From the public perception of a win or loss, Steve Susman prefers
plaintiff work because even when a lawyer wins for the defense, it is
not presented in the media as a win. For a defendant, the recognition of
a significant victory is frequently elusive. Many times, the client

resents it too, with the belief that, "I was innocent, why do I have to be punished by Susman and his fees?" He says in one case, for example, when he represented a large corporate client, the plaintiffs were seeking over $50 million in damages. The jury returned an actual damage award of $10,000 and a punitive damages award of $2 million. He is currently appealing the punitive award. But overall, it was a major victory for the client. "Of course, it was written up in a newspaper as a loss . . . I'd rather use my energy doing plaintiff work."

For Phil Corboy, a win has numerous definitions. One definition is getting more than what was offered to settle.

If I get an offer to settle a case for a million dollars and I try the case and I get a million, one hundred thousand dollars, you might say that's a win.
—Phil Corboy

Costs must also be calculated.

> But it may not be if it cost two hundred thousand dollars to try the case. So the win is only determined by whether the dollar in the client's pocket is more than the dollars offered.

Sometimes a win occurs when a precedent is established that alters the nature of the playing field. Corboy tells a story of how a horse changed a state statute.

> Years ago, I tried a case for a person who owned a horse. The horse was killed out at Arlington Racetrack. I tried the case and got a ninety thousand dollar verdict for the horse at a time when the Illinois Wrongful Death Statute allowed us thirty thousand dollars for the death of a human being. Two years later, we got the statute changed. Today there is no limitation on dollars you can get in a wrongful death action.

In another case, Corboy won after turning down $9 million.

> I tried a case several years ago where I was offered nine million dollars and I got nine-and-a-half million dollars. I was not offered the nine million dollars until the jury went out. Well, a lot of people might say, "That wasn't a win. You ran the risk of everything to get an additional five

hundred thousand dollars." Well, it was a win because the nine million dollars didn't come until the jury was out and my client wanted to let it go and he did and we got nine-and-a-half million dollars. Not many people turn down nine million bucks.

Once Corboy had put the case before a jury, he was intent in living by the jury's verdict. Even when he was offered a huge sum of money to settle at the eleventh hour, while the jury was deliberating, he took the verdict, and received even more. This was not a gamble on Corboy's part, it was a rational decision based on vast experience.

Joe Jamail is a man of few words when it comes to defining a win. "When I get about twice as much as the client thought I was going to get, for me, it's a win."

To Jim Brosnahan a conviction on a minor count in a case in which serious felonies have been charged is a win. And of course, so is acquittal, except in the criminal field, where a hung jury can be a win. If a case is tried, the jury is hung, and the prosecution decides not to try the case again, that, according to Brosnahan is a win.

That's a win if they dismiss it after that hung jury. A hung jury is not a loss, but it is not a win either if the case has then got to be re-tried.

—Jim Brosnahan

Brosnahan defines a win for the defendant in civil cases according to a neat formula. On the civil side, less than the offer made to settle is a win; settling between the offer and the demand is a draw; and anything above the demand is a loss. In discussing a near win he states:

> I lost a case one time. It was a takeover case. We almost won the goddamn thing. We weren't supposed to win, but we almost did and came home and one of my partners said, "We really won that case because the price of the stock went up in our client's benefit." I said, "We did not win the case."

Brosnahan did not care that the stock went up. From his perspective, he did not win the issues in the dispute at trial.

Arthur Liman, like his colleagues here, is committed to the idea of

355

"accomplishing something for a client" when talking about a win. One cannot simplistically state the result as a defendant's verdict or a plaintiff's verdict. A plaintiff's verdict can be less than a settlement offered earlier, or less than what should have been obtained in a trial. A defense win might involve a verdict for the plaintiff, but if, as Liman suggests, it is "a six-cent verdict," then the defendant is still way ahead. If he can achieve something for a client that could not have been achieved by another lawyer, then that is a win.

Steve Susman, as in many of his other calculations, sees the financial factor as primary. But it is clear from the way he states his case that subjective issues are important to him as well. A win is something to be celebrated.

> The best win is representing a plaintiff where you recover a lot of money for them and a lot for you. That's the best win. That is a real win. The next best win is to represent a defendant where you vindicate him or get them off with a lot less than they expected, where they are essentially happy, real happy, and you celebrate. Those are how I define wins.

For Bob Warren winning is defined in terms of the client's satisfaction. A win should not be taken as a personal victory by the lawyer.

> I define a win as achieving a result that is, or should be, satisfactory to that client. The purpose of taking a case for a client is not to achieve a personal win. The idea of taking a case for a client is to have it turn out in a manner that is tolerable to that client.

In the case of a business that gets into serious trouble, it may simply mean managing the case in such a fashion that when it is all over the business continues to be viable. This may entail, for example, getting enough of the damages recovered to enable a project to go forward or business to resume. Warren continues, in this regard, to take a cool, objective approach to his role as trial attorney. He is probably the most thorough rationalist among the fourteen. A win is not defined in terms of whether there is a personal vindication for the lawyer, or a grand moment when the lawyer gets to stand there and the judge announces a verdict in his favor. A win on paper for the attorney, a "W," or a notch on the gun, might be anything but a win for the client. Warren paints a rather Kafkaesque scenario of how a win can really be a loss.

There are many instances in which the correct jury verdict can be a terrible loss for the client in terms of having spent countless hours, preoccupation with a lawsuit for a substantial number of years in personal terms. It may be that five years of that person's life has been essentially pissed away thinking about nothing but the lawsuit. So, five years spent in preoccupation with a lawsuit, you win it at the end. Well, big deal, if you could have spared the client three out of those five years, it would have been a service.

—Bob Warren

Pat McCartan defines winning as achieving the client's objective, however that needs to be done.

> The plaintiff, unlike the defendant, can at least measure the outcome, almost always in monetary terms, by calculating recovery against cost. As a plaintiff, it's relatively easier because you can, at the end of the game, measure what you've achieved against what it has cost. I mean, more cost than expenditures on fees, experts, etc. That is relatively easier to measure.

For the defendant, calculating the outcome is more ambiguous. In many respects it is difficult for a defendant to win. Plaintiff's claims may be rebuffed, but there is always the question of the expense and time involved in the defense of a lawsuit.

> As a defendant, as a rule of thumb, if you hold a verdict or judgment within the range or below what you would have settled for, that is not a bad way to look at it. But it is ambiguous.

An example of McCartan's point is the antitrust case MCI brought against AT&T. Bob Hanley tried the case for MCI. He used mock juries to test his case themes, developed jury profiles with the assistance of his trial consultants, tested his exhibits, and won $1 billion, 800 million for his client. After an appeal, the case was remanded for retrial and a new team of lawyers from the same law firms retried it. The second lawyer representing AT&T held the

357

judgment to $100 million. To many it was considered a win. A lawyer close to the case stated:

> As you know, Hanley really hit George Saunders and AT&T. The next time Blair White tried it, they got hit for a hundred million and it seems to me that that was a win. I thought Blair did a masterful job from what I know of that case and I would say he won.

But the judgment for the plaintiff in the second instance has to be placed in perspective.

> It's hard to say that [Hanley's colleagues at] Jenner & Block lost when they got a hundred million, but in a sense they did. I try a case and get a ten million dollar verdict. Let's say another lawyer would have tried and got a fifty million dollar verdict. If you could evaluate the outcomes with certainty, I would have lost the client forty million dollars.

As Pat McCartan says "it ain't like baseball; statistics are much harder to keep."

Jim Neal accepts the prevalent view that winning for a plaintiff in a civil suit is getting more than expected, and, for the defendant, paying less than anticipated. He raises the question of whether or not a win can sometimes involve finding an alternative to a trial, and answers in the affirmative. He mentions, for example, of finding a "livable" solution for a criminal defendant in a federal case.

> I generally believe, because I work in the federal system in the main, in developing alternatives for the client. I try to assess the chances of winning, and I say forty-sixty with the federal government is a good shot. I try to develop alternatives to going to trial and the consequences of going to trial and I try to be objective, and then I let him do it. Now, if he says, "I just can't do it, that's not livable," and frequently you find something that's not livable, we go to trial.

It is not livable for a physician to be convicted of a felony.

> In the Elvis Presley's doctor case if [the doctor] was convicted of a felony, he loses his license, if he is convicted of a misdemeanor, he may not. I tried to work out a plea bargain for a misdemeanor. It was a tough-looking case. I got absolutely rejected. Went to trial. Victory. That's easy to determine.

The prosecution alleged that the doctor was simply a supplier of drugs to Presley. Neal argued that Presley was indeed an addict, but that the most prudent medical course of action at this time was to wean him slowly off the drugs. The jury accepted Neal's version and interpretation of the facts.

In another case for Neal, the definition of a win narrowed to a single possibility, acquittal. Neal considers it the toughest case he has ever tried.

> My client was charged with hijacking and kidnapping, intimidating the crew of the aircraft, going armed aboard an aircraft, all of that. At that time in seventy-two, kidnapping was a capital offense under the federal system. Also, air piracy, hijacking, was and still is, a mandatory twenty-five years. This case was so bad I went to the government, with my client's permission, and offered to plea to intimidating the crew of the aircraft and take ten years. The government says, "Hell, no, we've never tried a hijacking case all the way through. We're going to try this." He was acquitted on all counts.

Sometimes, both sides win. Or at least they can say they did. When the United States Football League (USFL) sued the National Football League (NFL), claiming the latter was a monopoly in restraint of trade, both sides "won" in the sense that they had their construction of the matter upheld. In fact, it was the lawyers for the USFL who really won. But Bob Fiske, as an attorney for the defense, was nevertheless happy with the outcome.

> You take the NFL case, both sides in perfectly straight face can say they won that. I mean, Harvey Meyerson would say, "We won." The jury found the NFL was a monopoly and, indeed, later on, Judge Leisure awarded the USFL attorney's fees something like six million dollars because they "won the case."

The actual judgment against the NFL was one dollar. Since it was an antitrust case, the damages were tripled. The ultimate award was three dollars. Notwithstanding the fact that the judge ruled that the NFL had to pay the plaintiff's attorney fees of six million dollars, Fiske felt that the client had obtained a major victory.

Finally, Max Blecher adds his agreement to a number of points made about winning. "Putting the client back in a functioning position," seems to be the most meaningful definition of a win. This may or may not involve money. Blecher thinks winning is basically "co-extensive with the gratification of the client."

Satisfying Cases

From their own perspective, what then are the most *personally* satisfying cases for these fourteen trial attorneys? It is a little different for each. Most, as we have already seen, focus on what has been done for the client. Yet, there are other dimensions. Some focus on specific legal achievements. Some value power and control more. Some value the intellectual fulfillment. Others such as Joe Jamail thrill to winning "unwinnable" cases.

Renee Webster Verdict

Little Renee Webster was riding on the back of a three-wheeler Honda-made off-road vehicle and they wouldn't pay a dime. She was paralyzed from the neck down. Honda's arrogance to me and their attitude, "Well, just a bunch of drug-crazed American teenagers who don't know how to operate these Japanese vehicles." And they had tried a couple of dozen of these cases around the country and won them. And I took little Renee over there and knocked their ass off for sixteen-million, six-hundred thousand and they pulled them off the market. That was gratifying.

—Joe Jamail

Phil Corboy felt that he had experienced numerous satisfying experiences in his professional career. Earning the gratitude of a client is an important value.

> I've been very fortunate in being blessed with the emotional ups of this business. I've had so many grateful clients. I've been so fortunate in being able to do well and do good for people. I've had literally hundreds of clients who would have been either penniless or would have had much less in compensation except for my efforts. I've had so many

people write me letters, thanking me...just to be so grateful that the high of it is, the dessert was not in winning the verdict—which I was supposed to do anyhow—but the gratitude of these terribly injured or demoralized or bereft people.

One of Corboy's most important cases did not involve enormous amounts of money by most standards, but for the two widows who were involved, "it represented the difference between eating well and just eating." He represented two Hispanic women in a suit against Equitable Life Insurance. Their husbands had "gone out one night, got drunk, and shot each other dead." There was a double indemnity clause in the $15,000 insurance policy that allowed for double payment in the event of an accidental death. There was also, however, a felony exception in the policy. If they were killed during the commission of a felony, the widows would recover nothing. Although Corboy won the case before a jury, regrettably for his clients it was reversed on appeal. "Neither widow got the fifteen thousand dollars, and in effect the result was very, very unhappy for them. But that certainly was an important case to me. It taught me something about winning and persuading and also about making a record."

For David Boies, winning and the intellectual stimulation of the case are great sources of satisfaction. When he defended CBS against charges of libel by General William Westmoreland it was enormously satisfying because it was difficult, because he was successful, and because he felt he had accomplished something that was morally right. It was a technical tour de force.

Because of his reputation for integrity and thoroughness, Fred Bartlit felt gratified at having been asked to head the famous Greylord investigation in Chicago.

> A federal judge of the Northern District of Illinois asked me to be the special prosecutor investigating the testimony of the Greylord lawyer witnesses. If you look into that, you'll see that the names involved are very big names and they wanted somebody who would get it right, who wouldn't make mistakes, wouldn't bring or recommend cases be brought just for the headlines...I was very honored because it was so sensitive, but it had to be done with integrity.

Bob Warren also describes the tremendous satisfaction of coming from behind and winning against the odds.

> The most satisfying to me was the verdict in the Ramada case. That's not necessarily the best example of some kind of legal work of solving a terrible problem, but a feeling of satisfaction of having fought it out for nearly six months; being way behind at points in the case almost surely; having so much riding on it; having it be in an area that I had devoted so much of my legal practice to; having the judge think we were going to lose and then pulling out that unanimous twelve-person verdict.

For Pat McCartan his most satisfying experiences also relate to verdicts achieved after a long period of intense effort.

> The Mobil-Marathon case. You can't imagine the level of activity, the intensity of the effort, that was brought to bear in that case. I had staff volunteering to work all night. Everybody in the law firm wanted to work on the case. I mean, it was a cause. A very satisfying win.

In another case, McCartan worked hard to save the reputation of Stanley Clark.

> The case probably brought me as much if not more satisfaction than anything I have ever done, that was the first major patent case that I tried. The patent counsel at what was at that time The Firestone Tire and Rubber Company was a fellow by the name of Stanley Clark. He was a good person and I liked him very much.

Firestone had been found guilty of committing a fraud on the court in Baltimore when the company, at Clark's direction, resisted transfer of the case to the Northern District of Ohio.

> This was a very serious matter for him. He had a heart attack as a result of it. He was a decent, honorable man and it was a terrible thing to do to him. The case had been transferred to Cleveland, and when it came to Cleveland, with thousands of exhibits and a record of almost two years of trial in Baltimore, we were asked to take on the case in midstream. The case involved the Government's Rubber Reserve Program during World War II and the history of synthetic rubber.

There was a steady string of losses.

> We finished trying the case for five-and-a-half months in the Northern District of Ohio. I can't think of one trial

ruling that went in our favor. The client was found guilty of fraud on the court without any additional evidence from that which the Baltimore court had found insufficient to find fraud and we lost the case on the merits. The company faced a staggering liability because just about every tire that had been made since nineteen fifty incorporated this formulation of synthetic rubber. Every day we went down to that courthouse knowing we were going to get hammered, but my job was to make a record.

However, McCartan's tenacity prevailed.

I was determined to win this case and we did. We eventually got judgment on appeal. And talk about personal identification with the client, I wanted to win that case for that guy more than anything in the world even though we were getting hammered day in and day out, I told our client and our team that "we will win this case," and we did.

A satisfying case for Arthur Liman is not always verdict oriented, but rather

---

...a special day in court and that can be a good argument, a good examination, a good opening, a good summation; something that was not quite planned, but the opportunity came and you did it in a way that leaves you with an enormous sense of satisfaction. I obviously get a lot of satisfaction out of helping people and accomplishing their goals, and that comes with this profession.

—Arthur Liman

In spite of the notoriety he achieved during the Iran-Contra hearings, Liman considers his most memorable case to be the R-46 subway car case for the City of New York. The verdict was $76 million for the city. Rockwell had made undercarriages for the city's subway cars. The castings were cracking. The cars were dilapidated and dangerous. The city felt it was Rockwell's responsibility. Rockwell blamed the problem on the design of the undercarriages, which were specified by the city. Liman feels this case was important, not only because of the monetary remuneration the city received, but also because the timing of the trial coincided with an especially low point, psychologically, for the City of New York. "I would regard this as clearly the most satisfying case. I was able to give something back to the city that I love at a time of its greatest need."

Max Blecher's satisfaction derives from helping people.

> I can't isolate any one instance that has been the most satisfying. I find sometimes even the smallest victory for someone I really like has been as exciting to me as one of the bigger, more high-profile cases.

For Harry Reasoner meeting his own standards and earning the respect of colleagues rank as important sources of satisfaction.

> I would have difficulty isolating a single experience. I think winning a big case, obviously there is a momentary thrill to it, but something like ETSI was peculiar, in that we had it on a contingent fee so that it was lucrative beyond any of the other experiences . . . and achieving a position that I feel at least I had earned respect and recognition but had satisfied my own standards to a degree. And, frankly, one of the attractions of trial practice is that it is kind of like bullfighting in the sense that you have to do it over each time and the bull doesn't give a shit how many bulls you've dealt with before.

For Steve Susman, his first big nationwide case gave him the most satisfaction.

> Probably the verdict on the Corrugated Container case would have to rank way up there because that was a big high. But, I don't really focus on it too much, because I think part of being a good trial lawyer is to even out the hills and valleys of your existence so that the lows aren't real low and the highs aren't real high and you just kind of blow with the wind and adjust.

Defeat

Notwithstanding the intellectual perspectives on winning and losing a court case, sitting at counsel table and hearing the jury's verdict against you is a painful and devastating experience. One asks, What went wrong? How did I fail? What could I have done differently? While there are many emotions associated with a loss for the men profiled here, the aspect of defeat they worry about most is the erosion of self-esteem, the threat to their self-image as winners. If any single professional event should cause a normal reaction of depression, certainly losing a case qualifies for a trial lawyer. Harry Reasoner comments on the impact losing has on many trial lawyers. "You see greatly talented trial lawyers, lawyers with great success who start to fear defeat to a degree that it leads them to excessive drinking or starts to affect their conduct or the way they handle themselves." But when facing the loss, according to Fred Bartlit, a good lawyer must put the feelings of defeat aside. "If you carry baggage with you, you won't be a happy trial lawyer and an unhappy trial lawyer is a bad one." Handling defeat is more difficult for some of the lawyers than for others, however, they all shared the ability to put the loss into perspective, to learn from it and to move on. Pat McCartan says he has "learned to tolerate, but never to accept losing" a case. Tom Barr expressed a similar philosophical approach to losing.

> I cannot tolerate losing. I just can't. It's not that it's going to end your life because you know that there are some things beyond your control. But it's not something that you're prepared to accept and fit in neatly. You know that this is an event that you will not be able ever to fit happily into your own psyche.

Phil Corboy describes his extreme reaction to a loss:

> Absolutely destroyed. Self-image terrible. Immediately had come in my mind in front of me the dozens and dozens of lawyers in this country who could have done a better job and won. I feel absolutely dejected. Lower than snail dirt. Distraught. Filled with loathing for me. Uncompromising in my disdain for me.

Bob Warren believes that with each defeat, a lesson is learned.

I've come to a conclusion, unfair as it may be, the great highs and wins are transitory, very pleasant, but transitory. Within two or three days, you're moving on thinking about other things. Defeats are very lingering. The warm glow of the high doesn't last as long as the icy bath of defeat. So, I think

that the way you handle defeat is to learn whatever lesson is to be learned and then move on.
—Bob Warren

Fred Bartlit is somewhat philosophical about defeat

> There are worse things than losing. You have to keep things in proportion and I'm all the time saying to myself, "Fred, everybody thinks this is a big deal, but in the scale of the world, it isn't." Every top trial lawyer has had a loss that really hurt. Losses make a man out of you. You have to lose to really be a winner.

Settlement

A reasonable approach to securing a successful outcome for your client is to instill a basic fear of failure in your opponent. Now, I'm not saying every case should be tried, but you don't get a good settlement unless there's a palpable, realistic inevitability that the case is going to be tried against you and it's going to be tried well. That's when you get your good settlements.
—Fred Bartlit

Obviously, cases can end in a number of ways. In addition to winning or losing, some cases will settle before going to trial. Others will settle in the course of the trial. In many instances, a verdict merely opens the door to the next phase of the dispute, the possibility of an appeal. Over the years I have heard trial lawyers say they do not care about the appellate process, "my job is to win this case in front of a jury, and that's all I care about." Those are the quintessential trial lawyers. On the other hand there are litigators who look for any aspect of the case that could lead to an appeal and prepare accordingly. These fourteen attorneys do both. However, in preparing to pursue the litigation through to its conclusion, they are pragmatists who are focused on what is ultimately in the client's best interest. This may mean securing the best possible settlement.

These fourteen men are aware of the way in which their egos and their opponents' egos play a part in the resolution of cases. This gives them a strategic advantage in settlement negotiations and clarity with regard to what is possible in a trial. Conflict frequently occurs between a lawyer's interests and the best interests of the client. "That's not sometimes, that's maybe mostly," according to Max Blecher.

> I have adopted a view that I like to have the settlement discussions between the clients. You put them in a room in which whatever they say is privileged. Most of the time they will come out with a solution. The lawyer can't do that because of his ego.

Lawyers' egos can cloud judgment. David Boies cites several instances where this can become a problem. One is an inability to admit defeat. Another is a lawyer's reluctance to present the prospects for success or failure in the cold light of day. For various reasons, the likely result is withheld from the client. Consequently, settlement offers, which are face-saving and in context reasonable, are not presented as real options. Boies thinks this was the case in the Westmoreland libel action.

> The other lawyer knew that we had, through discovery, built a more formidable defense than they may have anticipated at the time of the lawsuit. At the very beginning of the litigation, we had offered to give air time plus some money to pay for costs and stuff. By the time we went to trial, we had taken the money part off the table and we were just prepared to give air time, in part because the lawyer had recommended against the settlement originally.

Boies felt that Westmoreland's lawyers were reluctant now to tell Westmoreland to settle for less than he could have had before. "After the trial was essentially over, his attorney told Westmoreland that he really had no chance of winning and he ought just to walk away, which is what Westmoreland ended up doing with devastating results to him."

While defending *Time* against the allegations of libel from Ariel Sharon, Tom Barr was talking settlement with Sharon's lawyer

> Sharon was represented by a guy named Milton Gould who is an old-hand, cagey, court-smart, street-smart lawyer who I personally have always liked and enjoyed. We talked

> settlement all the time. Sitting together, we talked settle-
> ment while the jury was out. We talked in a way that was
> friendly and laughing, but we were serious.

Sometimes circumstances change as the trial develops. Although
some cases could have been settled for less than the ultimate result, in
many instances this could not really have been foreseen, no matter
how shrewd the attorneys for the defendant. Although the Milken case,
for example, could have settled for less in the beginning than was
ultimately paid, Boies has high regard for the defendant's counsel,
Mark A. Belnick and Arthur Liman, among others.

> I think the attorneys realistically faced up to that fact that
> circumstances had changed and were prepared to support
> and recommend a settlement that was a very large settle-
> ment but nevertheless, one that was a very good settlement,
> I believe, for the defendants.

Boies was looking at the matter from the perspective of the other side.
He was one of the attorneys negotiating against Milken

> It gave our clients a lot of money a lot faster than they
> otherwise had any hope of getting it, but it also gave
> Michael Milken peace and freedom. I think that he was
> quite well-served by his attorneys who were prepared to bite
> the bullet and say, "Even though we didn't buy the stock at
> ten and it's now twenty, we still think it's a good deal
> because we think it's going to forty."

Clearly, recommending settlement offers an arena in which a
lawyer's ego can clash with a client's best interests. Phil Corboy feels
the chances for such a conflict are greater with young, fire-eating
attorneys, hell bent on making a reputation. "But when you get
wizened enough and white-haired enough, you no longer ever try to
talk a client out of accepting dollars that are offered, even though I
point out that I believe the verdict may be more. But it's the client's
money." Corboy emphasizes the strategic nature of the settlement
issue. He does not make the final strategic calculation himself, but
considers it his obligation to give the client the best possible information on which a decision can be based. In terms of strategy, the plan is
to play for settlement until a particular moment is reached at which a
settlement offer is accepted or it is concluded that the case will go to
trial.

Jim Brosnahan claims to have witnessed some extreme examples in which an attorney wrapped up in his ego treated the client like a "total pawn. We're talking about individuals who are not sophisticated, are completely in the lawyer's control to a large extent, and they don't know what to do."

Arthur Liman has said of Joe Jamail, "Joe knows when to take the money off the table." Perhaps, but sometimes, according to Jamail, it is like "wrestling with the devil."

> You've got to say, "Back off ego." You know you've got it won. You know that this jury is going with you. You know the law is with you. You know this jury is going to give you fifty million dollars more than this client has asked or is wanting, or five million or five-hundred thousand or whatever. But hey, are you willing to underwrite this?" And ethically you can't.

Jim Neal has found himself on the horns of the same dilemma. It can come up in settlement issues in civil cases and in plea bargaining in criminal.

> There are a lot of cases I'd much rather try than have to settle. But I have to advise the client that the consequences of losing are so severe versus what he can get with a plea bargain and the chances of winning are problematical, that in my judgment, it's your best interest to settle this case although it's really disagreeable. It's ok to do that. That's no problem if you do it early on.

It is much more difficult if one goes through all the agony of preparation, gets right up to the day or a few days before trial, and then settles. For a trial lawyer, even though a good settlement is often better for the client "than even a favorable decision there is a sense of incompleteness when a case ends before verdict, particularly when the jurors tell you that they were in your corner and you should not have settled."

Arthur Liman has a technique for making the other side wake up and smell the coffee. Since he is prohibited from talking to the party on the other side, he will sometimes use a deposition to confront the opposing party with adverse evidence, even if there is no other purpose for the deposition. The idea is to precipitate a more realistic discussion. His firm is presently involved in a lawsuit in which the opponent's case is weak and will be expensive to win in court.

There is just absolutely no doubt that the other side ought to
accept the settlement proposal and we just cannot penetrate.
It's so expensive to see it through that our client's interest
really requires that we try, short of trial, to bring home to
the other side that their case has vanished.

Liman is one of those who believe some of his colleagues are not above
wringing money out of a case. At other times they just do not have the
nerve to confront the client with the truth.

You have some people who, because of the fact that they are
getting substantial fees, are incapable of settling until the
case has been milked. You have other people who are just
not realistic and you still have other people who aren't
strong enough to give the client a truthful assessment.

Seen from the perspective of a defense attorney, Tom Barr feels he
has been involved in lawsuits in which the plaintiff's attorney acted to
keep a losing case going. He is uncertain whether it was a mistake in
judgment or just an effort to get more money out of the client. This sort
of situation often eventuates in desperate, last-ditch efforts to settle.

I've seen a lot of lawsuits in which the plaintiff's lawyer,
particularly pressed, tried to settle, tried to get something
out of a client, in a case that was not worth anything. And
I've always thought it is very important to a corporation to
refuse any kind of tribute under those circumstances.

It may be a different matter with an individual, but Barr argues that a
corporation has a long-term interest in litigation, and ought to
establish a posture that says, "We will not pay off lawsuits that have no
merit."

Emotions breed erroneous judgment, according to Bob Warren, and
that, more than avarice or greed, is what sets a lawyer against his
client's best interests. He suggests that lawyers frequently get "wrapped up in combat and lose sight of the goal." Grandiosity, self-
righteousness, and greed, all are possible. Harry Reasoner reinforces
Warren's point. Getting "caught up in their own role in the process,"
can be a problem. Nor does Reasoner discount the possibility that a
lawyer may want to "churn the case."

Professional Disappointments

Pursuing the idea of self-image, one key element for all of these men is their belief that they are in control of what happens in the courtroom. Being in control is critical. Their greatest personal disappointments occur when events are uncontrollable. The unexpected is dangerous, whether it comes from the judge or from some other actor in the drama. As in competitive athletics, disappointment ensues when someone ceases to play by the rules. A surprising number of lawyers recount disappointments that revolve around unprofessional behavior of judges. Rather than anger, they express bitter disappointment that the system in which they work and in which they have faith, can be circumvented so cavalierly by one solitary individual. Although a negative experience with a judge causes disillusionment, perhaps those very experiences serve to shore up their confidence in themselves, and in the jury system. Gross judicial error, intemperance, or bias, illustrates the danger of having a single individual invested with the power to determine the outcome of the case. Juries, who actually decide the case, are not generally blamed for losses. Not one of these lawyers expresses disappointment with juries or the jury system. They believe that juries conscientiously try to get it right. But, when a judge is cavalier or ignorant, disrespectful or arrogant, these men find the transgressions of the values of fair play and high professional standards disheartening.

Harry Reasoner voiced a common sentiment, "Judges who are partisan, who simply don't respect the office, judges who are ideologues—I guess those have been the most disappointing experiences." The problem can be especially acute when regional biases come into play.

> I've been in situations in provincial areas or areas where you had a weak or unfair judge and having to deal with that process is distasteful and embittering. Going to situations where if you are unable to hire the right local counsel, you're in danger of being prejudiced by being *ex parte* and that is disillusioning and a distortion of the process. And to deal with those, you have to deal in ways that are unattractive.

For Jim Brosnahan, his most disappointing experience involved a judge, but was curiously intertwined with his most satisfying trial experience.

371

It was losing the Aguillar case [Tucson Sanctuary trial]. The one where the widow was convicted in two counts of felony and her only crime was taking food to the Salvadorian and Guatemalan refugees. The judge was just the worst judge I've ever encountered. I mean, he was just awful. He ruled out of order all of our defenses. He gave us nothing, almost directed a verdict in terms of intent. But the jury was out nine days. That's why when that young lawyer comes and says, "I want to be a trial lawyer twenty years from now." That's good, I want to encourage them. But I want to say to them, "You might sit in a courthouse next to your client for nine days waiting." That trial was an emotional roller coaster for six and a half months.

His strong belief in the system led him to continue to pin his hopes on the jury, even with the presence of a hostile judge. His personal emotional stake in the case made it all the more difficult to deal with a judge who did not exhibit the kind of competence and objectivity he expects of himself.

Pat McCartan recalls an incident that also involved unfair treatment by a judge. For him it was one of his worst disappointments.

I am somebody who really feels strongly about what I do and the way I think the system should function. Quite recently, I was presenting an appellate argument, and one of the judges on the panel was intent not only on asking me questions, but also interrupting me before I would complete the answer to his questions. When I persisted in answering completely, and kept making points, he leaned back and said, "Mr. McCartan, you make all this sound very simple, but I think you're just out to screw these people." The client was shocked. I was disappointed, but not shocked. The judge obviously had his own agenda and he was determined to see to it that we were going to lose that case, and he eventually wrote the opinion and got one of the other judges to go along with him.

In this case, McCartan felt a need to explain to his client that this was a profound distortion, and was not an outcome that could be explained by a "win some, lose some," philosophy. The system had been perverted.

We practice in an era of judge-dominated jurisprudence, and I've been in many situations where I knew judges were trying their darndest to take the case away from me. But for him to say something like that from the bench during argument was really offensive and I was embarrassed to be part of a system which could permit such conduct by a judge. It's one thing to come out of a case when you've lost it and say to the client, "Well, that's life," but to hear an appellate judge attribute that motive to the client, without any basis in the record, really bothered me, and it is ironic that this was in a court where the civility is supposed to prevail.

Arthur Liman also relates an incident that involved a terrible surprise by a judge. In this case the issue was later rectified, but he is still painfully reflective about the experience.

Probably the most disappointing experience that I ever had as a trial lawyer was the Milken sentence and that's because law is supposed to have an element of predictability. If you practice long enough, a client ought to be able to rely on your predictions and it was a very unhappy experience to find that in that instance, my prediction or forecast of what was within the range of being likely was so far off what really happened. Nothing had ever happened to me quite that way. You can expect to win, but you know you may lose a case. But when you are dealing with predicting a sentence and you have a whole history of experience in the court-house, it's almost inconceivable that you could be as far off as I and my colleagues were, in the prediction of that sentence... The judge gave ten years to my client. Everyone was stunned. No one expected it. Prosecutors didn't expect it. We didn't expect it. Nobody expected it. Later, the judge explained what she was doing, and I understood it because she intended a much smaller prison sentence. She said she intended thirty-six to forty months, but she gave ten years. You would get thirty-six to forty months by giving five years in prison. She was a new judge. Now, you take your risks whenever you have a new judge. But still, the stability of law depends upon predictability and I know nobody who came close to predicting this. I should have factored in more of the fact that she grew up with the guidelines. You see, the sentencing guidelines came in and she was trained under them, whereas I and almost all the other judges in the courthouse did not operate under the guidelines. It so

> happens that the judge has since rectified it, but I've never
> had an experience as disappointing as that.

These lawyers are rationalists, and they depend upon the system functioning in a predictable manner. When it does not, Liman suggests, "It causes you to have a lot of self-doubt and to question your own abilities and your profession and the predictability of your system."

Jim Neal says one of his most disappointing experiences is a case he lost where he thought he should have won, and he is quick to comment on the less than exemplary behavior of the judge.

> Now, I don't mean this case was the only one I ever lost, but
> it's the only case I can think of where I clearly thought I
> should have won. It was in Columbia, South Carolina, and
> everybody in the courthouse thought I'd won, and it was a
> two-count case. I guess I would have won it if the judge had
> done what he should have done and dismissed one count that
> I thought he should dismiss, but he didn't. The jury, after
> being out the total number of hours we were in trial, were
> praying and singing and all that, and they came back and
> convicted my client in a case that I thought I should have
> won. I always fault myself for that case.

Fred Bartlit does not associate his greatest disappointments with the judiciary. In fact, he suggests he has not experienced much injustice from the bench.

> Most judges are intelligent people who are trying their
> damnedest to get it right, just like I am. And I don't recall
> ever walking out saying, that venal son-of-a-gun, that
> crook, that dope. People are human, they see things
> differently. In thirty-one years as a trial lawyer, I have never
> seen a case tried through to the end that I could honestly say
> there was an injustice. We're not talking about people who
> use x-ray refraction techniques to measure something down
> to a millimeter. We're human beings with human issues and
> there's a zone of reasonableness that can go either way and
> the cases fall into that zone.

A disappointment for Bartlit is spending months of his life on a case and then the client "for perfectly good reasons decides to settle...you've done all the hard work that isn't the enjoyable or challenging part and then it's taken away from you."

For Bob Fiske his biggest disappointment came early in his career. A strong sense of responsibility permeates Fiske's account of what happened. He felt he had "let the government down," by failing to convict a man he was certain was guilty.

> I was much younger, but there was a very important criminal case that was brought right at the beginning of the Eisenhower Administration against a senior official in the Truman Administration and the main defendant was a Washington lawyer. He was a consummate fixer. The case was tried by a very able man who since then has become a federal judge, and four Assistant US Attorneys, who convicted him. It went to the Supreme Court and the Supreme Court reversed the conviction. It went back for a re-trial and by then, I had come into the office and I was the number–two person on the re-trial which ended up in a hung jury. The number-one assistant left the office and— then this is now the third time around—I tried it myself for six weeks and they were acquitted. And that was devastating. That was clearly the biggest disappointment I had, because I thought it was a great injustice. These guys were clearly guilty. I was very disappointed. I felt I'd let the government down. Also, it was the first major case I'd lost, and I think that must happen to every trial lawyer, the first one, it's a much bigger shock than if it happens the next time. I was very down for about three days.

David Boies looked back in disappointment upon a civil rights case which he believed he should have won. It was one of the most important cases of the Vietnam war era, the shooting of students at Jackson State College.

The case revolved around the children who were injured and the families of the children who were killed in the Jackson State College shootings following Martin Luther King's assassination. We had a case in which we had absolute proof that a group of police officers had just fired their guns into this dormitory of students, just shot up the dormitory. It was conceded that the shooting was unjustified. It was conceded that the shooting had

375

caused injuries of our plaintiffs and deaths of the students for whom the families were suing and yet, a jury was permitted to acquit and the acquittal was affirmed on appeal. The finding was for the defendant on the grounds that we could not trace a particular bullet to a particular gun. They were firing shotguns, which don't have ballistics and so we couldn't prove that any particular gun killed any particular student or injured any particular student. We argued from basic tort principles like if you've got two people, two hunters who shoot negligently and one of them hits a bystander, but you don't know which one, if they are both negligent, then both are joint and severally liable. And we said, "That sounds pretty good to us, that sounds the right way to go," and we were unable to win it at a trial, unable to win on appeal, and in the Supreme Court we got three votes for cert, but you needed four. That was probably my most disappointing result. It was really wrong. We should have won that case.

—David Boies

For Phil Corboy, some of his fellow colleagues have supplied him with his most disappointing experiences.

I've had lawyers go back on their word and lie and that's been a disappointment. I'm on a case right now, and I don't know whether I'm mad or just disappointed or whether it's both...early in the case opposing counsel asked me for a favor, or an accommodation, and I obliged him. Well, I wanted something from him the other day and he wouldn't give it to me. He's just being churlish, mean, snotty, bitchy. I reminded him of how he asked me to do something at the very beginning of this case for him. He denied ever calling me. Denied and said, "I don't remember that. I don't think that's what happened." But I'd learned that this guy is a liar and he pretends to be so honest and above-board. He's a very dishonest man. I guess that's the latest disappointment I've experienced...I don't revel in disappointments. I don't concentrate on the negative parts of my career. I don't concentrate on the badness or the evilness or dishonesty of other people. I don't remember those things. But I won't trust him for the rest of this trial.

Tom Barr, who remains hypercritical of himself, allows that it is forgivable for a trial lawyer to make misjudgments but that it is not acceptable for one to make a mistake. This recalls the French proverb, *c'est plus qu'un crime, c'est une faute* (it is more than a crime, it is a mistake).

> I had a case which was very complicated. There was one particular aspect that I just didn't understand and I didn't make the proper allowance for it. As a consequence, there was a big hole in the case. But what we had done, we were forcing the Norfolk and Western Railroad to buy the Erie Lackawana Railroad at a price to be set by the Interstate Commerce Commission and the trial was over what was that price. To reach that conclusion, we had to figure out what the earnings of the Erie Lackawana would be as a part of the merge to the Norfolk and Western system and therefore, what the stock was worth. I had not really realized, and I should have, nobody told me, but I should have realized it anyway, that the Erie Lackawana had been deferring maintenance on its track and property for a number of years and that that deferred maintenance had to be made up and that was going to be a large charge which would have affected the price. When I realized that, it was too late to correct it on our side because the evidence was already in. And that was a great problem because that would have destroyed the price. But I figured out how to demonstrate that the rate of deferred maintenance on the Norfolk and Western was just as great or greater than the Erie and, therefore, I had an argument that there didn't have to be any adjustment. And I got away with that. So, I was able to figure out a way to recover from that and once I did, it was all right.

Bob Warren's most disappointing experience was a libel case that he lost for a law firm. His witness was presenting a critical document, a letter.

> I recall that the trial was one of these standup things where I really thought we were all even-steven going along and the attorney who wrote the letter [a critical document in the

case] was on the stand and he was a man of very high integrity, a very nice man, but could appear somewhat cold and distant. The opponents obviously intended to keep him on the stand as long as they could hoping for something. I remember it like today. It was Friday afternoon and a certain question was asked and he answered it in a certain way, holding his finger out as he said it, and I just watched the lights go out in the jury box. I mean, click, click, click, click. I just knew it. I said so over the weekend. I said, "We've got to try to settle this. I think we lost it." Well, there were discussions about that but Monday came and the man came to me and said, "I think you were right. They aren't saying hello to me in the hall anymore." And the horrifying thing was, the trial still had four or five days to go plus the closing arguments. I felt just like one of those comedians who is up there dying... No matter how hard you try to tell a funny joke, nobody laughs and it gets worse and worse. Well, the whole rest of that case in front of that jury, I was convinced I was talking to stones that had been absolutely shot dead on Friday.

Max Blecher is disturbed and disappointed by what he saw as a trend of rapid deterioration in antitrust law over the last dozen years.

You work a whole lifetime to a point where, at the peak of your career you can really take off. And then all of a sudden, the law changes and "zap," your ability to win and even get cases to trial is just debilitated. It is like having ten years sucked out of my life. I think that's turning a corner now and hopefully the future looks a little better. That's my main professional disappointment. I built a group that I felt was really compatible and inspired and it became disappointing to lose with some consistency for the first time. One time I had a string going, I think eleven straight victories, and then it became impossible to win. The barriers were too great.

In Summation

When is a trial a win or a loss? This is a determination made with exacting care and these fourteen have their own reasoned perspective on this aspect of trial law, as on so many others. The exploration of winning and losing in this chapter revealed the extent to which a trial attorney's self-esteem and self-image are involved in losing. Money, prestige, and reputation may suffer, at time irreparably, through a well-publicized defeat. On the other hand, *sic transit gloria*. A win feels good but only for a few days and then it is on to the next battle.

It has been seen that a settlement can be a win, and that these men try to keep their egos at bay when settlement is at issue. Sometimes, a win can be measured in money. But a win might be no more than a convincing demonstration of moral superiority, or an acknowledgement of the fairness of one's claim. Primarily, winning is leaving the client better off than *before* litigation.

Disappointment for these attorneys hits them variously. Often, it takes the form of unfair treatment by a judge. Or, it may involve disillusionment with a colleague or an opposing attorney. Furthermore, making a mistake results in more than chagrin for a celebrity trial lawyer. More than most people, these men may torture themselves for days over something they feel should have been done differently, they may even castigate themselves for something not done and not even noticed by others. The anatomy of a win can be elusive and complicated, but in their hearts, these trial lawyers always know whether they have won or lost. Through it all, they are their own severest critics.

CHAPTER 10 ▒▒▒▒▒▒▒▒▒▒▒

The X Factor: The Secret Revealed

What's the difference between a .330 hitter and .360 hitter? He swings the bat a little faster, keeps his eye on the ball a little more.

—Bob Fiske

The fourteen men in this study are not psychologists or behavioral scientists. They responded to the questions about what makes a great trial lawyer with a single focus: what it takes to persuade a jury. Again and again, when talking to these men, one realizes the truth articulated by William James that "genius is concentration." A lawyer's fate is in the hands of the jurors, and it is with that in mind that every strategy and tactic, every fiber of a lawyer's being, must be aimed at the control of the jury.

There is clearly an extra edge involved in the difference between a good lawyer and a great lawyer. The men in this study mention a number of intangibles when it comes to influencing juries. There is a tautological character to answers like "great lawyers win,"or "great lawyers overcome obstacles." But there is the X factor. It is partly the unusual set of characteristics or traits discussed at various places in this book that distinguish these men from other trial lawyers. A particularly apt anecdote Bob Hanley once related to me about Fred Bartlit illustrates this extra something I am attempting to define here.

> Fred was cross-examining an expert in a jury case. The judge got up to look at a chart but in the process knocked over the American flag. Fred dove the full length of the floor and caught the flag. The jury clapped. Only Fred would do something like that.

This extra edge also comes from the careful observation of the successes and failures of others as well as through disciplined self-assessment. Phil Corboy advanced the model of the school of "hard knocks" as the basis for making a great trial lawyer. He has "never met a really good trial lawyer whose old man had any money, except for my son, Flip!" Are these men the product of Social Darwinism? Did they make an adaptation to adversity from which their incredible strength arose? There are suggestions of this type of thinking among the fourteen. Max Blecher's distrust of Ivy League schools, Joe Jamail's emphasis on courage and discipline are examples. The working-class ethics of Pat McCartan and Fred Bartlit is another suggestion. Blecher referred at one point to an ethnic factor, identifying the immigrant groups from the first decades of this century as the spawning ground for exceptional trial lawyers, the Irish, the Italians, the Eastern-European Jews.

It is fitting therefore that these men define the ingredients of their success. In doing so, they elucidate the difficult-to-define qualities that separate an exceptional career from the basic achievements of their less-illustrious colleagues; and in the process they have proven to be unusually thoughtful, reflective, and articulate. Schooled in the art of self-presentation, the skeptic might say these advocates know how to make themselves appear in the best possible light. But I believe that in the interviews with me and in the answers to the confidential questionnaires, they responded sincerely and candidly to questions about their professional lives. Many of them found the work for this book an opportunity for a degree of self-examination. All of them expressed a deep sense of obligation to their profession and they enjoyed relating their experiences.

In Their Own Words: The Marks of a Great Trial Lawyer

The fourteen lawyers were asked three specific questions about what it takes to be a superstar of the trial bar: What separates you from the other 65,999 members of the litigation section of the American Bar Association? What is the difference in your mind between a great trial lawyer and a good trial lawyer? And, do you draw a distinction between a trial lawyer and a litigator? The following is a digest of their perspectives on these questions.

Intelligence and ability, along with luck and opportunity (see

Figures 10-1 and 10-2), are key elements that separate great lawyers from the not so great. The talent for trial lawyering also consists of the ability to communicate and to maintain strict self-discipline. Specifically, with regard to reaching a jury, David Boies believes the skill required for major litigation is the ability to present facts in a lively manner, which is the antithesis of what one is taught in law school. In law school one typically learns about appellate cases, reasoning about what the law is, and what the law should be under specific fact situations. Most of the work of the trial lawyer, however, involves establishing what the facts are. The trial lawyer must select the facts to be emphasized, and then succeed in proving these designated facts as true. Boies observes that facts are in a sense, to paraphrase Aldous Huxley, the ventriloquist's dummy.

> And we all know that things get "proven in court" that are at variance with the real world, whatever that is, and they get proven *because what matters is what is presented to the jury*. Some things don't get presented because of rules of evidence. Some things don't get presented because the lawyer just isn't alert enough or hasn't marshalled the information, doesn't have it ready.

Intensity is a factor that one way or another all these men acknowledge as a component of greatness. Along with intensity of effort, Pat McCartan points to creativity and imagination as factors that separate the best from the merely good. Intensity of effort involves being hard on one's self. "I don't pay much attention to what others may think of the effort or my product. I listen mostly to myself. I know when I'm satisfied and when I'm not."

Thorough preparation and total commitment are crucial factors. Personal involvement is also essential. But above all it is an attorney's ability to present a version of the case that jurors will accept. Harry Reasoner states "great trial lawyers must have the analytic ability to simplify and be persuasive." Joe Jamail feels that part of his edge over others is that he cares more about what he is doing than other advocates. His intensity partly consists in being fiercely competitive. He also claims to be oblivious to the opinions of others regarding his courtroom behavior. Jamail feels that he plays by the rules and is ruthless in his desire to defeat his opponent, to annihilate anyone or anything that stands in the way of a favorable outcome for his client. He knows he has been criticized for being too abrasive and too

Luck & the Verdict

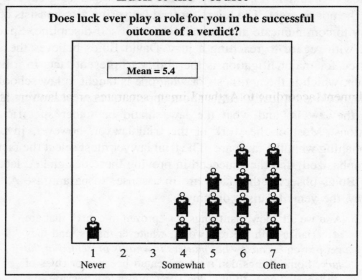

figure 10-1

Superstition

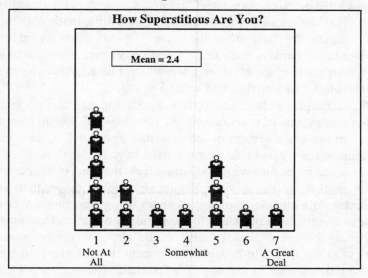

figure 10-2

punishing to his adversaries, but he is confident that he has the respect of colleagues and judges. On the spectrum of competitiveness, Joe Jamail is definitely a lawyer with a killer instinct. It is no accident that Percy Foreman was an early idol. Perhaps more than any of the other fourteen lawyers in this book, Jamail fits the public's image of a great trial lawyer.

Judgment, according to Arthur Liman, separates great lawyers from those who are only competent. Liman guesses that the best of the personal-injury bar could probably try criminal cases superbly because of their finely honed judgment and knowledge of courtroom procedure. Liman remembers when there were no specialists, no antitrust departments, security departments, or patent departments. In that context, the person who could try one case well could try any case well.

Courtroom judgment feeds on immediacy. When a trial is in progress, tactical agility, the need to make snap judgments in the face of a contingency is the difference. According to Bob Warren, "you don't have the leisure of making slow deliberate judgments when matters come up that are sudden and immediate in trial...There are an incredible number of very bright people who cannot focus on a course of action, 'Well, there are these factors on this side, and there are these factors on the other side.' 'Yes, but what do you think we ought to *do*?'"

Along with superb judgment, flexibility, foresight, and imagination are other distinguishing marks. Flexibility is the willingness to make sacrifices in order to win. One can learn to be disciplined. That is a skill. But flexibility is an attitude.

> Flexibility is what, to some extent, makes you able to do the work that discipline requires, and do it happily. If you're not happy at it, something will eat you up: the tension, the pressure, the hours, the work, the missed opportunities. Something will begin to erode the level of confidence, the ability, the judgment that you need to succeed.
>
> **—David Boies**

Flexibility means, for example, that one can change plans, and shift quickly into another mode of thought. This is also something Boies does not think can be learned, but falls more into the realm of innate capacity. It is a quality of the imagination that allows the few to see the outcome or end product of their work at an early date. Lesser lawyers see the case in segments, as a series of pleadings, interrogatories, depositions, and so forth. The case moves in one direction and then another, to no particular purpose. The ability to anticipate how something will play out down the line requires a degree of imagination that many lawyers do not possess. Imagination, however, must be combined with perseverance, a quality not typically found among trial lawyers, except for the truly exceptional.

Jim Brosnahan believes in the power of reading and study. "I am totally devoted to the process. I respect it. It's something I believe in. I've got three thousand books on trials, trial lawyers all the way back to the Greeks, the Romans. Those materials are not only interesting, but they are tremendously informative." While away on holiday, Brosnahan might practice speaking by reading the classics or poetry out loud. In general, Brosnahan feels his edge over other attorneys is his tremendous level of energy.

Great trial lawyers are able to perform publicly and enjoy doing so. Many cannot, and do not. Part of being able to perform in court is being dedicated, getting results, finishing a task, and bringing matters to a conclusion, "tying shoes," as Phil Corboy likes to put it. Corboy knows what most separates him from the pack is his orientation toward results rather than process. By process, Corboy means the details of discovery, the jousting, and the harassment, "the doggerel, the nonsense, the perfidiousness that's available. Most lawyers are content with going out of their way to make legal work and make it pay." He considers himself an "absolute, competent expert in the field of persuasion." He is not afraid to try a case in court, and he is not afraid to lose. He argues that a great lawyer has to be able to do both, go to trial, and accept the possibility of losing.

Most lawyers do not want to put either themselves or their posture or their dignity in jeopardy and as a result of that they don't get into the types of battles that people like my stripe do. And I think that that's where we are different.

—Phil Corboy

Enthusiasm for each case is a characteristic that marks an exceptional advocate. A case is not approached as typical work at a day job. Top lawyers derive a *joie de vivre* from their work. (See Figure 10-3). For others, law school and big firms have reduced law to dry-as-dust pedantry, wringing all the joy and excitement out of the discipline. Fred Bartlit recalls an article Gerry Spence wrote in *The American Bar Association Journal*.

> He said some of the most motivated and highly qualified young men and women in America go to law school. Before they go to law school, if you ask them what Jim Smith is like, they'd say, "Oh, he's a great guy." After they've spent three years with the undertakers, get out of law school, and get in a big firm, you ask them what Jim Smith is like and they say, "Well, his spleen is a half-inch long and it's located three-eighths of an inch from his kidneys."

Emotions Felt During Trial

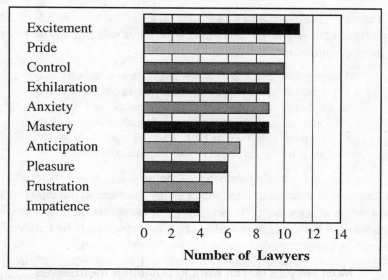

figure 10-3

Maintaining consistent and effective engagement in each case is necessary to excel in trial law. This is especially true among attorneys whose deep subjective inclination is to stand up for the plaintiff.

> I think to be a plaintiff's lawyer you have to have a certain sense of compassion or sympathy. You see lots of people come through your office in a lifetime whose businesses have been totally ruined or destroyed and it impacts their personal life. And there has to be some identification with these people above and beyond looking at them as an opportunity to make money...you have to have a sense of commitment to say, "These people have been wronged and these people need someone to represent them." As my friend Teddy says, "Aggressive fighting for the right is the noblest sport the world affords." That's really a very eloquent way of saying the way I feel about it.
> **—Max Blecher**

Passion, compassion, solicitude, and empathy are all related aspects of effective advocacy. Phil Corboy is a solicitor whose byword is indeed solicitude.

> The people who come to us are mostly upset. It's very easy to get mad at our clients because they are upset and they talk about things and they labor over minutiae and they are critical of us and sometimes untrusting of us. But we have to remember that they're hurt. They're mad at the world. And they hired you hopefully to acquire compensation.

Max Blecher wants to transmit to the jury, and make them commit to "a sense of emotional attachment or involvement to the client and to the case, and hopefully," he suggests, "it moves them." He wants the jurors to see his dedication and to see how passionately he believes the client has been trampled on by an indifferent system.

Empathy is closely related to passion. Lawyers admire it in their peers and hope to have it themselves. Although Harry Reasoner has seen trial lawyers succeed without empathy, the lawyers who have impressed him the most have a sensitivity and an ability to relate to people. Empathy is "that process where you get inside that person's skin or into the middle of that situation and feel what they feel, act the way they would act, understand what they are experiencing." The higher degree of empathy, the more effective the trial lawyer is in the courtroom.

Another important aspect of empathy is putting another's interest ahead of one's own. David Boies insists that the attorney must subordinate his or her personality to that of the client.

> How a jury thinks of you and how a judge thinks of you will affect how the jury or judge thinks of your client. And so you want the jury or judge to have a good opinion of you, but you've got to keep in mind that that is not an end in itself. It's a means to an end. Sometimes it works and sometimes it is counter-productive. The very worst thing that can happen is for a jury to go into a jury box thinking, "Gee, that guy was really a great lawyer. He did so well with such a difficult case."

Jurors are not going to give you points for being a good lawyer, they are going to give you points for being a good human being who makes their job easier. They also want to like a lawyer's case and to sympathize with his or her client. Ideally you want the jurors to think, "That guy really had a great case and he presented it well and simply. He was pleasant to us. It must be nice to have such a great case."

Joe Jamail identifies the ability to project credibility to a juror, to educate and persuade, to be believable in the highest sense as qualities that distinguish great trial lawyers.

> What doesn't make a good trial lawyer is...I've seen hundreds of them, literally hundreds of them [who] have a way of insulting a jury without knowing it—it's just unbelievable. They *want* to be condescending. They talk down to a jury. That is bullshit. A juror knows when you are doing it. I mean, the dumbest of us know that, OK? And they resent it.

Jamail is one of the great tacticians of the courtroom. For him, the nexus between lawyer and juror is the anvil upon which trial lawyers are forged.

All the lawyers are bound by a strong belief in the importance of sincerity. Qualities dependant upon knowledge of the facts in a given case. "A lot of people can't understand the facts of cases," Susman states, "but can very quickly figure out whether you're bullshitting them or not...sincerity is real important." And according to Reasoner, humility is fundamental. One should never forget life's complexities, vicissitudes, and the "thin difference between winning and losing. And juries relate to that common humanity. They sense when you are getting arrogant."

Jim Neal sees relevance and the imagination as necessary to compel a jury his way.

> I think in terms of skill, a highly developed sense of relevance and I don't know where one gets this. Certainly from some intelligence, but I have seen very bright people in other disciplines have a terrible sense of relevancy. I think the ability to communicate, a highly developed sense of relevancy, and imagination.

Others mentioned creativity and inspiration as the decisive defining quality of the great lawyer. Harry Reasoner thinks a great lawyer, on the strength of imagination, can create something wonderful and amazing out of a welter of incoherent information. Reasoner theorizes that "if you got half a dozen playwrights and gave them a detailed history of a family, a great playwright might create a play that would move you and the other five might write something utterly pedestrian."

Arthur Liman defines this ability to influence and move people as inspiration. Great trial lawyers have an *extra something* beyond preparation and understanding. "A great trial lawyer is inspired. There is just a something that, when you see it, you know it. I don't know how else to put it." Liman gives an example of inspiration from the practice of the legendary F. Lee Bailey. Bailey wanted to prove to a jury that a witness could not possibly have written a phone conversation down verbatim.

> An FBI agent said that he was taking notes which he produced while he was listening in on a conversation. And Lee Bailey, believing that that was untrue, took a telephone and handed it to the agent. Now remember, this is a courtroom environment, so it's not quite real, but Bailey understood that. He gave the agent a pencil and talked in his conversational way and had the agent say, "You're going too fast, you're going too fast," and finally Lee Bailey got down to the point of saying, "Can-we-meet, m-e-e-t, Tuesday?"

Liman allows that Bailey might have thought of this in advance, but it also could have been an inspiration of the moment.

He probably did not think too much in advance but he had the prop in court, but that's a great trial lawyer... What did he understand? He understood that the agent was going to get rattled in a court and that even if that agent had been able to take notes faster than he was in the courtroom, he would never be able to replicate it.

The ultimate difference between great and merely good is, other things being equal, courtroom performance. The ability to react in that environment in a way that carries the day, that overcomes the hurdles.

Litigators and Trial Lawyers

To a large extent the fourteen men represented in this book make an invidious distinction between litigators and trial attorneys. By looking at what they say on this subject, the qualities of a great trial attorney can be inferred.

> ...let me put it this way. There's as much difference between a litigator and a trial lawyer as there is between chicken shit and chicken salad. OK? Litigators are guys who couldn't cut it and can't cut it... I'm going to tell you something. I don't think there are what, fifty real trial lawyers in America? Real, dedicated trial lawyers who do it all the time and do it real well. And there may be five-hundred thousand litigators, but these are guys who go before committees and boards and agencies. That's different, my friend, that's different.
>
> **—Joe Jamail**

For most of the three-quarter of a million attorneys in the United States the idea of appearing in court and going to trial is so anxiety provoking that they do not entertain the notion. And it is the courage to overcome fear that these trial lawyers see that sets them apart from their colleagues. For our fourteen, litigator, if not a term of contempt, at least connotes an inferior species. Where litigators are concerned the question of courage is not at issue. Jamail continues:

These are not people who go down and face the barrel of a gun. That's what a lawyer is doing. His reputation is on the line. Defense and plaintiff...His reputation is that he is in there for a reason. He is dedicated to try to do what is right for that person...He's got those peoples' life and property in his hands. I don't think litigators look at it that way.

To the great trial lawyers, their kind is a breed apart, and must never be confused with mere litigators. The reason for this is simple according to Jamail.

That's a plain bald truism. There are not many people who can do what we do. Most of them know it in their hearts and won't say it. Why do you think they run to us every time something really important happens? I'm proud of the trial lawyers. Nobody appointed me to be their spokesman, but you just think about it. Trial lawyers build with ideas and creativity. Engineers build bridges and the things rust and fall down. The Statue of Liberty had to get fixed...and here's the Constitution. It's still working. Got no machinery to it. There's the Bill of Rights. It's still working. It's lawyers, my friends.

For Tom Barr, the term "litigator" is a euphemism for lawyers who do not go to trial. Litigation means conducting a battery of pretrial machinations. "A litigator has just become a word that people use really to hide from the world that they don't try cases." Even among those who call themselves trial lawyers, Barr supposes only a small number actually conduct trials. There are about 70,000 members of the trial lawyers bar. "I'll bet you there aren't ten percent of those who would qualify, in anybody's mind, as experienced trial lawyers." Arthur Liman's view of the matter is similar. Litigators fight their battles on paper—the discovery wars. They do not see it in terms of how "it's going to play on Broadway before a jury, they see the discovery process as an end in and of itself." Phil Corboy's scorn for the litigator however is more forgiving.

Litigators are interested in the process. Trial lawyers are interested in the result. Litigators do not know the result. Trial lawyers do know the result. Litigators never want the case to end. Trial lawyers can't wait until it ends. Trial lawyers know how to

> tie the shoes and know what shoes to wear.
> Litigators don't even know there are shoes there.
> All they know is there are rules. Litigators really
> are process oriented. They love the process of
> arguing motions—because they get paid for it.
>
> **—Phil Corboy**

For Bob Fiske, trial lawyers can do what litigators do, but not the reverse. Fiske knows many lawyers who are outstanding litigators in the sense of drafting pleadings, writing briefs, arguing motions, taking depositions, negotiating settlements, but who could not be called trial lawyers partly because they have done very little of it but also "some of them are uncomfortable actually going into a trial, particularly a jury trial." On the other hand, the litigator's work holds no mystery or terror for a trial lawyer.

Brosnahan likens litigators to brain surgeons who prepare for surgery, but never operate. ("I hope there are no brain surgeons who prepare for brain surgery and don't do brain surgery," he says wryly.) Brosnahan identifies the typical career path of a litigator. They become experts in pretrial procedures. "But they don't go to trial. It's amazing to me, but there are thousands of very competent people who are in that category who are very good lawyers." In Brosnahan's view, lawyers become a standard corporate acquisition, and are sometimes given responsibility for trying a case in court, even though they have no prior trial experience. They are brain surgeons operating for the first time. "People will actually hire someone to handle one of their biggest cases who has either never tried a case or has tried only two or three cases, give them that case, and tell them to go to court."

For Harry Reasoner there is a high percentage of immensely talented people (quite common on Wall Street) "who might do terrifically in front of juries if their practice ever took them there." There are others, however, who would not do well in trials. They spend their careers at the deposition discovery stage, motion stage, arguing. "It's a process of dispute resolution that seldom leads to the actual trial of cases." Bob Warren backs into the distinction, but suggests that some lawyers just do not have what it takes to go to trial.

> I think sometimes that the distinction is overdrawn, and
> sometimes by people who enjoy being in court but don't
> like the nitty gritty of putting together a case, as a way of

sneering at those who handle larger matters that stretch out. But, nonetheless, I do believe it is true that a substantial amount of people practicing trial law do not have the ability, in actuality, to try the case.

Whatever they are called, in Warren's view, they will shy away from going into court. "You can call them a litigator if you want, but the truth is that those people will, in some fashion, avoid having a case go to trial."

Pat McCartan hates the distinction between trial lawyer and litigator. He thinks it is a "dichotomy that does not do justice to either classification." He sees a positive interplay and cross-fertilization between the two roles. He does however acknowledge a functional differentiation.

If, as I think most people believe, the trial lawyer is the file jockey who is in court day in and day out and the litigator is the person who is shuffling paper, briefing, drafting motions for years, maybe deposing occasionally and arguing motions, yeah, there is a difference. I think I am more of a litigator than a trial lawyer because I spend more time out of court than I do in court, but when I go into court, I think I'm better prepared, my skills are probably just as well-honed as people who are in there on less sophisticated matters on a more routine and daily basis...I think that the first-rate litigators are first-rate trial lawyers. They have to be.

—Pat McCartan

By asking the lawyers to probe the difference between litigators and trial lawyers like themselves, considerable light has been shed on what they value about their identity. Honing in on what it takes to be a rarity, it is clear that it involves an ability to take charge, take responsibility, and be a fearless advocate in a public forum.

Getting There: Advice to Young Attorneys

All but two of the lawyers agree that the most important thing a young lawyer could do to help him or herself become a great trial lawyer is to get as much courtroom experience as possible. All fourteen agreed that law school does *not* prepare a lawyer for trial work. However, where a lawyer might obtain courtroom experience is subject to some disagreement. Most feel that in today's litigation environment this can be difficult for a young lawyer. Most cases settle, and in many jurisdictions it may take years for a civil case to reach the courthouse due to enormous numbers of criminal cases that have priority on the docket. All the lawyers here agree that it was easier to get into the courtroom and to develop courtroom skills when they were beginning their careers than it is today.

Jim Neal advises first "to be prepared to give up everything else in your life. Then, go walk on your knees to a place where they will put you in court. Don't go with the big firm. Go to a district attorney's office, go to a public defender's office, go to a US Attorney's office, go where you can get in court and take whatever you can get, and offer to do it for nothing if you have to." It does not matter what size and kind of cases one tries, Neal says, as long as you learn to figure out a defense or prosecution theory, however simple it may be; as long as you get to direct witnesses, cross-examine witnesses, sum up, and submit proposed instructions. And the "only difference between a trial that takes only a day and one that takes six months is a matter of stamina and logistics."

Arthur Liman agrees and suggests the place to get courtroom experience is at a prosecutor's office. "Try as many cases as you can, or go to a personal-injury law firm where you have volume and try as many cases as you can. Do that for two, three, four, five years." Learn how to examine a witness, how to read a jury and a judge, build self-confidence. Even then "You'll always have anxiety but the minute the curtain goes up, boy, you better be a different person. And you're not going to get that by trying one case every three years."

After this experience a young lawyer has to be noticed by judges and other members of the bar who will provide the word-of-mouth referrals for the big, important cases that a lawyer needs to build a reputation. Of course, a young lawyer would not get talked about and offered those cases unless he or she is perceived as really good to begin with.

> An incestuous relationship exists between district attorneys and judges, or judges and senior partners in firms. You start getting calls from the judge saying, "There's this kid, he

> was just out of this world. He was one of the best young trial lawyers I have ever seen." You then put him on your important case. Or the defense bar, if he's a prosecutor, starts saying, "This kid is fantastic. You ought to get him." I have called law firms and said, "You know, I've had a case with so and so and he is fantastic."

Bob Fiske shares the view that extensive experience in the courtroom is necessary to achieve prominence in trial law. To that recommendation, he adds the benefits of working closely with the best. "Go to the US Attorney's office or work for someone like Arthur Liman. There, you will be with somebody who will attract the major cases."

Another possibility is to look for a mentor, an attorney who will allow you to work with him or her to get the hands-on courtroom experience. A mentor relationship gets harder and harder to establish today since there are fewer courtroom opportunities. As indicated earlier, less than five percent of the cases that are filed go to verdict. Pat McCartan formalizes both approaches, working where one has immediate responsibility, and working with a good trial lawyer, into a two-step process. It is only with reservation and caution that he advises going to the US Attorney's office. Getting the experience that you need to become a great trial lawyer is tough to accomplish today, because the practice has changed so much. The garden-variety cases of the kind that McCartan and others cut their teeth on are just not available. Judges try to limit the number of cases tried. Cases "are being processed like insurance claims. A young lawyer has to kick, scream, and fight—generally first with his client—to get into a courtroom on any case."

From McCartan's perspective, starting out in private practice is the best route to develop rudimentary lawyering skills. Only after these skills are mastered would he advise a young attorney to risk going into the US Attorney's office or the county prosecutor's office. The risk is that bad habits can develop. The young attorney may be given more responsibility than he or she can handle, and have an unrealistically heavy work load, often functioning independently, without a mentor. And senior lawyers are too busy to play this role. "The mentor system is dead throughout the profession. So it's going to be working on your own, developing these skills. They ought to take every opportunity to observe and to critique more experienced trial lawyers."

Three or four years is long enough in such a position. Five years, according to McCartan, is too long. McCartan goes on to point to an irony that he has noticed in his firm—young lawyers who really want to have courtroom experience seem to find a way to get it. "They work around the system, and before you know it, they're down there in federal court trying a Title VII case. It's a pattern. They come out of the cracks somewhere. They convince somebody that they should have a case."

Harry Reasoner feels that the really important lessons are learned in working with *and* against exceptional trial lawyers. He sees a real danger in succumbing to routine, becoming sloppy, and losing sight of the complexities involved in trial law. There are a breadth of skills and abilities that need to be mastered. Jury skills are important, but these must be supplemented with procedural and legal knowledge.

> Ideally, you want to play on all of the jury skills that you have, but at the same time, you want to structure the case legally both to give you a record you can sustain on appeal and also to minimize your burdens, to focus the points, to get a charge that puts the minimum burden on you that the law requires. In training, you need a steady progression of responsibility.

Bob Warren, likewise, extols the virtues of working with excellent practitioners.

> Get in a milieu where you are working with people who stretch you and challenge you and instruct you, just by virtue of what they're doing, never mind whether they're instructing you in any formal sense. And get in an environment where trials are going on, where cases are going on, where you can participate in a very meaningful way.

Steve Susman said his first reaction to a young lawyer who wanted to become a great trial lawyer would be to offer some words of caution, "They can be great lawyers. They can be great second-chair people, but ninety percent haven't a chance to be a great trial lawyer."

Susman, like others, recognizes that work in a district attorney's office is double-edged. There will be an opportunity to try a lot of cases, but the work will be repetitive, the cases will not require a great deal of ingenuity, and the quality of the opposing forces will not be high. After spending some time in a firm like his own, Susman guesses that a year or two in the office of the district attorney could be valuable.

David Boies recognizes that young lawyers differ a great deal in their natural ability. He believes that the kind of training and experience a young lawyer needs is dependent upon the abilities and talents he had right out of law school. He differentiated the "talented" from the "not-so-talented," and suggested different approaches for each. For a very talented attorney, courtroom experience early on in one's career is important. "In general, my advice would be to get lucky, by that I mean, get good training, which you can get at a lot of different places. When you've had enough experience so that you can put that together with your ability, then get some good opportunities."

In the case of a lawyer who does not have great natural ability to be effective in the courtroom, work in a major law firm will afford an opportunity to see if such a capability develops, and in the meantime other valuable experience will be obtained. This experience will be valuable, whether or not a lawyer emerges as lead trial counsel or stays in the background in major litigation. There are many things to be learned, according to Boies, from an association with a large firm, "how to master large fact situations, how to organize, how to think, how to analyze, how to take care, be precise, and achieve perfection."

While first-hand experience is ideal, young lawyers can observe experienced trial partners in their law firms by working on a trial team, watching court T.V., or participating in NITA programs. Jim Brosnahan suggests an unusual idea not advanced by any other lawyer. He distributes a reading list. The books included are *Jury* by Victor Villansenor (the minute-by-minute jury deliberations in the first Juan Corona murder trial), works from antiquity by Demosthenes, Cicero, and Quintilian, trial books, and more trial books.

> There is a set of eighty-four notable British trials and I have eighty of them and I have probably read forty or fifty of them. These are beautiful transcripts by English barristers. So reading all that is a borrowed kind of experience and you really begin to understand what this is all about.

Two of the lawyers here, however, did not feel that courtroom experience was the best way to learn about or train for becoming a trial lawyer. Joe Jamail advises a young lawyer not to go immediately into the courtroom, but to observe the great ones in action. He emphasizes not so much learning pragmatic skills, but the development of an individual courtroom style or persona.

> Never try to imitate. Try to see what you like best about
> yourself and try to make people see you the way you want to
> be seen when you are representing somebody, because the
> client has no voice. Others see the client through you. So,
> young lawyers should watch great trial lawyers.

Tom Barr offered a unique perspective. He also did not feel that extensive courtroom experience was the best training for a young trial lawyer. He agreed with several of the other lawyers that the potential to be a truly great trial lawyer is rare. Perhaps as a challenge, his advice to a young lawyer who held aspirations to become great, would be, "'Don't do it. You can't be.' I've seen a lot of people come through here. We get twenty-five people every year and all of them say 'I want to become a great trial lawyer.' One or two of them has a chance." If Barr does perceive the necessary talent he recommends that they get close to someone who does trial law well and work closely with this person. Gaining a mastery of many pretrial aspects of going to court is vital.

> Learn the right way to prepare for getting into the court-
> room. Learn the organization. You want to do the small
> things of litigation. You want to learn how to do those things
> perfectly. You want to learn how to produce documents. You
> want to learn how to take a deposition, answer interrogato-
> ries, make the motions—do all those things perfectly all
> the time. The courtroom work will come fairly easily once
> you've learned to do the small things well.

Barr feels that going immediately into the US Attorney's office is *not* a good idea. A young lawyer is left too much on his or her own "to try bullshit criminal cases . . . And you are left in the hands of lawyers who don't know what they're doing."

What does the future hold for potential trial lawyers? Many will be called, and few chosen. It will be increasingly difficult to mimic the paths followed by those who are now at the top, and there is no certainty that new paths will develop.

The X Factor: Beyond the Born Versus Made Debate

For all these lawyers, there exists conflict between the belief that they possess an absolutely inspired, innate gift, and the belief that their trial skills are something they have learned and that others can learn as well. Clarity, accuracy, and speed in thinking, in speaking, and in advocacy in general, are habits or skills that trial lawyers must master to be successful. Further elements in a lawyer's effectiveness are the ability to project commitment, a sure sense of what is relevant, and a degree of imagination in formulating a theory of the case. These can be learned, and are part of what jurors perceive as credibility in an advocate. In addition to innate credibility and sincerity, there are certain skills that must be learned or at least honed and refined through experience. Fred Bartlit, for example, identifies capabilities that are genuinely attained skills as opposed to innate character traits.

> The ability to read really fast is what keeps me alive and I learned this by taking a speed reading course and practicing. But the quickness, in other words, if you are a contemplative person who says every time there's a decision, here's six reasons to do this and seven reasons to do that, you're not going to be a good trial lawyer. You have to make judgments. Every time I've gone against my gut, I've wished I hadn't, and every time I've gone with my first reaction and done what I thought was the right thing to do, I've been pleased. So be quick and read fast.

Experience is part of this extra ingredient. Bob Fiske says, "the fact that a lawyer has tried two hundred cases doesn't put him in this top group. On the other hand, anybody who is in it wouldn't be in it unless they've had a lot of training and experience as well as having innate abilities, so I think it is really a mixture." David Boies has a similar point of view. He tends to see what is learned as something built up on a substratum of innate ability that does not change much over time.

I've learned some things, happily, over the last twenty-five years. I've learned how to avoid distracting the jury, I've learned about clothes. I've learned how to relate to particular people in particular ways. I've learned a lot at the margin. But I think that my basic skills, my basic approach hasn't changed that much and I think the same thing is true for people as disparate as Steve Susman and Joe Jamail and Tom Barr. Although we would all say we've learned a lot as we've grown up, I think we should also say that some of our best work was when we were young and we still had the basic skills to do it well. For me, I think most of the attributes that make me a good trial lawyer are attributes that I had twenty-five years ago.

—David Boies

Joe Jamail suggests just how difficult it is to separate what is learned from experience from what is in place at birth.

> I think it is a combination. If I had to pick, I would say (and this is crazy because there never was a lawyer in my whole family history line) a lot of this is innate, which makes me think that you don't have to go to law school to be a good lawyer. You've got to go to learn the rules, but who's to say you [Vinson] couldn't be the best lawyer that ever lived? I guess I'm saying that a lot of this is innate, but when I say innate, it may be innate because you picked it up as a child or along your way through some experience.

Phil Corboy touches upon all these themes in coining the term, "X factor," the unknown quotient that predicts greatness.

There is an X factor that makes people great trial lawyers as compared to those who are just good trial lawyers. There's too much room in the world of trials for only the great trial lawyers to be trying cases. There are too many cases being tried physically to attract the attention of only the great trial lawyers. So it's like the difference between Ryne Sandberg and just another second baseman. What's the difference between Michael Jordan and another All-American who's playing basketball? There's some X factor that makes them better. They are usually better at communication. They are usually better at persuasion. They usually have more integrity. They are much more capable of cutting through the nonsense and reaching the decision that jurors have to reach... They are afraid to lose, but know that they

> have to be afraid to lose and that fear of losing is probably what stimulates them to being completely prepared to try the case.
>
> **—Phil Corboy**

According to Corboy, however, trial lawyers must also be trained. One must have the innate ability that supplies the technical ability to be a good trial lawyer. The X factor must be present, but it is not enough, one must still be trained as a trial lawyer.

Arthur Liman, a dedicated teacher, refers to an intuition or sixth sense that all great lawyers possess. This sixth sense can come out, for example, in cross-examination.

> All trial lawyers are taught when they cross-examine not to ask a question where they don't know the answer. I teach that. [But] I've never known a really good trial lawyer who did not ask such a question. Now I would tell you that when I asked that question, I know that answer. And how do I know the answer? I'm on a roll with that witness and it's almost a hypnotic experience . . . so if that witness is under my control and there is that momentum, I know that I can take it that extra half a step and then I'm going to get that answer.

Knowing how far to go is crucial, as is knowing when the job is done. Liman asked an artist and novelist, "How do they know when your painting is finished? How do you know when your book is finished? . . . it's that same type of instinct that some people have it, and some don't."

Moving from aesthetics to athletics, Bob Warren makes an interesting comparison with sports. Some athletes have abundant natural ability, but cannot win.

> You can name some tremendously gifted tennis players who have an incredible array of great shots, but never win tournaments. They have this innate, technical ability but because they cannot bring themselves to devote themselves single-mindedly to achieving real greatness and they do not have these qualities of intense perseverance, desire, and ultimate belief in their ability to win regularly . . . that difference in athletics is also a difference in trial law.

Pat McCartan believes he can train a young attorney to an acceptable level of performance, but over and above that level one can no longer teach. He jokes that he can watch a young attorney walk down the hall and will be able to tell whether he or she is going to perform as a trial lawyer. "But I don't have to work very long with them to see whether they have that practical sense, that sense of irony that is so essential in this practice... I think we are always looking for an edge, the difference, the line, the seam that separates them from others." A sense of irony is the final ingredient: "it magnifies all the skills... it is a juxtaposition of facts that provides the most effective and compelling way to see your way through the case."

Jim Brosnahan also notes the ability on the part of good trial lawyers to deal with situations instinctively, to react correctly to the immediate situation.

> There is a shortstop for the Dodgers right now who has got the league record, I think, for errors. He just doesn't have good baseball in him, probably a hell of an athlete, he doesn't have the instincts. Courtroom instincts, I don't quite know what I mean by that, but just the, "Oh, I see, here's what's happening." That's a very important skill. You can't be sitting there thinking about yourself as some people want to do. So that instincts, trial instincts, are crucial.

Fred Bartlit states the predominant view among his colleagues that whatever a lawyer's skills need to be, there is a core within them which is innate. Some trial lawyers will, through dint of extremely hard work, become better than ninety-five percent of the lawyers in America. "But in terms of the extra special, I think those skills are probably mainly innate."

Totally innate. It's just like asking me, "Could you teach somebody to hit like Willie Mays or pitch like Sandy Koufax?" No, of course not. It's just something that's in the arm or in the eye or in the physical coordination. I think this is something in the genes. It just comes. It's just the combination.
—**Max Blecher**

Even so, innate skills for Blecher are not always obvious. One has to use them to develop them.

> Sure, you can sharpen these skills up, you can try to teach people, "Be more discriminating, don't put in every fact that you've collected, think about a story line that you're going to develop for the jury, make it easy and understandable and clear to them," but then doing it is a second thing. Telling somebody what to do and doing it are two different things. I just think it is pretty much a talent rather than a learned or acquired trait.

Tom Barr seems to recognize that the basic decision-making power of a trial lawyer is grounded more in intuition than logic.

> How do you decide to hook the witness, I mean, set the hook in his mouth and then to pull it slowly so that you bring the fish in and land it? How do you decide what particular kinds of arguments are going to appeal to a judge's psyche and what are not? Sometimes I say to people, "You've got to trust the force." If you feel it, feel it as opposed to think it, then if you have the skill, if you have the ability, it's that feeling that you have to trust . . . there is a feeling, a sense, a gut reaction that really good trial lawyers have and everybody doesn't have that . . . you also have to have a passion of some kind. A passion that says, "I will not make any mistakes."

The Response to Fear

> It is like living inside a rotary lawn mower. That's what it's like. [A client once] said to me, "It's not money that gets you up at four thirty, Fred, it's the absolute fear of fucking up." Nothing more complicated than that.
>
> **—Fred Bartlit**

Throughout their careers these fourteen men have displayed extraordinary initiative. They have shown no fear in dealing with powerful people, nor of entering into intense, highly charged adversarial situations. They have not been afraid to take on responsibility for controversial outcomes or to risk vilification in the press. (And they have not been afraid to charge fees that were commensurate with their ability.) As Joe Jamail reiterates again and again, all this requires courage.

> Good lawyers take heat. Good lawyers, like me, thrive on it. If you're not bitching at me, I've done something wrong. I mean, what am I doing? Have I gotten lazy? Complacent? But that's the number one thing—courage.

It is not that these men are impervious to fear, or fear of failure. They all admit to such fear. But they can dismiss it, overcome it, rise above it, and be driven by it. Jim Brosnahan makes the point that although courage is particularly equated with the plaintiff, "it's also true in the defense bar. Just the courage that it takes to say, 'OK, we're going to do this.'" Along with courage comes dedicated and passionate advocacy, Jamail's song.

> You're going to have to find a way to make sure that you're one hundred percent dedicated to see that justice is done for your client. And I'm talking about advocacy. Advocacy makes the big difference between the great trial lawyer and the good trial lawyer or ordinary lawyer. And advocacy is not anything you learn in law school...And a sense that you need to preserve what is sacred—a jury trial. It's the greatest drama on earth.

Jamail compares this kind of fierce advocacy to the way in which a mother stands up for her child. To be an advocate is a life lesson not everyone can learn.

> Advocacy is something you learn from your mama, from your childhood friend, from every experience you've ever had. Courage, advocacy, the willingness to continue to learn, a fear for the right reason, and a fearlessness. If you're afraid of losing just because of losing, you're in the wrong place. If you try enough of them, you're going to lose. But the fear of losing because you've let somebody down is a stimulant for me....

The response to fear is another aspect of the X factor that separates great attorneys from the near great. The men in this study feel the presence of the fear of defeat, and muster the courage to overcome this fear. Pat McCartan says the good trial lawyer "must dare to fail." Part of the fear is that the jury will not "love" them, that they will not be found brilliant, and so forth. Phil Corboy zeroes in on this aspect of the profile. The trial lawyer:

> Loves to be loved. Wants to be loved. Wants to be accepted. Wants to be shrewd. Does not want to be criticized. Fearful of defeat, yet brave enough to face defeat. Unconcerned concern. Very concerned of what people think of him or her until it is said, but then when it's said, doesn't like it unless it's good. Thin-skinned, pretends he's not. Pretends bravery but he's really scared. Scared but really brave.

Tom Barr had a case early in his career, in the sixties, in which he almost made a terrible blunder.

> It scared the hell out of me. I think there is a higher level of thinking, of intuitive thinking that you get to only with some amount of emotion—some challenge, some fear, some desire—and I can feel it step up.

Barr reiterates how correct decision making is driven by emotion tempered by detachment, the lawyer's magic formula.

> I know when it's stepped up and I know that's the time when I feel like I could really make all the decisions and they're going to be right. And that comes about sometimes because of fear and it comes about sometimes because of the emotion of the situation.

Barr sees the intimate connection between emotion and intuition. When the emotion or feelings are real in a given situation, the intuition functions at a high level.

> When the Telex decision came down...on the front page of *The New York Times*, and the stock market went...IBM lost fifty points. That was a disaster. My reaction to that was, "Hey, it's never going to get any worse than this," and I sat down that day and laid out exactly what we were going to do and, within ten days, we had the judge pulling the decision back.

The question arose of where to get the energy to come back at this problem.

> Now the decision was wrong and I knew it was wrong and I knew what was wrong about it...but you've got to get up to that level. You've got to get yourself going and sometimes that gets hard. Sometimes it's hard to operate on the higher level because the lawyer on the other side isn't any good, or the

---

judge is not good, but you've got to get up to that level and you've got to keep yourself out of it.

Barr raises a theme encountered earlier, that the lawyer must identify with the client, get driven by that, but all the while maintain objectivity. Winning can come when the other side cannot sustain the tension between identification and objectivity.

David Boies gets on the edge, but it is more a form of excitement. Is there fear in it?

> ...I don't think so. I mean, it certainly puts you on edge. My hands are not perspiring now. You will never see me in court during a trial with hands that are dry. My hands are always perspiring from the tension...and it is partly from anxiety about what's going to happen and partly it's just from the tension of trying to figure out what is happening next and where things are going to go....

It is almost a state of egolessness, somewhere in between the no-ego of total identification and the ultimate ego of total objectivity.

You've got to be comfortable with yourself. I think you've got to be confident. You either got to have no ego or an enormous ego. You have got to have enough...you've got to have a drive to succeed, to achieve...You can't be a totally self-satisfied person. If you're totally satisfied, I think you don't have the urge to go out and achieve, to conquer...That drive comes from some desire, some need to do something you haven't done, achieve something you haven't achieved, fill in some piece of your puzzle that's missing.

—David Boies

Ego: The Real X Factor?

The lawyers in this study have made a number of provocative and insightful comments when asked to speculate on the psychological profile of the gifted lawyer. Clearly, some of what they say represents things they believe to be true about themselves. Quite probably there are some elements of idealization and projection in these answers. Some of the lawyers are reluctant to indulge in what is in a sense an excursion into pop psychology. Others do it with great relish. It comes as little surprise to learn that these men consider their peers, and by implication themselves, to be egocentric, competitive, and driven. The mix of psychological elements necessary to produce, motivate, and enable trial lawyers to endure the pressures of the work includes an unusual drive to succeed. Where does this drive come from? And how is it sustained? This is really the problem addressed by all of these men in response to questions about greatness. Earlier in this chapter comments revolved around the skills and human qualities necessary to *accomplish* the work of trial lawyering. Here the lawyers comment on the human qualities that make them *want* to do it. Jim Brosnahan considers that a person who has performed admirably for a long time will of course be somewhat egocentric. "At some level, they need to succeed and there could be very complex and very different reasons as to why that is. But you don't persevere in this business unless you are egocentric."

Bob Warren draws the line at calling himself and his peers monomaniacs. And he wants to qualify the definition of egocentric before he will own up to it.

> I don't think monomania is an essential characteristic of trial law. I don't think narcissism is an essential element of a trial lawyer or great vanity. I don't think that this self-preoccupation is essential or even beneficial. What is true, however, is that I cannot imagine somebody being a trial lawyer who does not have an ego that says that I am confident of my ability to do well. I respect my opponent, but I am not of the view that he is a better lawyer or person or anything else than I am . . . I don't think that's the kind of sick ego that people are talking about sometimes with trial lawyers.

Tom Barr suggests that great trial lawyers are fighters who cannot tolerate losing. They may motivate themselves with either optimistic or pessimistic scenarios. Trial lawyers are people with

> Pretty secure egos. People who can't tolerate losing, who are fighters . . . some people will motivate themselves by pessimism and some motivate them by optimism. Some

will say, "I'm going to lose, I'm going to lose, I'm going to lose," and some people will say, "We're going to win, we're going to win, we're going to win." I've always been an optimist. I've always been somebody who believed we were going to do it.

Barr's confidence is born of a combination of intuition and logic. A successful trial lawyer relies on "his own intuition and has a very good understanding of inductive reasoning and of logic and so forth, but who does not rely on that very much to tell him what to do." The combination is interesting. For Barr, the understanding of inductive reasoning and logic is secure, but it is intuition that tells him what to do. Intuition is sharpened by an intense identification that stimulates productive thinking in the courtroom. At times the advocate becomes virtually "transformed." Barr even thinks a kind of transforming intuition can function at all times during the trial. "There is an ego factor and I don't know what this magical quality is that enables you to relate to juries, but most trial lawyers I know sort of are transformed in the courtroom. They're different, there is a different presence in that courtroom."

This ability to get into a particular psychological and emotional zone in the courtroom is something all these men have experienced. Being able to enter this zone each time one goes into court, even in the later stages of one's career, is essential, for David Boies. "Great trial lawyers keep their edge, their desire to win as they get older." He says that after success some lawyers become too relaxed or unconcerned in the courtroom, and lose their edge.

In defining the psychological profile of a gifted trial lawyer, Joe Jamail is completely consistent with his earlier comments about personal qualities and skills, whether talking about himself or anyone else. There is no disparity between what he thinks is necessary, what the others have, and what he himself possesses. It is all of a piece, integrated, consistent. "If you don't have a well-defined ego, you haven't got much of a trial lawyer. I really believe that. And I've been with them. I've seen them. And, I'm one of them."

A Final Word

Identifying the specific qualities that lead to phenomenal success as a trial lawyer is both obvious and elusive. Ego. Drive. Intelligence. Empathy. These fourteen men do indeed share a number of common traits. Nevertheless, their individuality betrays easy generalization about the achievements that have propelled them into national prominence. They are all masters of strategy and tactics that integrate advocacy with the rules and procedures that govern the resolution of disputes in our system of justice. This is the area in which their unique insight, creativity, and judgment reside. So while we have been able to isolate commonalities among these superstars of the trial bar, we have also seen that there exists a self-described X factor associated with their approach to what they do. It is clear that this X factor, in combination with their personalities and experience, defines success.

Beyond descriptions of achievement or explanations for its occurrence, we do know one thing that is unequivocally common to these men—their love for what they do. Phil Corboy poignantly expressed it when he said, "I was lucky to get into something that I excelled at and enjoyed doing. I suppose that I'm like the baseball player who says, 'God, I'd play baseball even if they didn't pay me.'"

It is doubtful that any of Corboy's colleagues would disagree.

APPENDIX 1: ███████████

Profession Survey

[This survey was sent to four hundred members of the legal profession that included lawyers, judges, in-house corporate counsel to nominate lawyers for this book]

Trial Lawyer Research Project

I. In my view, the following individuals possess national reputations as exceptionally skilled trial lawyers:

Name	**Location of Their Office**
_____	_____
_____	_____
_____	_____
_____	_____
_____	_____
_____	_____
_____	_____

II. Is there any specific trait or characteristic that you believe is common to these people?

_____
Your Name
(please print)

APPENDIX 2: ██████████████████

Questionnaires

[These four questionnaires were sent to the fourteen trial lawyers profiled. When completed, they were sent to Peter Frank at Price Waterhouse. The completed questionnaires were identified only by the attorney's individual ID code and sent to Dr. Vinson for analysis.]

On the following pages you will find questions pertaining to your work and lifestyle preferences. Please check any or all options which apply to you, and feel free to add any options or comments which you deem to be important.

When responding to this type of scale:

Agree : ___ : ___ : ___ : _✓_ : ___ : ___ : ___ : Disagree

mark the space which most nearly reflects how you would rate along the continuum.

WORK STYLE

"By working faithfully 8 hours a day, you may eventually get to be a boss and work 12 hours a day."
—Robert Frost

~ Do you prefer to work:
 ( ) at home
 ( ) at your office
 ( ) no preference
 ( ) other _____

~ Do you prefer to work:
 ( ) mornings
 ( ) afternoons
 ( ) evenings
 ( ) late evenings
 ( ) all night
 ( ) no preference

~ What are your usual office hours? _____

~ When you are not in trial, how many hours a day, on the average, do you work? _____

~ Is it typical for you to work on Saturdays?
        (   ) no
        (   ) yes   How many hours? _____

~ Is it typical for you to work on Sundays?
        (   ) no
        (   ) yes   How many hours? _____

~ How much do you enjoy using the telephone in your work?

Enjoy a lot : ___ : ___ : ___ : ___ : ___ : ___ : ___ : Do not enjoy at all

~ Do you prefer to work:
        (   ) alone
        (   ) with others

~ What type of clients comprise the majority of your cases?
        (   ) individuals
        (   ) small companies
        (   ) large companies
        (   ) insurance companies
        (   ) organizations

~ Do your clients tend to be:
        (   ) plaintiff
        (   ) defense
        (   ) both equally

~ Which do you find more professionally challenging?
        (   ) plaintiff
        (   ) defense
        (   ) both equally

~ In preparing for trial, do you prefer:
   ( ) to be personally involved in every aspect of trial
       preparation
   ( ) to delegate a large number of trial preparation re-
       sponsibilities

~ Have your family, friends or colleagues ever teased you about being *too* organized?

   Frequently : ____ : ____ : ____ : ____ : ____ : ____ : ____ : Never

~ When keeping appointments, how punctual do you tend to be?

   Always early : ____ : ____ : ____ : ____ : ____ : ____ : ____ : Always late

~ Do you tend to procrastinate?

   Always : ____ : ____ : ____ : ____ : ____ : ____ : ____ : Never

~ Do you enjoy having friends or relatives in the courtroom while
   you are trying a case?

   A great deal : ____ : ____ : ____ : ____ : ____ : ____ : ____ : Not at all

~ If you account for your time by the hour, how many billable
   hours would constitute a typical year? _____

~ Do you tend to enlist someone other than a colleague (e.g.,
   spouse or a close friend) as a sounding board for case strategies
   and tactics? If yes, who?

   _____

~ What law magazines do you read?

( ) *Inside Litigation*
        ( ) read every issue, cover-to-cover
        ( ) read most of each issue
        ( ) read some of each issue
        ( ) browse each issue
        ( ) peruse only when I have time

( ) *Litigation Magazine*
        ( ) read every issue, cover-to-cover
        ( ) read most of each issue
        ( ) read some of each issue
        ( ) browse each issue
        ( ) peruse only when I have time

( ) *The ABA Journal*
        ( ) read every issue, cover-to-cover
        ( ) read most of each issue
        ( ) read some of each issue
        ( ) browse each issue
        ( ) peruse only when I have time

( ) *For the Defense*
        ( ) read every issue, cover-to-cover
        ( ) read most of each issue
        ( ) read some of each issue
        ( ) browse each issue
        ( ) peruse only when I have time

( ) *Trial*
        ( ) read every issue, cover-to-cover
        ( ) read most of each issue
        ( ) read some of each issue
        ( ) browse each issue
        ( ) peruse only when I have time

( ) *American Lawyer*
    ( ) read every issue, cover-to-cover
    ( ) read most of each issue
    ( ) read some of each issue
    ( ) browse each issue
    ( ) peruse only when I have time

( ) *The National Law Journal*
    ( ) read every issue, cover-to-cover
    ( ) read most of each issue
    ( ) read some of each issue
    ( ) browse each issue
    ( ) peruse only when I have time

( ) Other: _____

~ Which journal do you like best? _____

~ How much do you like or dislike doing your own legal research?

    Like a lot : ____ : ____ : ____ : ____ : ____ : ____ : ____ : Dislike a lot

~ Do you do your own legal research or do you enlist others for
  that purpose?
    ( ) I do my own
    ( ) others do it for me

~ Do you personally use a computer in your work:
    ( ) no
    ( ) yes

~ Have you ever used a trial consultant?

        ( ) no
        ( ) yes

        For what kinds of assistance?

        ( ) help with development of trial themes
        ( ) jury selection
        ( ) change of venue issues
        ( ) preparation of witnesses
        ( ) development of demonstrative exhibits
        ( ) jury instructions
        ( ) preparing oral arguments
        ( ) preparing opening statements
        ( ) preparing closing arguments
        ( ) presentations to clients
        ( ) post-trial jury interviews
        ( ) jury verdict form

~ Overall, how would you rate the value of "trial consultant" services?

Extremely valuable : ___ : ___ : ___ : ___ : ___ : ___ : ___ : Not at all valuable

~ While trying a case, you may experience many different emotions and moods. Please circle those you experience *OFTEN*.

exhilaration	anxiety	exhaustion	fear
loneliness	relaxation	hostility	disgust
impatience	joy	anticipation	pleasure
frustration	mastery	anger	pride
excitement	control	tranquility	isolation

other _____

_____

_____

~ There are times when anger or hostility toward an opponent can actually contribute to an extreme motivation to win. Have you ever found yourself becoming and remaining particularly angry or hostile at the opposing counsel throughout the course of a trial?

( ) no

( ) yes

If yes, how common an occurrence is this?

Very common : ___ : ___ : ___ : ___ : ___ : ___ : ___ : Very rare

~ When in trial, do you adhere to any unique daily routine or activities that you do not follow when not in trial, e.g., changes in your food or exercise regimes? If yes, what are they?

~ Have you ever been told that your temperament changes while you are in trial? If yes, in what ways?

~ Many lawyers feel that a certain attire is necessary for a lawyer to appear credible to a jury. How much do you believe that to be true?

Absolutely : ___ : ___ : ___ : ___ : ___ : ___ : Not at all

~ If you have guidelines for attire in the courtroom, what are they?

~ When you travel on business, how often do you fly first class?

Always : ___ : ___ : ___ : ___ : ___ : ___ : Never

~ Over the years, have you involved yourself with any aspect of a law firm's governance or management?

Please check: If so, how much do you enjoy those activities?

( ) **Administration** Enjoy a   Do not
great deal : __ : __ : __ : __ : __ : __ : __ : enjoy at all

( ) **Training** Enjoy a   Do not
great deal : __ : __ : __ : __ : __ : __ : __ : enjoy at all

( ) **Recruiting** Enjoy a   Do not
great deal : __ : __ : __ : __ : __ : __ : __ : enjoy at all

( ) **Compensation** Enjoy a   Do not
great deal : __ : __ : __ : __ : __ : __ : __ : enjoy at all

( ) **Other**

_____ Enjoy a   Do not
great deal : __ : __ : __ : __ : __ : __ : __ : enjoy at all

_____ Enjoy a   Do not
great deal : __ : __ : __ : __ : __ : __ : __ : enjoy at all

~ To which legal organizations do you belong?

423

~ Have you found active participation in those legal organizations
  or societies to be a valuable use of your time?

  Very useful : ___ : ___ : ___ : ___ : ___ : ___ : ___ : Not at all useful

~ About how much time do you devote in a month to these organizations? _____

~ How long have you been with your current firm? _____

~ If you have been with your current firm less than 5 years, how
  long were you at your previous firm? _____

~ How many different firms have you been with during your legal
  career? _____

~ Do you tend to specialize in any particular area of litigation? If
  so, what? _____

  _____

~ Have you ever worked as a lawyer for the government?
           ( ) no
           ( ) yes
           If so, in what capacity?

~ How would you rate the value of that experience in preparing you
  for your current practice?

  Extemely valuable : ___ : ___ : ___ : ___ : ___ : ___ : ___ : Not at all valuable

ATTITUDES TOWARD LAW AS A CAREER

"I would sooner fail than not be among the greatest."
—John Keats

~ At what age did you decide to become a lawyer? ____

~ Did you ever seriously consider a different career?
    (   ) no
    (   ) yes
        What?_____
        When? _____

~ How much did you like or dislike law school?

Liked it a lot : __ : __ : __ : __ : __ : __ : __ : Disliked it a lot

~ How satisfied are you with law as a career?

Very satisfied : __ : __ : __ : __ : __ : __ : __ : Very dissatisfied

~ A large law firm affords a trial lawyer many advantages in material resources and staff support. In your opinion, how important are these perquisites to a trial lawyer's success in the courtroom?

Very important : __ : __ : __ : __ : __ : __ : __ : Very unimportant

~ Looking back upon your legal career and knowing what you know now, is there anything you would have done differently in your professional life?

~ Success seldom comes without some sacrifice; what price have
  you paid for your success as a trial lawyer?

~ In the seventeenth century, Shakespeare's rebel recommended, "First thing we do, let's kill all the lawyers." Do you see current "lawyer bashing" as a continuation of this old tradition or as something truly new? What do you believe to be the genesis of the current climate of negativity toward lawyers as a professional group?

~ When you first began practicing law, did you have a mentor?

    ( ) no

    ( ) yes, and he is still alive today

    ( ) yes, but he is not alive today

~ In a few words, could you describe the most valuable aspects of your relationship with your mentor?

~ Do you find yourself in a mentor's role today?

    ( ) yes

    ( ) no

~ If you could somehow spontaneously change your career today, would you want to be anything other than a trial lawyer?

    ( ) no

    ( ) yes

    What? _____

~ At some point in your career, would you like to be a judge?

    ( ) no

    ( ) yes

~ Would you or have you advised a son or daughter to go into law as a career?

    ( ) have not given advice

    ( ) have advised *for* becoming a lawyer

    ( ) have advised *against* becoming a lawyer, because:

~ If you had the opportunity to retire right now, would you prefer to do that or go on working?

    ( ) retire

    ( ) continue working

    ( ) semi-retire; continue working but at a more leisurely pace.

~ As you reflect upon your career as a lawyer, of which of your accomplishments are you particularly proud?

ROLE OF MONEY

"The world is his, who has money to go over it."
—Ralph Waldo Emerson

~ Do you know, off-hand, exactly how much your income was last
  year?
  ( ) no
  ( ) yes

~ Some professionals enjoy the technicalities of money management and investment decisions, while others prefer to leave those
  decisions to someone else. How much do you enjoy "hands-on"
  dealings with your financial matters?

Enjoy a great deal : ___ : ___ : ___ : ___ : ___ : ___ : ___ : Do not enjoy at all

~ Having no intrinsic value of its own, money symbolizes different
  things to different people. To some it may represent "time" or
  "freedom," to others it may represent "status" or "security."
  Some may view it as a barometer of success, while others may
  see money as a necessary prerequisite for living the successful
  professional's life. How do you tend to view the role of money in
  your life?

~ Are you more or less successful financially than you ever thought
  you would be?
  ( ) more than I expected
  ( ) less than I expected
  ( ) about what I expected

~ The relative *importance* of money is different for different people. Please rate the importance or unimportance of money for
your:

Father   Very important : __ : __ : __ : __ : __ : __ : __ : Very unimportant

Mother   Very important : __ : __ : __ : __ : __ : __ : __ : Very unimportant

Spouse   Very important : __ : __ : __ : __ : __ : __ : __ : Very unimportant

Self   Very important : __ : __ : __ : __ : __ : __ : __ : Very unimportant

~ When was the last time you bought a "gift" for yourself?
- ( ) days ago
- ( ) weeks ago
- ( ) months ago
- ( ) years ago
- ( ) never

LEISURE TIME

*"The secret of being miserable is to have the leisure
to bother about whether you are happy or not."*
—George Bernard Shaw

~ How much do you enjoy your:

Work

Enjoy a great deal : ___ : ___ : ___ : ___ : ___ : ___ : ___ : Do not enjoy at all

Leisure Time

Enjoy a great deal : ___ : ___ : ___ : ___ : ___ : ___ : ___ : Do not enjoy at all

~ When you find yourself with leisure time, what things do you especially enjoy doing?

~ Do you find you have the time to serve on business or philanthropic boards or foundations? If so, please list:

Business: Philanthropic:

_____   _____

_____   _____

_____   _____

~ Do you have an active interest in politics or political activities?
     ( ) yes
     ( ) no

~ Have you in the past few years, served on political campaign committees or on political fundraising efforts?
     ( ) yes
     ( ) no

~ Do you generally contribute to political candidates?
     ( ) yes
     ( ) no

~ If you make political contributions, are they to:
     ( ) local candidates $_____ per year
     ( ) state candidates $_____ per year
     ( ) national candidates $_____ per year

~ How politically liberal or conservative do you consider yourself
to be?

Very liberal : ___ : ___ : ___ : ___ : ___ : ___ : ___ : Very conservative

~ When you read literature not related to work, what kinds of books do you like?

~ Who is your favorite author(s)?

~ What magazines do you read that are not related to work?

( ) read every issue ( ) read, but not every issue ( ) just peruse when I have time	( ) read every issue ( ) read, but not every issue ( ) just peruse when I have time
( ) read every issue ( ) read, but not every issue ( ) just peruse when I have time	( ) read every issue ( ) read, but not every issue ( ) just peruse when I have time
( ) read every issue ( ) read, but not every issue ( ) just peruse when I have time	( ) read every issue ( ) read, but not every issue ( ) just peruse when I have time

~ What newspapers do you read?

~ Approximately how often do you take a vacation?
  ( ) more than once a year
  ( ) once a year
  ( ) once every couple of years

~ How many days do you spend on vacation in a year? _____

~ When you take vacation time, it is for:
  ( ) rest and relaxation solely
  ( ) a combination of business and pleasure

~ When taking vacation trips or personal flights, how often do you fly first class?

Always : ___ : ___ : ___ : ___ : ___ : ___ : ___ : Never

~ Do you ever have trouble relaxing while on vacation?

Always : ___ : ___ : ___ : ___ : ___ : ___ : ___ : Never

~ Do you enjoy exercising or participating in athletics?

A great deal : ___ : ___ : ___ : ___ : ___ : ___ : ___ : Not at all

Check those you enjoy: Circle how frequently you engage in them:

(   ) Golf   daily   4-6/weekly   2-3/weekly   1/weekly   less

(   ) Tennis   daily   4-6/weekly   2-3/weekly   1/weekly   less

(   ) Jogging   daily   4-6/weekly   2-3/weekly   1/weekly   less

(   ) Racquetball   daily   4-6/weekly   2-3/weekly   1/weekly   less

(   ) Swimming   daily   4-6/weekly   2-3/weekly   1/weekly   less

(   ) Bicycling   daily   4-6/weekly   2-3/weekly   1/weekly   less

(   ) Mountain climbing   daily   4-6/weekly   2-3/weekly   1/weekly   less

(   ) Boxing   daily   4-6/weekly   2-3/weekly   1/weekly   less

Other:_____   daily   4-6/weekly   2-3/weekly   1/weekly   less

Other:_____   daily   4-6/weekly   2-3/weekly   1/weekly   less

~ Rate in importance for you, the following reasons to exercise:

Good Health

Very important : ___ : ___ : ___ : ___ : ___ : ___ : ___ : Very unimportant

Physical Appearance

Very important : ___ : ___ : ___ : ___ : ___ : ___ : ___ : Very unimportant

Physical Stamina

Very important : ___ : ___ : ___ : ___ : ___ : ___ : ___ : Very unimportant

Enjoyment

Very important : ___ : ___ : ___ : ___ : ___ : ___ : ___ : Very unimportant

Quiet/Alone Time

Very important : ___ : ___ : ___ : ___ : ___ : ___ : ___ : Very unimportant

~ Of how much concern to you is your physical health?

Of great concern : ___ : ___ : ___ : ___ : ___ : ___ : ___ : Of little concern

~ Has your health ever suffered because of your work?
       ( ) no
       ( ) yes, a little
       ( ) yes, a lot

~ How many hours a night do you generally sleep?_____

~Do you need or want more sleep than that?
       ( ) no
       ( ) yes

~ Are you particularly concerned about your eating and drinking habits?

Greatly concerned : ___ : ___ : ___ : ___ : ___ : ___ : ___ : Unconcerned

      Is your concern due to:
      ( ) motivation to avoid future health problems
      ( ) concern with personal appearance
      ( ) current health problems
      ( ) wanting to feel better
      ( ) other _____

~ What kinds of recreational activities do you enjoy?
      ( ) boating
      ( ) hiking
      ( ) hunting
      ( ) shooting
      ( ) sky diving
      ( ) motorcycling
      ( ) auto racing
      ( ) equestrian
      ( ) flying
          ( ) have pilot's license
          ( ) still fly
      ( ) other: _____

~ What kind of music do you like?
      ( ) jazz
      ( ) blues
      ( ) country
      ( ) easy listening
      ( ) rock and roll
      ( ) swing
      ( ) classical
      ( ) other: _____

~ What kind(s) of food do you like?

~ When not in trial, where do you dine?
        ( ) at home
        Who prepares the meals? _____
        ( ) restaurants
        How many times per month? _____
        What type of restaurants?

~ When you dine out, what do you estimate to be your average bill, including tip, for a party of 4?

~ Do you "collect" anything, e.g., art, antiques? If so, what?

~How many homes do you own? _____

~ What kind of home is your principal residence? (e.g., townhouse, apartment, condominium, single family, etc.)

_____

~ What kind of home is (are) your other home(s)?

_____

_____

~ How large is your primary residence?
       ( ) under 4,000 square feet
       ( ) 4,000–8,000 square feet
       ( ) over 8,000 square feet

~Do you have a FAX at home?
       ( ) no
       ( ) yes

~ Do you have a FAX at your vacation home?
       ( ) no
       ( ) yes

~ How many cars do you own? _____

~ How many car phones do you own? _____

~ What are the makes and colors of your cars?

~ Do you employ a driver?
       ( ) no
       ( ) yes

~ What mode(s) of transportation do you use daily?

SOCIAL RELATIONSHIPS

"Tell me thy company, and I'll tell thee what thou art."   **—Cervantes**

~ It takes a great deal of time to maintain close personal relationships. Do you find that you have time for:
  ( ) many friends
  ( ) only a few close friends
  ( ) only one close friend
  ( ) acquaintances rather than close friends

~ Reflecting on your social contacts, are *most* of your social interactions with:
  ( ) other professionals who, like yourself, are involved in law
  ( ) people not involved in law
  ( ) other _____

~ When you entertain at home, who normally makes the plans and arrangements?
  ( ) self
  ( ) spouse
  ( ) both of us
  ( ) other _____

~ When you dine out, who normally selects the restaurant?
  _____

~ Who normally makes the reservations?
  _____

~ Who plans the menu for a dinner party?
  _____

SPOUSE

"Never feel remorse for what you have thought about your wife. She has thought much worse things about you."
—Jean Rostand

~ What is your marital status?
        ( ) single (never married)
        ( ) married
            ( ) first marriage
            ( ) second marriage
            ( ) third marriage
        ( ) divorced
            ( ) from first marriage
            ( ) from second marriage
            ( ) from third marriage
        ( ) separated
            ( ) from first marriage
            ( ) from second marriage
            ( ) from third marriage
        ( ) widowed
            ( ) from first marriage
            ( ) from second marriage
            ( ) from third marriage

~ Do you have any children? ( ) no ( ) yes Ages?_____

~ **If you are currently not married, please answer the following questions as they would pertain to your former spouse:**

~ How would you describe the social status of your wife's family?
        ( ) upper class
        ( ) upper-middle class
        ( ) middle class
        ( ) lower-middle class
        ( ) lower class

~ What is your wife's highest attained educational level?
       ( ) high school diploma
       ( ) some college
       ( ) BA degree
       ( ) some graduate school
       ( ) graduate degree

~ Is your wife employed outside the home?
       ( ) no
       ( ) yes
       What is her occupation?
       _____

~ Does your wife identify with any particular ethnic group?
       ( ) no
       ( ) yes
       Which? _____

~ Can you specify any ways in which your spouse has had an influence on your career?

~ How interested in the specifics of your cases is your wife?
Not at all interested : ___ : ___ : ___ : ___ : ___ : ___ : ___ : Very interested

~ *ANSWERING FOR YOUR WIFE:* To what extent has your career as a lawyer detracted from the quality of your family life?

Detracted a great deal : ___ : ___ : ___ : ___ : ___ : ___ : ___ : Not detracted at all

~ To what extent do you and your wife have similar or dissimilar views on the following:

Politics   Very similar : __ : __ : __ : __ : __ : __ : __ : Very dissimilar

**Leisure
Activities**   Very similar : __ : __ : __ : __ : __ : __ : __ : Very dissimilar

**Religious
Orientation**   Very similar : __ : __ : __ : __ : __ : __ : __ : Very dissimilar

**Food
Preferences**   Very similar : __ : __ : __ : __ : __ : __ : __ : Very dissimilar

Value of Money   Very similar : __ : __ : __ : __ : __ : __ : __ : Very dissimilar

**Importance of
Material
Possessions**   Very similar : __ : __ : __ : __ : __ : __ : __ : Very dissimilar

~ To what extent does your wife enjoy entertaining or socializing with clients?

Enjoys a great deal : ___ : ___ : ___ : ___ : ___ : ___ : ___ : Does not enjoy at all

~ How often does your spouse travel with you on business trips?

Always : ___ : ___ : ___ : ___ : ___ : ___ : ___ : Never

~ How accurate is your spouse at judging a person's character?

Very accurate : ___ : ___ : ___ : ___ : ___ : ___ : ___ : Very inaccurate

~ What are the traits you admire most in your wife?

~ Do you feel it would be difficult to be married to a lawyer?

Very difficult : ___ : ___ : ___ : ___ : ___ : ___ : ___ : Not at all difficult

~ Some aspects of being married to a trial lawyer must be very positive while some are undoubtedly negative. What do you believe
are the positive and negative aspects for your spouse?

Positive: _____

_____

_____

_____

Negative: _____

_____

_____

_____

~ How much does your wife enjoy spending social time with other lawyers?

Enjoys a great deal : ___ : ___ : ___ : ___ : ___ : ___ : ___ : Does not enjoy at all

~ Does your spouse affiliate with any religious group? If so, which?

_____

~ In what year was your wife born? _____

FAMILY

"Lawyers, I suppose, were children once."
—Charles Lamb

~ Are there other lawyers in your family?
      ( ) no
      ( ) yes
      Who?
         ( ) grandfather
         ( ) father
         ( ) mother
         ( ) uncle
         ( ) aunt
         ( ) brother
         ( ) sister
         ( ) spouse
         ( ) son
         ( ) daughter
         ( ) other _____

~ When you were growing up, who was the dominant personality in your family?
      ( ) father
      ( ) mother
      ( ) both equally dominant
      ( ) other _____

~ Who was the disciplinarian?
      ( ) father
      ( ) mother
      ( ) discipline shared equally
      ( ) other _____

~ How would you describe your family environment as you were growing up?

happy : ___ : ___ : ___ : ___ : ___ : ___ : ___ : unhappy

tense : ___ : ___ : ___ : ___ : ___ : ___ : ___ : relaxed

warm : ___ : ___ : ___ : ___ : ___ : ___ : ___ : cold

active : ___ : ___ : ___ : ___ : ___ : ___ : ___ : passive

religious : ___ : ___ : ___ : ___ : ___ : ___ : ___ : agnostic

emotional : ___ : ___ : ___ : ___ : ___ : ___ : ___ : reserved

wealthy : ___ : ___ : ___ : ___ : ___ : ___ : ___ : poor

loving : ___ : ___ : ___ : ___ : ___ : ___ : ___ : indifferent

conservative : ___ : ___ : ___ : ___ : ___ : ___ : ___ : liberal

healthy : ___ : ___ : ___ : ___ : ___ : ___ : ___ : unhealthy

work oriented : ___ : ___ : ___ : ___ : ___ : ___ : ___ : leisure oriented

education emphasized : ___ : ___ : ___ : ___ : ___ : ___ : ___ : education not emphasized

rural : ___ : ___ : ___ : ___ : ___ : ___ : ___ : urban

~ If you grew up in an urban setting, how large was the community?
( ) small (under 10,000)
( ) medium (10,000-50,000)
( ) large (over 50,000)

~ As you remember it, how would you describe your relationship with your father?

       Very close : ___ : ___ : ___ :___ :___ :___ :___ : Not at all close

~ As you remember it, how would you describe your relationship with your mother?

       Very close : ___ : ___ : ___ :___ :___ :___ :___ : Not at all close

~ Are your parents still living?
         ( ) no
         ( ) yes
         ( ) only my _____

~ If one or both of your parents are still living, how frequently or infrequently do you talk with them over the phone?

      _____

~ How often do you see them?_____

~ Do they live nearby? ( ) no ( ) yes

~ Are you still close to them today? ( ) no ( ) yes

~ When you were growing up, what do you recall as being your family's reward for good behavior?

~ What do you recall as being their punishment for bad behavior?

~ Were there any special values, principles or goals that received particular emphasis in your family as you were growing up?

~ What was your father's highest attained educational level?
- ( ) elementary school
- ( ) junior high school
- ( ) some high school
- ( ) high school diploma
- ( ) some college
- ( ) BA degree
- ( ) some graduate school
- ( ) graduate degree

~ What was your mother's highest attained educational level?
- ( ) elementary school
- ( ) junior high school
- ( ) some high school
- ( ) high school diploma
- ( ) some college
- ( ) BA degree
- ( ) some graduate school
- ( ) graduate degree

~ Do you consider yourself more or less successful, financially, than your father?
- ( ) more successful
- ( ) less successful
- ( ) about the same

~ How would you describe your family's social status while you
  were growing up?
      ( ) upper class
      ( ) upper-middle class
      ( ) middle class
      ( ) lower-middle class
      ( ) lower class

~ How many brothers and sisters did you have?
      ( ) None
      ( ) Brother(s)
          ( ) older   how many? ___ ages? _____
          ( ) younger how many? ___ ages? _____
      ( ) Sister(s)
          ( ) older   how many? ___ ages? _____
          ( ) younger how many? ___ ages? _____

~ Are you particularly close to them today?
      ( ) no
      ( ) yes, to all of them
      ( ) yes, to some of them

~ Generally, do you consider yourself more or less *professionally*
  successful than your siblings?
      ( ) more successful
      ( ) less successful
      ( ) about equal

~ Generally, do you consider yourself more or less *financially* successful than your siblings?
      ( ) more successful
      ( ) less successful
      ( ) about equal

~ As you were growing up, how would you rate your popularity with:

Other kids your own age?

Very popular : ___ : ___ : ___ : ___ : ___ : ___ : ___ : Not very popular

Older kids?

Very popular : ___ : ___ : ___ : ___ : ___ : ___ : ___ : Not very popular

Younger kids?

Very popular : ___ : ___ : ___ : ___ : ___ : ___ : ___ : Not very popular

~ As a child, how athletic were you?

Extremely athletic : ___ : ___ : ___ : ___ : ___ : ___ : ___ : Not at all athletic

~ Do you affiliate with any particular religious group?
      (   ) no
      (   ) yes
      If yes, what? _____

~ Do you identify with any particular ethnic group?
      (   ) no
      (   ) yes
      If so, which? _____

~ What is your age? _____

GENERAL PHILOSOPHY

"I have gained this by philosophy: that I do without being commanded what others do only from fear of the law." **—Aristotle**

~ What do you consider to be the most important thing that has happened to you in your life?

~ What is the riskiest thing you have ever done (outside the military)?

~ When you were growing up, was there anyone in particular in whom you felt you could confide? If so, please describe that person(s):

~ What are the traits you greatly admire in others?

~ When you were growing up, did you have heroes (real or fictional)? If yes, who were they?

~ Today, is there anyone in particular for whom you have a great deal of admiration? If yes, please name (or, if you prefer, describe) that person and what it is you admire about him or her.

~Are there any specific values that you feel are important to teach children?

~ How much do you believe in luck?

    A great deal : ___ : ___ : ___ : ___ : ___ : ___ : ___ : Not at all

~ Does luck ever play a role for you in the successful outcome of a verdict?

    Often : ___ : ___ : ___ : ___ : ___ : ___ : ___ : Never

~ How superstitious do you consider yourself to be?

Very superstitious : ___ : ___ : ___ : ___ : ___ : ___ : ___ : Not at all superstitious

~When was the happiest time of your life?

ACADEMIC BACKGROUND

"I learned law so well, the day I graduated I sued the college, won the case, and got my tuition back."

—Fred Allen

~ Looking back to elementary school, high school and college, what do you think you **WOULD HAVE DESCRIBED** as your major accomplishments **AT THAT TIME**?
For example, while in the third grade, you might have been very proud of an award for perfect attendance.

Elementary School:

High School:

College:

Law School:

~ Did you participate in athletics in:

      ( ) Elementary School
      What? _____

      ( ) High School
      What? _____

      ( ) College
      What? _____

      ( ) Law School
      What? _____

~ Did you belong to organizations or extracurricular groups in high
school, college or law school? If so, please list and include any
offices that you held:

High School:

College:

Law School:

~ Were you employed while you were in college?
        (   ) during the school year
           approximate number of hours per week ____
        (   ) during the summer
           approximate number of hours per week ____

~ If you were married while you attended law school, did your spouse work?
        (   ) no
        (   ) yes
           What did she do?_____
           _____

           Are you still married to her?
           (   ) yes   (   ) no
        (   ) not married during law school

~ What was your major in college? _____

~ In school, what subjects did you enjoy the most?

In High School: In College:

_____   _____

_____   _____

_____   _____

~ What subjects did you *not* enjoy?

In High School: In College:

_____   _____

_____   _____

_____   _____

~ How did you do academically, prior to law school?
  ( ) upper 10% of class
  ( ) upper 25% of class
  ( ) upper 50% of class

~ How did you do academically in law school?
  ( ) upper 10% of class
  ( ) upper 25% of class
  ( ) upper 50% of class

~ College may serve many functions; it may serve an educational function, although not always. For some, college might be more important as a socialization experience, for others as a time to lay foundations for networks which will be utilized later in their careers. Looking back, what do you consider to be the role of college in your life?

~ What do you consider to be the role of law school in your life?

~ Did you ever serve in the military?

      (   ) no

      (   ) yes

          what branch? _____

          (   ) enlisted

          (   ) officer

          (   ) drafted

          (   ) volunteered

          (   ) peace time

          (   ) war time

          (   ) lawyer duties

          (   ) other duties _____

~ Reflecting back on your military experience, how much did you like or dislike the military?

    Liked it a lot : ___ : ___ : ___ : ___ : ___ : ___ : ___ : Disliked it a lot

~ In general, how would you rate the overall value of that experience to you?

Extremely valuable : ___ : ___ : ___ : ___ : ___ : ___ : ___ : Not at all valuable

~ How would you rate the value of your military experience in terms of preparation for a career as a trial lawyer?

Extremely valuable : ___ : ___ : ___ : ___ : ___ : ___ : ___ : Not at all valuable

~ If you felt it was a valuable experience for career preparation, in what ways was your military service helpful?

SELF-EVALUATION

Below are 24 adjectives which are often used to describe an individual's personality. For each adjective, please rate how much it describes or does not describe **YOUR PERSONALITY**.

1. Assertive
Describes Me
Very Well : ___ : ___ : ___ : ___ : ___ : ___ : ___ :
Does Not Describe
Me at All

2. Hostile
Describes Me
Very Well : ___ : ___ : ___ : ___ : ___ : ___ : ___ :
Does Not Describe
Me at All

3. Creative
Describes Me
Very Well : ___ : ___ : ___ : ___ : ___ : ___ : ___ :
Does Not Describe
Me at All

4. Self-conscious
Describes Me
Very Well : ___ : ___ : ___ : ___ : ___ : ___ : ___ :
Does Not Describe
Me at All

5. Modest
Describes Me
Very Well : ___ : ___ : ___ : ___ : ___ : ___ : ___ :
Does Not Describe
Me at All

6. Depressed
Describes Me
Very Well : ___ : ___ : ___ : ___ : ___ : ___ : ___ :
Does Not Describe
Me at All

7. Anxious
Describes Me
Very Well : ___ : ___ : ___ : ___ : ___ : ___ : ___ :
Does Not Describe
Me at All

8. Active
Describes Me
Very Well : ___ : ___ : ___ : ___ : ___ : ___ : ___ :
Does Not Describe
Me at All

9. Vulnerable
Describes Me
Very Well : ___ : ___ : ___ : ___ : ___ : ___ : ___ :
Does Not Describe
Me at All

10. Compliant
Describes Me
Very Well : ___ : ___ : ___ : ___ : ___ : ___ : ___ :
Does Not Describe
Me at All

11. Disciplined
Describes Me
Very Well : ___ : ___ : ___ : ___ : ___ : ___ : ___ :
Does Not Describe
Me at All

12. Warm
Describes Me
Very Well : ___ : ___ : ___ : ___ : ___ : ___ : ___ :
Does Not Describe
Me at All

13. Excitement-
seeking
Describes Me
Very Well : ___ : ___ : ___ : ___ : ___ : ___ : ___ :
Does Not Describe
Me at All

14. Altruistic
Describes Me
Very Well : ___ : ___ : ___ : ___ : ___ : ___ : ___ :
Does Not Describe
Me at All

15. Competent
Describes Me
Very Well : ___ : ___ : ___ : ___ : ___ : ___ : ___ :
Does Not Describe
Me at All

16. Orderly   Describes Me   Does Not Describe
Very Well : ___ : ___ : ___ : ___ : ___ : ___ : ___ : Me at All

17. Impulsive   Describes Me   Does Not Describe
Very Well : ___ : ___ : ___ : ___ : ___ : ___ : ___ : Me at All

18. Positive   Describes Me   Does Not Describe
Very Well : ___ : ___ : ___ : ___ : ___ : ___ : ___ : Me at All

19. Straightforward   Describes Me   Does Not Describe
Very Well : ___ : ___ : ___ : ___ : ___ : ___ : ___ : Me at All

20. Gregarious   Describes Me   Does Not Describe
Very Well : ___ : ___ : ___ : ___ : ___ : ___ : ___ : Me at All

21. Deliberate   Describes Me   Does Not Describe
Very Well : ___ : ___ : ___ : ___ : ___ : ___ : ___ : Me at All

22. Achieving   Describes Me   Does Not Describe
Very Well : ___ : ___ : ___ : ___ : ___ : ___ : ___ : Me at All

23. Dutiful   Describes Me   Does Not Describe
Very Well : ___ : ___ : ___ : ___ : ___ : ___ : ___ : Me at All

24. Tender-minded   Describes Me   Does Not Describe
Very Well : ___ : ___ : ___ : ___ : ___ : ___ : ___ : Me at All

Please rate each of the following six inclinations in terms of its overall importance in your life.

1. Fantasy   Very Important : ___ : ___ : ___ : ___ : ___ : ___ : ___ : Very Unimportant

2. Aesthetics   Very Important : ___ : ___ : ___ : ___ : ___ : ___ : ___ : Very Unimportant

3. Feelings   Very Important : ___ : ___ : ___ : ___ : ___ : ___ : ___ : Very Unimportant

4. Actions   Very Important : ___ : ___ : ___ : ___ : ___ : ___ : ___ : Very Unimportant

5. Ideas   Very Important : ___ : ___ : ___ : ___ : ___ : ___ : ___ : Very Unimportant

6. Values   Very Important : ___ : ___ : ___ : ___ : ___ : ___ : ___ : Very Unimportant

Is there anything you would like to add about yourself or about the practice of law, that you believe would be helpful to this study?

Directions: The following is a list of values which people consider important in their lives. They are not all considered equally important; some are very important to some people but of little importance to others. After each statement, mark its relative importance to you in the space along the continuum.

A comfortable life (a
prosperous life)
Very
Important : ___ : ___ : ___ : ___ : ___ : ___ : ___ : Unimportant
Very

An exciting life (a
stimulating, active life)
Very
Important : ___ : ___ : ___ : ___ : ___ : ___ : ___ : Unimportant
Very

A world at peace (free of war
and conflict)
Very
Important : ___ : ___ : ___ : ___ : ___ : ___ : ___ : Unimportant
Very

Equality (brotherhood, equal
opportunity for all)
Very
Important : ___ : ___ : ___ : ___ : ___ : ___ : ___ : Unimportant
Very

Freedom (independence, free
choice)
Very
Important : ___ : ___ : ___ : ___ : ___ : ___ : ___ : Unimportant
Very

Happiness (contentedness)
Very
Important : ___ : ___ : ___ : ___ : ___ : ___ : ___ : Unimportant
Very

National security (protection
from attack)
Very
Important : ___ : ___ : ___ : ___ : ___ : ___ : ___ : Unimportant
Very

Pleasure (an enjoyable,
leisurely life)
Very
Important : ___ : ___ : ___ : ___ : ___ : ___ : ___ : Unimportant
Very

Salvation (saved, eternal life)
Very
Important : ___ : ___ : ___ : ___ : ___ : ___ : ___ : Unimportant
Very

Social recognition (respect,
admiration)
Very
Important : ___ : ___ : ___ : ___ : ___ : ___ : ___ : Unimportant
Very

True friendship (close
companionship)
Very
Important : ___ : ___ : ___ : ___ : ___ : ___ : ___ : Unimportant
Very

Wisdom (a mature
understanding of life)
Very
Important : ___ : ___ : ___ : ___ : ___ : ___ : ___ : Unimportant
Very

A world of beauty (beauty of
nature and the arts)
Very
Important : ___ : ___ : ___ : ___ : ___ : ___ : ___ : Unimportant
Very

Family security (taking care
of loved ones)
Very
Important : ___ : ___ : ___ : ___ : ___ : ___ : ___ : Unimportant
Very

Mature love (sexual and
spiritual intimacy)
Very
Important : ___ : ___ : ___ : ___ : ___ : ___ : ___ : Unimportant
Very

Self-respect (self-esteem) — Very Important : ___ : ___ : ___ : ___ : ___ : ___ : ___ : Very Unimportant

A sense of accomplishment (lasting contribution) — Very Important : ___ : ___ : ___ : ___ : ___ : ___ : ___ : Very Unimportant

Inner harmony (freedom from inner conflict) — Very Important : ___ : ___ : ___ : ___ : ___ : ___ : ___ : Very Unimportant

Ambitious (hard-working, aspiring) — Very Important : ___ : ___ : ___ : ___ : ___ : ___ : ___ : Very Unimportant

Broadminded (open-minded) — Very Important : ___ : ___ : ___ : ___ : ___ : ___ : ___ : Very Unimportant

Capable (competent, effective) — Very Important : ___ : ___ : ___ : ___ : ___ : ___ : ___ : Very Unimportant

Cheerful (lighthearted, joyful) — Very Important : ___ : ___ : ___ : ___ : ___ : ___ : ___ : Very Unimportant

Clean (neat, tidy) — Very Important : ___ : ___ : ___ : ___ : ___ : ___ : ___ : Very Unimportant

Courageous (standing up for your beliefs) — Very Important : ___ : ___ : ___ : ___ : ___ : ___ : ___ : Very Unimportant

Forgiving (willing to pardon others) — Very Important : ___ : ___ : ___ : ___ : ___ : ___ : ___ : Very Unimportant

Helpful (working for the welfare of others) — Very Important : ___ : ___ : ___ : ___ : ___ : ___ : ___ : Very Unimportant

Honest (sincere, truthful) — Very Important : ___ : ___ : ___ : ___ : ___ : ___ : ___ : Very Unimportant

Imaginative (daring, creative) — Very Important : ___ : ___ : ___ : ___ : ___ : ___ : ___ : Very Unimportant

Independent (self-reliant, self-sufficient) — Very Important : ___ : ___ : ___ : ___ : ___ : ___ : ___ : Very Unimportant

Intellectual (intelligent, reflective) — Very Important : ___ : ___ : ___ : ___ : ___ : ___ : ___ : Very Unimportant

Logical (consistent, rational) — Very Important : ___ : ___ : ___ : ___ : ___ : ___ : ___ : Very Unimportant

Loving (affectionate, tender) — Very Important : ___ : ___ : ___ : ___ : ___ : ___ : ___ : Very Unimportant

Obedient (dutiful, respectful) — Very Important : ___ : ___ : ___ : ___ : ___ : ___ : ___ : Very Unimportant

Polite (courteous,
well-mannered)
Very
Important : ___ : ___ : ___ : ___ : ___ : ___ : ___ : Very Unimportant

Responsible (dependable,
reliable)
Very
Important : ___ : ___ : ___ : ___ : ___ : ___ : ___ : Very Unimportant

Self-controlled (restrained,
self-disciplined)
Very
Important : ___ : ___ : ___ : ___ : ___ : ___ : ___ : Very Unimportant

Directions: The statements below represent values which people consider important in their work. These are satisfactions that people often seek in their jobs or as a result of their jobs. They are not all considered equally important; some are very important to some people but of little importance to others. Indicate how important each statement is for you by marking the space which most nearly reflects how you would rate along the continuum.

WORK IN WHICH YOU...

1. ...have to keep solving new problems.

Very Important : ___ : ___ : ___ : ___ : ___ : ___ : ___ : Very Unimportant

2. ...help others.

Very Important : ___ : ___ : ___ : ___ : ___ : ___ : ___ : Very Unimportant

3. ...are financially successful.

Very Important : ___ : ___ : ___ : ___ : ___ : ___ : ___ : Very Unimportant

4. ...are continually faced with a changing milieu.

Very Important : ___ : ___ : ___ : ___ : ___ : ___ : ___ : Very Unimportant

5. ...have complete freedom.

Very Important : ___ : ___ : ___ : ___ : ___ : ___ : ___ : Very Unimportant

6. ...gain prestige in your field.

Very Important : ___ : ___ : ___ : ___ : ___ : ___ : ___ : Very Unimportant

7. ...need to have artistic expression.

Very Important : ___ : ___ : ___ : ___ : ___ : ___ : ___ : Very Unimportant

8. ...enjoy interacting with other professionals.

Very Important : ___ : ___ : ___ : ___ : ___ : ___ : ___ : Very Unimportant

9. ...know your professional expertise will always be in demand.

Very Important : ___ : ___ : ___ : ___ : ___ : ___ : ___ : Very Unimportant

10. ...lead the kind of life you most enjoy.

Very Important : ___ : ___ : ___ : ___ : ___ : ___ : ___ : Very Unimportant

11. ...like the surroundings in which you work.

Very Important : ___ : ___ : ___ : ___ : ___ : ___ : ___ : Very Unimportant

12. ...can evaluate the results of your efforts.

Very Important : ___ : ___ : ___ : ___ : ___ : ___ : ___ : Very Unimportant

13. ...have authority over
others.

Very
Important : ___ : ___ : ___ : ___ : ___ : ___ : ___ : Very
Unimportant

14. ...contribute new ideas to
your field.

Very
Important : ___ : ___ : ___ : ___ : ___ : ___ : ___ : Very
Unimportant

APPENDIX 3: ▮▮▮▮▮▮▮▮▮▮▮▮

Personal Interview Guide

[These questions were asked of all fourteen lawyers.]

I. Your Personal Background

- How did you decide to become a trial lawyer?

- Looking back, what experiences in your personal life best prepared you for what you do today?

- What aspects of your training and/or experience as a young lawyer were the most beneficial to your career?

- What do you like most about being a trial lawyer? What do you like least?

- How many cases have you tried?

- What was your largest plaintiff verdict or your most prominent defense verdict?

- There are more than 800,000 lawyers in the United States. Modesty aside, how do you see yourself as different from these people?

- Do you consider yourself more of a private person or a social person?

- Have you found your prominence as a lawyer or the publicity associated with your success to be a burden in any way?

- What do you enjoy doing in your spare time?

- Are you involved in any particular community activities?

- Do you enjoy talking about your cases with friends or relatives?

– How do you relax?

– How would you describe a dreadfully boring weekend?

– If you were to plan a perfect vacation, what would you do?

– If your best friend were asked to criticize something about you, what would he say?

II. The Legal Profession

– What are the personal qualities of a good trial lawyer?

– What particular talents or skills must a good trial lawyer possess?

– Do you draw a distinction between trial lawyers and litigators?

– What is the distinction between a good trial lawyer and a great trial lawyer?

– Are the defining skills of gifted trial lawyers acquired through training and experience or are they innate?

– What kinds of people make the best trial lawyers?

– How would you describe the psychological profile of the truly gifted trial lawyer?

– Some people refer to trial lawyers as modern day "gun slingers." Do you agree?

– Why are so many young people attracted to the legal profession today?

– When you hire young kids out of law school, have you detected any patterns in hiring successes or failures?

– What is the best way to train a young lawyer?

– Will the country have more or fewer talented trial lawyers in 20 years?

– Why do you think that TV shows and movies about trial lawyers have become so popular?

– What kind of influence has this type of entertainment had on the jurors?

– Why do people dislike trial lawyers so much?

- Why has America become such a litigious country?

- In what ways has the legal profession changed from the time that you first began practicing law?

- What are some of the major challenges that will confront the legal profession in the future?

III. The Practice of Law

- How do you decide whether or not to accept an engagement?

- Do you "like" most of your clients? Is this important to you?

- Within your area of expertise, are there any kinds of cases or people that you would not represent?

- To what extent do your personal, social, or political views influence the cases you accept?

- In deciding whether or not to file a lawsuit, what kinds of issues do you consider?

- How do you define a win?

- Have you encountered instances where the lawyer has difficulty maintaining a perspective on what is ultimately in the client's best interest versus the lawyer's desire to win?

- Should more cases be settled?

- How can lawyers facilitate settlement?

- Why do you think there is a growing tendency for acrimony, hostility, and discourtesy among lawyers today?

- How do you prepare for trial?

- How does your life change?

- What kind of help do you need?

- How do you develop your theory of the case?

- What do you like least about going to trial?

- As a trial lawyer, what are the advantages/disadvantages of being in a large firm? A small firm?

- As a trial lawyer, what has been your most satisfying experience?

- What has been your most disappointing experience?

- How do you personally handle defeat when you lose a case?

- Could you describe in some detail one of the most challenging cases you've tried?

- What are some of the high profile cases you've tried?

- Can you think of an instance when you were caught "off guard" or really surprised by something during a trial?

- Can you think of an instance where an opponent was too clever and tripped himself up?

- What is the worst thing that has happened to you in a courtroom?

- What is your feeling about trying cases in other parts of the country?

- What aspects of trial practice do you enjoy the most? Which do you enjoy the least?

- I've heard trial lawyers use the term "burn-out."
     What is "burn-out"?
     Have you experienced it?
     How do you personally overcome or avoid it?

- Can you recall any particularly humorous or funny experiences you have encountered in the courtroom, with clients, or with other lawyers?

IV. Trial Strategies and Tactics

Could you comment on some of the strategic and/or tactical considerations you feel are important for each of the following aspects of the trial process? Can you give some examples from cases you've tried?

A. Pretrial Issues

- Venue

- Jurisdiction (State/Federal)

- Selection of Witnesses

- Discovery

- The Process - Depositions - Interrogatories

B.   The Trial

- Voir Dire

- Jury Selection

- Witness Preparation

- Opening Statements

- Direct Examination

- Cross Examination

- Exhibits

- Instructions

- Closing Arguments

C.   Relationships/Demeanor

- Clients

- Opposition Counsel

- The Difficult Judge

- The Jury

What are some of the typical mistakes lawyers make in each of these areas?

V. Juries

- What are your thoughts about effective courtroom communication and jury persuasion?

- What are some of the more common mistakes lawyers make with juries?

- Is it important for the jury to like you? To like your client?

- Do you have any views on appropriate attire for the courtroom?

- Over time, have you observed any traits or characteristics that differentiate jurors you like from those you don't?

- What are some of the best ways to handle:

  - A dull, boring, or technical case

  - – An antagonistic, sarcastic or hostile witness
  - – A large number of paper depositions
  - – Video depositions
  - – An antagonistic opponent
  - – A hostile judge
- How do you use demonstrative exhibits?
- What are your reactions to the new courtroom visual display techniques such as computer animation and laser disc systems?
- What is the impact of this technology on:
  - – Jurors
  - – Lawyers
  - – The Court
  - – The System
- Are there any cases that juries cannot or should not hear?

APPENDIX 4: ███████████

Psychological Analysis

Four personality measures were administered to the lawyers in this study. Collectively they assessed two major areas of interest for describing prominent trial lawyers. First, an understanding of the participants' personalities was deemed important. If indeed there were dispositional characteristics that the members shared in common, illuminating what they were would aid in an understanding of why this group of lawyers was unique. Additionally, and perhaps just as important as identifying the consistent traits among the participants, was determining what variations occurred among their personalities. In other words, what traits were not shared in common by successful trial lawyers. The NEO Personality Inventory—Revised Version (NEO-PI) was used to gauge the lawyers' personalities. It assessed general personality traits along five dimensions. The dimensions were then used to generate a profile of an individual's personality. From the individual profiles, a group profile was then plotted. The aggregated profile, while addressing individual differences among the scores, allowed generalizations to be made about the group as a whole. As an adjunct to the NEO-PI, an Adjective Check-List was also developed. It loosely corresponded to the facets of the NEO-PI. The checklist was useful in comparing the overt self-concept of each individual with the more behaviorally oriented self-report generated by the NEO-PI.

NEO-PI

For decades, psychologists have believed that there were five basic traits, or dimensions, underlying personality. It was felt that if the dimensions could be measured then a consistent description of an individual's disposition could be made. Various assessment instruments have been developed over the years that aimed at measuring the five global traits. However, not all researchers in the field of personality assessment have been in total agreement as to which traits should be included in the "big five." In general, though, traits which reflected degrees of *neuroticism, extroversion, conscientiousness, openness*, and *agreeableness* have been accepted as major personality components. For the ratings of the lawyers in this study, see Chart 1 below.

Chart 1. Five NEO Traits
Aggregated for the 14 Lawyers

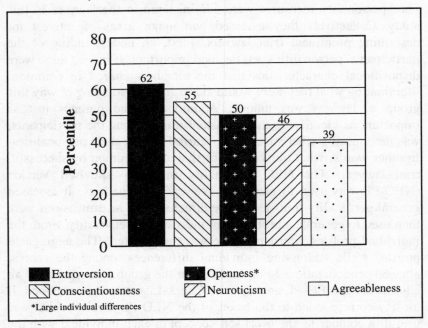

Until recently, the instruments that have been used to measure the five traits, have not been especially helpful to researchers because they lacked "reliability," that is, stability over time. If an instrument purports to measure stable traits, then it should generate similar scores for the same individual tested on different occasions at different times. Recently, thanks to computer-assisted analyses involving huge amounts of normative data, the dimensions of personality have been reliably measured. The NEO-PI is one of the most reliable measures of personality traits.

The NEO-PI is *not* a measure of psychopathology. Instead, it was developed and standardized on normal people. It is used to describe healthy rather than pathological individuals. In addition to the five global dimensions of personality, the NEO-PI allows a finer more detailed description to emerge regarding the traits. Each of the five traits is made up of six "facets." The facets describe in greater depth what characteristics are involved in the major traits. It is possible for an individual's scores to vary on any given trait. For example, a person might score in the high range on four of the six facets and moderately or low on the remaining two. When this pattern occurs, it is necessary to look at the facets separately to give a more accurate description of the person. The traits and their respective facets are listed in Table 1.

Table 1.
The Five "Traits" and Their Respective "Facets"

Neuroticism	Extroversion	Openness	Agreeableness	Conscientiousness
Anxiety	Warmth	Fantasy	Trust	Competence
Angry-Hostility	Gregariousness	Aesthetics	Straightforwardness	Order
Depression	Assertiveness	Feelings	Altruism	Dutifulness
Impulsiveness	Activity	Actions	Compliance	Achievement Striving
Self-Consciousness	Excitement-Seeking	Ideas	Modesty	Self-Discipline
Vulnerability	Positive Emotions	Values	Tender-Mindedness	Deliberation

The respondents read 240 statements which make up the NEO-PI. After each statement, they indicated the degree to which they agreed or disagreed, by circling one of five alternatives: "strongly disagree," "disagree," "neutral," "agree," or "strongly agree." A profile was then plotted for each person. It displayed their relative standings on the five traits as well as their standings on the thirty facets. The scores were then compared to the normative scores to determine percentile ranking. The percentile ranking denoted whether a particular score fell in the "very high," "high," "average," "low" or "very low" category. The profiles do not provide "cutoff" scores for the traits, i.e. if the person is over a predetermined amount he has the trait, if he is under it he does not. Instead the profiles allow descriptions to be made for all levels of the trait. As much information is provided when an individual scores low on a trait as when he scores high on a trait. The combined results of the NEO-PI on each facet of the five major dimensions are presented in Charts 2 through 6 for the fourteen lawyers in the study.

Chart 2. The Extraversion Facets

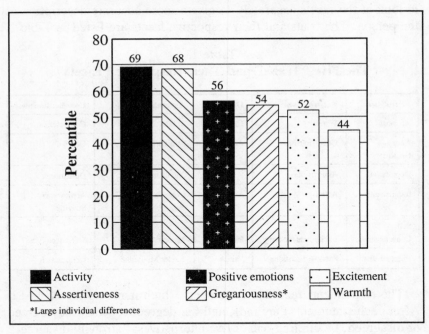

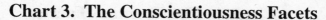

Chart 3. The Conscientiousness Facets

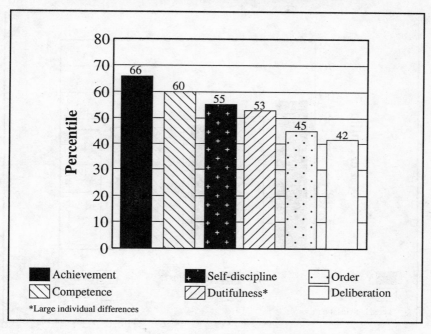

Chart 4. The Openness Facets

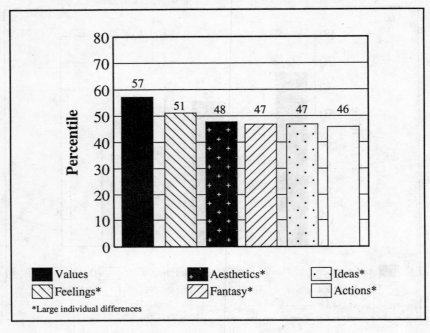

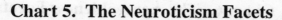

Chart 5. The Neuroticism Facets

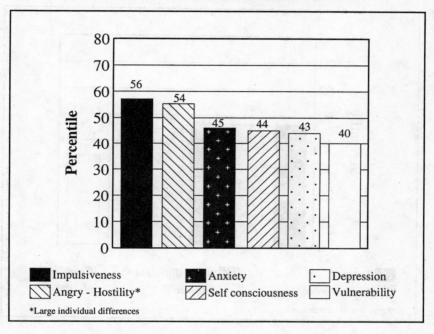

Chart 6. The Agreeableness Facets

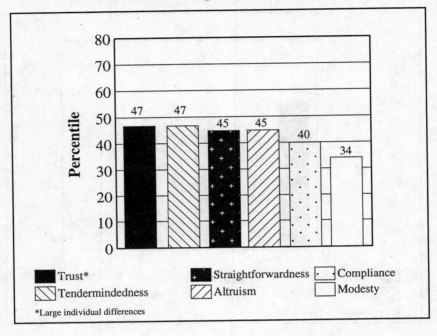

Adjective Checklist

An Adjective Checklist was also completed by the lawyers. The adjectives that were chosen were loosely based upon the scales found in the NEO-PI. Rather than being a duplication of effort, the adjective checklist is a further refined gauge of the traits. The NEO-PI focuses on behavioral indicia of traits, while the adjectives themselves more directly represent the actual trait. It was felt that a comparison of the two might prove fruitful in understanding the lawyer's own self-perceptions. Here, the lawyers rated themselves on how much or how little the adjectives were an accurate description of who they were as people. The adjectives were rated on a seven-point scale ranging from "does not describe me at all" to "describes me very well." The adjectives are listed in Table 2.

Table 2. Self-Evaluation Adjective Checklist

Assertive	Excitement-seeking
Hostile	Altruistic
Creative	Competent
Self-conscious	Orderly
Modest	Impulsive
Depressed	Positive
Anxious	Straightforward
Active	Gregarious
Vulnerable	Deliberate
Compliant	Achieving
Disciplined	Dutiful
Warm	Tender-minded

Six additional "inclinations" were included in the check-list. They correspond to the remaining facets on the NEO-PI that did not lend themselves to an adjective format. These were also rated on a seven-point scale which ranged from "very unimportant" to "very important." They are listed in Table 3.

Table 3. The Six Inclinations

Fantasy	Actions
Aesthetics	Ideas
Feelings	Values

It is important to point out that the scores on the personality instruments discussed in this Appendix, are aggregated scores. Whereas the comments made here are descriptive of the group of participants as a whole, the evaluations may not accurately or completely describe any particular individual. There are individual exceptions and varying degrees of standing on the traits that were measured. The aggregated information does not describe specific individuals, but attempts to draw a composite portrait of the personality of a successful trial advocate.

Results

Table 4. Self-Evaluation Adjective Checklist

The adjectives are considered "high" if they were rated a 6 or a 7 on a seven point scale, "moderate" if their rating was 3, 4, or 5, and "low" if their rating was a 1 or a 2.

High (6-7)	Moderate (3-5)	Low (1-2)
Achieving	Excitement-seeking	Anxious *
Competent	Warm	Hostile
Active	Dutiful	Compliant
Straightforward	Gregarious	Depressed
Positive	Deliberate *	
Assertive	Orderly *	
Disciplined	Altruistic *	
Creative	Impulsive *	
	Tender-minded *	
	Self-conscious *	
	Vulnerable *	
	Modest	

*Large individual differences were seen on these variables.

The way the lawyers rank themselves on the self-evaluation checklist is above. The adjectives that have the highest degree of descriptive fit for them are: *achieving, competent, active, straight-forward, positive, assertive, disciplined,* and *creative.* Inclinations that rank highest are *values* and *ideas.* Lowest, are *aesthetics* and *fantasy.* See Table 5.

Table 5. Ranking of the Inclinations

1. Values

2. Ideas

3. Actions

4. Feelings

5. Aesthetics*

6. Fantasy*

* Large individual differences were seen on these variables.

When the underlying personality traits, as revealed in the objective data collected in this study, are closely analyzed, certain clear relationships emerge. The lawyers rank high on traits and attributes that are closely related to what they say it takes to be a gifted lawyer, and low on attributes that would interfere with their success. In their personality profile, for example, they rank as a group high on achievement, competence and self-discipline, low on self-consciousness and vulnerability. They are low on modesty, and high on extroversion, highly oriented toward successful interactions with others in which they are seen in a positive light. Objectivity is manifested in their openness to values. Their courage and competiveness is manifest in part by their low ranking of themselves on traits such as anxiety, hostility, compliance, and depression.

Table 6. Descriptive Statistics for the Questionnaire's "Self-Evaluation"

	MEAN	STDEV
Competent	6.727	0.467
Active	6.500	0.674
Achieving	6.455	1.214
Straightforward	6.364	0.809
Positive	6.273	0.786

Assertive	6.250	1.215
Disciplined	6.167	0.937
Creative	6.000	1.477
Gregarious	5.455	1.128
Excitmnt-seek	5.417	1.975
Warm	5.333	1.371
Dutiful	5.300	1.160
Deliberate	5.273	1.421
Orderly	3.917	1.621
Vulnerable	3.750	1.913
Anxious	3.000	1.907
Modest	3.000	1.549
Hostile	2.083	1.084
Depressed	1.583	0.900
Compliant	1.417	0.669
Values	6.727	0.647
Ideas	6.727	0.467
Actions	6.545	0.688
Feelings	5.800	1.619
Aesthetics	5.091	2.212
Fantasy	4.455	1.864

Values

An area of interest for this study was concerned with determining what values were considered important by successful trial lawyers. Values are those qualities which are regarded as intrinsically desirable. They are qualities people want and seek out in the activities in which they engage. Two kinds of values were salient for this study: work values and life values. The Work Values Inventory and the Rokeach Value Survey were chosen to identify the relative importance of values for prominent trial lawyers.

Work Values Inventory

We asked whether the highly successful trial lawyers might have work values included in this study that are different from those held by other lawyers included in the national survey. The Work Values Inventory, which assesses different values related to work, was chosen for this task. The original Inventory measured fifteen work values. It was felt that one category, "supervisory relations," was not relevant for the lawyers who participated in this study, so it was eliminated. The remaining fourteen values are listed in Table 7. In responding to questions about the work they do, the lawyers indicated the degree to which each of the values was important. This was done by rating each statement on a seven-point scale, ranging from "very unimportant" to "very important." As seen on Table 8, are the results.

Table 7: Work Values

1. Altruism	8. Authority over others
2. Aesthetics	9. Economic returns
3. Creativity	10. Security
4. Intellectual stimulation	11. Surroundings
5. Independence	12. Associates
6. Achievement	13. Variety
7. Prestige	14. Way of life

Respondents (the fourteen in our study as well as those in the national survey) indicated the degree to which each of the values was important in the work they did, by rating each statement on a seven-point scale, ranging from "very unimportant" to "very important."

Table 8. Work Values Results

The rank order of work values for the current sample of trial lawyers and for lawyers in general.

The Fourteen Lawyers	General Group of Lawyers
1. Intellectual stimulation	**1. Achievement**
2. Way of life	2. Intellectual stimulation
3. Achievement	3. Way of life
4. Prestige	4. Creativity
5. Economic return	5. Economic return
6. **Security in job**	6. Prestige
7. Creativity	7. **Authority over others**
8. Independence	8. Surroundings

9. Associates

9. Independence

10. Surroundings

10. Altruism

11. Variety

11. Associates

12. Altruism

12. **Security in job**

13. **Authority over others**

13. Variety

14. Aesthetics

14. Aesthetics

Of particular importance is the difference in relative value for the fourteen group of lawyers for *authority over others* and *security in job*. The fourteen lawyers did not feel it important for them to have authority over others in their work. In general, they did not feel comfortable delegating a lot of responsibility for their trial work to colleagues. Instead, they preferred to do the work themselves, or at least have first-hand experience with most of the preparation.

Surprisingly, job security was more important for the fourteen than for average lawyers. This may be reflective of their need constantly to achieve in their profession. They always needed to be on top and they always wanted to be in demand professionally. There are no striking differences between the great trial lawyers and their less-prominent colleagues. The top three work values are the same for both groups. It is interesting that our group of fourteen ranks *intellectual stimulation* above *achievement*, while the reverse is the case in the general group.

Rokeach Value Survey

Of interest also for this study, was the topic of life values. Comparable to values that are concerned with work, life values, likewise, represent desirable qualities, but they are not limited to the work situation. Life values are much broader in scope and reflect an individual's philosophy about himself and his position in the world. They summarize an individual's goals, ideals and desired behaviors. The Rokeach Value Survey was chosen for this purpose. The instrument was developed by one of the leaders in the field of values research, Milton Rokeach. The scale measures eighteen "terminal values," or goals in life and eighteen "instrumental values," or modes of conduct. The eighteen "terminal values" and the eighteen "instrumental values" are listed in Table 9. As in the Work Values Inventory, the fourteen lawyers rated each life value as to its importance for themselves. They responded to each of the thirty-six values, on a seven-point scale, ranging from "very important" to "very unimportant."

Table 9. Rokeach Value Survey

Terminal Values	Instrumental Values
A comfortable (prosperous) life	Ambitious (hard-working, aspiring)
An exciting (stimulating, active) life	Broadminded (open-minded)
A world at peace (free of war)	Capable (competent, effective)
Equality (brotherhood, equal opportunity)	Cheerful (lighthearted, joyful)
Freedom (independence, free choice)	Clean (neat, tidy)
Happiness (contentedness)	Courageous (standing up for your beliefs)
National security (protection from attack)	Forgiving (willing to pardon others)
Pleasure (an enjoyable, leisurely life)	Helpful (working for the welfare of others)
Salvation (saved, eternal life)	Honest (sincere, truthful)
Social recognition (respect, admiration)	Imaginative (daring, creative)
True friendship (close companionship)	Independent (self-reliant, self-sufficient)
Wisdom (a mature understanding of life)	Intellectual (intelligent, reflective)
A world of beauty (beauty of nature and the arts)	Logical (consistent, rational)
Family security (taking care of loved ones)	Loving (affectionate, tender)
Mature love (sexual and spiritual intimacy)	Obedient (dutiful, respectful)
Self-respect (self-esteem)	Polite (courteous, well-mannered)
A sense of accomplishment (lasting contribution)	Responsible (dependable, reliable)
Inner harmony (freedom from inner conflict)	Self-controlled (restrained, self-disciplined)

Tables 10A and 10B display how the fourteen lawyers as a group ranked the thirty-six life values from most to least important. It is important to note that the numerical ratings for each value were calculated as an average score across all of the fourteen and then the *average* ratings were rank ordered.

Table 10A
Terminal Values: Goals in Life

1. Self-respect (self-esteem)	6.857
2. Sense of accomplishment (lasting contribution)	6.857
3. Exciting life (stimulating, active)	6.786
4. Freedom (independence, free choice)	6.643
5. Family security (taking care of loved ones)	6.643
6. Wisdom (a mature understanding of life)	6.571
7. Mature love (sexual and spiritual intimacy)	6.429
8. Happiness (contentedness)	6.143
9. Comfortable (prosperous) life	6.071
10. True friendship (close companionship)	5.714
11. National security (protection from attack)	5.571
12. Equality (brotherhood, equal opportunity)	5.571
13. Social recognition (respect, admiration)	5.5
14. Inner harmony (freedom from inner conflict)	5.5
15. Pleasure (an enjoyable, leisurely life)	5.357
16. A world at peace (free of war)	5.357
17. A world of beauty (beauty of nature and the arts)	5.0
18. Salvation (saved, eternal life)	3.214

Table 10B

Instrumental Values: Modes of Behavior

1. Courageous (standing up for your beliefs)	6.643
2. Capable (competent, effective)	6.643

3. Independent (self-reliant, self-sufficient)	6.571
4. Honest (sincere, truthful)	6.571
5. Responsible (dependable, reliable)	6.429
6. Imaginative (daring, creative)	6.286
7. Broadminded (open-minded)	6.143
8. Ambitious (hard-working, aspiring)	6.071
9. Intellectual (intelligent, reflective)	6.071
10. Self-controlled (restrained, self-disciplined)	5.857
11. Logical (consistent, rational)	5.643
12. Loving (affectionate, tender)	5.643
13. Cheerful (lighthearted, joyful)	5.571
14. Forgiving (willing to pardon others)	5.286
15. Helpful (working for the welfare of others)	4.929
16. Clean (neat, tidy)	4.786
17. Polite (courteous, well-mannered)	4.357
18. Obedient (dutiful, respectful)	3.714

Of interest here is the relatively lower rating of social recognition (thirteen out of eighteen) for the Terminal Values. This confirms the lawyer's internalized reward system. They do not look to others, generally, for a sense of their own worth. They instead set up their own personal reward system that serves them in the oftentimes lonely tasks they must perform. Similarly interesting is the relatively lower rating of two more hedonistic goals, *inner-harmony* and *pleasure*. The lawyers do not enjoy harmony, as displayed by their preference for competition. Likewise, pleasure, as in a leisurely life, is totally incongruent with their high-activity levels. *Family security* ranks fifth, behind *self-respect, sense of accomplishment, exiting life,* and *freedom.* This is an indication of an important aspect of the lawyers' personal philosophy. Down the list are such things as *true friendship, social recognition,* and a host of altruism-related values. The fact that the lawyers do not rank highly values such as *equality (brotherhood* and *equal opportunity), national security,* or *a world at peace,* is in contrast to the values of attorneys such as Darrow, or in our own time William Kunstler or Ralph Nader, who see themselves as social crusaders.

With respect to instrumental values or modes of behavior, it is hardly a surprise that *courage, capability, honesty*, and *independence* rank highest. Of particular interest is the relatively lower ratings of *self-controlled* and *logical*. *Honesty* was valued more highly than *self-control*. These men would rather be truthful in their expressions than restrained. Similarly, they do not highly value being logical, consistent and rational above being broad minded or imaginative. In their communications to jurors or to judges they did not feel that logic was especially useful. Instead, an imaginative approach to presenting the facts, they felt, was often more useful than a strictly logical approach.

The Instrumental Values that they value least, are all concerned with being less than brutally honest. For example, *forgiving, cheerful, obedient, polite, clean*, and *helpful*. These values have as a commonality the social graces and amenities that tend to negate the total veracity of the individual. We have seen that the fourteen lawyers in this book prefer honesty to obsequiousness. In a sense where values are concerned, everything seems to converge on the objective of achieving an ultimate goal or objective, or in the case of their trial practice—a favorable verdict. The psychological profile, reflected in values, is probably closest to that of a warrior or championship athlete. Achilles does not ask if the Greek cause is just. If he comports himself with self-respect, honor, and courage that is enough. And above all he must win.

Sources:

Costa, Paul T. Jr. & McCrae, Robert R. *Professional Manual Revised NEO Personality Inventory (NEO-PI-R) and NEO Five-Factor Inventory (NEO-FFI)*. Psychological Assessment Resources: Odessa, Florida, 1992.

Rokeach, Milton *The Nature of Human Values*. Consulting Psychologists Press: Palo Alto, CA, 1973.

INDEX

— A —

— B —

— C —

— M —

— N —

— O —

— P —

— R —

— S —